LOOKING
BEHIND THE
LABEL

GLOBAL RESEARCH STUDIES

is part of the Framing the Global project, an initiative of Indiana University Press and the Indiana University Center for the Study of Global Change, funded by the Andrew W. Mellon Foundation.

Advisory Committee

Alfred C. Aman Jr.   Patrick O'Meara

Eduardo Brondizio   Radhika Parameswaran

Maria Bucur   Heidi Ross

Bruce L. Jaffee   Richard R. Wilk

LOOKING
BEHIND THE
LABEL

*Global Industries and the
Conscientious Consumer*

TIM BARTLEY

SEBASTIAN KOOS

HIRAM SAMEL

GUSTAVO SETRINI

NIK SUMMERS

INDIANA UNIVERSITY PRESS   *Bloomington & Indianapolis*

This book is a publication of

INDIANA UNIVERSITY PRESS
Office of Scholarly Publishing
Herman B Wells Library 350
1320 East 10th Street
Bloomington, Indiana 47405 USA

iupress.indiana.edu

The paper used in this publication
meets the minimum requirements of
the American National Standard for
Information Sciences—Permanence of
Paper for Printed Library Materials,
ANSI Z39.48–1992.

Manufactured in the
United States of America

Cataloging information is available
from the Library of Congress

ISBN 978-0-253-01648-5 (cloth)
ISBN 978-0-253-01656-0 (paperback)
ISBN 978-0-253-01662-1 (ebook)

1 2 3 4 5   20 19 18 17 16 15

CONTENTS

Acknowledgments   *vii*

List of Commonly Used Acronyms   *ix*

Introduction: Rules, Responsibilities, and Rights in the Global Economy   *1*

Part I: Making Sense of Conscientious Consumerism

1   The Making of Conscientious Consumers:
    Individual and National Patterns   *37*

2   The Dilemmas of Conscientious Consumerism   *60*

Part II: Behind the Label: Global Production and the Meaning of Standards

3   Wood and Paper Products: Searching for Sustainability   *85*

4   Food: Global Agriculture and Local Institutions   *112*

5   Apparel and Footwear: Standards for Sweatshops   *146*

6   Electronics: The Hidden Costs of Computing   *179*

Conclusion: Beyond Conscientious Consumerism   *209*

Appendix   *227*

Notes   *235*

References   *243*

Index   *277*

ACKNOWLEDGMENTS

THIS BOOK REPRESENTS THE COLLABORATIVE EFFORT OF THIS TEAM of authors. Some of us came to the project with expertise on consumer behavior and debates about conscientious consumerism, while others had focused more on the application of standards in global industries. We have learned a great deal from one another, though a series of conversations and through an iterative process of sketching, writing, and rewriting the manuscript.

The team of authors also benefited from a much larger set of people who supported our research in various ways. The full list is too long to mention, and it would include numerous people we have interviewed in the field. We thank them for being generous with their time and knowledge. A partial list of others who supported our research, took it in new directions, or otherwise facilitated our work includes Graeme Auld, Suzanne Berger, Teri Caraway, Ben Cashore, Greg Distelhorst, Kevin Doran, Niklas Egels-Zandén, Deborah Fitzgerald, Thomas Kochan, Kai Lee, Richard Locke, Sarah Lyon, Errol Meidinger, Ethan Michelson, Tad Mutersbaugh, Ruth Norris, Hari Nugroho, Timea Pal, Michael Piore, Christian Resch, Ben Rissing, Mari Sako, Ulrike Samer, Andrew Schrank, Binbin Shu, Peter Sprang, Edward Steinfeld, Judith Tendler, Eric Thun, Zhuo Wang, and Lu Zhang, as well as members of Hewlett-Packard's social auditing team, the Center for International Forestry Research (CIFOR), and the Department of Sociology at Sun Yat-Sen University.

Valuable feedback on conceptualization and writing was provided by Christi Smith, Rachel Schurman, and the "Framing the Global" Fellows, who are Manuela Ciotti, Deborah Cohen, Stephanie De Boer, Lessie Jo Frazier, Zsuzsa Gille, Anne Griffiths, Rachel Harvey, Prakash Kumar, Michael Mascarenhas, Deirdre McKay, Sean Metzger, Faranak Miraftab, Alex Perullo, and Katerina Teaiwa. We thank this group (of which Bartley was a member), its intrepid leaders, Hilary Kahn and Deborah Piston-Hatlen, and its funders at Indiana University and the Mellon Foundation for support and encouragement throughout the project.

Our editor at Indiana University Press, Rebecca Tolen, deserves a great deal of credit for helping us conceptualize the project and integrate its various pieces and for very effectively moving the project toward publication. Others at the press, including Mollie Ables, Nancy Lightfoot, and Janet Rabinowitch, also made key contributions. We thank Jill R. Hughes for copyediting and Susan Storch of Illuminating Indexing for preparing the index.

COMMONLY USED ACRONYMS

ACFTU   All China Federation of Trade Unions

APP   Asia Pulp and Paper

APRIL   Asia Pacific Resources International Limited

ATOs   Alternative Trading Organizations

AZPA   Azucarera Paraguaya

BSCI   Business Social Compliance Initiative

CCC   Clean Clothes Campaign

CSA   Community Supported Agriculture

CSR   Corporate Social Responsibility

DAP   Desarollo Agricola Paraguaya

EICC   Electronic Industry Citizenship Coalition

ETI   Ethical Trading Initiative

FLA	Fair Labor Association
FLO	Fairtrade Labelling Organization
FSC	Forest Stewardship Council
FWF	Fair Wear Foundation
ILO	International Labor Organization
INGO	International Nongovernmental Organization
LOHAS	"Lifestyles of Health and Sustainability"
NGO	Nongovernmental Organization
PEFC	Programme for the Endorsement of Forest Certification
RSPO	Roundtable on Sustainable Palm Oil
RTRS	Roundtable on Responsible Soy
SAI	Social Accountability International
SFI	Sustainable Forestry Initiative
UNITE	Union of Needletrades, Industrial, and Textile Employees
WRAP	Worldwide Responsible Accredited Production
WRC	Worker Rights Consortium
WTO	World Trade Organization
WWF	previously World Wildlife Fund or Worldwide Fund for Nature

LOOKING
BEHIND THE
LABEL

INTRODUCTION

Rules, Responsibilities, and Rights in the Global Economy

THE FURNITURE SHOPPING TRIP WAS MORE COMPLICATED THAN expected. Searching for a new headboard, my wife and I (Bartley) hoped we would find something that was well made, preferably under decent conditions. When we asked about items made from wood certified by the Forest Stewardship Council, we mostly got blank stares or information that seemed intended to divert our attention. One saleswoman was telling us proudly about the store's furniture being made in the USA when we saw "Made in Vietnam" stamped in large letters on the back of one piece. We knew that logs were being harvested illegally—not to mention unsustainably—in Laos, Indonesia, and Russia and shipped to factories in Vietnam and China to make furniture for consumers in North America and Europe. We also knew that the young women and men working in these factories endured health hazards and long hours to meet the low prices and fast delivery times that retailers demanded. Not that "Made in the USA," even if we could find it, would be a perfect guarantee either, since labor laws are frequently violated here as well, and unsustainable forestry is not unique to developing countries.

After much head scratching, we stopped browsing and bought a cheap used headboard from a Craigslist ad. We might have even felt good about this for a moment, since we could claim to be resisting a culture of disposability and overconsumption. But we knew we wouldn't keep the slightly ugly headboard for long and would soon find ourselves back in the same conundrum.

Little dilemmas like this have become increasingly common, especially in the markets of North America and Europe. Many consumers claim to "shop with a conscience," and a huge number of eco- and social-labeling programs have sprung up to assure them that factories, farms, forests, and fisheries around the world are in some sense "sustainable" or "fair." One project to track eco-labels has found more than 450 different labels worldwide.[1]

Yet it is clear that consumers often abandon their ideals for low prices, and even conscientious consumers can be confused by the barrage of labels and misleading claims. Some labels are issued by independent initiatives with stringent standards, such as Fair Trade certification and the Forest Steward-ship Council, but what lies "behind the label" is a far cry from what consumers imagine when they see images of a smiling coffee farmer or a green tree in a lush forest. What does it mean if consumers "vote with their pocketbooks" by choosing products that are labeled as "fair" or "sustainable"? Can global production processes really be transformed by standards that are voluntarily adopted by profit-seeking companies to please fickle consumers? As some people strive to be "conscientious consumers," are they just fooling them-selves, engaging in small acts of charity while ignoring larger structures of power and inequality that shape the lives of workers, citizens, and commu-nities locally and globally? Is a consumerist logic of "one dollar, one vote" displacing the democratic principle of "one person, one vote?"

This book explores these dilemmas by looking at the links between con-sumption and production processes in global industries. Celebrations and critiques of "ethical consumption," "political consumerism," and the related issue of "corporate social responsibility" have abounded in the past decade. Yet rarely do these treatments look closely at the links between consumer markets, voluntary standards, and production processes in different indus-tries and locations. We believe it is crucial to examine the dynamics of both consumption and production in order to understand if and when "shopping with a conscience" is likely to make a difference in global industries. Doing so has taken us not only into analyses of consumer behavior and market structures but also into footwear factories in China, sourcing offices in Hong

Kong, smallholder farms in Paraguay, timber operations in Indonesia, electronics factories in Malaysia, activist organizations in the United States, and beyond. As a group, we have conducted more than four hundred interviews across four continents. We have talked with a variety of practitioners in the world of global standards, from managers responsible for making changes to auditors charged with judging compliance; from workers and smallholder farmers to the representatives of global brands and international nongovernmental organizations (INGOs). We have also analyzed a variety of data on consumers, firms, and industry dynamics. In this book we have sought to integrate a large amount of information into straightforward analyses and rich case studies.

THE DEBATE OVER CONSCIENTIOUS CONSUMERISM

Can consumers contribute to a fairer, more sustainable model of globalization? Should they, or is this a foolish way to bring about social change? These questions are central to the scholarly debate about what we call "conscientious consumerism"—that is, consumers viewing their purchases as a way to express some sense of ethical, or perhaps even political, responsibility. Some theorists have treated conscientious consumerism as an attractive and viable way for individuals to express their values, likening consumption to activism, political engagement, and active citizenship (Micheletti 2003). At a minimum, paying attention to how consumer products are made may enhance consumers' sense of global connection and help to "de-fetishize" commodities (Seyfang 2005). Others have argued that conscientious consumerism is a shallow form of engagement that detracts from other pathways to social change; expresses parochial, self-serving values; and legitimates overconsumption (Guthman 2007a; Maniates 2001; Maniates and Meyer 2010; Szasz 2007). In between, some theorists have argued that individuals can be hybrid "citizen-consumers" whose consumer choices contribute in small ways to a broader sense of social and political engagement (Williams 2006; Willis and Schor 2012).

These debates are important, and we stake out our own position here, since any treatment of conscientious consumerism must grapple with its personal and political meanings. But by focusing almost exclusively on the culture, politics, and meanings of conscientious consumerism, existing research has had little to say about two key factors—(1) the *structures* of conscientious consumption and (2) its *consequences* at the point of production. First, consuming products labeled as "fair" or "sustainable" is not just a matter of individual "reflexivity," regardless of whether one views this as noble or self-absorbed. It is structured by the constraints and opportunities that consumers face. This refers in part to factors such as income, education, and social class that make conscientious consumerism far from universal. But it also refers to differences across countries. Even among fairly affluent countries in North America and Europe, there are significant differences in the size and shape of markets for products whose labels claim they are fair or sustainable.

Second and even more striking is the degree to which the discourse on conscientious consumerism has sidestepped questions about the implementation of the standards that consumers are supporting. Many forms of conscientious consumption rely on assurances that certain production standards have been followed. Consumers cannot see for themselves whether their food has been farmed in a fair and sustainable way, whether their furniture originated in deforestation, or whether their smartphones are the product of heavily polluting high-tech sweatshops. But scholars of conscientious consumerism have failed to interrogate these standards and assurances. They usually either accept them at face value or dismiss them altogether as "greenwash" or "fairwash." Other scholars have begun to study the implementation of voluntary production standards, typically in order to evaluate "private governance" systems (Locke 2013; Ponte 2008; Seidman 2007) or what some have called "transnational private regulation" (Bartley 2007b). But research on standards "on the ground" remains rare, and comparisons of different industries and locations are just beginning to emerge.

As one does look behind the label, this much is clear: claims of fairness and sustainability that seem straightforward to consumers become significantly murkier as one looks at the farms, factories, and forests where the products originate. Fair trade coffee may not be so fair for the casual laborers that farmers hire to toil in organic farms (Jaffee 2007).[2] A decade of "corporate social responsibility" in the apparel industry did not prevent more than eleven hundred workers from dying when the Rana Plaza complex of factories in Bangladesh collapsed in 2013. Certified sustainable forests have sometimes turned out to be sites of illegal logging and violence against local residents. But it is also clear that not all assurances are the same. Some initiatives are more stringent and credible than others; some parts of an industry are more open to reform than others; and some places are more likely to support decent conditions than others. We find more variation and complexity in global industries than would be expected by either simplistic celebrations of corporate social responsibility or by condemnations of greenwash/fairwash. Our goal is to document, grapple with, and hopefully sort out some of that complexity.

The debate about conscientious consumerism is to some degree colored by the different terms that scholars have used to describe it. Some use the term "political consumerism" (Micheletti 2003), which has become the standard term for researchers in much of Europe. We believe it is premature to label shopping with a conscience as a political act, at least until far more is known about how consumers understand this act and its consequences. Others prefer the term "ethical consumerism," which appears to be more common in British and American discourse (Barnett et al. 2005; Goodman, Maye, and Holloway 2010). But this seems to imply that consumers have a coherent ethical rationale. We use the term "conscientious consumerism" (and "conscientious consumption") to reflect our view that concerned consumers are more often acting on a vague sense of trying to do good in the world than on a specific political or ethical commitment. This does not mean that conscientious consumption cannot be highly principled. In some cases it clearly is. But in many cases we suspect that consumers are uncertain and grasping—a reasonable response to the perplexing world of labels and global industries. And sometimes scholars question whether seemingly ethical purchases might actually be self-serving and insular (Szasz 2007). We see "conscientious" consumer activity as open to both more and less principled ethical/political commitments. Grappling with the pitfalls of this activity, in this book we argue that an overarching ideology of conscientious consumerism as a vision of social change is vacuous. Consumers and scholars should not rely on shopping to change the world. Nevertheless, we argue, specific practices of conscientious consumption can sometimes be meaningful as part of multifaceted strategies for reforming global industries. Careful attention is needed, then, to both consumer behavior and the effects of voluntary production standards.

In the remainder of this introduction we sketch our approach to the analysis of conscientious consumption and standards for global industries. We begin by discussing the processes through which claims of "fairness" and "sustainability" have become common features of shopping aisles. This includes some of the most significant changes in the global economy and polity over the past four decades, including the rise of global supply chains, transnational advocacy networks, and neoliberalism as an ideology of governance. We then move on to critique three common frames for understanding conscientious consumption and related global standards. This sets the stage for our own framework for analysis, which emphasizes industry structures, the constituencies behind standards, global-local linkages, and what we call the "puzzle of rules" in the global economy. Following this introductory chapter, we turn to an analysis of consumer behavior in the United States and Europe. This is followed by an attempt to unpack the dilemmas of conscientious consumerism—and our interpretation of what is harmful and helpful about it. Then, in part 2 of the book, we shift from consumption to production and develop case studies of four types of products: timber, food, apparel, and electronics. All have been subject to standards for "fair" or "sustainable" production, yet the results have rarely been what reformers hoped for.

FROM CAMPAIGNS TO LABELS

The story usually begins with a social movement. While twentieth-century social movements often targeted national states and public policy, by the turn of the twenty-first century, environmental, labor, and human rights activists were also "shaming the corporation" and contesting markets directly. Often this meant exposing well-known transnational corporations' complicity with exploitation of workers (especially young women), natural environments, and indigenous people in locations around the world. Anti-sweatshop groups "named and shamed" Nike, Walmart, H&M, and many other companies to draw attention to unsafe working environments; physical and verbal abuse; and a high-pressure, low-wage model of production in the apparel and footwear industry. Eventually this approach spread to the electronics industry as activists showed how Apple, Hewlett-Packard, Samsung, and others rely on harsh labor conditions in Asia as well as "conflict minerals" from war-torn areas of Central Africa. Environmentalists had long been targeting companies like The Home Depot, B&Q, and Mitsubishi because of their contributions to tropical deforestation, not to mention campaigns against Shell, Chevron, and other oil companies with reputations for pollution and environmental injustice. Food markets became especially politicized. Environmentalists showed how beef consumption threatened the Amazon rain forest, how seafood sales contributed to the depletion of species and destruction of ocean habitats, and how "factory farms" polluted local environments. They also raised concerns about pesticides and genetically modified organisms (GMOs) in the supply chains of many food brands and retailers. Human rights and development organizations linked Hershey, Nestlé, and others to bonded labor in cacao farms and connected Coca-Cola, Pepsi, and Cargill (a large soybean producer) to land grabs that forcibly displaced small farmers in South America, Asia, and Africa.

In response, retailers and brands increasingly have adopted voluntary rules for their supply chains. Apparel, footwear, and electronics companies have adopted "ethical sourcing" policies and "codes of conduct," sending auditors around the world to assess their suppliers' compliance. Some have joined initiatives like Social Accountability International (SAI), the Fair Labor Association (FLA), Business Social Compliance Initiative (BSCI), or the Electronics Industry Citizenship Coalition (EICC), which have their own sets of rules and auditing procedures. Food producers and retailers have similarly joined initiatives like the Roundtable on Responsible Soy (RTRS) or the Roundtable on Sustainable Palm Oil (RSPO), both of which address the environmental and social implications of large-scale agricultural plantations. Sellers of paper and furniture have turned to products certified by the Forest Stewardship Council (FSC) (or its competitor, the Programme for the Endorsement of Forest Certification [PEFC]) to demonstrate their green credentials, while some food retailers have agreed to sell seafood certified by the Marine Stewardship Council. These are just a few examples of how pressure from social movements has led to the proliferation of ethical standards. Some of these standards take the form of policies that companies adopt, while others are governed by external associations, like those mentioned above. Typically these associations are created either by coalitions of NGOs and a few leading firms or by groups of companies hoping to fend off further pressure.

In some instances social movements have not merely pressured companies to improve their practices; they have sought to endorse alternative models of production. Organic agriculture was a movement before it was a market, and it helped to legitimate forms of farming that do not rely on pesticides. The fair trade movement originated with the goal of supporting small farmers who were organized into democratically run cooperatives, and it sought to use certification to direct greater resources toward these farmers, not to improve conditions on large plantations (Linton, Liou, and Shaw 2004). Although labor rights advocates have been hesitant to label companies as "good," groups like the Worker Rights Consortium (WRC) and the Fair Wear Foundation (FWF) have begun to build market support for factories in which workers are represented by independent unions. Similarly, some of the impetus for the Forest Stewardship Council came from foresters, environmentalists, and indigenous rights groups hoping to support small-scale community forestry operations, not simply to improve industrial timber operations (Bartley and Smith 2010). These kinds of initiatives are "in the market but not of it" (Taylor 2005) and insert alternative "orders of worth" into market decisions (Boltanski and Thévenot 2006). Yet as activists have sought to build market support for these production models, they have encountered dilemmas of "mainstreaming" alternatives. Under pressure, larger companies have agreed to sell certified products, including Starbucks and Fair Trade coffee or The Home Depot and FSC-certified lumber. But as activists have discovered, there is a fine and often blurry line between building market support and becoming dependent on big companies in a way that leads to the weakening of standards.

As our case studies show, the world of voluntary standards, whether for alternatives or "best practices," involves a constant struggle for the power to define legitimate standards and to determine how strictly they should be applied in the field. There is an "NGO-Industrial Complex" that underlies most conscientious consumption and production initiatives (Gereffi, Garcia-Johnson, and Sasser 2001), but it is multifaceted and contentious.

The ultimate impacts of conscientious consumption and production projects are often hard to discern, but this much is clear: taken together, these activities amount to a vast new set of standard-setting projects for the global economy. Promoted by a mix of NGOs, companies, and trade associations, they seek to use global production networks—or "global value chains"—rather than the national state to promote rules about fairness, justice, and sustainability (Cashore, Auld, and Newsom 2004; Guthman 2007b; Ponte 2008; Seidman 2007). "Lead firms" in these global value chains—that is, large retailers and brands from Apple to IKEA to Zara—have the power to set styles, prices, and delivery schedules for their suppliers, so, advocates argue, they should also be able to influence the conditions of workers, communities, and the environment. Companies frequently adopt standards to fend off activist pressure and the media spotlight, but adoption does not mean implementation. In some cases alternatives have found a niche in the market, and in other cases voluntary initiatives have proliferated while the logic of production—and exploitation—has remained largely unchanged.

Scrutiny of global industries has also spawned tools to help consumers make sense of all of these claims and to smartly vote with their wallets. *Consumer Reports* magazine can trace its origins to a much earlier wave of muckraking (Rao 1998), and with the recent proliferation of competing eco-labels it has sometimes stepped in to referee, as have publications from Co-Op America in the United States and *Ethical Consumer* magazine in the United Kingdom. The Monterey Bay Aquarium in the United States has long published a list of seafood for environmentally conscious consumers to prefer and avoid. Online guides and smartphone apps have made these types of guides more elaborate. Goodguide.com, developed by some leading researchers before being sold to Underwriters Laboratories (UL), compiles a wide array of information to rate products and companies for their health, environmental, and social impacts. Smartphone apps even allow consumers to trace products to parent companies and investors, as with apps that enable consumers to boycott the conservative Koch Brothers, avoid the biotech giant Monsanto, or support companies that recognize lesbian, gay, bisexual, and transsexual rights (O'Connor 2013).

Of course, these consumer guides are only as good as the information that goes into them, and as our case studies show, meaningful, accurate information is often difficult to come by in complex global industries. Furthermore, as our analyses of consumer behavior show, only particular subsets of consumers have indicated an interest in boycotting or "buycotting," and there are real questions about how many will pay more for guarantees of fairness and sustainability. Before diving into these issues, we must consider the larger context in which the rise of conscientious consumerism has occurred.

RECONFIGURING RESPONSIBILITIES, RIGHTS, AND RULES

Debates about consumers, producers, and ethical standards are vexing in part because they are tied up with a larger reconfiguration of responsibilities, rights, and rules in the global economy. National and multinational corporations have become transnational corporations with activities stretching across national boundaries without being deeply rooted in them. National states, once the main makers of rules and arbiters of rights, are increasingly just one of many actors issuing rules and claiming to enforce rights. International NGOs and global standards associations have sought to issue rules and enforce rights as well, although their effectiveness in doing so is unclear. More broadly, the goal to turn the world into "one big market"—associated with neoliberal ideology—has challenged earlier conceptions of what national states can and should do to protect or empower citizens, workers, and the environment. Conscientious consumption and production projects are to some degree the result of these changes. In a world of vertically integrated companies and strong, responsive states, there would be far less demand for voluntary standards supported by consumers. But these changes have not simply paved the way for conscientious consumerism; they have complicated its meanings and impacts in a variety of ways.

The Supply Chain Revolution

Capitalism in the twentieth century was characterized by the growth of vertically integrated corporations, which controlled raw materials, manufacturing, and distribution, and by the growth of horizontally integrated corporations and conglomerates, in which multiple businesses were combined in the same corporate structure. By the 1980s these models were giving way to the "supply chain revolution," in which large firms contract with independent suppliers rather than owning an entire production process. Nike built its fortunes by being an early adopter of the "manufacturer without factories" model, and Walmart became a dominant retailer by making its supply chains work faster and cheaper than retailers had previously. In what Robert Feenstra (1998) called the "integration of trade and disintegration of production," companies in industries from apparel to electronics to furniture shed their factories, contracted with independent manufacturers, and focused on building their "brand" images.

While some contracting and subcontracting happened within national borders, scholars pointed out that many production processes were being turned into "global commodity chains," and especially "buyer-driven" global commodity chains, in which companies nearest the distribution end of the chain (retailers and well-known brands) exercised the greatest power over production processes and extracted the greatest profit from them (Gereffi 1994, 1999). Other terms, such as "global production networks" and "global value chains" described similar phenomena, and as many industries shifted to a supply chain model of some sort, these different traditions of research began to merge and more nuanced ways of describing power and coordination in global value chains were articulated (Bair 2008; Gereffi, Humphrey, and Sturgeon 2005). This supply chain revolution was facilitated by technological changes that made contracting more efficient and by legal changes that opened more parts of the world to foreign investment. Of course, in some industries, such as agriculture, large, consumer-facing companies had long relied on networks of suppliers—from coffee farmers to growers of corn, wheat, and other commodity crops. Yet these industries have been reconfigured to some degree by the growth of mega-retailers that have cut out middleman distributors.

Most important at this point is to recognize how the supply chain revolution both highlighted and blurred the responsibilities of transnational corporations. On one hand, contracting and subcontracting networks tied retailers and brands in the United States and Europe to sites of production—and exploitation—around the world. To be sure, multinational corporations like Nestlé, ITT, and PepsiCo had been shamed for the actions of their foreign arms in the 1970s, but the networked transnational corporations of the 1990s had more extensive ties, and thus greater vulnerabilities. On the other hand, the lines of responsibility—and especially legal liability—were blurry, since brands and retailers exercised a great deal of power over their suppliers but did not own those sites of production. Initially when sweatshops, child labor, and prison labor were uncovered, brands like Nike and Walmart denied responsibility on the basis that they did not own the factories where such abuses occurred. As pressure mounted, these and other lead firms in global value chains began to accept "soft" forms of responsibility by adopting codes of conduct and pledging to monitor and improve conditions in their supply chains. Those same companies, however, fiercely resisted attempts to make them *legally* liable (Bartley 2005; Shamir 2004).

For the most part, this remains the situation in the forest products, food, apparel/footwear, and electronics industries. When pressed, retailers and brands have publicly accepted some responsibility to improve conditions in their supply chains, but their commitments are rarely binding. Suppliers are often allowed to slip by with tiny improvements, and retailers and brands can backtrack on their voluntary commitments when necessary. They may face other sanctions if they do so, such as loss of sales from conscientious consumers, delisting from socially responsible investment indexes, or additional social movement pressure, but even if this sort of pressure materializes, there is no guarantee it will bear enough force to effect real change. For better or worse, this is the terrain in which conscientious consumption and production projects operate.

Neoliberal Globalization

To a great extent globalization has been a project to turn the world into "one big market," not only by increasing countries' openness to foreign investment and orientation to international trade but also by making it possible for firms and investors to operate more smoothly across borders than ever before. It is not just technology and the search for cheap labor and natural resources that has driven the globalization project; it is the ideology of neoliberalism. In its most basic form neoliberalism emphasizes the power of so-called free markets to improve well-being and to solve social problems. The focus of the neoliberal globalization project, then, is to keep states from interfering with global markets by convincing (or coercing) them to tear down barriers to foreign investment and reduce subsidies, tariffs, and "non-tariff barriers to trade," such as regulations that discriminate against foreign firms. Of course, neoliberalism has its own tensions and contradictions. As Greta Krippner (2007) argues, governments often face a "neoliberal dilemma": "Policymakers are anxious to escape responsibility for economic outcomes, and yet markets require regulation to function in capitalist economies. . . . [The result is] a continual process of institutional innovation in which functions are transferred to markets, but under the close control of the state" (478).

As this dilemma illustrates, the world is far from being a fully integrated "free market." But many global value chains, including the ones studied here, do function as integrated "global factories" that depend on the smooth and integrated flow of inputs across national borders. Yet while these industries have a transnational scope, the structures for authoritatively regulating markets have remained largely national in scope, especially when it comes to issues of fairness and sustainability. The World Trade Organization (WTO) has endorsed protections for intellectual property rights, but it has left only narrow spaces for governments to protect workers and environments, and it has refused to address labor rights directly. Bilateral and multilateral trade agreements sometimes include labor and environmental standards, but these are limited in scope and enforceability. International organizations such as the United Nations and the International Labor Organization promote conventions for governments to adopt, but these organizations rarely have any power to demand enforcement. National governments are constrained in part by a global economy in which firms and investors can move from one jurisdiction to another but perhaps even more by ideological commitments to neoliberal globalization and the rules of the WTO (Evans 1997; Rodrik 2011). As we argue, it is a mistake to think that governments are powerless or irrelevant in the face of globalization, but there is no doubt that the dearth of binding international regulation of production conditions has led many to look to the private sector as a way of enforcing standards. NGOs, for instance, have often turned to voluntary standards and conscientious consumption as second-best alternatives to intergovernmental systems of regulation.

Neoliberalism can be credited not only with helping to hollow out the state but also with promoting an individualization of responsibility. In a process that theorists have called "responsibilization," individuals are treated as having the duty and capacity to take responsibility for things that should rightly be seen as the result of social structures. This can be seen, for instance, in attempts to reform welfare states to make welfare recipients take responsibility for their own fates (Rose 2000). The moralization of markets has also been a responsibilization process, in which individual consumers are told they have the duty—and the ability—to solve the world's social problems through their purchases. While some scholars use the language of responsibilization to dismiss conscientious consumption as misguided, we do not see this as the most appropriate response. We recognize that individual consumers are being asked to take responsibility for problems that would often be better served by more collective and robust solutions, including revitalized states and labor unions. But it is at least possible that responsibility-taking by consumers could help to support more durable solutions in the future, especially

if governments, NGOs, and consumers themselves have a clearer understanding of what is and is not being affected by conscientious consumption
and production initiatives.

INGOs and Transnational Advocacy Networks

Since the end of World War II, NGOs have become key actors in national,
international, and transnational governance. By the turn of the twenty-first
century, NGOs were carrying out most of the tasks of governing complex societies: delivering development assistance, mediating social conflicts, setting
standards for business, developing expert knowledge, and reconstructing
societies after natural and social disasters. By some accounts the proliferation
of NGOs and their incorporation into development and governance projects
amounts to an associational revolution that "may constitute as significant a
social and political development of the latter twentieth century as the rise of
the nation state was of the nineteenth century" (Edwards and Hulme 1996, 2).

International NGOs (INGOs), such as Greenpeace, Oxfam, or Human
Rights Watch, have mobilized attention to a variety of global problems, from
climate change to new forms of bonded labor. They have garnered media
attention to these problems and have pushed governments and intergovernmental organizations to take action. In addition, the growth of transnational
networks of advocates and experts has sometimes allowed domestic activists
to gain leverage over their governments. In what Margaret Keck and Kathryn
Sikkink (1998) dubbed the "boomerang effect," domestic activists can reach
past indifferent or hostile domestic governments and appeal to transnational
advocacy networks that in turn exert pressure on those governments.

Since the 1990s INGOs have increasingly sought to put pressure on transnational corporations and restructure markets, not just state policies. They
have led efforts to build product certification initiatives, from the Forest
Stewardship Council to the Marine Stewardship Council, and they have
coordinated "market campaigns" to convince large retailers to support these
initiatives. In addition, the traditional boomerang effect has been supplemented with what Naomi Klein (1999) called the "brand boomerang," in
which grassroots labor or environmental activists call on their international
allies to put pressure on a well-known company that is operating in (or buy-

ing from) that location. Through these processes, INGOs have become important architects, advocates, and watchdogs of conscientious consumption and production projects.

The rise of INGOs does raise conundrums, however, especially about the relationship between professional advocates based in Amsterdam or Washington, D.C., and grassroots activists in developing countries. To some extent INGOs have become sensitive to these power disparities, and local NGOs have become savvy about working with foreign partners. But the power of INGOs to organize transnational campaigns, attract media attention, and shame global companies does carry the danger that more locally oriented strategies, or those directed to domestic governments, are being neglected (Seidman 2007).

Standards for Markets and Markets for Standards

Without the supply chain revolution, neoliberal globalization, and the growth of transnational advocacy networks, it is hard to imagine the rise of conscientious consumption and global standards for fairness and sustainability. Yet just because initiatives for auditing, certifying, or reporting on sustainability or fairness have emerged, that does not mean they will have integrity or impact. Typically, conscientious consumption and production projects are organized as private, voluntary initiatives. They attempt to set standards for markets, but they also exist within markets. Like all voluntary programs, they depend on participation from companies, and there can often be a trade-off between the stringency of standards and the number of participants (Potoski and Prakash 2009). All voluntary initiatives are structurally dependent on their corporate participants, so one should take the language of independent, "third-party" initiatives with a grain of salt. Furthermore, as private initiatives they have no monopoly on standards for a particular topic (as a government would have). This means competing standards initiatives can easily emerge. For some observers the private, voluntary character of these initiatives is reason enough to give up on them (e.g., Seidman 2007), while for neoliberal advocates of market-based solutions, these same features make such initiatives especially attractive. As we argue below, our approach seeks to unpack variation in the organization of these initiatives and the contexts in which they operate. At the same time, as our case studies show, there are certainly limits on what private, voluntary initiatives have been able to accomplish.

THREE FRAMES AND THEIR SHORTCOMINGS

Given the rise of conscientious consumerism and the growth of standards for global industries, scholars and advocates are racing to promote simple frames for making sense of them. In this section we discuss three frames that are often invoked. Each captures a slice of something important, but each ends up obscuring as much as it illuminates, or more.

The Empowered, Sovereign Consumer

Scholars and advocates often adopt a celebratory tone in discussing conscientious consumerism. They argue that consumers are being empowered to "vote with their dollars" and that these small changes in the habits of affluent consumers can change, or even "save," the world. As Ruth Stokes (2013) writes in the *Ecologist* magazine, "I believe that changing the way we shop—voting with our money—can help to change the world. . . . Companies respond to the habits of shoppers. We all have consumer power; we just have to make sure we use it wisely." If consumers have been manipulated by companies in the past, they are increasingly being empowered by new sources of information, argues Dara O'Rourke (2011). Theorists of "political consumerism" have argued that this mode of political expression is especially empowering for individuals who are alienated from formal politics, such as young people and women (Micheletti 2003). Furthermore, as companies compete for the support of conscientious consumers and the coveted "lifestyles of health and sustainability" (LOHAS) niche (Emerich 2011), many observers argue that they will become transparent, responsible corporate citizens (Porter and Kramer 2006; Smith 1990; Zadek, Pruzan, and Evans 1997).

Such celebrations often rest on an idealized framing of consumer agency—that is, the ability and willingness of the "sovereign citizen-consumer" to be the prime mover of social change (Jacobsen and Dulsrud 2007). The "sovereign consumer" is an old concept that is intended to suggest that consumer tastes are the driver of all economic activity. As scholars have observed the growth of conscientious consumption, the sovereign consumer has become the sovereign citizen-consumer, or what Roberta Sassatelli (2007) dubbed the waking of the "sleepy giant of the sovereign citizen-consumer" (188). Social theorist Ulrich Beck, perhaps the most prominent theorist of consumption as a form of politics, argues that "citizens discover the act of shopping as one in which they can always cast their ballot—on a world scale, no less" (qtd. in Sassatelli 2007, 188). Michele Micheletti (2003) takes the provocation even further:

> Conflicts over what and where to consume are now central for understanding the functioning of affluent Western societies. This can even mean that consumers participating in boycotts can, for instance, be likened to resistance fighters. Yet unlike resistance or revolutionary conflicts of the past, citizen-consumers tend to direct their attention toward the market rather than state actors. (16–17)

Even if one gets past the hyperbole, treating consumer tastes as king or queen is problematic in several respects. First, consumers' attitudes turn out to be only one ingredient in the construction of conscientious consumption markets. As we show in this book, the opportunities for conscientious consumption are not distributed evenly across individuals or across countries. Social inequality and differences in market structures mean the social context of consumption is just as important as individual attitudes. Consumer tastes may make a difference, but it is difficult to see them as a true prime mover.

Second, it is naive to assume that a change in consumer tastes translates directly into a change in the production processes of global industries. As Margaret Willis and Juliet Schor (2012) argue, many accounts of conscientious consumerism take a "naïve aggregationist" approach to markets, assuming that if a large enough number of consumers is interested in alternative products, the market will simply change to deliver them. A quite different story is told by research on industries, technologies, and organizations over time. Production processes are often "locked in" by a system of interrelated technologies and expectations, making them difficult to change. Paul David (1985) famously illustrated this by considering the persistence of the inefficient QWERTY keyboard on typewriters and computers. Even if production practices are not strongly locked in, companies, like all organizations, rarely abandon their core routines and technologies (Hannan and Freeman 1989). Perhaps the biggest problem is that those who celebrate the transformative power of new consumer tastes assume that industry practices are changing, but they almost never actually investigate this assumption. The disconnect between theories of conscientious consumerism and empirical research on industry practices is stark, and it is one thing that we hope to remedy with this book.

Finally, by celebrating the empowered, conscientious, politicized consumer, one obscures the ways that *unreflective* consumer choices influence labor and environmental conditions in global industries. As much as some consumers are becoming more conscientious about *some* of their choices, especially when it comes to food and drinks (e.g., organic produce, fair trade coffee), much consumer activity is routine and habitual, and some of the ethics of consumption are opaque to all but the most committed individuals. Conscientious consumers might be careful to recycle, avoid disposable plastic water bottles, and buy organic vegetables, but then eat beef without thinking of its massive natural resource demands and the contributions of cattle production to global warming. As environmentalists have pointed out, encouraging consumers to make their purchases more environmentally friendly carries a risk of legitimating overconsumption in affluent markets, which is the foundation of many forms of environmental degradation (Maniates and Meyer 2010). The issue may not be just the amount of consumption but its pace as well. As will become clear later in this book, the rise of "fast fashion" and "fast electronics"—that is, the rapid churning through fashionable styles of clothing and different models of smartphones—appears to be a root cause of labor exploitation in the apparel and electronics industries.

Greenwash/Fairwash

While some have celebrated conscientious consumerism, others have dismissed voluntary standards, eco-labeling, and social labeling as "greenwash" or "fairwash." As Sharon Beder (2001) puts it, "The attempt to provide a 'green' and caring image for a corporation is a public relations strategy aimed at promising reform and heading off demands for more substantial and fundamental changes and government intervention" (253). Claims about fair and sustainable production, in this view, simply provide cover to companies that are engaged in fundamentally unfair and unsustainable activities. The codes of conduct, sustainability reports, and information disclosures that are highlighted in celebratory accounts of transparency may actually be forms of "disinformation" that obscure companies' actual practices.

The term "greenwash" took off among environmentalists in the late 1980s as a description of advertising campaigns that portrayed companies as protectors of the environment (Beers and Capellaro 1991). Greenpeace argued that transnational corporations like Shell, DuPont, and Mitsubishi had "embraced the environment as their cause and co-opted its terminology," even while contributing massively to environmental degradation (Greenpeace 1992, 2). The analogue for corporate claims about incomes, livelihoods, and justice—"fairwashing"—entered the lexicon later, in the wake of the fair trade movement. As fair trade certification was becoming "mainstreamed" and imitated, scholars and activists began worrying that fairwashing was on the horizon (Conroy 2007; Lyon and Moberg 2010). Observers have also criticized the images produced in the name of "corporate social responsibility," arguing that these are "merely a public relations game . . . lulling us into a false sense of security" (Doane 2005, 29). Common to all these diagnoses is the sense that most assurances one finds on a product are nothing more than public relations efforts.

The greenwash/fairwash critique captures two key features of conscientious consumption and global standards. First, when faced with criticism, companies would prefer to be able to improve their images without altering profitable practices. A public relations campaign is typically the first line of defense. Companies may also hire outside organizations—auditors, consultants, and sometimes NGOs—to lend some credibility to their campaigns. They may also fund seemingly independent standard-setting initiatives that can endorse their corporate social responsibility programs or label their products. As we will see, this is how the US timber industry's Sustainable Forestry Initiative got its start, and it helps to account for the role of apparel and footwear brands in the Fair Labor Association. One must always take assurances of sustainability and fairness with a grain of salt. The dosage of salt depends in part on whether claims come from companies themselves, initiatives that they control, or more independent initiatives. (If initiatives depend on the voluntary participation of companies, they can never be *fully* independent, but there are gradations.) In our analyses of standards (in part 2 of this book), we are attentive to who has created a particular initiative, how it is funded, and how dependent on companies it is. Second, there is nearly always some hypocrisy present when companies take up greening or fairness initiatives. Simply because one product or one aspect of a company's production has earned some credentials does not mean that the company's operations overall can be considered green or fair. As David Vogel (2005) has argued, we often yearn for simple pronouncements of "good" and "bad" companies. But companies, like people, are complex, multifaceted, and often contradictory. One part of a company may be developing green production processes while another part lobbies against environmental regulation.

On the other hand, we see simple distinctions between greenwash/fair-wash and "true" reform as a poor match for the current state of global industries and labeling projects. Eco-labeling and social labeling may once have been the domain of public relations personnel, but they have become their own specialized world, in which credibility depends on "multi-stakeholder representation" and extensive amounts of accreditation, auditing, and verification. Companies might prefer to respond to criticism with public relations campaigns, but they are often pushed by activists and investors to go further and achieve some kind of external assurance. For instance, if confronted by labor rights abuses, apparel and footwear companies no longer simply hold up a code of conduct; instead they refer to sophisticated factory monitoring programs, external certifications, and "capacity-building" projects (Locke 2013). Rather than simply co-opting the language of environmentalism, many retailers have been pushed to sell products that are independently certified (Conroy 2007). Furthermore, the world of voluntary certification has become increasingly formalized. For instance, to judge compliance with the standards of the FSC, an auditing organization (e.g., Scientific Certification Systems, SmartWood, or the Soil Association) must be accredited by a separate oversight body (Accreditation Services International). Furthermore, the FSC belongs to an umbrella organization—the ISEAL (International Social and Environmental Accreditation and Labeling) Alliance—which defines best practices for credible certification initiatives. To be sure, all of this certification of the certifiers of the certifiers (and beyond) is not guaranteed to bring about meaningful improvement. Indeed, we describe cases where this formalization has been counterproductive and where seemingly credible initiatives have failed spectacularly. But it does mean there is more "checking" than there is simple "washing." As Peter Dauvergne and Jane Lister (2012) put it, "Corporate sustainability goals . . . include measurable targets, are audited by independent groups, and are integrated into the core business . . . [through] life-cycle assessment, supply chain tracing, eco-certification, and sustainability reporting" (38). We concur with them that all of this measurement and reporting often skirts the root causes of problems, but one cannot seriously assess conscientious consumption without investigating this activity. If the world were as simple as it was when the "greenwash" frame was first coined, a book like this would not be necessary.

Most importantly, the greenwash/fairwash frame leaves a key question unanswered: if a claim is *not* just greenwash/fairwash—in other words, if it is backed by stringent standards and credible verification processes—then what is it? It would be tempting to assume that the converse of greenwash/fairwash is something like "real sustainability/fairness" on the ground. But as our case studies show, it is possible to have stringent standards and credible assessment but still not generate much reform of global industries. Our goal is to provide some tools for making sense of these complex (and common) intermediate scenarios.

Importing Standards into Empty Spaces

Another problematic frame concerns the implementation of global standards, including those supported by conscientious consumerism. It is tempting to see global standards as introducing new rules into otherwise empty spaces. For instance, one might think of labor codes of conduct as introducing labor rights into factories that would otherwise be completely unregulated and chaotic. Or one might think of global sustainability standards as introducing environmental norms into settings where businesses would otherwise be free to pollute with impunity. As Alison Brysk puts it, global rule-making projects often "concern areas previously ungoverned or even unknown" (Brysk 2005, 120). Indeed, scholars and practitioners often portray private rules as filling a "regulatory void" as they are put into practice, especially in developing countries (Sabel, O'Rourke, and Fung 2000). For some, developing countries are so lacking in the rule of law as to constitute "areas of limited statehood," in which private rules must serve as a substitute for public authority (Börzel and Risse 2010). Sociologists in the "world society" school start from different assumptions but nevertheless argue that global norms about environmental protection, child labor, and human rights are imported into developing countries as novel concepts that are completely alien to the locals (Meyer et al. 1997).

The problem with this approach is not only, as Gay Seidman (2007) argues, that "stateless regulation" usually lacks enforcement power. A more fundamental problem is that this frame obscures the institutional arrangements that *are* in place in developing countries. Developing countries are not empty, anonymous, uniform places. They are populated with different business systems, cultures of production, and political institutions. What may look from afar like a relatively empty space turns out on closer inspection to have a dense set of preexisting relationships, organizations, and rules. These local circumstances can reconfigure global rules in myriad ways (Halliday and Carruthers 2009; Merry 2006). For instance, in chapter 4 we look at fair trade certification and its consequences in Paraguay, a place where earlier ways of organizing agricultural operations set the stage for fair trade projects and shaped their results. Fair trade standards were not simply imported to this setting, they were layered onto an existing set of institutions. In fact, a thicker "layering" of rules, with varying consequences, has been a common result of global standards (Bartley 2011). An "empty spaces" assumption also obscures ongoing political struggles at the point of production. As we will see, INGOs and conscientious consumers are far from the only actors concerned with labor rights, sustainability, or the fair distribution of resources. For instance, recent years have seen a rising tide of strikes in China and mobilization of garment workers in Cambodia and Bangladesh (Alam 2013; Dara and Willemyns 2014; Friedman 2013). The land rights of indigenous people in Brazil and Indonesia are a concern not only of backers of global sustainable forestry standards but also of burgeoning movements of indigenous people themselves (Gerber 2011). Social movements in developing countries may struggle to influence powerful global industries, but they cannot simply be ignored.

When it comes to governmental regulation, it is true that developing countries often lack the resources and administrative capacities to effectively regulate production processes, as do many governments in affluent countries. Moreover, the logic of global production in some ways gives them disincentives to do so: aggressively implementing regulations may cause investors—and orders from brands and retailers—to flee the country, and the rules of the WTO make some forms of regulation untenable. But "developing countries" are diverse. In nearly all parts of the world there are laws related to labor, the environment, and the rights of citizens. Scholars are beginning to find increased enforcement of these laws in some surprising places, from revitalized state labor inspection in the export processing zones of the Dominican Republic (Schrank 2013) to aggressive environmental regulators in Brazil and China (Coslovsky 2011; McAllister, Van Rooij, and Kagan 2010). In other instances, law can be repressive—restricting the rights of workers or indigenous communities, for instance (Lee 2007; Li 2010). Again, the influences of local structures can vary, but one should not assume a blank slate.

A ROUGH GUIDE TO UNPACKING CONSCIENTIOUS CONSUMPTION AND PRODUCTION PROJECTS

How, then, can one make sense of projects to promote conscientious consumption and fair or sustainable production? The first step is simply to accept that there is a great deal of variation. There is variation across individuals and locations in conscientious consumer behavior. There is variation across products and labeling initiatives in the "on the ground" implications of global standards. There is variation across industries (and even within them) in systems of production, and these intersect with national (and even subnational) differences in industry organization. To understand whether conscientious consumption and fair/sustainable production projects can contribute to meaningful alternatives, we must look closely at these industrial and political contexts. A second starting point is to accept that the influence of global standards for fair/sustainable production is typically highly circumscribed or contingent on other factors. As will become clear, even the most stringent standards and most credible initiatives do not transform global industries. They sometimes influence certain parts of an industry, but even this cannot automatically be assumed.

To unpack conscientious consumption initiatives and the global standards they endorse, we bring four factors to the foreground: (1) structures of production and consumption, (2) the constituencies of standards, (3) global-local linkages, and (4) the coexistence of rule making and unruliness.

Structures of Production and Consumption

Industry structures shape both the opportunities for conscientious consumption to occur and the consequences of rule-making projects at the point of production. To start, some industries are more likely than others to become targets of activism, which is typically the catalyst for rule-making and conscientious consumption projects.

Lead firms in global value chains, especially when they are large and have salient corporate reputations, make attractive targets for social movements (Bartley and Child 2014). Industries that lack powerful and well-known brands tend to attract less scrutiny. For instance, the manufacturing of bricks, especially in developing countries, is often a highly polluting and exploitative industry. But because there are not well-known global brands in this industry, it has received little international attention. In other cases activists have highlighted a problem, but without powerful and recognizable brands to link this to, rule-making projects have not emerged. The production of cheap costume jewelry is rife with exploitation, as shown in the documentary *Mardi Gras: Made in China,* but this has not become a site of extensive rule making and conscientious consumerism. In some circumstances the existence of large, high-profile retailers can compensate for a more fragmented or poorly known set of manufacturers. Anti-GMO activists, for instance, have pressured manufacturers like Monsanto by going through large retailers like Marks & Spencer (Schurman and Munro 2009). Our analysis of global food distribution (in chapter 4) is consistent with this observation, but it also suggests that the locus of consumer and activist pressure depends on the specific product.

When activists do press lead firms to make their supply chains fairer or more sustainable, the consequences seem to depend in part on the structure of that supply chain. If suppliers can easily find alternative buyers who are not demanding changes—that is, if there are few suppliers and many buyers—they will have little incentive to comply with a particular lead firm's rules. Going further, by many accounts, when lead firms have a great deal of power over "captive" suppliers, they should be able to demand that those suppliers make improvements (Mayer and Gereffi 2010). On the other hand, some research has questioned whether this power is truly effective or whether it merely spurs a game in which suppliers pretend to be making improvements (and lead firms nod in approval) (Locke, Amengual, and Mangla 2009). We suspect that the power of lead firms does make a difference but that more significant changes are possible when lead firms and suppliers are mutually dependent and work together over long stretches of time. (Our analysis of the apparel industry in chapter 5, though, suggests that long-term collaboration is rare.) In addition, when global value chains are fairly simple in their structure, without too many intermediaries, this should make it easier for standards to "travel" through them. There is a conundrum here, however, since it is often in industries with a high degree of subcontracting (such as apparel) that global standards are in the highest demand. If global industries were dominated by vertically integrated firms rather than dispersed supply chains, the world of conscientious consumerism would look quite different. Furthermore, sometimes the lack of action by large lead firms can leave a space for activists and entrepreneurs to carve out a small market niche based on fairness or sustainability. This is how fair trade–certified coffee began, and some new projects appear to be emerging in electronics (Fairphone, as discussed in chapter 6) and apparel (the Alta Gracia factory, as discussed in chapter 5). After looking more closely at our four industries—timber, food, apparel/footwear, and electronics—we return to questions about industry structure in the book's conclusion.

Industry structures also matter for consumers. As we show in the next chapter, opportunities to engage in conscientious consumption are just as important as motivations to do so, and these opportunities depend in part on the structure of the retail sector in a particular country. Generally we suggest that having larger retailers will facilitate consumer purchases of eco- and social-labeled products. In part this is simply because larger retailers offer a wider array of choices overall—that is, different versions of the same product—while smaller retailers offer fewer choices. To be sure, small stores can specialize in "alternative" products and large stores can fail to carry them. But given the trend toward "mainstreaming" of alternatives (see Jaffee 2012), large retailers have become key points of sale for eco- and social-labeled products. Furthermore, oligopoly in the retail sector—the dominance of a small number of large companies—also seems to magnify the power of activists to influence the market. As Rachel Schurman and William Munro (2009) found, the existence of a small number of large food retailer chains in the UK allowed the anti-GMO movement to flourish there while it foundered amid the larger number of supermarket chains in the United States.

Constituencies and Standards

Global standards for fairness and sustainability may sound universal, but they spring from the priorities of particular individuals and groups. A crucial step in understanding these standards is to examine the founders of initiatives that make rules, audit compliance, and certify products as fair or sustainable. Some such initiatives, such as fair trade certification, originated largely with NGOs or others outside of the industry. Others, such as the Electronics Industry Citizenship Coalition and the Sustainable Forestry Initiative, were founded almost exclusively by industry associations or other groups of companies, often in response to the actions of NGOs. In between are a number of initiatives developed by coalitions of NGOs and companies, from the Forest Stewardship Council to Social Accountability International. Founders are not everything. NGO-initiated programs can become watered down as they are mainstreamed, and industry-initiated programs often evolve into formally independent organizations. Most programs seek credibility by calling themselves "multi-stakeholder" initiatives. We maintain, however, that founding constituencies leave deep imprints on the content of standards and on the distribution of power within rule-making initiatives. Rules can get ratcheted up or down over time, but these are usually marginal revisions to a core approach. Furthermore, even when initiatives become formally independent from the constituencies that created them, informal ties, revolving doors, and financial contributions often persist.

Generally we expect that industry-initiated programs will have standards that depart in relatively small ways from the normal practices of the industry. Companies may want to improve labor conditions or environmental performance of their suppliers, but they will be loath to push so far as to disrupt production or force a major change in their sourcing practices. As a result, the greater the influence of companies in the founding of an initiative, the more likely it is to use either a "best in class" approach or a "continuous improvement" approach. In the first, companies are recognized (through certification or other endorsement) for demonstrating that they are above average in their industry. This often skirts the issue of whether they meet a stringent definition of a fixed standard. As Scott Nova (2011) has noted, a "best in class" model is like grading on a curve, even if average performance is quite low. The second approach allows companies to start with a relatively lax standard and encourage gradual improvement over time.[3]

When industry outsiders have power in the initial design, standard-setting initiatives should look somewhat different. First, their standards are likely to depart more substantially from normal practices in the industry, to a greater or lesser degree depending on the power of these outsiders. Second, these initiatives are more likely, though certainly not guaranteed, to endorse an alternative model of production rather than to just reward the best in class or push for continuous improvement. Fair trade certification and its emphasis on democratically managed producer cooperatives (as described in chapter 4) is the clearest example of this. Third, and because of this, initiatives spawned by outsiders are likely to either remain small or face dilemmas of mainstreaming as they grow. If they seek a large market presence, "alternative" programs will inevitably become more dependent on large companies. The result may be a watering down of standards, although as the case of the FSC shows (in chapter 3), this can be counteracted to some degree.

For most products there are multiple competing attempts to define fairness and sustainability. For instance, there are several ways of certifying the fairness and sustainability of coffee or of assessing the labor conditions of apparel companies.[4] Usually this competition reflects the struggle between companies and NGOs. Some scholars believe that such competition dooms voluntary initiatives, since it confuses consumers and lets companies choose their own standards (Seidman 2007). Others believe that it strengthens governance by spurring a "ratcheting up" of expectations (Sabel, O'Rourke, and Fung 2000). Our analysis of four global industries suggests that different sets of standards can often coexist, not exactly peacefully, but with moderate interaction or in different market niches. Competition is inevitable, but it seems to neither doom nor guarantee meaningful standards for fairness and sustainability. It must be noted that initiatives that began with high bars—namely, Fair Trade and the FSC—have not been pushed out of the market by their competitors.

Localized Globalisms and Globalized Localisms

Specifying links between "the global" and "the local" has proven difficult, and scholars have often fallen prey to two types of conceptual dangers. First, in focusing on the global diffusion of a given idea or norm, some have portrayed domestic settings as little more than passive receivers of a global project. The language of domestic settings as "receptor sites" for global models (Frank, Hironaka, and Schofer 2000) is one example of this. Pinpointing this problem, researchers are increasingly focusing on how local actors appropriate and "indigenize" global models to make them useful or meaningful

(Halliday and Carruthers 2009; Merry 2006). Second, scholars of globalization often equate the global with universalism (and often progress) and the local with particularism (and often backwardness). In so doing, scholars uncritically accept the most dominant model as "the global" and obscure the power that was exercised to establish its dominance.

To deal with these problems, we adopt Bonaventura de Santos's language of "globalized localisms" and "localized globalisms" (Santos 2006; Santos and Rodríguez Garavito 2005). The first refers to a process in which a *particularistic* set of ideas and practices becomes a dominant global norm. Santos (2006) provides examples such as "the transformation of the English language into a lingua franca, the globalization of American fast food or popular music or the worldwide adoption of the same laws of intellectual ownership, patents, or telecommunications aggressively promoted by the USA" (396). For our purpose the key issue is how particular understandings of rights, rules, and enforcement have become institutionalized as global norms. Concretely, the notion of a "globalized localism" sensitizes us to processes by which particular sets of reformers (NGOs, companies, or others) have turned their projects into "global" standards for fairness and sustainability. Our point is not to join the chorus that argues that "Western" standards are being illegitimately forced on people and companies elsewhere. There have long been calls for decent work and responsible natural resource management in many different parts of the world. But the global standards supported by conscientious consumers in North America and Europe embody particular approaches to these issues.

The second concept, "localized globalism," refers to the incorporation of these global models into local routines and expectations. The concept sensitizes us to the work involved in turning global standards for fairness and sustainability into a concrete practice in a factory, forest, or farm in some particular location. As we have noted, scholars too often portray these sites as empty spaces. We believe it is preferable to start from the opposite premise: that sites of implementation are crowded with different actors and agendas, only some of which are likely to line up with global standard-setting initiatives. Some elements of global standards are easily incorporated into local practices while others are fiercely resisted. But a recognition of localized globalisms also has methodological implications. It is rare for researchers to actually study these locations in detail. It is easier to conduct distant and decontextualized studies of CSR or to focus only on the creation of standards rather than their local implementation. Our analyses of the global timber, agricultural, apparel, and electronics industries include attention to specific locations, from the sugarcane farms of Paraguay to the electronics factories of Malaysia.

The Puzzle of Rules: Rule Making and the Persistence of Unruliness

One can better understand conscientious consumption and production projects by recognizing what Tim Bartley (2014a) has called the "puzzle of rules" in the global economy: simply put, global capitalism can be "unruly," but it also generates many rule-making projects.

The expansion of global markets has facilitated a number of rule-making projects, from the standardization of accounting procedures to the rules for fairness and sustainability discussed in this book. The volume of rule making by both public and private actors has increased over the past three decades. Many scholars have pointed to these trends as evidence that global capitalism is not manic or ungovernable as it was initially framed. Marie-Laure Djelic and Kerstin Sahlin-Andersson (2006) argue that "the proliferation of regulatory activities, actors, networks or constellations leads to an explosion of rules and to the profound re-ordering of our world" (1), and they see global capitalism as "marked by more—not less—rule-making activity" (376).

On the other hand, the explosion of rule making has often been geared toward the expansion of markets rather than their restriction, and in many respects global capitalism has remained unruly. In many industries investment and orders can and do move quickly across locations, often undermining attempts to impose rules. Even more socially controlled European varieties of capitalism have had their foundations chipped away (Streeck 2009). Furthermore, for all of the efforts of NGOs to build rules for fairness, sustainability, and human rights, many corners of global industries remain largely unscrutinized and unaffected by these rule-making projects.

As our case studies illustrate, even as standards for fairness and sustainability have risen to prominence, global industries have remained volatile and exploitative. Certification of sustainable forestry rose to prominence from 1995 to 2010, but so did illegal logging, and deforestation worsened in many places. The global apparel industry has come to be governed by numerous codes of conduct and factory monitoring initiatives, but it has also continued to move quickly from one location to another in search of low wages and more docile workers. The rapid and inconsistent pace of the global electronics industry has undermined attempts to improve working conditions, while rapidly changing agricultural markets have threatened the livelihoods of many smallholder farmers.

The puzzle of rules can be solved through an analysis of neoliberalism (see Bartley 2014a), but it also provokes a simple conclusion about the prospects for global fairness and sustainability: global industries often have contradictory tendencies, so we should not expect either complete "greenwash"/"fairwash" or serious transformation. Fair trade certification has not transformed the logic of commodity trade, but it has improved conditions for some farmers in some circumstances. FSC certification has not made the timber trade sustainable, but it has supported improvements in some forests. As we develop these findings (in part 2 of the book), we hope to speak not only to scholars of conscientious consumerism but also to citizens and consumers themselves. Consumers often want to feel like their purchases are "clean" of exploitation, but this is unrealistic. We believe it would be more promising if consumers shifted from a deterministic to a probabilistic approach: conscientious consumption may increase one's probability of contributing to improvements and decrease the probability of contributing to the most extreme forms of exploitation. This does not answer the question of how large those probabilities are (which surely varies by product and label) or the question of how significant those improvements can be. But only if consumers shift from an all-or-nothing view of "clean" versus "dirty" production (that is, sustainable versus destructive, fair versus exploitative) can they come to an accurate understanding of what their purchases can and cannot achieve.

WHAT LIES AHEAD

Part 1 of this book focuses on dynamics and dilemmas of conscientious consumerism. In chapter 1 we look at why some American and European consumers are more likely than others to practice conscientious consumption. Using survey data on thousands of individual consumers, our quantitative analyses focus on factors that shape two forms of conscientious consumption: boycotting and "buycotting"—that is, preferring a product for some political or ethical reason. Some patterns are related to consumers' beliefs and the extent to which they can afford to be choosy. But individual differences are only a small part of the story. *Where* consumers are has a great deal to do with whether they engage in conscientious consumption or not. We therefore connect the individual survey responses with measures that capture national economic, political, and cultural contexts. Overall, this initial portrait shows that conscientious consumption is widespread but far from universal, with key differences rooted not only in individual characteristics but in different structures of consumption as well.

Having sketched some general patterns, we delve deeper into the meanings and implications of conscientious consumerism in chapter 2. Our analyses in chapter 1 are based on what consumers *say* they do, but there are reasons to doubt that consumers will follow through on what they say, or that what they say truly captures the social meaning of their actions. Yet we show that there *is* evidence of consumers being willing to pay for eco-labels and social labels. Consumers are most likely to do so when their "ethical" choices also serve their self-interest, such as saving on energy costs or eating safer, healthier foods. But even for those forms of conscientious consumption that have no short-term, direct benefit for consumers, there is mounting evidence that some consumers will pay more. For labeling enthusiasts this is a good thing. But the "one dollar, one vote" logic of conscientious consumerism and the status-symbol character of some "ethical" products are potentially danger-ous in that they can exacerbate social, economic, and political inequalities among consumers. Moreover, there is a danger that conscientious consumer-ism can displace other forms of political engagement, promoting individual consumerism at the expense of democratic citizenship and collective social movements. Working through these debates, we argue that conscientious consumerism as an ideology is regressive and counterproductive, but specific practices of conscientious consumption can sometimes be consistent with other forms of political engagement.

Of course, the real test of conscientious consumption comes at the point of production. To what extent do voluntary standards forged in response to consumer concern make a difference "on the ground" in global industries? We tackle this question in part 2 of the book by looking at the global produc-tion of four types of products—(1) wood and paper products, (2) food (espe-cially the agri-food industry), (3) apparel and footwear, and (4) electronics.

Each of these case studies is rooted in the interviews that we have conducted with local actors and other fine-grained information on the organization of production. These chapters apply the framework sketched above (and a common organizational template) to allow for comparative insights.

Chapter 3 looks at the rise of forest certification and its effects in the global timber industry. Like fair trade, the FSC is one of the oldest and most established certification and labeling initiatives. It was founded more than twenty years ago, and it spurred a number of imitators and competitors. Yet it is not well known among conscientious consumers, and its impacts have been far less than originally intended. We trace the rise of forest certification, with particular attention to the founders and constituents of the FSC and how they leveraged the structure of the forest products industry to "make a market" for certified wood and paper. Yet applying sustainability standards to the production of some wood and paper products has barely influenced global deforestation. A closer look at FSC certification in the tropical forests of Indonesia illustrates both the contradictions of certifying in a shifting and contentious context and the limited ability of forest certification to influence the main drivers of deforestation.

Next, in chapter 4 we turn to agricultural production and the fairness and sustainability projects that have emerged in this setting. Consumers attach a variety of meanings to food, and the politics of food consumption has exploded in the past decade. In addition to sketching the structure of agri-food production and consumption in general, we focus on two types of rule-making projects: fair trade certification and an increasingly popular "commodity roundtable" approach. Looking more closely at two crops—sugar and soy—in one country, Paraguay, we are able to illustrate the consequences of different models of certification and the crucial role of local context. Global food politics are being layered onto preexisting institutional arrangements, and it is largely these institutional arrangements that determine whether certification is meaningful or not. For instance, fair trade certification seems to matter most when smallholder farmers are already organized into democratically effective cooperatives or when local organizing allows them to upgrade their production capacities over time. The contingent effects of conscientious consumption come into focus in this chapter.

Chapter 5 considers how the rise of anti-sweatshop activism in the early 1990s led to various attempts to monitor and improve working conditions in apparel and footwear factories. A rough indication of how these initiatives have fared is provided by the occurrence of factory fires in 2010–2013 and the death of more than eleven hundred garment workers in the 2013 collapse of the Rana Plaza building in Bangladesh. Our chapter examines the constituencies behind different factory auditing and certification initiatives, the ways standards were implemented, and the reasons why their effects have been minimal. The structure of apparel and footwear production in many ways created the demand for codes of conduct, but the structure and the mobility of the industry have undermined meaningful improvements. Looking more closely at factories in China, we show how attempts to certify particular factories have fallen short. In recent years several new projects to provide ethical apparel have emerged, but there remain few credible alternatives in this industry.

Finally, chapter 6 takes us into the fast-paced world of the electronics industry, where companies produce new models of smartphones, laptops, and other devices at breakneck speed. Yet recently this industry has become a focus of attention for the exploitation of production workers, especially after a series of worker suicides (and later strikes) at Foxconn factories in China and mounting scrutiny of Foxconn's buyer, Apple. Electronics brands have also been accused of using "conflict minerals" in the production of smartphones. The electronics industry is populated by well-capitalized companies that at times have demonstrated good intentions to make the labor process safer and more humane. Yet the industry has struggled to make improvements and find tenable solutions. We argue that the solution to this puzzle lies in the architecture of production and, to a large extent, ultimately in the organization of electronics consumption. This is a case in which conscientious consumerism has been slow to develop, and unreflective consumerism has been a powerful constraint on significant improvement. Using detailed data on factories producing for Hewlett-Packard, we show how the industry continues to demand extraordinarily "flexible" labor markets and excessive working hours in its factories in Southeast Asia.

We have tried to provide a sense of the complexity of these cases and settings while still drawing out clear implications. Along the way readers should get a clearer sense of the structure and operation of global value chains, the varied geographies of production, and the circumscribed consequences of eco-labels and social labels. In a concluding chapter we compare our four sets of products and consider what has been learned.

PART I
MAKING SENSE OF
CONSCIENTIOUS CONSUMERISM

1 – THE MAKING OF CONSCIENTIOUS CONSUMERS

Individual and National Patterns

THREE DECADES AGO A CONSUMER BUYING COFFEE WOULD HAVE found several roasts from a few major brands on the grocery store shelves, perhaps Maxwell House or Folgers in the United States or Douwe Egberts in Europe. Marketers had not yet invented the category of "specialty coffee," so the price and quality differences between coffees were small. In addition, the global coffee market was regulated by the International Coffee Agreement, which stabilized the prices that coffee farmers around the world received for their beans. Fast-forward thirty years and that grocery shelf would include a variety of specialty coffees, some with labels promising fair or sustainable production methods. After the International Coffee Agreement collapsed in 1989, coffee prices became highly volatile. As coffee farmers in developing countries fell into extreme poverty, religious groups and peace activists in Europe and the United States developed a label to help support them—what would soon become the fair trade label. In response to the environmental effects of coffee production, organic, shade-grown, bird-friendly, and rain forest–friendly labels also became common.

In short, that grocery store aisle has become a place where consumers may express their consciences. Some choose mainly on the basis of price or quality, but others find those assurances of fairness or sustainability appealing. Why? Furthermore, might the chances of being a conscientious consumer depend on where you live are? In some countries those labels are found on only a few expensive varieties, but in others they are more mainstream.

In this chapter we examine the factors that make consumers in Europe and the United States more or less likely to engage in conscientious consumption, whether that means buying coffee because it is certified as fair trade and organic, choosing an environmentally sustainable piece of furniture, or avoiding a clothing company that exploits its workers. We use a simple and broad definition of conscientious consumption at this point, before probing deeper and looking at different products in subsequent chapters. Like many other researchers, our focus here is on two types of consumer behavior. First, consumers may *boycott*—or intentionally not support—a particular product or company for political or ethical reasons. Boycotts have been waged for hundreds of years, from the Boston Tea Party to grape boycotts called by farmworkers' unions in the United States to boycotts in the UK against apartheid in South Africa. Whether organized or individual, conscientious consumption often means avoiding particular purchases.

More recently a second form of conscientious consumption has become widespread—that is, *buycotting,* or intentionally purchasing a product for political or ethical reasons. Consumers might support locally produced goods because they believe local economies are more sustainable or responsive than large-scale systems of trade. They might prefer a particular type of food—perhaps with an eco- or social label on it—that they believe is fairer or more sustainable than others. Or they may seek out clothes made domestically because they believe doing so reduces the chances that the garment was made in a sweatshop. These are just a few examples of buycotting. Our later chapters delve into these cases, but for now our initial goal is to develop a general portrait of conscientious consumption as practiced through individual boycotting and buycotting.

To begin this portrait, we have analyzed data from two large-scale surveys: the US "Citizenship, Involvement, Democracy" (CID) survey (conducted in 2005) and the European Social Survey (ESS) (conducted in 2002–2003).[1] Both surveys were conducted through face-to-face interviews with probability samples of adult residents. The CID data comes from a sample of 1,001 individuals across all regions of the United States. The ESS data covers 26,981 individuals in nineteen European countries.[2] Both surveys ask about boycotting and buycotting in the following way. Starting with a preface ("There are different ways of trying to improve things or help prevent things from going wrong"), individuals are asked, "During the last 12 months, have you done any of the following?" with answer choices that include "Boycotted certain products" and "Deliberately bought certain products for political, ethical or environmental reasons." Obviously, these questions are asked in a quite general way, and this data does not allow us to probe for specific examples.[3] Nevertheless, the data reveal variation in conscientious consumption that deserves to be explained. Only 18 percent of all respondents said they had boycotted in the past year, and only 29 percent said they had buycotted. By this measure most individuals in the United States and Europe are not especially conscientious consumers. Why are some people more likely than others to engage in conscientious consumption?

TOWARD A MULTILEVEL EXPLANATION

Most fundamentally we argue that explaining conscientious consumption requires attention to consumers' motivations, beliefs, and opportunities. Consider the introductory example of buying coffee. How can we explain the action of a consumer who has paid two dollars more for fair trade–certified coffee? One factor might be a pro-social *motivation,* such as the desire to help coffee farmers in poor countries. In addition, and for this motivation to matter, the individual needs to hold a *belief* that fair trade really does help farmers, or at least that conventional coffee is exploitative. Finally, the greater the *opportunity* to buy fair trade–certified coffee—or on the flip side, the fewer the constraints—the greater the likelihood of the purchase occurring. Constraints on conscientious consumption exist at the individual level (in the form of disparities in discretionary income, for instance) but can also be embedded in the social context (as with differences in retail structures).[4]

By the end of this chapter we will have drawn a general portrait, rooted in our survey data, of the individual and contextual factors that make Europeans and Americans more or less likely to engage in conscientious consumption. We start with individual characteristics—not only motivations and beliefs but also variables such as income and social class. Many of these factors are salient, casting doubt on perspectives that treat ethical consumer identities as fully individualized—that is, divorced from "old" social structures such as social class (Beck 1994). However, individual differences are but a small part of the picture, since conscientious consumer activity varies quite substantially across countries. For our second set of analyses, then, we combine the ESS data with data on the political, economic, and cultural characteristics of different countries.[5] Conscientious consumption, we find, is not just an individual behavior; it is structured by national differences in affluence, retail structures, and governance.

But first we begin by taking the example of fair trade a bit further. Markets for fair trade products have evolved quite differently in different countries. Through a brief comparison of the UK, Germany, and the United States, we illustrate how similar kinds of projects can evolve into different market structures. These structures of consumption have profound implications for individual acts. In addition to being revealing in their own right, these brief case studies pave the way to a cross-national analysis of our survey data.

Movements and Market Structures: The Example of Fair Trade

When it comes to the consumption of fair trade products, British consumers stand alone. In 2010 British consumers spent the equivalent of approximately $32 per capita on fair trade–certified products, compared to around $15 per capita in Sweden and Denmark, $10 per capita in the Netherlands, and $6–7 per capita in Belgium and France. German consumers spent $5 per capita and Americans spent only $4 per capita, although this was higher than some countries, such as Spain, where spending was less than $1 per capita (calculations based on data from FLO 2011). Fair trade–certified coffee, tea, chocolate, and fruit are widely available in the UK, and NGOs linked to the broader fair trade movement, such as Traidcraft and Oxfam, are well established there (Nicholls and Opal 2005). As figure 1.1 shows, growing sales of fair trade–certified products in the UK has far outpaced sales in Germany and the United States.

To some extent the UK's leadership on fair trade could be attributed to critical voices in media and NGOs that stirred up debate about globalization.

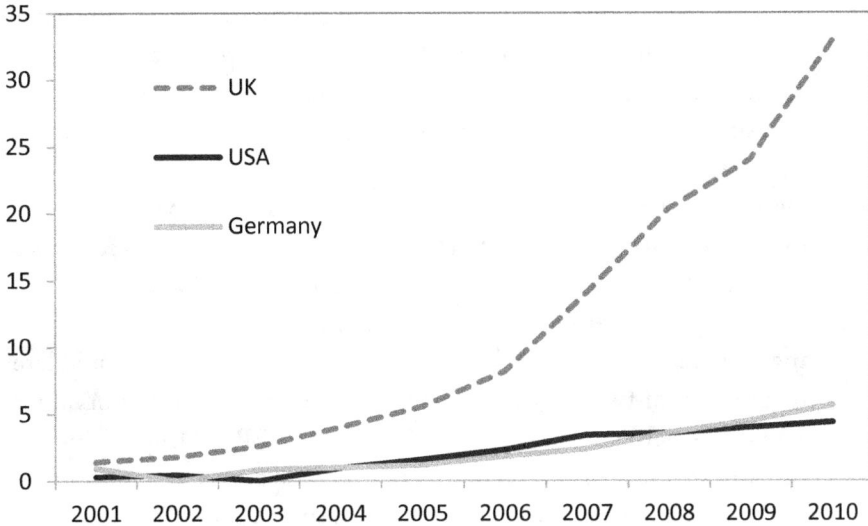

Figure 1.1: Per Capita Spending on Fair Trade–Certified Goods in the UK, USA, and Germany (in US $). *Note:* Values have been converted from € to US $ and standardized by population size as per capita spending. *Sources: Fairtrade Annual Report* (FLO 2005, 2006, 2007, 2008, 2009, 2010, 2011) and reports of national labeling organizations.

In addition, since the 1980s, British governments have promoted a neoliberal set of policy agendas that endorsed voluntary "corporate social responsibility" and consumer "responsibilization" (Kinderman 2012; Shamir 2008). On the other hand, British consumers are not the most "responsibilized" on all dimensions. When it comes to the consumption of organic food, the UK ranks far below Scandinavia, Germany, the United States, and France.[6] The pattern becomes easier to understand if we look at how fair trade movements, retail structures, and consumer choices have co-evolved. If we compare the UK, Germany, and the United States, we see that what looks like a global market actually has nationally distinct movements behind it.

Common to all fair trade projects are the goals of (1) building stronger relationships between consumers and producers and (2) setting prices that provide a premium to producers (and are more stable than market prices). In addition, farmers and artisans typically receive some sort of subsidy (or "social premium") to support infrastructure and services for their communities.

In these ways the fair trade movement has sought to provide an alternative to both the vicissitudes of so-called free trade and the paternalism of charity. Of course, it has also been accused of retaining undesirable elements of both. [7] (For our analysis of the consequences of fair trade certification in agriculture, see chapter 4.)

In the United States the fair trade movement dates to the 1940s, when Mennonite religious groups began a fair exchange program with makers of handicrafts in Puerto Rico (Grimes 2000). Soon after, the Church of Brethren began using a similar model to support World War II refugees in a "Sales Exchange for Refugee Rehabilitation" program. These projects would later fuel the creation of two religiously affiliated alternative trading organizations (ATOs)—Selfhelp: Crafts of the World and SERRV International—which acted as importers and retailers of handmade goods from developing countries (Grimes 2000). Selfhelp was later renamed Ten Thousand Villages, which now has hundreds of stores. In the UK fair trade can be traced to Oxfam—a famine relief charity founded in Oxford—which began selling handicrafts from developing countries as early as 1964 (Oxfam 2013). It did this in its own stores, which were initially designed for selling donated clothes and books. In Germany fair trade dates to 1972, when Campaign Third World groups were founded by Christian youth groups. After initially importing goods through a Dutch organization, the German groups founded their own alternative trading organization, Gepa, which allowed them to import, stock, and sell items on a much larger scale.

The existing infrastructure of Oxfam shops in the UK helped fair trade to get off the ground. In the United States and Germany there was a gradual shift from selling through church groups to setting up new fair trade shops, or "world shops," mostly staffed by volunteers. Importantly, fair trade crafts in the United States and Germany remained closely tied to Christian organizations (Fridell 2004; Raschke 2009).

Starting in the late 1980s the fair trade movement became not only about crafts but about agriculture as well. In response to volatile world coffee prices, German Third World groups and American peace activists (via Equal Exchange) began selling what would be become fair trade coffee. British activists soon followed, developing the Cafédirect line of Fairtrade coffee. New organizations, like Transfair (United States, Germany, and others) and the Fairtrade Foundation (UK) emerged to standardize the labeling process (Linton, Liou, and Shaw 2004). As of 2001 the US market had 120 fair trade licensees (companies allowed to use the Fair Trade or Fairtrade mark on their products), Germany had 57, and the UK had 39 (Krier 2001). But by 2009 that number had increased by around 3.5 times in Germany, nearly 7 times in the United States, and roughly 10 times in the UK. Rapid growth in sales in the United States and Germany were no match for the nearly 1200 percent growth in the UK (as shown in fig. 1.1). Even as fair trade was becoming "mainstream," mission-driven organizations (e.g., Equal Exchange, Gepa, and Cafédirect) persisted and expanded their offerings. As of 1997, sales by Oxfam and Traidcraft in the UK far outpaced sales from similar organizations in Germany and the United States (Martinelli 1998).

So why did fair trade grow so much more in the UK than in Germany or the United States? There are surely several pieces to a full answer. Matthias Varul (2009) argues that the legacy of British colonialism left British consumers with a peculiar sense of obligation. We argue that another important factor has to do with the legacies of early movements and their links to retailing structures, as described above. In the United States and (especially) Germany, the fair trade movement and its specialized distribution structures had a religious image. In the UK there had not been a broad base of "world shops." Oxfam shops had been used, but these were never exclusively focused on fair trade. This left more leeway for the "branding" of fair trade and its mainstreaming through supermarkets. British fair trade advocates successfully lobbied large retailers to stock Fairtrade-certified goods, and some supermarket chains even transformed their own coffee and chocolate brands to Fairtrade (Barrientos and Smith 2007). There has been a trend toward concentration in British retailing—toward a small number of very large retailers with big investments in their own brands—and this likely amplified the efforts of fair trade activists, much as it did for the anti-GMO activists studied by Rachel Schurman and William Munro (2009).

Returning to our opening vignette about a coffee purchase, a consumer in a grocery store in the UK would find numerous options for fair, ethical, or sustainable coffee. A consumer with similar motivations and beliefs in the United States or Germany would face a different set of opportunities for conscientious consumption. This leads us to ask about the individual and contextual factors that shape these consumers' behavior. Our analysis of survey data sheds considerable light on this issue, allowing us to look at both individual-level and national-level factors.

WHO ENGAGES IN CONSCIENTIOUS CONSUMPTION? INDIVIDUAL-LEVEL PATTERNS

Motivations and Beliefs

What motivates conscientious consumer behavior? This question has spawned a range of answers, emphasizing factors from environmentalism to particular conceptions of morality (Arndorfer and Liebe 2013; Copeland 2014; Daugbjerg and Sønderskov 2012; Guido, Pino, and Prete 2009; Neilson 2010; Shaw 2005; Stolle, Hooghe, and Micheletti 2005; Sunderer and Rössel 2012). Studies of particular forms of political consumption, such as buying fair trade goods, have also highlighted the influence of specific attitudes (Guido 2009; Ozcaglar-Toulouse, Shiu, and Shaw 2006; Shaw 2005) and identities (Arndorfer and Liebe 2013; DuPuis 2000; Varul 2009). In addition, there is some evidence that religious identities matter, with Americans who were raised as Protestants being more likely to buycott and those who reject evolution (in favor of a literal biblical account of creation) being less likely to boycott (Starr 2009).

But the most widespread general argument is that conscientious consumption reflects deeper "post-materialist" orientations, such as self-actualization and autonomy, that become possible when individuals move beyond "materialist" concerns, such as economic well-being and physical security. By some accounts rising affluence has led industrial democracies to undergo a fundamental value shift over the past decades from materialist to post-materialist concerns, including environmental protection, creative expression, and human rights (Inglehart 1997; Norris 2002). One need not subscribe to a full value-shift theory to appreciate that individuals with more post-materialist values may be more likely to be conscientious consumers. Indeed, our analyses find that among European consumers, individuals who express strong post-materialist values—that is, "understanding, appreciation, tolerance and protection for the welfare of all people and for nature"—are far more likely than others to boycott or buycott. Holding other factors constant, an increase of one standard deviation in the measure of post-materialism increases the likelihood of buycotting by 7 percent and the likelihood of boycotting by 4 percent. Compared to the least post-materialist individuals, those with the strongest post-materialist value orientations are 58 percent more likely to buycott and 34 percent more likely to boycott.[8]

This pattern, like the others reported in this chapter, is statistically significant, meaning there is less than a 5 percent chance that it could have occurred just because of random variation in the sampling of particular American and European consumers to participate in the surveys. In addition, this pattern (again like the other reported patterns) holds when controlling for other individual factors, such as income, gender, age, social class, trust, political interest, and political efficacy, each of which we discuss below. That post-materialism matters is becoming well established in research on European consumers (Daugbjerg and Sønderskov 2012; Guido 2009; Koos 2012; Stolle, Hooghe, and Micheletti 2005). Unfortunately, the CID survey did not measure post-materialist attitudes, so we cannot examine them directly among American consumers. But in some recent research, Lauren Copeland (2014) finds that Americans with post-materialist values are significantly more likely than others to engage in buycotting.

When it comes to belief in the efficacy of conscientious consumerism, scholars have made a strong case for focusing on trust. Individuals who are more trusting of others have greater confidence that their political and civic activities will be effective, accepted, and reciprocated (Nannestad 2008). They should be more likely to act as conscientious consumers as a result (Koos 2012; Neilson and Paxton 2010). Our analyses show that generalized trust in others does indeed shape conscientious consumption among American and European consumers. A one standard deviation increase in generalized trust raises the likelihood of buycotting by almost 3 percent. Those who report the highest levels of trust are 15 percent more likely than the least trusting to engage in buycotting. (The differences are smaller, and only significant at the 10 percent level, for boycotting.)

While generalized trust facilitates conscientious consumption, trust in institutions should have the opposite effect. If individuals distrust core social institutions, such as government, to solve social problems, they may be more likely to "do it themselves" in the marketplace. Our analyses find some support for this idea: respondents who report the least trust in political institutions (such as their country's parliament/legislature, legal system, or politicians) are 11 percent more likely than those with the most trust in political institutions to engage in a boycott. On the other hand, no such relationship can be detected for buycotting, suggesting that consumers may not see "voting with your dollars" as a substitute for political authority.[9] Individuals' sense of political efficacy, especially their sense of personal political competence, may also shape their likelihood of engaging in conscientious consumption.[10] Researchers have found that people with a strong sense of personal efficacy are likely to get involved in both conventional and unconventional forms of political participation (Stolle, Hooghe, and Micheletti 2005; Verba, Schlozman, and Brady 1995), so we would expect this to shape their likelihood of boycotting and buycotting. Our analyses find support for this among Europeans. Europeans with the highest sense of personal political efficacy have a 20 percent higher likelihood of boycotting and a 25 percent higher likelihood of buycotting than those with the lowest feelings of efficacy. The survey data do not allow us to measure personal political efficacy in the United States. But both surveys measure political *interest*, which is typically associated with political engagement (Almond and Verba 1989; Stolle, Hooghe, and Micheletti 2005; Verba, Schlozman, and Brady 1995). When it comes to conscientious consumption, we find that Americans and Europeans who are "very" or "quite" interested in politics have a 7 percent higher likelihood of boycotting and a 9 percent higher likelihood of buycotting than people who are "hardly" or "not at all" interested in politics. In these senses conscientious consumption can be viewed as intertwined with political life. On the other hand, other research suggests that the political party affiliation of Americans (Democrat or Republican) is not related to the likelihood of buycotting (Starr 2009).

In sum, we can identify several general types of motivations and beliefs that shape conscientious consumption: post-materialist values pay a major role, while trust, personal efficacy, and political interest matter to a somewhat lesser degree. These, of course, are overarching patterns that do not include more specific motivations and beliefs that matter for particular consumer choices. Other research has shown how the purchase of certified products depends on consumers' knowledge of and trust in labeling and certification processes (Daugbjerg and Sønderskov 2012; De Pelsmacker and Janssens

2007). More strikingly, the choice to buy organic food relies heavily on the belief that it is healthier, more nutritious, and safer (Hughner et al. 2007; Zanoli and Naspetti 2002). The connection to personal well-being is an issue we return to in the next chapter, when we consider the evidence for the motivational capacities of self-interest and altruism.

Resources and Constraints: Social Structures of Consumer Choice

Much of the writing on conscientious consumerism frames it as an individual "choice," but from a sociological perspective that choice is obviously heavily constrained. Most noticeably, those with little disposable income may need to base their consumer decisions mainly on price, while those with more disposable income may have the luxury of considering other factors. Our analyses support this expectation, as illustrated in figure 1.2. Across Europe, individuals with near-mean household income (between 80 percent and 120 percent of the country average) have a 3 percent higher likelihood of buycotting than those with less than 80 percent of their country's mean income. Those with higher income (more than 120 percent of the country average) have a 6 percent higher likelihood of buycotting than those in the lowest income group (see fig. 1.2). This basic finding, a statistically significant but not substantively huge relationship, is the same in the United States (Starr 2009). When it comes to boycotting, on the other hand, higher income is not associated with increased participation. This may reflect a difference in the logic of these forms of conscientious consumption. Buycotters must often pay a premium for ethical/sustainable alternatives, but boycotters may be able to forego a purchase altogether or find a similarly priced substitute.

More importantly, though, the effect of income is far more muted than one might expect. Other kinds of resources, and other forms of inequality, must also be considered. One relevant resource is education, which we expect to increase consumers' interest in and understanding of complex global production processes, and perhaps also to provide skills for civic engagement (Verba, Schlozman, and Brady 1995, 305; Ferrer and Fraile, 2006; Goul Andersen and Tobiasen, 2004). We find that consumers in Europe and the United States who have completed secondary education (e.g., high school degree) have a 4 percent higher likelihood of boycotting and 8 percent higher

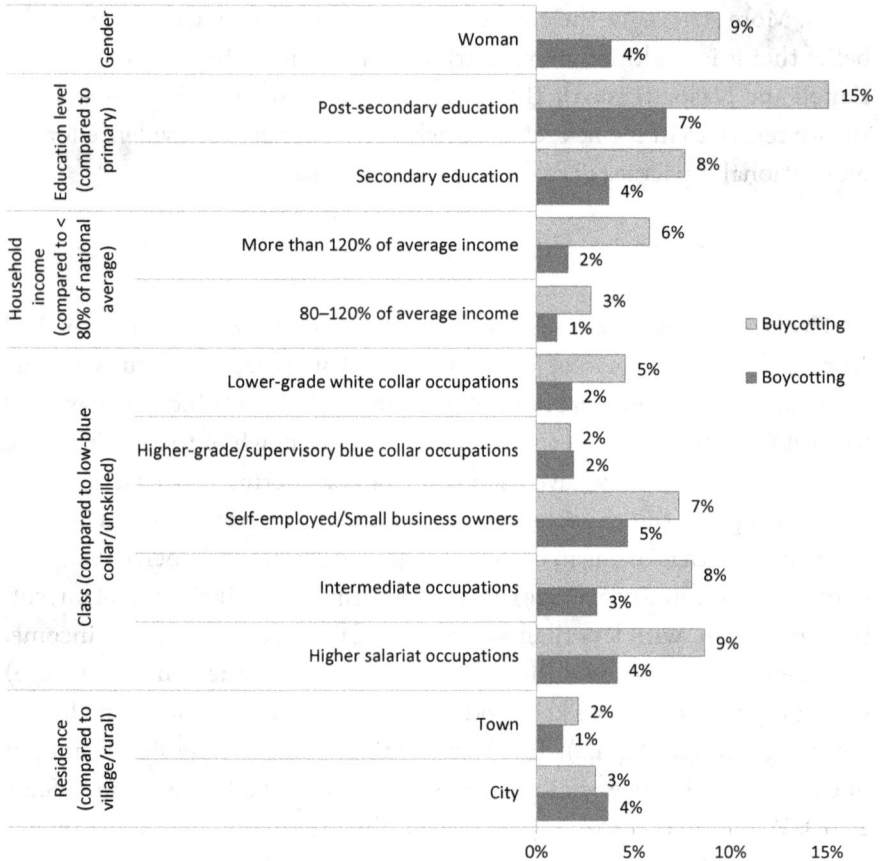

Figure 1.2: Factors Shaping the Likelihood of Boycotting and Buycotting among European Consumers. *Note:* Shown are predicted probabilities (in %) for individual variables, keeping all other variables at their mean. Details of our logistic regression models are available in the appendix.

likelihood of buycotting than those with less education. Having a university degree increases the likelihood of boycotting by 7 percent and of buycotting by 15 percent compared to the least educated group.

Beyond income and education, conscientious consumption may be rooted in social class. As Thorstein Veblen (1949 [1899]) and Pierre Bourdieu (1984) have argued, consumption can be a form of class distinction. Specifically, consumption activities that conspicuously demonstrate a "distance from necessity"—that is, "an experience of the world freed from urgency" (Bourdieu

1984, 54)—are powerful ways of establishing and reinforcing the boundaries of social class. A great deal of conscientious consumption demonstrates this kind of distance from necessity, since it subordinates function and price to higher-order ethical concerns. As such, the consumption of fair trade, organic, and eco-labeled products may be contributing to a new form of class distinction (Johnston 2008; Johnston, Szabo, and Rodney 2011). Elites may strategically use consumption practices to symbolically differentiate themselves, but they may also unintentionally enact a class-based "habitus" that profoundly shapes their tastes and dispositions and normalizes their values.

In the next chapter we consider the meaning of conscientious consumption in light of class distinction. But first we must assess whether class position affects a person's likelihood of boycotting and buycotting, especially when education and income are held constant. We adopt Robert Erikson and John Goldethorpe's (1992) model of occupation-based class positions, which are measurable in our European data. As illustrated in figure 1.2, there are indeed major differences, especially for buycotting. Compared to individuals in blue-collar or unskilled occupations, those in the "higher salariat" positions (professionals, upper- and mid-level managers), intermediate occupations (low-level managers and office workers), and self-employed/small business owners have a higher likelihood of buycotting (9 percent, 8 percent, and 7 percent higher, respectively) and of boycotting (4 percent, 3 percent, and 5 percent higher, respectively). Those in lower-grade white-collar positions (cashier, salesperson) are also more likely to engage in buycotting. Those in skilled or supervisory blue-collar occupations are fairly similar to their unskilled counterparts in terms of boycotting and buycotting.

In short, class matters, even when holding income and education constant. This finding stands in contrast to the image of the "sovereign consumer" as promoted in writing about the "individualization" thesis (Beck 1994; Pakulski and Waters 1996). Scholars in this tradition have argued that conscientious consumerism is tied up with a process of "reflexive modernization" that has dissolved class-based tastes and replaced them with individual projects of identity construction (Beck 1994). While we do not deny that individual agency and identity work is involved in becoming a conscientious consumer, social class clearly remains important in structuring opportunities and tastes.

Racial and ethnic inequality may also influence conscientious consumption. As we discuss in the next chapter, some prototypical sites of conscientious consumption, such as community farmers markets, are often racially exclusionary (Guthman 2008). In the United States there is evidence that white consumers are somewhat more likely than nonwhite consumers to engage in buycotting (Starr 2009). Unfortunately, researchers have yet to address how race and ethnicity might matter across different countries, in part due to challenges in comparing distinct configurations of racial and ethnic inequality.[11]

Another traditional axis of difference and inequality—gender—does generally structure conscientious consumption. We find that women in the United States and Europe are 10 percent more likely than men to buycott and 4 percent more likely to boycott. The result for Europe alone, shown in figure 1.2, is similar. This gender difference has become well established in the research literature (Goul Andersen and Tobiasen 2004; Koos 2011, 2012; Stolle, Hooghe, and Micheletti 2005; Strø msnes 2005). The reason for it, however, is not as clear. It could stem from the fact that women typically have a greater responsibility for shopping. For instance, insofar as women are still disproportionately in charge of domestic duties, they may be more inclined to purchase eco- or organically labeled products in an attempt to protect their families from danger (Szasz 2007). One study, however, found a gender difference even when holding the amount of shopping constant (Stolle and Micheletti 2013, 82). Michele Micheletti (2003) has argued that women are more likely to be conscientious consumers because they are marginalized or alienated from other, more formal modes of political participation. This is a plausible explanation, but other possibilities should also be considered. On average, women are more religious than men (Collett and Lizardo 2009; Roth and Kroll 2007), and they have different views on a range of social and environmental policy issues (Bolzendahl and Olafsdottir 2008; Xiao and McCright 2014). These factors might account for different patterns of boycotting and buycotting without having to presume that women think about conscientious consumption in fundamentally different ways.

If the "ethical consumer" ideology has become more prominent in the past few decades, as many theorists argue (Stolle, Hooghe, and Micheletti 2005), then we would expect younger cohorts to be more likely to engage in it. In our analyses of American and European consumers, we find that the relationship between age and conscientious consumption takes the shape of an inverted U. Up to around age thirty-five, older consumers are more likely than younger ones to engage in boycotting and buycotting. After that the likelihood of boycotting and buycotting decreases with age. We suspect that younger cohorts have learned to consider conscientious consumption as a routine part of shopping (Koos 2011, 2012; Strømsnes 2005), but the more mature members of these cohorts are most likely to be mindful of their consumption habits.

Finally, consumers' location matters, though not overwhelmingly so. Americans and Europeans who live in cities are 4 percent more likely to boycott and 3 percent more likely to buycott than those who live in small villages or rural areas. Those in cities are likely to have more shopping choices in general, and those in rural areas tend to have less access to co-ops, "world shops," and other alternative markets.

In sum, individuals' motivations and beliefs are only one part of the story. Education and income facilitate boycotting, and especially buycotting, and conscientious consumption remains structured by social class, gender, and (to a lesser extent) location. We see these findings as a rejoinder to the image of the "sovereign consumer," unconstrained by anything but his or her devotion and imagination. In addition, the opportunities for conscientious consumption also vary cross-nationally. It is to these national contexts that we now turn.

CROSS-NATIONAL DIFFERENCES IN CONSCIENTIOUS CONSUMPTION

Even comparing affluent Western countries to one another we can observe quite large differences in the extent of conscientious consumerism. Figure 1.3 shows the distribution of conscientious consumerism for a number of countries. In nearly all of them consumers are more likely to buycott than to boycott. But the differences across countries are striking. The Scandinavian countries and Switzerland have the highest rate of boycotting and buycotting, while Southern and Eastern European countries tend to be at the lower end of the distribution. In between, American consumers are slightly above the European average when it comes to boycotting and slightly below this average when it comes to buycotting.

Why do consumers in some countries have a higher propensity to boycott/buycott than consumers in other countries? We argue that opportuni-

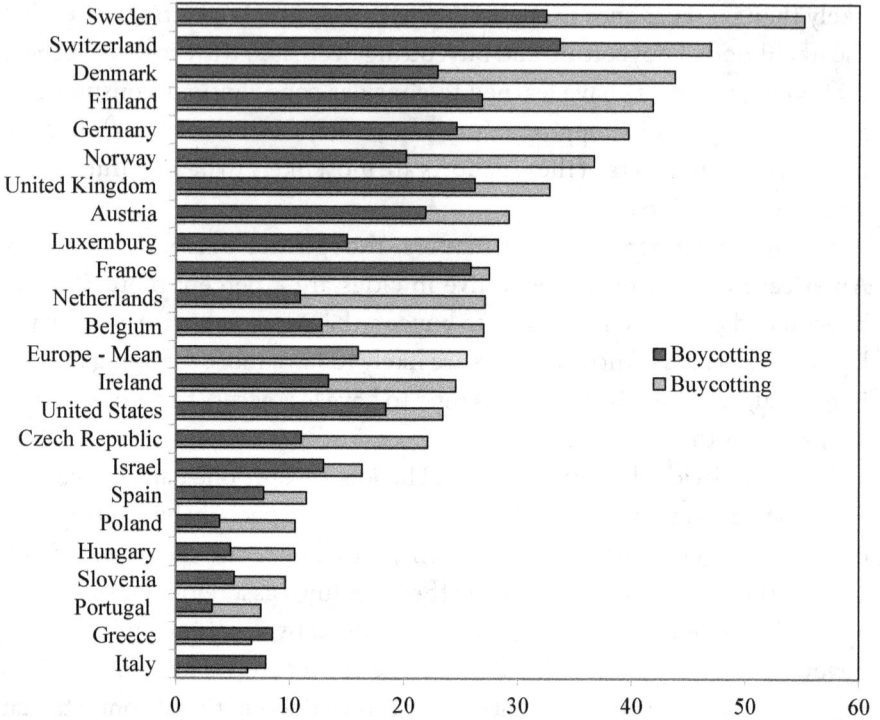

Figure 1.3: Boycotting and Buycotting across Countries (in %).

ties matter, and we highlight three types of "opportunity structures" for conscientious consumption. First, *political opportunity structures* refer to the extent to which states and social movements make conscientious consumption a priority for citizens. For instance, in countries with a strong "statist" political culture, citizens may treat channels other than the market, such as state policy, as more appropriate targets of conscientious behavior. Second, *economic opportunity structures* refer to factors like the country's affluence and the availability of alternative products, such as those with eco- or social labels. Returning to our earlier example, the greater availability of fair trade–certified products in the UK may constitute an economic opportunity for conscientious consumption. Third, countries may have different *cultural opportunity structures* for conscientious consumption. Things like trust and post-materialist values are not merely individual attitudes; they also may be institutionalized in dominant meanings and discourses at the national

level. By some accounts such collective meanings can be even more important than individual orientations (Durkheim 1898 [1995]; Meyer et al. 1997).
Overall, by looking at these types of opportunities we can assess the extent
to which conscientious consumption is structured mainly by cultural and
political differences (as emphasized by Balsiger 2010; Beck 1997, 2000; Inglehart 1997; Neilson and Paxton 2010; Norris 2002) or largely by differences
in the size and organization of markets (as stressed by Koos 2012; Seyfang
2009; Sønderskov 2009).[12]

Political Opportunities and Their Consequences

Affluent democracies differ greatly in how their political systems are organized and their markets are governed. In the United States and Great Britain,
for instance, the state has a comparatively limited role in rectifying social
and environmental problems. In these two countries the state tends to lean
heavily on civil society (nonprofit organizations and voluntary associations
of citizens) to correct market failures and administer social services. In Germany and France, in contrast, the state plays a more direct role. Markets are
more heavily controlled by state agencies, who tend to have a strong hand in
regulating companies. Statist systems, we suspect, should discourage conscientious consumerism, since citizens will be more likely to look to the state for
necessary action. On the other hand, citizens in non-statist/"societal" systems should be more accustomed to thinking of voluntary individual action
as the appropriate response to social or environmental problems (Schofer
and Marion 2001). This is indeed what our analyses find when we compare
statist and "societal" countries, as identified by Ronald Jepperson (2002).
Controlling for individual factors, as well as the other cross-national differences discussed below, living in a statist country reduces a consumer's
likelihood of buycotting by 8 percent. (However, there is not a statistically
significant effect on boycotting.) Thus, the historically developed institutional arrangements of states provide different political opportunities for
conscientious consumption.[13]

    As discussed in the introductory chapter, conscientious consumption ini-
tiatives are typically spawned by social movements. Environmental, labor,
and human rights movements have all been active in "naming and shaming"
companies and encouraging consumers to be mindful of the implications of

their shopping. Social movements, and the NGOs that often guide them, may shape consumer behavior in several ways. First, social movement campaigns provide new information about injustices and unsustainable practices, and they mobilize individuals to respond to this information. In addition, NGOs often help to construct alternative markets, by promoting eco- and social labels, for instance. Third, social movements play a key role in framing social and environmental problems so that they resonate with citizens and consumers (Benford and Snow 2000; Holzer 2006). Boris Holzer (2007) shows, for instance, how Greenpeace, Amnesty International, and other activists inspired a boycott by framing the complicity of Shell with human rights abuses in Nigeria. Philip Balsiger (2010) illustrates how the Clean Clothes Campaign in Switzerland staged events to inform consumers and frame global labor rights issues.

Thus, one might expect countries where social movements have a greater presence to have higher rates of boycotting and buycotting. We have assessed this by measuring the percentage of residents who say they are members of an environmental, peace, or human rights organization (based on the European Values Survey). Using this measure we find no link between the presence of social movements in a country and the likelihood of conscientious consumption. This does not mean that social movements are irrelevant, but it does mean that national membership patterns alone do not capture their effects. In part 2 of this book we show how some particular NGOs and social movements have fostered conscientious consumerism, for better or worse.

The Importance of Economic Structures

National economic circumstances can shape both the demand for and supply of alternative products (Clarke et al. 2002). On the demand side, a country's overall affluence may shape the "degrees of freedom" in consumer decisions—that is, the amount of aggregate discretionary income. If consumers must spend most of their income on basic subsistence, we would not expect a country to be a hotbed of buycotting and boycotting. In countries where consumers have more discretionary income, the pool of money available for eco- or social-labeled goods, or for finding substitutes to boycotted products (Baumol, Oates, and Blackman 1979), should be much greater. In other words, conscientious consumerism grows in affluent markets. Our analysis finds strong support for this idea. An increase of one standard deviation in a country's affluence increases consumers' likelihood of both buycotting and boycotting by approximately 6 percent. People in the richest countries in Europe, such as Switzerland, have an almost 18 percent higher likelihood of conscientious consumption (buycotting or boycotting) than people in the least affluent countries, such as Poland. Importantly, this is above and beyond the role of household income discussed above.

On the supply side, the choices available to potential conscientious consumers depend on the "infrastructures of provision" (Southerton, Chappells, and Van Vliet 2004) that are in place in a country. Eco- and social-labeled products are available to some degree almost everywhere, but countries differ a great deal in the extent to which they are available. In line with our emphasis on opportunities and the earlier discussion of fair trade, we would expect that greater availability of these products is linked to a greater likelihood of conscientious consumption (see also Terragni and Kjærnes 2005). To assess this assumption we developed a measure of the supply of eco-, organic-, and fair trade–labeled goods that were available in each country in 2001 (relative to the size of the country's market; see appendix for details). We find that availability does matter. A one standard deviation increase in the supply of these products in a country is associated with a 4 percent higher likelihood of consumers engaging in buycotting.[14]

The availability of products may also be influenced by the structure of the retail sector in a given country—that is, the type of sales outlets and their concentration. Large supermarkets, or even hypermarkets, that are common in Northern Europe and the United States (Grunert et al. 1996, 130) offer a large variety of brands and goods. This may make it easier for consumers to avoid certain products, or penalize certain companies, and find a substitute. In addition, if the overall number of consumer choices is larger, then we would expect there to be more room for differentiation—that is, having at least a few items that speak to consumers' consciences. In contrast, smaller independent stores and local markets that dominate Southern and Eastern Europe (Clarke et al. 2002, 49) often have a limited selection of goods, sometimes originating from nearby. Whatever else one thinks about this approach, we would expect it to provide limited opportunities for making a deliberate choice to avoid or prefer a particular item. In other words, for all the criticism of large oligopolistic retailers, much of it justified, they may make it easier for consumers to follow their conscience while on the shopping floor. In addition, as emphasized by Schurman and Munro (2009), when a country is dominated by a small number of very large retailers, this can actually make it easier for activists to find good targets and push them to introduce new products.

Our results, based on measuring the prevalence of small retailers in a country, are consistent with this idea. Markets with numerous small retailers tend to have lower rates of boycotting and buycotting. Consumers in European countries where retail markets are highly concentrated, with a few dominant large-scale retailers have a 12 percent higher likelihood of buycotting and an 8 percent higher likelihood of boycotting.

Overall, economic opportunities—based on retail structures, the supply of products, and especially national affluence—have major implications for the seemingly "individual" act of boycotting or buycotting. As discussed in the introductory chapter, most discussions of conscientious consumerism have overlooked this in favor of what we see as overly psychologized, overly voluntaristic treatments of the sovereign consumer.

Do Cultural Opportunities Matter?

Finally, even though there is great diversity within countries, there may be overarching patterns of national culture that make it normal or abnormal to engage in conscientious consumption. Here we return to the idea of post-materialism. By many accounts post-materialism is not just an individual orientation; it is also a societal one (Inglehart 1990, 1997). As post-materialism becomes dominant in a country, one might expect markets to shift from price and quality considerations to more expressive notions of value, including environmental sustainability and global fairness. Yet our results do not provide support for this idea. When controlling for economic opportunity structures, there is no statistically significant association between a country's overall level of post-materialism and its rate of boycotting or buycotting.[15] Similarly, returning to our earlier discussion of trust, it is plausible that "high trust societies," in which many citizens find others trustworthy, would make more fertile ground for conscientious consumption. Some have argued that trusting societies are more easily able to come to cooperative, mutually beneficial solutions (Putnam, Leonardi, and Nanetti 1994; Sønderskov 2009). Once again, though, our evidence does not portray societal trust as important for conscientious consumption when controlling for economic opportunities. Other factors aside, European consumers in more trusting countries (e.g., Denmark) are no more likely than those in less trusting countries (e.g., Greece) to engage in boycotting or buycotting.

These results are interesting given that at the individual level, both trust and post-materialism shape conscientious consumption. Overall our analyses demonstrate that national differences are important, but these are more traceable to political systems and (especially) economic structures than to cultural differences. It is tempting to attribute differences in consumer behavior to "culture," but this is misleading. Individual attitudes matter, but when it comes to national differences, the key factors are political and economic.

Combined Effects of Individual-Level and Country-Level Differences: Post-Materialist Values and Economic Opportunities

The results so far raise the question of whether cross-national differences interact with individual-level differences. Do national opportunity structures amplify the role of individual attitudes? Or would attitudes matter in basically the same way everywhere? Answering this question fully would require a number of more complex analyses, but we can provide some insight by considering the so-called low-cost hypothesis (Diekmann and Preisendörfer 2003). This hypothesis claims that value orientations matter only when the costs of taking action are not too high. To the extent that the social context supports conscientious consumption, individual values should matter a great deal. But if the social context makes conscientious consumption difficult, then what a person believes may not make much of a difference.

Since we found individual post-materialist values to be an important predictor of buycotting, we take those as our focus. At the country level we found that affluence matters a great deal. The low-cost hypothesis would expect post-materialist values to matter a great deal in affluent countries and to hardly matter at all in less affluent countries. Figure 1.4 shows the interaction between these two factors and sheds light on the interplay of these two

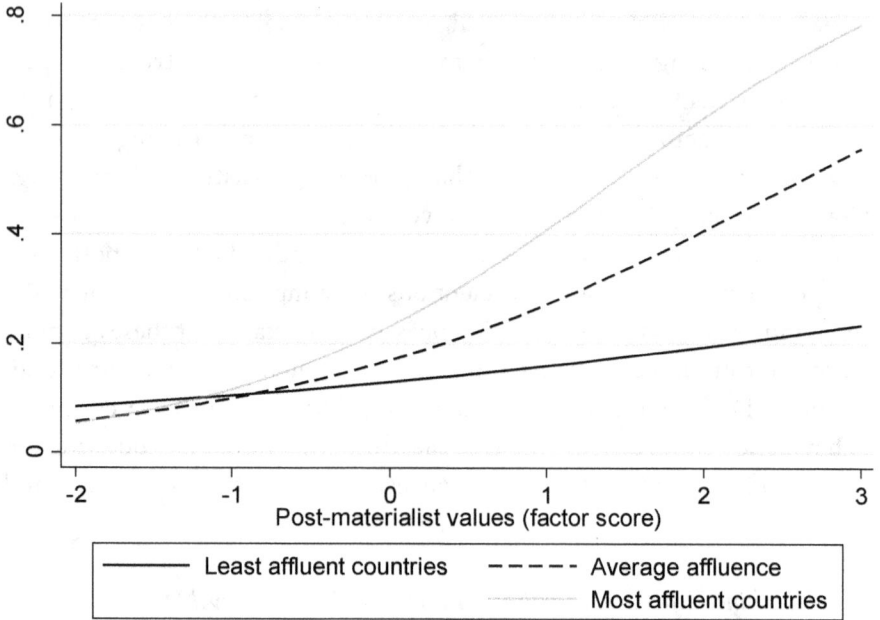

Figure 1.4: Predicted Probabilities of Buycotting by
Individual Post-materialism and Societal Affluence.

levels of analysis. As shown in the figure, in the most affluent countries, such
as Switzerland and Sweden, individual value orientations have a large impact
on buycotting. The likelihood of buycotting in such countries increases from
6 percent for the least to almost 80 percent for the most post-materialist
people. If we turn to the less affluent European countries, such as Poland and
Portugal, we observe that value orientations still matter, but to a much more
limited degree. In these countries, an increase from the lowest to the highest
level of post-materialism is associated with an increase in the likelihood of
positive buying from only around 8 to 24 percent. Looking at it slightly differently, if someone were a strong post-materialist, that person's likelihood
of buycotting would be 50 percent higher if he or she lived in the wealthiest
European countries than in the least affluent parts of Europe. On the other
hand, for an individual with the lowest level of post-materialism, it makes no
difference if one lives in a more or less affluent European country.[16] Overall,
some places clearly provide more space than others for individuals to become
conscientious consumers.

CONCLUSION

Conscientious consumption can be a very individual act. Consumer choices are often made alone in a store and only occasionally as part of a coordinated campaign. It is our hope that in the process of reading a book like this, individuals will consider their priorities and values as well as their understandings of social change. As the next chapter discusses, the individual character of consumption has generated a great deal of debate among scholars. Some have celebrated conscientious consumption as an empowering form of "individualized collective action" (Micheletti 2003), and others have decried it as a death knell for the coordinated collective action of vibrant social movements (Maniates 2001). These debates are important, but as we have shown in this chapter, conscientious consumption is not entirely individualized after all. To be sure, the portrait of boycotting and buycotting that we have developed reveals that individual orientations matter. A person's level of post-materialism and personal efficacy helps to explain whether he or she is likely to engage in conscientious consumption or not. So do characteristics such as gender, household income, education, and social class. Boycotting and buycotting are not elite activities, but neither are they universal among individuals in the United States and Europe.

But social context—and especially the landscape of opportunities for boycotting and buycotting—also matters a great deal. In this sense conscientious consumption is not just an individual act but a societal phenomenon as well. Even the structural characteristics of the retail sector can shape whether an individual becomes a conscientious consumer or not. As we move further in this book, we build on the theme that industry structures matter and, more broadly, that we must understand conscientious consumerism *in context.* In part that means digging deeper into the meanings of this activity for consumers and political life, as discussed in the next chapter. But it also means digging into different products and standards along with the assurances that consumers receive about those standards. Even the most conscientious consumer is only as effective as the standards he or she supports.

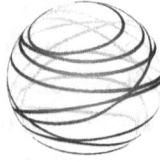

2 – THE DILEMMAS OF
CONSCIENTIOUS CONSUMERISM

IN 1995 AND 1996 SWEATSHOPS WERE HITTING THE HEADLINES IN American news media. Federal agents had found indentured Thai immigrants working in an apartment in El Monte, California, producing apparel to be sold at major retailers. Soon after, labor rights activists had shown that child workers in Honduras were producing Kathie Lee Gifford's line of clothing for Walmart. Amid the surge in attention, several researchers began asking Americans if they would pay more for clothes to be made in decent conditions. One study found that 84 percent of respondents would pay a dollar more for a twenty-dollar garment (Marymount University Center for Ethical Concerns 1999). Other studies found that 76 percent would pay five dollars more (University of Maryland 2000) and 33 percent would pay as much as ten dollars more (Hertel, Scruggs, and Heidkamp 2009). With markets for organic food, fair trade coffee, and a variety of green products growing, many observers hoped that a market for "sweat-free" apparel would follow (Elliott and Freeman 2003). But could these survey responses be taken seriously? Would consumers really pay more, or would they revert to a search for low prices once they were in the store? Furthermore, if some consumers were actually willing to pay more, what exactly would this mean? Would it represent a deep concern about working conditions and social justice around the world, or would sweat-free just become a status symbol, a way for well-off consumers to feel superior to those who shop at Walmart and other discount retailers?

In this chapter we delve into these types of meanings and dilemmas of conscientious consumerism. Our analyses in the previous chapter focused on individuals' answers to survey questions—asking them if they had "purchased a product for political, ethical, or environmental reasons." Their responses provided a revealing look at the overall patterns of conscientious consumerism. But those analyses could not tap into either individuals' actual behavior or the larger social meanings of conscientious consumption. Simply put, people may buycott far less than they say they do. Or their purchases of eco- or social-labeled products may have more to do with self-interest and social status than with ethical commitments. To deepen our analysis and inquire into the promise and limitations of conscientious consumerism, this chapter takes on two main tasks. First we look more closely at markets for eco- and social-labels, including evidence about whether consumers are willing to pay more for assurances of fairness and sustainability. Then we take a critical look at the cultural meanings and political implications of conscientious consumerism. Ostensibly "ethical" acts may turn out to be merely self-serving or contrary to their supposed goals.

Popular satires hint at some of the dilemmas of conscientious consumerism. The IFC television show *Portlandia* has satirized the quixotic quest for local, sustainable, and "authentic" food with a couple who, while ordering in a restaurant, begin to ask about the origins of the chicken on the menu. Unsatisfied with the server's answer, they leave the restaurant to inspect the farm for themselves, and they end up falling under the spell of a charismatic farmer-guru and living "off-the-grid." For its part, Comedy Central's *South Park* devoted an episode to the cloud of "smug" that emerged from the moral superiority of hybrid car owners. These depictions suggest that self-satisfaction and a certain style of elitism are bound up with conscientious consumerism.

Whatever one thinks of these particular depictions, there are good reasons to be concerned that conscientious consumerism can reflect the priorities of the privileged and have antiegalitarian consequences in consumer markets. Food consumption, for instance, has become highly stratified, with affluent consumers in the United States enjoying the "ecological cornucopia" of the Whole Foods grocery chain (Johnston 2008) while poorer consumers are stigmatized for poor taste and the "moral decrepitude" of obesity (Guthman 2007a). Furthermore, if some consumers are convinced that they can sufficiently protect their families or change the world simply by "voting with their dollars," they may disengage from civic and political life, undermining the foundations of collective rights and state regulation. We argue that an overarching ideology of conscientious consumerism is indeed counterproductive. Yet specific practices of conscientious consumption can sometimes be consistent with an egalitarian, socially engaged form of citizenship. To consider how, we begin with a closer look at consumer behavior, including the extent to which it is tied up with self-interest and altruism. We then consider the key dangers of conscientious consumerism as well as evidence that these dangers are very real but not entirely overwhelming.

MARKETS FOR STANDARDS: MAKING
SENSE OF CONSUMER BEHAVIOR

In many ways the market for eco- and social-labels has boomed. The number of sustainability labeling initiatives worldwide has grown from fewer than 50 in 1990 to nearly 450 in 2012.[1] While some labels have struggled to find a market, other labels have found significant niches, or in a few cases have even become dominant. Consider the growth of the Energy Star label in the United States, which identifies products that meet energy efficiency standards set by the Environmental Protection Agency. As of 2000, Energy Star appliances accounted for around 11 percent of the sales of dishwashers, 9 percent of clothes-washing machines, and 27 percent of refrigerators. By 2009 the vast majority of dishwashers sold in the United States were Energy Star models, and its share of clothes-washing machines and refrigerators had increased to nearly 50 percent and 35percent, respectively (US Environmental Protection Agency 2002, 2010).

Consider also the growing market for organic food. Sales of certified organic food in the United States increased from $1 billion in 1990 to over $29 billion in 2011 (Organic Trade Association 2011). On a per capita basis Americans went from spending an average of $13 per year on organic food in 1997

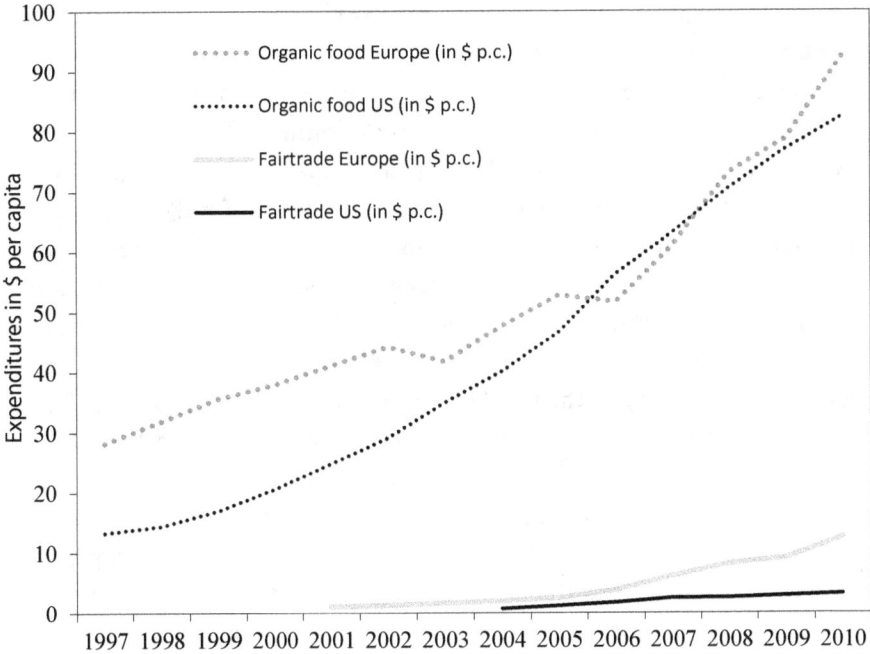

Figure 2.1: Per Capita Annual Consumption of Organics and Fair Trade Products in Europe and the United States. *Sources: Fairtrade Annual Report* (FLO 2005, 2006, 2007, 2008, 2009, 2010, 2011); "The World of Organic Agriculture" (Richter and Padel 2005; Schaer 2009; Willer and Kilcher 2009, 2012; Willer and Toralf 2004; Willer and Yussefi 2007).

to an average of $82 in 2010. As figure 2.1 shows, European consumers were already spending more than Americans on organic food, and their purchases continued to grow over that period. Across eight European countries, per capita spending on organic food went from $27 to $92 on average from 1997 to 2010.[2] Organic food remains a small part of the larger food and beverage market—less than 5 percent in the United States (Organic Trade Association 2011)—but it nevertheless represents a striking shift in consumer tastes. Advocates of other eco- and social-labels often point to the rise of organic food as evidence that there is robust consumer demand for alternative production processes, even when it means paying more.

Yet a closer look at these examples suggests that the market for sustainability is more fragile than it first appears. Both energy efficiency and organic food are cases in which consumers may perceive a direct private benefit from the purchase of a labeled product. A desire to save money on their energy bills may lead consumers to buy energy-efficient appliances. Even if this is only one factor, saving money surely amplifies any desire consumers might have to promote energy efficiency for broader environmental reasons.

Consumers may also have self-interested reasons to buy organic food. Many consumers prefer organic fruits, vegetables, and milk because they are perceived as safer, healthier, or more nutritious (Johnston and Szabo 2011; Hughner et al. 2007; Szasz 2007; Zanoli and Naspetti 2002). In fact, moments of heightened concern about personal and child health have helped to build the market for organic food. For instance, concerns about the safety of milk from cows injected with the rBGH hormone led to a "not in my body" reaction that greatly facilitated the growth of the organic milk market (DuPuis 2000). Eating organic food does reduce consumers' exposure to pesticides with health risks to some degree (Holzman 2012), but it is telling that for many consumers the perception of organic food is so tied up with personal health that they overlook the fact that organic standards are fundamentally environmental standards. The organic farming movement began with concerns about industrial agriculture's consequences for soil fertility (Guthman 2004), and organic standards ban synthetic pesticides and fertilizers in large part to safeguard groundwater, soil, and biodiversity. Yet some consumers are either unaware that organic standards are environmental standards or are attracted to organic food for reasons that have nothing to do with environmental protection. For instance, in a survey of 555 randomly selected undergraduate students at Indiana University in 2009 and 2010, we found that 43 percent of them reported buying items labeled as organic often or very often in the past year. But strikingly, only 65 percent of this subgroup said they had bought a product labeled as environmentally friendly (often or very often in the past year). In other words, at least 35 percent of those who commonly bought organic products did not appear to think of the organic label as an eco-label. Furthermore, less than half of the frequent organic purchasers (41 percent) reported frequently buying something deliberately for "political, ethical, or environmental reasons." In fact, 20 percent of them said they had never (in the past year) deliberately purchased something for these reasons. Taken together, these findings suggest that it was common for students to be frequent organic consumers without thinking of this as an environmental or ethical decision.[3]

In general the eco-labeled products that have developed the largest markets are mainly those that consumers understand as satisfying their own self-interest. Many other labels do not promise direct private benefits, apart from the possible psychic benefit of feeling good about one's altruism. They ask consumers to contribute to fairness or sustainability goals that can, at best, have long-term and indirect consequences for those who purchase the products. For these labels consumer demand tends to be much lower, though not necessarily insignificant.

For instance, the introduction of dolphin-safe tuna labels helped to slow the decline in tuna sales in the early 1990s (Teisl, Roe, and Hicks 2002). Saving dolphin populations can preserve ocean habitats, and consumers may see dolphins as especially worthy of sympathy and protection, but there are no direct private benefits of consuming dolphin-safe tuna. Similarly, although there are probably no health benefits when it comes to organic *clothing*, when Patagonia switched to organic cotton, its customers proved willing to pay significantly more for cotton flannel shirts (Casadesus-Masanell et al. 2009). Even though it costs more, office paper made from recycled pulp has developed a sizable market. For tissue paper, American consumers have clung to varieties made from virgin pulp, but European consumers have been more willing to pay a bit more for recycled content (Walsh 2009). There is evidence that some Americans are willing to pay more for recycled paper products (Guagnano 2001), but on the other hand, even after twenty-five years of wide availability, recycled paper products have remained only a small part of the American market.

"Fair trade" is the clearest example of a label that does not offer private benefits to consumers, often costs more, but nevertheless has a significant market. As discussed in chapter 1, fair trade markets have become especially large in the UK. Sales of Fairtrade-certified coffee in the UK grew by more than 700 percent from 2002 to 2012, ultimately accounting for roughly a quarter of the coffee market (Fairtrade Foundation 2013). Fairtrade bananas and chocolate, which were barely available in 2002, were outselling Fairtrade coffee in the UK by 2012, with one-third of bananas sold being Fairtrade (Fairtrade Foundation 2013). In the United States, Fair Trade–certified coffee amounts to only around 3 percent of the total coffee market, but its sales boomed in the 2000s. The volume of coffee certified by Fair Trade USA (previously TransFair USA) increased from only around 76,000 pounds in 1998 to

163 million pounds in 2012. Per capita fair trade consumption in Europe and the United States increased over time as well. Across eight European countries, per capita yearly spending on fair trade items grew from $1.32 in 2002 to $12.60 in 2010. In the United States it grew from $1.16 in 2005 to $3.15 in 2010.

But as figure 2.1 illustrates, fair trade sales have remained far below organic sales. On a per capita basis, American consumers spent twenty-six times more on organic than fair trade products in 2010, and European consumers spent over seven times more. In the United States, sales of Fair Trade products are estimated to amount to roughly one-fortieth the size of the organic industry (Hainmueller, Hiscox, and Sequeira 2011; Transfair USA 2009). We see fair trade as the exception that proves the rule: consumer demand for ethical production does exist, but to a much lower degree when consumers do not view those products as having direct private benefits.

Are consumers willing to pay more for products that do not directly benefit them, such that conscientious consumption initiatives might truly be a viable way to improve global labor and environmental conditions? Will consumers actually pay price premiums? If not, or if the size of the premium they will pay is small, then the promise of conscientious consumption may be quite limited. To address this question we consider the existing evidence—fragmentary as it is—on consumers' willingness to pay more for labeled products.

Willingness to Pay

Using surveys, researchers have often estimated that 60–80 percent of consumers in North America and Europe are willing to pay more for fair or sustainable products. But these numbers are obviously hard to square with the limited size of actual markets for fairly or sustainably produced goods. The reason is rooted largely in some combination of "social desirability bias," meaning that individuals adjust their answers to match societal expectations, and the "attitude-behavior gap," wherein even honest intentions are set aside in practice (Vermeir and Verbeke 2006). One step toward better measuring willingness to pay through surveys has been to consider the importance of standards relative to other features of the product (size/shape, quality, etc.). When researchers have conducted such surveys by using "conjoint analysis" (a technique in marketing research) or other, similar methods, they have found that something more like 10–16 percent of consumers are willing to pay price premiums for ethically made products (Auger et al. 2003; Auger et al. 2008; De Pelsmacker, Driesen, and Rayp 2005; Dickson 2001; Loureiro and Lotade 2005).[4]

Yet these results still rely on self-reporting about hypothetical purchases. Field experiments, in which consumer behavior can be observed directly, have become the gold standard for estimating whether consumers are willing to pay premiums for labeled products. Of course field experiments are difficult to carry out, since they depend on finding stores that are willing to let researchers manipulate their products and prices. In addition, some attempted experiments have turned out to suffer from design problems and practical challenges (Arnot, Boxall, and Cash 2006; Hiscox, Broukhim, and Litwin 2011; Hiscox and Smyth 2006; Prasad et al. 2004).[5] For instance, Roy Anderson and Eric Hansen (2004) worked with two Home Depot stores in the Pacific Northwest to compare sales of FSC-certified and noncertified plywood. When prices were identical, the certified wood far outsold the noncertified; when a 2 percent price premium was added, the certified wood's sales fell dramatically but still amounted to 37 percent of the total sold. Unfortunately, in addition to the small scale of the experiment and the small premium, incomplete labeling in one store left the researchers uncertain about the actual willingness to pay for certified wood. Monica Prasad and her colleagues' (2004) experiment sought to compare sales of identical athletic socks—one set labeled for "Good Working Conditions"—that sat side by side in a department store in a working-class neighborhood of Detroit. Roughly 25 percent of customers were willing to pay a premium for the labeled socks, up to a 40 percent premium. Unfortunately, however, using identical socks with only one set labeled could easily have confused consumers or led them to question the legitimacy of the label. Moreover, the baseline price of the socks had to be reduced to just one dollar in order to generate enough sales to complete the experiment in the allotted time, so a 40 percent premium meant consumers were spending only forty cents more.

In a more sophisticated experiment, Jens Hainmueller and Michael Hiscox (2012) worked with Banana Republic to randomly assign 111 stores around the country to place signs emphasizing the company's labor standards next to selected products. This allowed the researchers to compare sales in these stores to sales of the same products in other Banana Republic stores. Their findings provide a mixed picture of consumer interest in labor standards.

Emphasizing labor standards increased sales of a $130 women's linen suit by 14 percent, but sales did not increase for cheaper products, such as an $18 pair of women's yoga pants or a $12 men's T-shirt. It seems that Banana Republic consumers interested in cheaper goods were not especially attracted to labor standards, but those interested in more expensive goods were. Unfortunately, in this case the researchers were not able to add price premiums to the labeled products to assess whether consumers would pay more for standards.

In an experiment involving Fair Trade coffee, Hainmueller, Hiscox, and Sandra Sequeira (2011), were able to add premiums, though this experiment was conducted on a somewhat smaller scale, involving twenty-six stores that were part of an upscale grocery chain. An initial goal was to understand the influence of the Fair Trade label on sales at existing prices, so the researchers randomly assigned half of the stores to attach a label to the bulk bins for Fair Trade French roast and Colombian blend coffees, while the other stores sold the same coffees at the same prices but did not label them. Labeling increased the sales of the Colombian blend by 13 percent and of the more expensive and popular French roast blend by 8 percent. A second goal was to estimate the elasticity of demand when prices were increased. Half of the stores were randomly assigned to raise the prices of the two Fair Trade blends by $1 (to $12.99 per pound for French roast and $11.99 per pound for Colombian) and to display a label that linked the higher price to Fair Trade certification.[6] The other stores sold the same coffees at the original price with a similar label.[7] When the price was increased, sales of the popular French roast coffee actually increased by 2 percent, showing that consumer demand was quite *inelastic* to a price increase. But sales of the Colombian blend decreased by 30 percent, revealing the *elasticity* of consumer demand for this product. A cheaper and unlabeled alternative, Colombian Supremo, saw a 16 percent increase in sales when the premium for the fair trade Colombian blend was added, suggesting that consumers readily switched to a substitute when confronted with a price increase. Since the French roast coffee was more expensive to start with, Hainmeuller and his colleagues suggest that consumers who are not especially cost-conscious are willing to pay more for ethical guarantees—a finding that mirrors the results at Banana Republic. With Fair Trade French roast coffee amounting to around 11 percent of this company's total bulk coffee sales, the segment of consumers willing to pay more was not trivial, but neither was it especially large. This experiment is perhaps the most rigorous test of consumers' willingness to pay more, and the researchers went to great lengths to rule out alternative explanations (like seasonal trends) and examine substitution patterns.

Of course, these experiments measure only what consumers are willing to do for a particular purchase at a single point in time. Over the course of multiple purchases of different products, we would surely find a larger number of consumers who are willing to pay more at some point. Generally the research to date shows that some segment of consumers is willing to pay more for standards that do not directly benefit them, but the size of this segment varies across products and settings and probably amounts to a minority of consumers in affluent countries. The percentage surely lies below the rosy estimates of 60–80 percent from survey research but above the lower estimates of around 10 percent that can be extrapolated from field experiments at single points in time.

While adding a dose of realism to the celebration of conscientious consumerism, this evidence also holds room for optimism that consumers *will* support alternative production methods, even if these cost more and do not have clear benefits for the consumers themselves. Shopping can be consistent with altruism, not just through gift giving or tipping but also through a willingness to pay more in support of standards for the production process. Of course, as our later chapters examine, the simple assurances of labels are often a poor match for the complexities of production, and consumers' mainly unreflective actions may outweigh their occasional conscientious ones. But these are not the only implications of conscientious consumerism that are open to doubt. The rise of conscientious consumerism may exacerbate inequality or depress political engagement among consumers. Sorting through these dilemmas is essential.

THE POLITICS AND PERILS OF
CONSCIENTIOUS CONSUMERISM

"Voting with your dollars" is, by many accounts, an important form of political activity. As Michele Micheletti and her colleagues have emphasized, it can expand the sphere of politics, attracting more individuals to political issues and ultimately subjecting companies to more extensive oversight (Micheletti 2003; Stolle, Hooghe, and Micheletti 2005). The market in this account is an

especially important "venue for political action" for those who are marginalized in—or alienated from—conventional political channels (Micheletti
2003, 12). As individuals become engaged consumers, their consciousness
of public concerns at both local and global scales may expand (Barnett et al.
2005; Clarke et al. 2007). Furthermore, consumer concern may politicize
products and question dominant production practices when governments
are paying scant attention to these issues. Changing consumer preferences
may also insert new urgency into gridlocked domestic or international negotiations. When activists "name and shame" companies and mobilize consumer concern, it brings these companies and issues into public debates that
would likely not occur if political engagement were limited to conventional
channels (Micheletti 2003).

Seeing consumption as a new form of political engagement has been especially attractive in light of concerns that traditional forms of political and
civic engagement are on the wane. Most famously illustrated by Robert Putnam's (2001) "bowling alone" metaphor, scholars in the 1990s increasingly
argued that citizens in advanced democracies were joining fewer voluntary
associations, voting less, and participating in fewer social clubs than they had
in previous eras. Yet while proponents of this "decline thesis" worried about
the demise of collective civic life and the vitality of democracy (Macedo et
al. 2005), others argued that citizens were simply engaged in new and different ways, which were not captured by researchers' typical metrics (Dalton
2008). Seen in this light, being a conscientious consumer may be a new mode
of political and civic engagement. Added to this, globalization and the rise of
neoliberalism have led many to hope that consumption can be a meaningful
form of *global* politics. In an era of globe-trotting companies and "thinned"
nation-states, perhaps consumer concern can regulate global industries to
some degree. If standard-setting programs are a form of "transnational private regulation" (Bartley 2007b), then conscientious consumption may be a
way of "voting" for regulatory controls.

The Trouble with "One Dollar, One Vote"

One important objection lies in the inequality that is built into conscientious consumption as a mode of political expression. To put it simply, while
the underlying idea of democratic citizenship is "one person, one vote," the

corollary for conscientious consumerism is "one dollar, one vote." In an era of vast economic inequalities, both globally and in most domestic contexts, the power for the wealthy to influence industries far outstrips the economic "voting power" of the disadvantaged. In this sense conscientious consumerism is necessarily at odds with egalitarianism. Even if "voting with your dollars" were widespread, some people would have more votes, and thus louder voices, than others. It is hard to see this as a model for a reinvigorated form of democracy. Although democratic institutions have their own problems of participatory inequality, they are at least characterized by normative appeals to equality, which are largely absent in markets (Bryant, Goodman, and Redclift 2008; Friedland, Rojas, and Bode 2012). To the degree that political participation drifts toward the market and away from political institutions we may be drifting farther away from the ideal of democracy. In this way, conscientious consumerism may be contrary to the idea of citizenship (Reich 2008).

This objection has a practical side too: Relatively wealthy, highly educated consumers value different things than other consumers and citizens. As discussed in chapter 1, "post-materialist" values such as environmental protection are closely linked with the practice of conscientious consumerism. If poor and working-class people had an equal role in defining "ethical" production, social justice and labor rights would arguably be more central (Johnston, Szabo, and Rodney 2011). As Margaret Gray (2014) shows, demands for local and sustainable food have largely overlooked the often dire conditions of migrant agricultural workers on small farms. In general, by catering to the preferences of affluent consumers, standard-setting initiatives may marginalize some voices and create very partial and skewed forms of regulation. In other words, the problem with "one dollar, one vote" is not merely that it reproduces inequality in an abstract sense, but that those with ten dollars will vote (multiple times) for something different from what those with one dollar would have voted for.

Status and Distinction

Conscientious consumerism may also exacerbate inequality by symbolically excluding or marginalizing some populations. More than just personal status symbols, consumer goods communicate signals about social class and reinforce class inequality. People have long used consumption to distinguish themselves from others, creating symbolic boundaries that mark high-status and low-status groups (Bourdieu 1984; Veblen 1949 [1899]; Lamont 1992). In the nineteenth-century United States, elites used the consumption of "high culture" to distance themselves from the masses, using orchestras and art museums to valorize their class position and consolidate their power (DiMaggio 1992). Though less stark, there are reasons to worry about upper-middle-class consumers using conscientious consumption as a way to valorize themselves and symbolically marginalize those in lower-class positions.

Scholars have been especially attuned to the development of symbolic boundaries around food. They have argued that what counts as ethical, high-quality, authentic, and generally "good" food has been defined by privileged groups who emphasize eating locally, eating organic food, and treating animals humanely (Johnston, Szabo, and Rodney 2011). What is most problematic is when these definitions of "good" food also come to define who is and is not a "good" person. In this way, symbolic boundaries are drawn between classes, and the lack of "good" eating by those who are less privileged is attributed to a lack of morality or good taste as opposed to structural constraints or biased standards (Johnston, Szabo, and Rodney 2011). As Julie Guthman (2007a) has pointed out, much moralizing about healthy, sustainable food ends up treating obesity as a symbol of moral decrepitude, and even dehumanizing those who are overweight. In addition, patronizing attitudes among privileged white proponents of sustainable food have often made spaces where it is celebrated, such as farmers markets, exclusionary of poorer and nonwhite individuals (Guthman 2008).

Such dynamics are not unique to food. Catherine Dolan's (2007) interviews with consumers of Fairtrade flowers suggest that while the fair trade movement has hoped to build reciprocal relationships between producers and buyers, for consumers, buying fair trade may solidify a sense of moral and economic superiority. In her analysis, "while the act of buying a Fairtrade flower (coded as 'giving') confirms the piety, prestige and moral rectitude of the consumer, it also reproduces the consumer's power in the relationship [with a poor farmer]" (256). Looking historically, it is not difficult to find examples of seemingly conscientious consumption being used to draw exclusionary boundaries. In the late 1890s the National Consumers League created its "White Label" for undergarments "made under clean and healthful conditions." This was partially an attempt to improve working conditions, but it also exploited wealthy consumers' fears of "dirty" and "diseased" immigrant workers in tenement sweatshops (Sklar 1998; Wolfe 1975). At various points in the twentieth century, "buy American" campaigns have been used for narrow nationalistic purposes, exploiting antiforeigner sentiments (D. Frank 2000). In subtle and not-so-subtle ways, then, conscientious consumerism can be parochial and exclusionary, and it can exacerbate inequalities on the basis of both social class and racial categorization.

The Death of Politics?

Although some see it as expanding the sphere of politics, there are also reasons to worry that conscientious consumerism could represent a retreat from political engagement, ultimately diminishing the prospects for strong social movements. One possibility is that conscientious consumerism could "crowd out" other forms of engagement and displace other conceptions of activism. Michael Maniates (2001) has argued that the rise of eco- and social labels is part of a dangerous move toward an "individualization of responsibility" for social and environmental problems. This individualization atrophies the collective efficacy of citizens and narrows their imaginations about how to achieve social change. If people believe they are doing their part to achieve social change through their purchases, they may feel less compelled to participate in protest, join social movement organizations, or push policy makers to enact strong regulation (see also Reich 2008). Moreover, if one sees individual acts of consumption as the key to social change, then the observation that not everyone is acting as a conscientious consumer may lead to scorn or resignation. This can lead environmentalists, for instance, to "heap disdain on those who do not . . . recycle or drive small cars or otherwise live sustainably" as opposed to building a strong, unified social movement (Maniates 2013, 261).

Relatedly, the rise of eco-labels may foster continued overconsumption and delude people into thinking that severe environmental problems can be solved without some degree of sacrifice by wealthy consumers (see Maniates and Meyer 2010). The message of much "green consumerism" is that we can minimize environmental damage not by consuming less but by consuming *more* (Dauvergne and Lister 2012; J. Johnston 2008). Josée Johnston (2008) argues that at the same time Whole Foods claims to promote environmental responsibility it undermines that goal by offering a cornucopia of choices for consumers while neglecting issues like food miles and consumption reduction, not to mention labor conditions in agricultural industries. Whole Foods shoppers seem to view the store mainly in consumerist terms, appreciating the aesthetics of the store and the variety of foods available more frequently than the environmental or social implications of the products (Johnston and Szabo 2011). Many environmental organizations have also aggressively adopted consumption-oriented narratives about change while muting their earlier messages about the dangers of overconsumption (see Bartley 2007a). As Peter Dauvergne and Jane Lister (2012) argue, eco-labeling, green marketing, and pleas for individuals to behave responsibly—the mainstays of the green consumerism industry—may deliver tiny successes but obscure alternative, more productive paths to change. Without a serious challenge to consumerism and poorly regulated capitalism—and the knotty, arduous, contentious, and collective efforts that this will require—it is difficult to see how major environmental challenges can be met.

More broadly, by turning to the market to fight for the good society, citizens may be turning away from democratic institutions that were built to handle such fights and are uniquely equipped to challenge powerful economic actors. It may be possible for consumer action to nudge markets here and there, but governments are uniquely able to mandate large-scale, systematic changes that last over time. State policy can translate the desires of citizens into binding law that forces companies to take actions they would otherwise avoid. In addition, state policy allows citizens to force themselves to take actions they believe in (from driving safely to supporting decent working conditions) but are tempted to shirk (Reich 2005). Of course, governments are not always willing to pass such policies, and regulations may be poorly enforced. Thus, significant social change requires the strengthening of democratic institutions and regulatory capacities. Anything less is, as Robert Reich (2008) puts it, "frolic and detour" (14).

Going further, some critics have charged that what appears to be conscientious consumption can actually be a retreat from social engagement altogether—that is, the construction of a "protective bubble" that shields wealthy consumers from danger. In *Shopping Our Way to Safety*, Andrew Szasz (2007) argues that consuming organic and "natural" products is, in essence, a desperate and defensive attempt to retreat from a world of environmental danger. As consumers construct an "inverted quarantine" to keep the unruly and dangerous world from affecting themselves and their families, they are turning inward and, in effect, giving up on creating society-wide solutions to environmental problems. While a traditional quarantine isolates a threat to protect the larger population, this "inverted quarantine" allows privileged individuals to isolate themselves from the larger threats—and the rest of the population. As Szasz argues, the recent rise of conscientious consumerism is in some ways analogous to the building of fallout shelters in the 1960s as a response, albeit a feeble one, to the threat of nuclear war. He also draws an important parallel to suburbanization and "white flight" over the past half century. To insulate themselves from so-called urban problems, affluent white residents have either fled to suburbs or strengthened social and physical barriers within cities to keep the "dangerous classes" away. The consequences for those who remained were clear: resources were depleted, and racial and economic segregation undermined the production of collective goods (like safety and education). By Szasz's account, fleeing to the protection of organics may allow environmental problems to fester in much the same way. "Because people believe . . . that they are protected, they are less likely to feel an urge to voice support for the kinds of regulatory controls that would be needed to really address the hazard" (Szasz 2007, 226).

BEYOND THE IDEOLOGY OF CONSCIENTIOUS CONSUMERISM

These critiques have exposed serious weaknesses in the ideology of conscientious consumerism—that is, the idea that the world can be "saved" through shopping. The implications of this ideology—that moral worth is defined by consumer choices and that consuming *more* is a solution to the world's problems—are at best vapid and at worst extremely regressive. If adding morals to markets means promoting an ideology of conscientious consumerism, then we believe there is indeed a danger that the actions of conscientious consumers, whether to protect themselves or even to altruistically address larger problems, will undermine the possibilities for serious reform. In addition, as part 2 of this book shows, consumer concern has inspired a number of standard-setting initiatives in global industries, but most are too weak for the tasks that face them. Other ways of regulating global industries, including reinvigorated regulation by national states and international organizations, are clearly necessary.

Yet perhaps *conscientious consumption* does not need to contribute to the ideology of *conscientious consumerism*. John Connolly and Andrea Prothero (2008) found conscientious consumers to be enthusiastic but ultimately uncertain about the impacts of their choices. Perhaps this is the appropriate stance, given the many unanswered questions about the influence of different standards. And perhaps consumers who boycott or buycott are not so enamored with the idea as to dismiss other approaches, such as state regulation or even reduced consumption. If consumers can be mindful of the limitations of eco- and social labels, politically engaged in a variety of ways, and not overly self-satisfied about "saving" the world, perhaps conscientious consumption can escape some of the pitfalls described above.

Indeed, as discussed below, we believe that the political critiques of conscientious consumerism are important, but they do not entirely damn a project of conscientious consumption. The critiques identify serious *potential* dangers, but evidence suggests that these are not always as threatening as they seem. Instead of crowding out, for instance, there is evidence that conscientious consumption can sometimes be part of a repertoire of political engagement. Furthermore, although there are definitely ways that conscientious consumption reproduces social and economic inequalities, it can also be compatible with egalitarian agendas.

The Crowding Out Problem

There is clearly a danger that the rise of conscientious consumerism could get in the way of other strategies of achieving social change. But there are two reasons to think that this danger is not as clear-cut as it initially seems. First, those who lament the turn to the market as a turn away from politics often invoke only disparaging images of market behavior and highly romanticized views of political engagement. Markets are not merely sites of self-interest seeking. Consumers frequently use purchases to express concerns for or connections with others (Willis and Schor 2012), and markets are often governed by moral codes that shape what consumers view as acceptable and unacceptable to buy or sell (C. Chan 2009; Zelizer 2013). Democratic politics, as Michael Schudson (2007) has pointed out, are usually based on narrow self-interest and are far from the welcoming beacon of egalitarian participation that critics of consumerism depict. Many of the same inequalities of partici- pation that plague conscientious consumerism also plague more traditional types of political and civic engagement (Brady, Verba, and Schlozman 1995). Furthermore, traditional political engagement can be alienating for citizens, so it should not be so surprising that they are attracted to markets as a way to express their politics (Schudson 2007).

As Margaret Willis and Juliet Schor (2012) argue, a clearheaded analysis of conscientious consumerism must avoid the "essentialist trap" of viewing the market as the self-regarding site of the consumer and the state as the other- regarding site of the citizen. It must view "sites" such as markets and politics as distinct from the "practices" that occur within them (see also Bowles and Gintis 2012 [1986]). The practice of consumption can be used to express political or ethical principles, even if markets as a whole—or the ideology of consumerism as a whole—are not dominated by this logic. We agree that consumption practices can potentially be meaningful forms of political ex- pression. On the other hand, it is important to keep the logic and limitations of different sites in mind. We see institutions of democracy as on the whole better suited than those of the market to host struggles to achieve common goods (Reich 2008). It is unclear, for instance, whether markets alone could ever be molded to reduce inequality to the same extent that the redistributive powers of the state can.

The second reason to believe that the crowding-out critique is overstated is that the evidence that exists, fragmentary as it is, points largely in the oppo- site direction, at least when it comes to individual patterns of engagement at a given moment. In the analysis of survey data, researchers have consistently found that individuals who engage in conscientious consumption are more likely than others to be politically engaged in other ways as well. In a sur- vey of university students in Canada, Belgium, and Sweden, Dietland Stolle and her colleagues (2005) found that conscientious consumers are more likely than others to attend protests or demonstrations and to be members of "checkbook-like" voluntary associations (that is, those in which members primarily participate by donating money). They are no different from others in terms of more conventional forms of political engagement: membership in political parties, participation in student elections, or contacts with offi- cials. But importantly, "there is not a single significant negative relation with other forms of political participation" (260), suggesting that conscientious consumers are not feeling so satisfied with themselves as to opt out of political engagement. In our own survey of Indiana University students, we found that students who recently had engaged in buycotting were slightly more likely than others to have participated in protest at some point, even holding their political views and a number of other factors constant. Those who had buycotted also had significantly less individualistic attitudes—in other words, they were less in agreement with the statement that "in our society, everyone must look out for him/herself. It is of little use to unite with others to fight for one's goals."[8]

These results are consistent with the view that conscientious consumption can be part of a repertoire of political engagement. Indeed, the students surveyed by Stolle and her colleagues saw voting and volunteering as more influential than consumption choices, and the conscientious consumers among them "seem to be quite realistic about the potential effectiveness of this participation instrument; it is an *addition* . . . and does not replace more conventional participation acts" (Stolle, Hooghe, and Micheletti 2005, 262; emphasis in original). Similarly, in our survey, students who had purchased a product labeled as environmentally friendly were more likely than others to perceive voting for an elected official as an effective way to promote environmental change, even controlling for environmental attitudes.

In larger, more representative samples, researchers have similarly found that conscientious consumerism and political engagement are sometimes positively correlated and never negatively correlated. As discussed in chapter 1, across a number of European countries individuals' sense of political efficacy and their interest in politics shape their likelihood of buycotting and boycotting. Lisa Neilson and Pamela Paxton (2010), working with similar data, find evidence that involvement in a voluntary association is a strong predictor of boycotting and buycotting. Although these studies seek to explain why people boycott/buycott rather than the consequences of doing so, their findings contradict simple images of self-satisfied conscientious consumers opting out of other forms of engagement. More pointedly, Willis and Schor (2012) find that for American adults in general, boycotting and buycotting are associated with higher degrees of political engagement. In a separate survey of those already sensitized to conscientious consumption, the researchers found that those who were more engaged as consumers were also more engaged as citizens. Directly responding to the critiques discussed above, they argue that "self-interest, as in the sense of attempts to protect personal health or the quality of products that one consumes, and public interest, such as trying to reduce environmental impact or support workers, do not appear to be mutually exclusive motivations" (180).

In addition to this large-scale survey evidence, studies have found synergies between consumption and politics within particular communities. Brian Obach and Kathleen Tobin (2013) surveyed a sample of "civic agriculture participants" in upstate New York (made up of Community-Supported Agriculture [CSA] members, farmers market patrons, and health food store shoppers) and compared this to a sample drawn from the general population in the same communities. Those involved in civic agriculture were far more likely than others to report a variety of political and civic engagements, including participating in political demonstrations (24 percent compared to 9 percent), being interested in politics (82 percent vs. 57 percent), attending a political meeting (43 percent vs. 21 percent), and volunteering (71 percent vs. 48 percent). Even the health food store shoppers, who were not necessarily strongly committed to environmental goals, were in many respects not so different from the more committed CSA members. In a study of a local organic food cooperative in the UK, Gill Seyfang (2006) found that 75 percent of customers cited health as a reason for purchasing the food, but environmental issues and localism were not far behind, at 70 percent and 65 percent respectively. It seems that at least within some communities of relatively committed consumers, individuals are not as easily distracted or deluded as many critiques suggest. Many environmental activists, for instance, criticize green consumption and discount its potential as a strategy for social change but nevertheless participate in it (Connolly and Prothero 2008).

Still, the existing evidence is only partial, and it does reveal some segments of consumers that act more as the critics predict. In our survey of Indiana University students, we found that nearly a quarter were so enthusiastic about recycling bottles and cans that they rated it as having a greater environmental impact than having not used those bottles and cans in the first place. Nearly 10 percent rated the environmental benefits of using eco-labeled products as higher than not buying those products in the first place. The argument that easy, market-friendly environmentalism may be confusing consumers and feeding overconsumption does receive some support from observations like

these. Some do see *more* consumption, not less, as a pro-environmental solution. In addition, even among more committed conscientious consumers,
being a good consumer sometimes serves as a rationale for not doing other
things. Take the individuals who work with Traidcraft, a fair trade organization in the UK that sells coffee, chocolate, crafts, and other items, not only
through world shops but through churches and other social networks. As
described by Nick Clarke and his colleagues (2007), these individuals are
socially engaged practitioners working collectively, not atomized consumers. On the other hand, in interviews with Clarke and his fellow researchers,
some explicitly used this activity as a rationale for *not* participating in political activism. One explained that she was not involved in a public campaign
that Traidcraft and others were sponsoring

> because I felt I supported it in other ways, through supporting fair trade . . . I admire all
> these young people who . . . go out and do things and go out and help in a crisis. . . . I'm not
> the sort of person, I wouldn't feel brave enough to do it myself, I would rather help in other
> ways. (qtd. in Clarke et al. 2007, 599)

Another described her fair trade work as political action, yet said:

> In the actual taking action, going out on the streets and going to rallies, that type of thing,
> and meetings as to what are we going to do, how are we going to approach this campaign,
> I don't go to the campaign meetings and I don't go out on the demos . . . I mean I'd love
> to, I'd love to but I don't have time. So on the practical side I feel I'm there to provide the
> stock, provide myself if that's required, and provide information if they want it, or I can
> point them in the direction to go. (599)

Perhaps these two people are unlikely to "hit the streets" for other reasons,
but their statements make it clear that their work with Traidcraft is not having the kind of "cognitive liberation" effect that social movement scholars
have identified as central to becoming a committed activist (McAdam 1982).

Ultimately the question of how conscientious consumption shapes other
political views and activities will have to be addressed by looking at individuals and political institutions *over time.* The evidence for the repertoire view
is convincing, but it only looks at individuals at a given point in time. It is
possible that people who conscientiously consume also report substantial
political engagements, as the existing evidence shows, but that consumer activities expand and political activities subsequently contract. In other words,
the crowding-out effect could take hold as individuals progress through their
lives or as larger historical changes shape the distribution of different forms
of engagement.

The Inequality Problem

If one cares not only about environmental protection or charity but also about promoting an egalitarian social order, then the logic of "one dollar, one vote" and the status dynamics of conscientious consumerism are indeed troubling. In our view an egalitarian agenda must be part of meaningful social change. Questions about the distribution of rights and privileges should be at the center of both how we evaluate consumer actions and how we understand the impacts of production standards (as in part 2 of this book).

Yet it would be wrong to dismiss conscientious consumption as *necessarily* inegalitarian. Not all forms of conscientious consumption are especially costly. Take the consumption of beef. Producing beef demands huge inputs of grain (and thus of water and land), contributes to pollution by factory farms, arguably distorts global grain markets, and in some regions of the world drives the destruction of natural forests as they are converted to cattle pasture or land to grow grain. A conscientious consumer might respond by paying more for local, grass-fed beef or other "sustainable" beef. But a conscientious consumer could also respond by simply eating less beef. Dietary substitutes such as beans and other legumes are typically much less expensive. Furthermore, consumers who boycott a particular product or brand can often find substitutes at similar price levels (Sandıkcı and Ekici 2009). To be sure, higher incomes will give consumers more options for expressing their values through their purchases, but it is a mistake to equate conscientious consumption with conspicuous consumption. Conscientious consumption may also be consistent with a rejection of consumerism—that is, a weakening of the link between consumer goods and one's conception of a good life—that helps consumers save money. In a few instances, at least, local food initiatives are becoming well integrated into low-income communities (Hinrichs and Kremer 2002; Johnston and Baker 2005). Symbolic boundaries are not easily erased, but some advocates of conscientious consumption are working to blur them.

On the whole the problem of conspicuous consumption, exclusionary symbolic boundaries, and status-oriented consumption seems to be more a problem of consumerism in general than of conscientious consumption in particular. We can see why critics would seize on the hypocrisy of status-driven, exclusionary behavior in supposed pursuit of fairness and sustainability. The LOHAS ("lifestyles of health and sustainability," as mentioned in the introduction) marketing industry provides plenty of fodder for status competition and for critique. But is conscientious consumption really more unequal and stratifying than consumerism in general? We suspect that status-driven and exclusionary consumer behavior is at least as widespread, if not more so, in the larger market, where consumers mark their status through luxury brands, homes, and cars. As Robert Frank (2010) has argued, consumerism in an era of rising wealth inequality has led standards for high-quality, high-status objects to keep ratcheting up, chasing the lifestyles of the ultra-wealthy. The most consequential status distinctions and expenditures of cultural capital have nothing to do with fair trade, organic, or sustainable forms of production; they have to do with elite education; family wealth; and durable race, class, and gender hierarchies. Our point is not to minimize exclusionary tendencies in the world of conscientious consumption, but they must be evaluated in context.

CONCLUSION

The key for both scholarship and practice, we believe, is to reject the *ideology of conscientious consumerism* and its suggestion that the world can be "saved" through shopping. This ideology reproduces inequality and obscures other, more meaningful pathways to social change. Yet specific *practices of conscientious consumption* can vary in their compatibility with egalitarianism, in their symbolic meanings, and in their political implications.

As part 2 of this book shows, practices of conscientious consumption also vary in their consequences "on the ground" at the point of production. Ultimately the assessment of conscientious consumption depends in large part on its practical consequences. How much difference does it make if consumers support fair trade in agriculture or sustainable forestry practices? What has consumer concern about sweatshops meant for labor conditions in the global apparel industry? What are the consequences when consumers are *not* conscientious—that is, when they do not reflect much on the consequences of their purchases? To a startling degree, debates about the dilemmas of conscientious consumerism have proceeded without really addressing these questions. It is this huge oversight that we attempt to remedy in the next part of this book.

PART II
BEHIND THE LABEL
Global Production and the Meaning of Standards

3 – WOOD AND PAPER PRODUCTS

Searching for Sustainability

IN 1989 *TIME* MAGAZINE CALLED THE DESTRUCTION OF THE AMAZON rain forest "one of the great tragedies of human history" (Linden 1989). The Amazon was burning, in large part to clear forested land for agricultural plantations and cattle ranching. Brazilian labor and environmental activist Chico Mendes had just been assassinated, and international observers were becoming increasingly concerned about the local and global consequences of tropical deforestation. Some were calling for boycotts of tropical timber not only from Brazil but also from Indonesia, Malaysia, and other places where "timber barons" were exploiting forests at the expense of local ecosystems, global biodiversity, and indigenous populations. Environmental organizations were targeting companies such as B&Q (a British home improvement retailer), Scott Paper, and Burger King, which was charged with supporting the conversion of rain forests to cattle pasture. These campaigns were part of a larger attempt to combat deforestation, which reduces biodiversity, makes local environments and forest-related livelihoods more fragile, and exacerbates global warming.

While sometimes calling for an overall reduction in the consumption of forest products, environmental organizations also hoped to highlight "good wood"—that is, products from well-managed forests harvested through low-impact and socially responsible logging. Out of these early attempts to identify "positive alternatives" to boycotts, a complex field of standard setting and certification eventually arose. Reformers founded the Forest Stewardship Council (FSC) in 1993 to oversee the certification of well-managed forests and the labeling of forest products. The FSC has stringent requirements across a range of issues, from minimizing the damage that logging can do to waterways and animal habitats to respecting the rights of indigenous communities and forest workers.

Starting from just 17 independently certified forests in 1995 (Upton and Bass 1996), by 2001 auditors had awarded FSC certificates to 281 forests, covering 21.5 million hectares of land (around 53 million acres) (Forest Stewardship Council 2001). By 2012 nearly 160 million hectares of forest area was FSC-certified, amounting to around 7.5 percent of all forest land worldwide that is designated for production or multiple use (Food and Agriculture Organization [FAO] 2010). Industry associations also developed their own certification programs to compete with the FSC (such as the Sustainable Forestry Initiative in the United States, the Malaysian Timber Certification Council, and a variety of European programs that would become part of the Programme for the Endorsement of Forest Certification [PEFC]). As a group, these associations had certified roughly 11 percent of eligible land by 2012. But the FSC survived the competition with these programs, and it was becoming increasingly visible in the marketplace. From 2001 to 2006 the number of factories with FSC "chain of custody" certification—which allows them to label products made with timber from certified forests—skyrocketed from less than one thousand to more than five thousand. In the UK the vast majority of timber and panel products sold were certified, mostly to FSC standards, by 2008. Throughout North America and Europe it was becoming common to find books (e.g., the Harry Potter series) and catalogs (e.g., Victoria's Secret and Crate & Barrel) printed on FSC-certified paper.

Despite the growth of forest certification, most consumers in the United States and Europe have at best a vague awareness of the FSC. Consumers are far more likely to know the Fair Trade label, and consumer demand for certified forest products has been slow to develop. Furthermore, even as forest certification grew in prominence, deforestation remained a serious problem. The global rate of deforestation increased from 1990 to 2000 and continued to increase, albeit at a slower rate, from 2000 to 2005 (FAO 2006). In some countries severe deforestation persisted; between 1990 and 2005, Brazil lost 9 percent of its primary forest land and Indonesia lost 31 percent, while Gabon lost 32 percent from 1990 to 2010 (FAO 2006, 2010). Global warming was becoming increasingly clear, but it was unclear whether enough forests could be preserved to act as significant "carbon sinks" or if the continued clearing of forests would exacerbate carbon emissions.

In short, the rise of the FSC's much-heralded eco-labeling program occurred without a great deal of demand from conscientious consumers and without transforming the dynamics of deforestation. This chapter considers how that happened. While we consider the rise of forest certification in general, we pay particular attention to the FSC, which has the most stringent standards and the most backing from environmental NGOs. As we will see, the FSC's standards have not always been perfectly implemented, but its requirements for forest management are far from empty greenwash. Yet its ability to slow deforestation has been quite limited. Forest certification has led to some reforms in the production of wood and paper products, but the links between the label and forest-level improvements are far more tenuous than most observers assume.

We begin our examination of the search for sustainable wood and paper by looking at the structure of the industry. We then look at the origins of the FSC and the attempts to globalize its standards and to build a market for certified forest products. Looking at the evidence on implementation reveals several reasons why forest certification failed to stem the tide of deforestation. A closer look at the implementation of FSC standards in Indonesia further clarifies the limits of the certification model.

THE STRUCTURE OF PRODUCTION AND CONSUMPTION

Approximately 30 percent of the world's land area is covered by forests. Much of this is concentrated in a few countries with especially large tracts of forest land. Russia alone contains 20 percent of the world's forest land, followed by Brazil (which has the largest area of primary natural forest), Canada, the United States, China, and the Democratic Republic of the Congo (FAO

2006). Most forest land around the world is publicly owned, and governments grant permits, or "concessions," to companies to harvest wood from particular areas. This harvesting can sometimes be quite destructive, even if it stays within the bounds of what is allowed by the permit. But as advocates of sustainable forestry have argued, natural forests can also be harvested in ways that allow for natural regeneration; preserve ecosystems; and minimize damage to waterways, habitats, and the livelihoods of local people. Wood and especially paper products may also originate from timber plantations—that is, planted forests. These monoculture plantations (commonly eucalyptus, acacia, or pine) lack most of the ecological benefits of natural forests, and the desire to develop large plantations often means the destruction of natural forests. Still, timber plantations can sometimes help to reduce pressures on natural forests and provide a steady supply of timber for pulp and paper manufacturing.

The global timber trade stretches back to the era of colonialism. But today's "global factory" has integrated different locations like never before. Timber harvested in Cameroon, Russia, or Malaysia may be shipped to factories in China or Vietnam to be manufactured into furniture for sale in the United States. Timber plantations in Brazil feed massive plants that manufacture wood pulp for the production of paper for the European market. Even timber harvested from North American and European forests may be shipped to other countries for manufacturing before being returned to those consumer markets.

Consumers in North America and Europe have a disproportionate influence on the world's forests. Roughly three-quarters of the world's wood products and two-thirds of the world's paper are consumed in affluent countries (with the United States and Japan being especially important) (Dauvergne and Lister 2011, 33). Despite the growth of recycled paper and non-wood building materials—and predictions of a "paperless office"—global timber production in 2012 was nearly 50 percent higher than what it had been in 1961 although lower than its peak in 1989.[1] Wood for construction, furniture, and flooring continues to be in high demand, but the shape of demand for paper products has changed. In the United States the total consumption of toilet paper has now surpassed consumption of newsprint, and Americans consume more toilet paper per capita than consumers elsewhere (European Tissue Symposium 2008; Levitz 2012). In addition, while some types of paper use are declining, the globalization of production has increased demand for paperboard/cardboard packaging and wood shipping pallets (Dauvergne and Lister 2011).

Companies based in North America and Europe still dominate the global timber industry, but many large pulp and paper manufacturers (e.g., International Paper, Stora Enso) have built plants in developing countries to take advantage of timber supplies, low labor costs, and access to those markets. Large retailers have also contributed to the global integration of the timber industry. Walmart has become the largest retailer of wood furniture in the United States, helping China to become the world's top exporter of furniture (Cao, Sun, and Eastin 2014; Dauvergne and Lister 2011). The role of American and European markets should not be overstated, however. With economic growth, China, India, and Brazil are becoming major timber markets, and companies based in the Global South (e.g., Asia Pacific Resources International in Indonesia, Fibria in Brazil) are beginning to challenge the dominance of the northern paper companies.[2]

The structure of production depends in large part on the product. Consider furniture, paper, and lumber. Furniture production has become a strongly "buyer-driven" global value chain, with a large number of manufacturers around the world selling to a small number of large retailers in North America and Europe, especially in the discount market. Walmart, IKEA, and other leading furniture retailers (e.g., Target, Pier 1, Pottery Barn, JYSK) source products from factories in China, Indonesia, Vietnam, and Poland, among others (Scott 2006),and they regularly shift from one supplier to another (Dauvergne and Lister 2011). In many ways the structure of production in this labor-intensive industry resembles the apparel industry as described in chapter 5.[3] In contrast, paper manufacturing is capital-intensive, with large investments necessary to operate pulp and paper plants. Partly because of this, many of the leading companies in this industry are vertically integrated, from the planting and harvesting of timber plantations to the production of tissue paper, office paper, diapers, and packaging materials.[4] The lumber industry lies somewhere in between. Lumber companies usually engage in harvesting logs and processing them into sawn wood (solid lumber) or plywood (made from multiple layers of wood). But the costs of setting up a sawn wood/plywood plant are low, so many factories without their own harvesting operations have also arisen around the world. In fact, some governments (e.g., Indonesia, Brazil, Ghana, and parts of the United States and Canada) have banned the export of raw, unprocessed logs in order to support domestic timber-processing industries.

Despite these differences in products, all of them have been subject to growing concentration and power in the retail end of the industry. For paper, Staples, Office Depot, Walmart, and other mega-retailers have become increasingly powerful, largely by contracting for their own private label lines of paper (Kumar and Steenkamp 2007). Sawn wood and plywood, which are essential to home construction and improvement, are increasingly likely to be sold through "big box" retailers such as The Home Depot and Lowe's in the United States or Kingfisher and its various outlets in Europe (B&Q, Castorama, and Brico Depot) (Dauvergne and Lister 2011; McDermott and Cashore 2009).

Concentration in the retail sector has had two main consequences. First, large retailers have gained the power to squeeze suppliers on price. Writing about furniture, Peter Dauvergne and Jane Lister (2011) describe this process:

> Big box retailers . . . are known to strike buying contracts with suppliers that take up a large fraction of a factory's production capacity. The supplier then invests in a redesign of its facility to meet the huge order. The following year the retailer may then offer the same purchase order, but now demand a lower price: say, a 5 percent discount. The supplier is then stuck, often having gone into debt to raise production to meet the first year's big order. (7)

Under pressure to keep prices low, some manufacturers have turned to cheap, illegally harvested wood. The rise of discount furniture manufacturing in China, for instance, has played a significant role in driving the rise of illegal logging in Asia and Africa (Lawson and MacFaul 2010). Even if the wood is of legal origin, price pressures and small profit margins make it difficult for forest management companies to invest in reduced-impact logging methods and other environmentally friendly practices. (As we will see, demand for low prices has limited the effectiveness of forest certification.)

Second, concentration in the retail sector has provided opportunities for environmental activists to mobilize public pressure against large, well-known firms. In the UK activists from Friends of the Earth set up giant inflatable chainsaws in the parking lots of B&Q stores in the early 1990s, linking that company to tropical deforestation. In the United States the Rainforest Action

Network used similar tactics in targeting The Home Depot over the destruction of domestic and foreign old-growth forests. As Staples was becoming the largest office supply retailer in the United States, it also became the target of campaigns over its paper suppliers' role in deforestation in Southeast Asia. These campaigns have revealed many destructive and shadowy aspects of the global forest products industry, including violence by logging companies against indigenous people, logging permits gained through patronage and corruption, harvesting methods that leave local environments devastated, and corporate structures that use "front companies" to shield owners from accountability. In addition, campaigns targeting well-known retailers have been used to build markets for alternative wood products, such as those that are certified by the FSC.

GLOBALIZED LOCALISMS: THE DEVELOPMENT OF GLOBAL RULE-MAKING PROJECTS

As discussed in the introductory chapter, global standards spring not from some abstract global order but from the projects of specific individuals and organizations. This is especially clear in the field of sustainable forestry, where particular communities of experts and environmentalists have sought to globalize their approaches to sustainability. Industry associations have also attempted to define global sustainability, and the result has been an expanding and contentious field of forest certification. Errol Meidinger (2003) called this "a loosely networked social field in which there are several centers of activity that closely monitor each other. . . . Relations among them involve a complex, shifting mix of mutual observation, direct communication, trust, distrust, mutual adjustment, cooperation, coordination, and competition" (276). In the following section we show how forest certification arose, with particular attention to the founding of the FSC and its growing market presence.

The Creation of the FSC

The Forest Stewardship Council was founded in 1993 by a coalition of environmental organizations, foresters, and companies (including several retailers and timber importers in the United States and Europe). To understand how this coalition came to agree on the need for forest certification, we must look back to the late 1980s and early 1990s. In response to consumer concern about deforestation and potential boycotts, tropical timber exporting companies and their governments began making a number of impressive-sounding but usually meaningless or unverified claims about "sustained yield" forestry (Upton and Bass 1996). Environmentalists sought to expose this as green-wash (WWF 1994 [1991]), but many environmental groups were also uncomfortable with boycotts, which they feared would punish forest-dependent populations or unintentionally promote *less-sustainable* alternatives to wood. Even those who supported boycotts, such as Friends of the Earth and the Rainforest Action Network, also began producing "Good Wood" guides to identify alternatives.

It was the search for "positive alternatives" to the "blunt tools" of boycotts that ultimately produced forest certification initiatives. Starting around 1989 a small group of environmentalists, indigenous rights advocates, foresters, and woodworking companies began to formulate plans for an independent association to certify sound forest management. The Woodworkers Alliance for Rainforest Protection, made up of small, craft-based companies in the United States and Europe, played an important role (Ecological Trading Company 1990). So did a small group of foresters who had worked together on community forestry projects in South America. Dubbed the "Peace Corps–Paraguay mafia" by their collaborators, this group saw greening markets in Europe and the United States as a "tremendous market opportunity for the 'wood producer projects' in the U.S. and overseas" (Donovan 1990). A few companies and nonprofit organizations, such as Scientific Certification Systems and the Rainforest Alliance, were beginning to certify forestry operations, and they too became part of the project to build a larger body to standardize and provide credibility for this activity. Environmental NGOs, especially WWF (which originally stood for "World Wildlife Fund"), soon took a leadership role in convening and expanding this group, partly due to frustration with the effort to build a binding intergovernmental forestry convention, which ultimately failed at the 1992 Earth Summit. In 1991 WWF organized the first of many "buyers' groups" of retailers, including B&Q, that would commit to selling certified products.

By 1993 these various players had founded the Forest Stewardship Council, which developed a set of "Principles and Criteria" for responsible forest management, a product label, and a system for accrediting certifiers. FSC members included companies, but they were limited to having a minority share in the voting and executive power of the organization. The FSC's architects were paying attention to the growth of certification in organic agriculture and fair trade, but they also sought to create a "unique new tool" that could take old conflicts between industry and environmentalists and "resolve that fight over here, with a completely new ground and completely new outlook."[5] The FSC's founders agreed on a fairly stringent set of standards that would require companies to minimize the environmental effects of logging, protect plant and animal habitats, respect the rights of indigenous people, generate benefits for local communities and forest workers, and much more. They hoped to give timber companies an "incentive that would tap into a very efficient engine, which is the market . . . and tap the power of the consumer to create change. [It was] a non-regulatory approach that took the power of the consumer and turned it into change—basically let people vote with their dollars."[6] Some even framed this as "a different kind of citizenship; it's like consumer citizenship, because people widely recognize that governments don't do what they're supposed to do, or that there are limitations on it."[7]

The FSC soon faced competition from other certification initiatives. In Canada the main forest products industry association (the Canadian Pulp and Paper Association) asked the Canadian Standards Association to develop a sustainable forestry standard, which was released in 1996. Dissatisfied with the limited space for industry involvement in the FSC, Canadian companies promoted this standard as an alternative (C. Elliott 2000). In the United States the American Forests and Paper Association, the main industry association, developed the Sustainable Forestry Initiative (SFI) and turned it into a certification program in 1998. Throughout Europe industry associations and owners of forest land organized their own certification systems, which soon joined together in the Pan-European Forest Certification (PEFC) system (Cashore, Auld, and Newsom 2004). By 2003 this group had expanded its scope beyond Europe (and changed its name to the Programme for the Endorsement of Forest Certification), consolidating in one umbrella organization most "homegrown" competitors to the FSC, including those in Malaysia, Chile, and Gabon, as well as the Canadian and American programs.

These programs generally had less stringent standards than the FSC, but through processes of comparison and competition some convergence occurred. PEFC-affiliated programs gradually strengthened their standards

(Overdevest 2010), while the FSC made it easier for products to bear its logo without originating entirely in certified forests. As we will see, the latter step helped the FSC increase its visibility in the market, although its quest for growth also led to some questionable certifications (Rainforest Foundation 2002). Still, the FSC did not reduce its stringent requirements for certification, and its advocates managed to convert opposition or ambivalence into support in some markets (Cashore, Auld, and Newsom 2004). Competition between the FSC and PEFC persists to this day. The FSC has greater support from major environmental NGOs (although some also criticize it) and from large retailers in the United States and Europe, but the PEFC has more certified forest land, more support from manufacturing industries, and a strong foothold in some markets. Although the standards of the two groups converged to some degree, some crucial differences remain. For instance, the FSC has stronger prohibitions on the conversion of natural forests to plantations and more stringent requirements on preserving "high conservation value forest" areas.

Building Support and Making Markets

Casual observers often assume that certification initiatives arise in response to demand from conscientious consumers. But in this case forest certification emerged before sizable demand from individual consumers, and its supporters had to work strategically to "make a market" for certified products. Retailers such as B&Q and The Home Depot hoped that consumer demand would eventually emerge, but they admitted that they were "putting the cart before the horse" in supporting the FSC.[8] "Industry-wide customer demand for certified wood is practically nil" (Caulfield 2001, 2), and "the momentum thus far has largely been in anticipation of customer demand, rather than in response to it" (Home Depot representative, qtd. in *Journal of Forestry* 1993). As Michael Conroy (2007) puts it, "The appearance of ever-greater quantities of FSC-certified wood in Home Depot and Lowe's stores in the US is not a response to hordes of consumers asking for FSC. If you doubt it, just ask the sales associates; you'll find that it is still rare for a salesperson to have any notion of what the FSC represents" (292). IKEA is a major supporter of FSC certification, having pledged to eventually use 100 percent certified wood for its furniture. But it does not apply the FSC logo to its products, reportedly because it does not want to distract from its own brand image.

Why, then, did major retailers make early commitments to stock FSC-certified products? The answer lies in social movement campaigns that publicly charged retailers with contributing to global deforestation and asked them to shift to certified wood in response. In the UK, Friends of the Earth organized pressure against B&Q, which became an early supporter of the FSC. In the United States and Canada, the Rainforest Action Network, Coastal Rainforest Coalition (later called ForestEthics), Greenpeace, and others used banner drops, store protests, and media campaigns to shame companies such as The Home Depot, Staples, and Victoria's Secret. In addition to the "stick" of protest and negative publicity, many campaigns implicitly or explicitly held out a "carrot" of an end to the campaign if a company supported FSC certification (Cashore, Auld, and Newsom 2004; McNichol 2006). As one leader of the Rainforest Action Network remarked, "It was like good cop/bad cop. We were the FSC's bad cop" (qtd. in Carlton 2000). A ForestEthics leader similarly explained its approach to certification: "It used to be that you either worked with companies or against them. But that's foolish and a false choice. We help companies change, but we don't take no for an answer" (qtd. in Caplan 2005).

Campaigns also had larger ripple effects. Once The Home Depot agreed to promote FSC-certified products, its competitor Lowe's soon followed suit. After Victoria's Secret agreed to use FSC-certified paper for its catalogs, Williams-Sonoma and Tiffany began to do so as well (Conroy 2007). Since the early 1990s WWF had been organizing "buyers groups" of companies that agreed to promote certification in their supply chains. The first of these, made up of British companies, was soon followed by buyers groups in North America, Germany, the Netherlands, Belgium, Switzerland, and Austria (Gulbrandsen 2010).

Still, without significant consumer demand, how did the FSC project garner enough resources to stay afloat? In part it was support from philanthropic foundations that kept the project going. From 1992 to 2001 foundations contributed nearly $40 million to forest certification initiatives. Most of this came from the Ford Foundation, Doris Duke Charitable Foundation, Rockefeller Brothers Fund, and several others that had formed a "Sustainable Forestry Funders" network to support the FSC, its constituents, and the development of buyers' groups (Bartley 2007a). In addition, supporters of the FSC were successful in getting government procurement offices to adopt a preference for certified products in public purchasing. The UK government's procurement office proved especially important in supporting FSC-certified products and in putting pressure on competing systems to strengthen their standards (Overdevest 2010). Advocates of the FSC also got its standards to be preferred in the US Green Building Council's LEED (Leadership in Energy and Environmental Design) standards for environmentally friendly buildings. As governments, companies, and universities built LEED-certi- fied buildings, the market for FSC-certified wood products grew, even with minimal knowledge among individual consumers.

To be sure, consumers were not completely uninterested in forest certifica- tion. A survey of American consumers in 1995 found a segment of individuals who said they were willing to pay significant premiums for certified forest products (Ozanne and Vlosky 1997). Other studies suggested that consumers in North America and Europe might be willing to pay premiums of 4 to 20 percent, depending on the product (Ozanne and Vlosky 2003). But an early study of the *sellers* of FSC-certified products in the United States found that most were not selling these at a premium price, and the few that were received premiums of 1–5 percent (Humphries, Vlosky, and Carter 2001). As discussed in chapter 2, there was a significant gap between consumers' attitudes and their market behavior. Furthermore, even as the volume of FSC-certified goods increased, consumer awareness of the FSC label remained low. The FSC and its supporters launched numerous consumer awareness campaigns, but their results were highly uneven. In recent materials the FSC has esti- mated the rate of basic consumer awareness of its label to be as high as 71 percent in the Netherlands but only 28 percent in Germany; 21 percent in the United States; and 14–15 percent in France, Sweden, and Australia (FSC 2013). (As a comparison, fair trade certification had achieved similar rates of consumer recognition as early as 2000: 74 percent in the Netherlands, 41 percent in Germany, and 13 percent in Sweden (Linton et al. 2004).)

A turning point for FSC's place in the market came when the organization altered its approach to labeling. Early on, the FSC had shifted from a purist model of certifying a product only if 100 percent of its inputs were certified to a percentage-based model, in which a product might be labeled as "FSC

70%." But then in 2004 the FSC introduced a "volume credit" system. This allowed a company that was getting, for instance, 50 percent of its wood or pulp for a particular product line from certified forests to apply the FSC label to 50 percent of the products in that line. In the aggregate the total amount of certified wood or pulp and the volume of labeled products should match, but a given product might carry the FSC label without necessarily coming from a certified forest. The noncertified inputs would need to be verified to the FSC's "controlled wood" standard, which prohibited the most destructive forms of logging (i.e., logging that was illegal, destroyed "high conservation value forests," violated local people's rights, or relied on GMOs). But this standard is far less costly and difficult for companies to comply with than the full FSC standard. This change made it easier for firms to match the supply of certified inputs with the demand for certified products and spurred the growth of the FSC label, especially on paper and packaging (Conroy 2007). For pulp and paper factories the new system meant the factory did not have to spend money keeping certified and noncertified inputs separate. This is one change that allowed the "mainstreaming" of the FSC label. As we will see in the next section, forest management standards themselves were also revised over time, further altering the meaning of the FSC label.

The FSC also increased its market visibility by, in effect, taking over the recycled paper market. Created in 2004, the "FSC Recycled" label allowed products made from recycled wood fiber (at least 85 percent of which must be post-consumer recycled material) to bear the FSC name. Since recycled paper first became common in the 1980s, manufacturers had been applying the classic three-arrow recycled label themselves, typically with some oversight from governments and sometimes with external certification. The FSC Recycled label and similar labels created by the PEFC have increasingly taken over this terrain. The incorporation of recycled material into the FSC has also fueled the growth of paper labeled as "FSC Mix," which is manufactured from a mixture of recycled content, pulp from an FSC-certified forest, or pulp from a "controlled wood" source (as discussed above). It is possible under this system that a paper product with the FSC logo may have no connection whatsoever to an FSC-certified forest. While consumers typically imagine a direct link between an eco-labeled product and its sources, the reality is far more complex, and by some accounts this muddies the goals of the FSC (Moog, Böhm, and Spicer 2014). On the other hand, the system has allowed

FSC Mix papers, some containing FSC-certified pulp, to gain a significant presence in the market, priced only slightly above completely noncertified paper from virgin pulp. Staples and Office Depot sell their FSC Mix paper (with 30 percent recycled content) for approximately 14 percent more than the most basic option (as of 2013). Similar 100 percent FSC Recycled paper was priced at a 38 percent premium.

Overall, the FSC and its supporters have had some success in building a market and fending off challenges from competing initiatives (see Cashore, Auld, and Newsom 2004). But the FSC did make some significant compromises along the way. These have helped to dramatically increase its market visibility, but they have also raised questions about its ultimate impact. To examine this further, we must look at the "on the ground" implementation of sustainable forestry standards.

IMPLEMENTING SUSTAINABLE FORESTRY STANDARDS

The "on the ground" effects of sustainable forestry standards depend on forest management companies deciding to seek certification. Typically this is in response to a request from a retailer or manufacturer. The hope of FSC supporters was that if retailers could charge a premium for certified goods, producers could also get a premium price for harvesting certified wood. Some even hoped that this premium would be enough to "add value" to forest management and reduce the temptation to convert a forest to agricultural uses. As we will see, producer premiums have been far from guaranteed, and this has made the link between product labeling and major on-the-ground improvements more complicated than originally expected. But that is just one of many complications in the implementation of FSC standards.

If a forest management company does want to get its operation FSC certified, it must hire an auditor accredited through the FSC system to assess compliance with the FSC's Principles and Criteria. If the auditors find that the company is in compliance, with no major unresolved problems, they grant a certificate that is valid for five years, subject to follow-up audits each year, or more frequently if necessary, to check on unresolved problems.

In part because the standards and auditing procedures are relatively strict, most of the initial growth of FSC certification occurred in the forests of North America and Europe, where legal requirements were relatively close to FSC standards and companies were accustomed to dealing with environmental demands. Recognizing that it was having a minimal impact in the tropical forests that initially inspired it, the FSC aggressively pushed for growth in the global south. A joint project between WWF and the World Bank sought to vastly expand the amount of FSC-certified forest area around the world. This project, as well as assistance from government aid agencies, retailers, and NGOs, helped to prepare companies for their audits and subsidize some of the costs of certification. In addition, in some cases governments directly supported certification, as in Bolivia, where the government introduced forestry regulations that were highly consistent with FSC standards and treated certification as proof of regulatory compliance (Nebel et al. 2005). Still, as of 2005 less than half of FSC-certified forest land was in developing or transitioning countries (e.g., Brazil, Russia, and Bolivia) (Cashore et al. 2006). But by 2012 Russia alone accounted for 48 percent of all FSC-certified forest land, with sizable amounts certified in Brazil, China, Poland, and a rapidly growing presence in several parts of Africa, including the conflict-ridden Congo Basin.

But what difference was certification making on the ground? To answer this question researchers have often examined the "corrective action requests" issued by auditors, which provide a window into the specific kinds of changes that companies must make in order to become (or remain) certified. These studies generally show that FSC certification requires a variety of changes, "sometimes minor, but sometimes involving radical departures from the previous management style in a region" (Nussbaum and Simula 2004, 19). For example, a study of FSC certificates in twenty-one different countries showed that auditors frequently demanded changes involving forest management plans, conservation areas, logging roads/trails, worker safety, and relations with local stakeholders, among other things (Newsom and Hewitt 2005). In certified community forests in Mexico, auditors frequently pushed forest managers to reduce the environmental impacts of logging roads/trails (Klooster 2006).

It is clear that becoming FSC certified is not easy, and auditors are not simply handing out certificates. (The quality of auditing in the FSC system has been higher, for instance, than in the factory certification initiatives discussed in chapter 5.) But four other issues temper this interpretation. First, a close look reveals that auditors more frequently require companies to formalize and document their management *processes* than to prove that the *performance* outcomes are improved (Nussbaum and Simula 2004). Auditors can easily require a firm to adopt a sound management plan, for instance (and often do), but they may not be able to assess whether the plan is fully implemented in the field. Second, a request for corrective action does not always mean an effective and durable change was made. Problems can persist or reappear over time, sometimes leading the certificate to be suspended, but sometimes leading to a long string of small improvements that never quite meet a strict reading of the standard (see Bartley 2012; WWF European Forest Programme 2005). Third, although the FSC covers a wide range of environmental and social standards, not all standards are equally scrutinized in the field. In particular, although the FSC calls for freedom of association—that is, the right of forest workers to form their own unions—our evidence suggests that this is rarely audited vigorously. In China, where freedom of association is prohibited by the state, audits for FSC have completely neglected this issue.[9] In their study of changes necessary for FSC certification, Deanna Newsom and Daphne Hewitt (2005) find that firms in developing countries typically had to address workers' safety, wages, or living conditions, but the researchers did not even mention issues related to freedom of association. The neglect of labor rights likely stems from the fact that the FSC's key founders and watchdogs are environmental and indigenous rights NGOs, not trade unions and labor rights groups. Finally, there is evidence that auditors sometimes tailor their judgments more to current best practices in the region than to the substantive requirements of the FSC standards (Cerutti et al. 2011; Schulze, Grogan, and Vidal 2008). In other words, where local best practices are well below a strict reading of the FSC standards, auditors tend to relax their interpretation of standards.

As this final point suggests, the character of FSC certification depends in part on where a forest is located. The FSC's global standards have to be "translated" into locally meaningful practices. This is supposed to occur through a multi-stakeholder national/regional standard-setting process, but this has not occurred in many regions, leaving auditors to do this work in a rather ad hoc fashion. Examining forest certification in Russia, Olga Malets (2013) notes, "It would be wrong to argue that companies simply had to identify practices that were not in compliance with FSC requirements and substitute them with the 'correct' practices. Rather, both activists and company forest managers experimented and combined global, external, and locally available, domestic 'elements'—i.e., legal requirements, global concepts, and on-the-ground practices—in different ways" (315). Even different regions of the same country can vary substantially. In the Russian far east, where illegal logging is common, industry and government fiercely resented the FSC's incursions, creating a challenging environment for auditors (Tysiachniouk 2012).

The Challenge of Mainstreaming

As discussed in the introductory chapter, the "mainstreaming" of alternative production standards often involves a watering down of standards and greater accommodation to the interests of large companies. In the case of the FSC, mainstreaming has influenced the meaning of certification on the ground in several ways. The FSC's decision to allow the certification of timber plantations, so long as they were not recently converted from natural forests, rankled some of its early supporters, who charged that monoculture plantations were not in line with the FSC's initial purpose. In addition, the FSC's original ban on logging in "primary" old-growth forests was later turned into a more nuanced set of standards for conserving "high conservation value forests," which has sometimes proven to be a slippery notion (Cashore, Auld, and Newsom 2004; Tollefson, Gale, and Haley 2008). Furthermore, with the FSC seeking growth and its certifiers profiting from conducting more audits, several highly controversial certificates have been awarded (Rainforest Foundation 2002).

Yet the FSC's mainstreaming has also been held in check by scrutiny from NGOs—both within and outside of the FSC membership—and decision-making rules that require support from nonindustry constituents to make changes. Even though the FSC sought to increase the amount of certified forest land, it took steps to ensure that its decision-making process remained open and that it did not lose support from environmental NGOs (Klooster 2010). As Dan Klooster puts it, "As certification systems mainstream, their alternative character is likely to erode; lower standards are a tradeoff for increased acceptability. The need to protect system legitimacy, however, provides countervailing pressure to maintain inclusiveness and rigorous standards" (11).

In addition, under pressure from NGOs, the FSC has recently disassociated itself from some companies that seemed to be using the FSC name to cover up a highly destructive set of operations. In Indonesia the pulp and paper giants APP (Asia Pulp and Paper) and APRIL (Asia Pacific Resources International) have routinely cleared natural forest land, disrupted endangered species, and relied on questionable sources of "mixed tropical hardwoods" to feed their pulp mills. But they had also gotten some areas verified as "controlled wood" and were preparing to sell paper labeled as FSC Mixed. In 2007, after journalists publicly exposed this plan—generating a storm of controversy—the FSC banned APP from using the FSC logo and soon developed a new policy to prevent this kind of association in the future (Wright and Carlton 2007). In 2013 the FSC invoked this policy in disassociating itself from APRIL after a complaint was lodged by Greenpeace, WWF, and the Rainforest Action Network. That same year, the FSC also disassociated itself from the European timber company Danzer over its activities in the Democratic Republic of the Congo. The impoverished and war-torn Congo basin was becoming a growth area for FSC certification, and a forest managed by Danzer had been approved as "controlled wood." But an investigation by Greenpeace charged that the company was engaged in illegal logging and complicit in violence against local residents (Greenpeace 2011). In these three cases, the FSC has clearly clamped down and sought to prevent mainstreaming from completely undermining its credibility.

The Failure of a Credible Initiative?

Despite its numerous shortcomings, FSC certification is a reasonably credible indication that forest management is at least better than average in some respect. But this does not mean forest certification has been effective in reducing deforestation. Indeed, even as certification gained steam, deforestation rates in many parts of the world continued to increase at alarming rates (FAO 2006). Generally, research on forest certification paints its overarching consequences as quite mixed (Auld, Gulbrandsen, and McDermott 2008). As R. E. Gullison (2003) puts it, there is "clear evidence that certification produces biodiversity benefits by improving management of *existing timber production forests* during the auditing process. In contrast, the incentives offered by certification are insufficient to prevent deforestation" (162; emphasis added). In Bolivia, for instance, FSC certification became quite popular, partly due to the government support mentioned above, but the increased rate of certification did not slow the rate of deforestation (Nebel et al. 2005).

To some extent deforestation persists simply because the vast majority of the world's forests are not certified. (As mentioned above, FSC certification covers roughly 7.5 percent of eligible land, and PEFC certification covers roughly 11 percent.) It is costly and onerous for forest management companies to obtain FSC certification, and most companies have not seen the benefit of doing so, either because their products are sold in markets with little demand for certification or because demands for certification are not being backed by premium prices. For some types of timber, such as rare, high-value tropical hardwoods, there is evidence that producers can receive sizable premiums for FSC certification (Espach 2009; Kollert and Lagan 2007; Nebel et al. 2005). But these same studies find that premiums are small or nonexistent for lower-value tropical hardwoods. For most forest management companies, market premiums have been uncertain or so small that they barely cover the direct costs of certification. Some retailers that support the FSC (e.g., IKEA and Walmart) also tightly squeeze prices in their supply chain, leaving little if any room for producer premiums. To compensate for the dearth of producer premiums, governments, NGOs, and companies in affluent countries have sometimes stepped in to subsidize the costs of certification in developing countries (Molnar 2003; Borneo Initiative 2014).

Yet a more fundamental reason for the limited influence of forest certification is that the main drivers of deforestation lie outside its sphere of influence. As mentioned earlier, a great deal of deforestation occurs through the burning or clearing of forest land so that it can be converted to agricultural uses. In South America the expansion of soy plantations (see chapter 4) and cattle ranching have contributed to the loss of natural forest land. In Southeast Asia what were large tracts of natural forest land have increasingly been converted to timber plantations or oil palm plantations. Initially some supporters of the FSC hoped that certification (unlike boycotts) would add value to managed forests and thus reduce the temptation to convert them to agriculture. But over time it has become increasingly clear that any market benefits available for harvesting certified timber are dwarfed by the money that can be made by converting land to agriculture, as we will see in the case of Indonesia below. Furthermore, governments have often prioritized agricultural development at the expense of forests. Forest certification, which has sought to "bypass" governments to instead enforce standards through supply chains, has had little influence on these decisions.

Forest certification has also failed to stem the tide of illegal logging. While certification has sought to improve and recognize good forest management, it has had little bearing on the lucrative illegal timber trade. In Indonesia illegal logging exploded during a turbulent political transition, and scholars estimated that one-half to three-quarters of all timber production in the late 1990s could have been illegal (Tacconi et al. 2004). In the far east of Russia unauthorized logging feeds into a complex and shadowy timber trade on the Chinese border. In Cambodia the rise of illegal logging led an international NGO, Global Witness, to be brought in as an independent monitor of the forest sector. But the illegal timber trade was so enmeshed with the ruling government and its elite supporters that Global Witness was soon dismissed and replaced with a more conciliatory monitor.

Much illegal timber soon finds its way into legitimate supply chains as it flows "from Russia, Africa, and Southeast Asia into China[,] where it is turned into 'legal' products for worldwide export" (Dauvergne and Lister 2011, 122). Estimates have suggested that more than a quarter of the wood imported to the European Union in the 2000s came from illegal or suspicious sources (Dauvergne and Lister 2011). Between 2008 and 2010, with growing international attention to illegal logging and concerns from some industry groups that it was depressing the prices of legally harvested wood, the United States and EU each passed laws that penalized the sale of products that can be traced to illegal logging. These striking legislative acts—a revision of the Lacey Act in the United States and the passage of the EU Timber Regulation—have generated a new set of debates about the meaning of legality and its enforcement.[10] This emerging timber legality regime will certainly influence the future of forest governance, but its rise has also served to illustrate the limited impact of voluntary sustainable forestry certification (Bartley 2014b). To further examine what certification is and is not capable of, we turn to a closer examination of forest certification in Indonesia.

LOCALIZED GLOBALISMS: CERTIFYING THE FORESTS OF INDONESIA

As research on sustainability is increasingly recognizing, global standards are modified and often muted as they are translated into practice in particular places (Malets 2013). Looking at what it takes to localize a global principle reveals a great deal about the practical implications of certification and labeling. In this section we show some of the contradictions of applying the FSC's standards in one crucial tropical forest context, Indonesia.

In addition to being the world's fourth-largest country by population, Indonesia has the world's third-largest amount of tropical forest land. Yet from 1990 to 2005 Indonesia lost 31 percent of its primary forest cover (that is, relatively undisturbed native forests) and 24 percent of all forested land (FAO 2006). Indonesia also went through a major political transition during that period. After ruling the country for more than thirty years, President Suharto was forced out of office in 1998, and the authoritarian "New Order" regime gave way to an era of democratization and "Reformasi." Soon thereafter Indonesia embarked on a set of reforms to decentralize control of natural resources, shifting some power from the central government to district governments. These ended up being devastating for forests and in some ways facilitating the rise of illegal logging. Indonesia is an important case for forest certification, but for these reasons among others, also a very difficult one.

Deforestation in Indonesia had been at the center of tropical timber boycott campaigns in the 1980s. In the 1990s, as a global field of forest certification began to emerge, the teak plantations of Perum Perhutani, the state forestry company, were among the first to be certified. Although the company had long had tense relations with local people (Peluso 1992), its scientific agroforestry methods were viewed positively by many environmentalists, and it was selling timber to Smith & Hawken, an American outdoor furniture company at the forefront of sustainable business initiatives (Taylor and Scharlin 2004). The original certificate, issued by the Rainforest Alliance, eventually led to a series of FSC certificates, and certified teak from Perum Perhutani flowed to a number of specialty furniture manufacturers. But in 2001, amid a rising tide of illegal logging and violence against local people by the company, Perum Perhutani's certificates were suspended (Donovan 2001). FSC certification, even with secure sales channels and premium prices, had proven insufficient to guarantee fair and sustainable conditions in the forest.

This case is a microcosm of sorts for the larger story of forest certification in Indonesia. In response to demands from retailers a few forests in Indonesia did achieve FSC certification. But a tumultuous domestic economic and political situation limited the number of firms that were interested and made it difficult for them to get—or stay—certified. At the same time that

FSC certification was beginning to cover 15–20 percent of eligible forest land in Russia and Brazil (Blaser et al. 2011; Malets 2011) it covered less than 2 percent of "production forest" land in Indonesia (as of 2009). Moreover, conflicts between timber companies and villagers were common in certified and noncertified forests alike. Forest certification could do little to counteract the rise of illegal logging and the conversion of natural forests. In short, the growing global market for certified wood and paper products had, at most, a minor effect on forest conditions in Indonesia.

Sustainable Plywood and the Tribulations of PT Intracawood

The clearest links between the growing market for certified wood and Indonesian forests occurred in the plywood industry. The Home Depot, like other home improvement retailers, was under fire for its sales of plywood from tropical forests. But as it began to demand FSC-certified products—and in some cases offer premiums for them—some plywood manufacturers in Indonesia were able to respond. Take, for instance, PT Intracawood, an Indonesian company with a marketing arm in the United States that supplied directly to The Home Depot. After failing its first attempt, in 2005 Intracawood successfully got its timber concession in East Kalimantan certified to FSC standards. Importantly, PT Intracawood, like several of the other Indonesian timber companies that became certified (e.g., PT Sumalindo, PT Suka Jaya Makmur), was an integrated plywood manufacturer, responsible for managing forests and manufacturing the logs into plywood. The simple structure of this part of the forest products industry made the link between demand and supply relatively straightforward. In contrast, in the furniture industry some retailers were demanding FSC certification, but this did not mean manufacturers could easily supply it. Furniture manufacturers in Indonesia were primarily buying timber from other companies and rarely in large enough quantities to influence how they managed the forest.[11]

Although PT Intracawood had a clear incentive to obtain FSC certification, the company's operations were in many ways difficult to reconcile with FSC standards, especially when it came to community rights. There was a history of tension with communities in and around the area where the state had given Intracawood the rights to harvest. As Indonesia transitioned to democracy these tensions became more visible. One villager claimed, "When

PT Intracawood first came here, we were not brave enough to say anything, because it was during the New Order regime. Since Reformasi we have spoken out" (qtd. in Colchester, Sirait, and Wijardjo 2003, 211). In some cases villagers seized machinery or blockaded roads, and the company in turn called in police and military forces (212).

The legal standing of Intracawood's concession was also problematic. The boundaries of the company's timber concession had not been completely finalized, and local governments had begun issuing a range of overlapping permits—that is, multiple permits for the same area of land—during a tumultuous set of decentralization reforms. Under pressure from certifiers for the FSC, the company successfully got these permits voided in 2002. But then in 2003 the national Ministry of Forestry suddenly declared Intracawood's permit invalid, in effect ceasing the certification process.

After getting its permit reinstated, Intracawood received FSC certification in 2005 (SmartWood 2006b). But the tense community relations were not wiped away, and the auditors asked the company to make "significant progress to resolve all community disputes dating from prior to certification" (SmartWood 2006b). The auditors came to be satisfied with compensation agreements that the company made with community leaders (SmartWood 2006a). The compensation of roughly twenty-seven cents per cubic meter amounted to roughly 0.3 percent of the cost of production (based on averages in that region, as reported by Ruslandi, Oscar Venter, and Francis E. Putz [2011]). This compensation, which was supplemented by charitable contributions, may be more than villagers would have received during the Suharto era. But it was far below the compensation (of roughly two dollars per cubic meter) that was being offered by small-scale (often illegal) loggers in the era of decentralization (Colchester, Sirait, and Wijardjo 2003, 215–16). FSC certification did put a spotlight on company-community relations, but it is difficult to judge how well these agreements fulfilled the FSC's substantive goals of supporting clear land tenure and indigenous peoples' rights. As Marcus Colchester and his colleagues argue, there is a danger that compensation payments to communities with no real land rights ends up reproducing colonial- and Suharto-era systems of domination.

After obtaining certification the company continued to struggle to meet standards for community relations, logging practices, and erosion control, leading to several temporary suspensions of the FSC certificate (SmartWood

2008b, 2012). In one instance auditors reinstated the certificate while admitting that similar (but not identical) issues remained problematic—in essence, finessing the decision so that the certificate could continue (Smart-Wood 2008a, 2008c).[12]

In the case of Intracawood one finds a bit of everything—some reform and some intransigence, some scrutiny that is quite serious and some that is less so—all set within a contested and rapidly changing local context. This is apropos for the case of forest certification in Indonesia, and it should serve as a reminder that the situation on the ground is always more complicated—and often more conflictual—than a simple eco-label can represent.

The Bigger Threat: Converting Natural Forests to Plantations

The small pockets of land that received FSC certification, imperfect or not, were ultimately a small piece of the larger story of deforestation in Indonesia. Deforestation was driven in part by the expansion of the pulp and paper giants such as APP and APRIL, as mentioned above. With the stated purpose of developing timber plantations, these companies cleared large tracts of natural forest land, using the "mixed tropical hardwoods" from the cleared forests to feed their mills (Barr 2001). Sometimes the forests were cleared and the timber used, but the plantation was never developed—what became known as the "plantation hoax" (Ekawati 2009; Human Rights Watch 2006). Recently, facing intense international campaigns, these companies have made "no deforestation" pledges, but their past actions make many observers skeptical.

Even more important has been the conversion of forests to oil palm plantations. Palm oil has become an increasingly popular ingredient in soaps and processed foods around the world, a cooking oil in China and India, and a potential biofuel. With rising prices the amount of land in Indonesia designated for the growing of oil palm trees increased by more than 600 percent from 1990 to 2010, making Indonesia the world's largest producer of palm oil by 2007 (Carlson et al. 2012; McCarthy and Cramb 2009). More than half of Indonesian oil palm expansion from 1990 to 2005 came from the conversion of forests (Koh and Wilcove 2008). Typically these forests had been categorized as "degraded" by government and thus eligible for conversion. But in the eyes of many foresters and environmental groups, these "degraded" lands were in fact rich, biodiverse forests. (In Malaysian Borneo, just across the border from Indonesian Kalimantan, researchers have found that "degraded" forests are nearly as rich in biodiversity as are primary forests [D. Edwards et al. 2011].) Moreover, as palm oil prices increased, some local governments recategorized tracts of natural forest as eligible for conversion.[13]

Even if a company could receive a significant premium from harvesting wood from a certified natural forest, which was by no means certain, the incentives to convert forests to oil palm plantations were high. One estimate suggests that an oil palm plantation in Kalimantan is worth nearly three times as much as a similarly sized logging operation there (Ruslandi, Venter, and Putz 2011). Yet it also happened that plantation development was used primarily as a ruse to clear an area and sell the resulting timber (Elson 2011; Gellert 2005, 1352).

Concerns about palm oil inspired a new certification initiative called the Roundtable on Sustainable Palm Oil (RSPO). In chapter 4 we argue that this type of "commodity roundtable" has a limited chance of institutionalizing alternative models of land use and economic development. Even if the RSPO succeeds in making some oil palm plantations more sustainable over time, it is clear that the growth of the palm oil industry has come at the expense of forests in Indonesia, among others, and the FSC was powerless to affect that. For consumers the politics of food and the politics of forests may appear to have nothing to do with each other. But on the ground, whether forest land will be harvested for timber or converted for use by the agri-food industry is tremendously important.

CONCLUSION

Forest certification has captured the attention of researchers; environmental NGOs; and many retailers of furniture, lumber, paper, and other forest products. But it remains at the margins of consumers' attention in most countries. In some ways the growth of forest certification demonstrates that eco-labeling initiatives are not entirely dependent on demand from individual conscientious consumers. The FSC grew largely through support from foundations and government procurement offices, with environmental activists' "good cop/bad cop" strategies goading retailers into support. In addition, the case of forest certification shows that a fairly credible eco-label can become prominent in the market but fail to solve the problems that originally inspired it. The growth and mainstreaming of the FSC did not result in a complete sellout, but neither did it significantly alter the dynamics of global deforestation.

Conscientious consumers often want simple assurances that their purchases are sustainable. But the complexities of industries and certification initiatives, let alone competing definitions of "sustainability," make such assurances essentially impossible. So what does buying an FSC-certified product really mean? We believe the material in this chapter provides at least an approximate answer, although it is not a simple one. First, if a product is labeled "FSC 100%," one can be reasonably certain that this purchase supports forest management practices that have been found to be consistent with a strict set of standards. The assessment most likely missed some problems and glossed over others, and in some regions those forest management practices may be just slightly above the norm. Nevertheless, buying this product rather than an uncertified one raises the odds of supporting decent forest management. Whether this is better than not buying the product at all is debatable, depending in part on what its substitute would be. Second, if consumers use products that are labeled "FSC Recycled" (e.g., office paper, toilet paper, paper towels, etc.), this may contribute to decreased demand for virgin pulp. But FSC Recycled products may not be significantly different from other products with high levels of post-consumer recycled material, and demand for virgin pulp could also be reduced by simply reducing one's use of paper products. Third, if the product is labeled "FSC Mixed," the link to certified forests is more tenuous, but this label still somewhat increases one's odds of supporting decent forest management and avoiding the most destructive forms of logging. On the other hand, if a company touts its FSC "chain of custody" certification on its website or in advertising materials, conscientious consumers should keep in mind that this means nothing unless the company is actually selling products made from certified wood or pulp.

Yet even if the market for "FSC 100%" products grew substantially, this would be unlikely to make a big impact on global deforestation, because deforestation is being driven largely by factors that are not affected by the FSC's label, such as conversion of forests to agriculture and government land-use policies. And even FSC-certified forests can leave a great deal to be desired when it comes to the rights of indigenous communities and forest workers.

It is hard to see how this can change without greater recognition of rights by governments. Unless it coincides with vigorous social movements and significant changes in government policy, buying eco-labeled forest products is unlikely to get to the root of problems of environmental degradation and social injustice. We generally concur with Johannes Ebeling and Maï Yasué's (2009) sobering yet not entirely pessimistic assessment of FSC certification:

> Conservationists need to have realistic expectations about the potential of forest certification and other market-based strategies to improve management practices on the ground. Certification is clearly no silver bullet, but could be a valuable tool in a comprehensive conservation strategy for tropical forests, which would also include enhanced environmental law enforcement, effectively implemented and ecologically-minded land-use planning, expanded protected area networks, and agricultural policy reforms. Importantly, a comprehensive forest conservation strategy must not be limited to the forestry sector itself but instead address all drivers of deforestation and forest degradation. (1153)

Perhaps the prospects for governmental action are not entirely dim. The EU and the United States have taken aggressive legislative action against illegal logging, and intergovernmental climate change initiatives such as the UN-REDD program (Reducing Emissions from Deforestation and Forest Degradation) continue to evolve. The question, which we take up in the conclusion, is whether the concerns of conscientious consumers might be redirected into projects that expand the rights of citizens, strengthen the democratic and administrative capacities of states, and restructure industries to reverse the intense downward pressure on prices at any cost. As a start, conscientious consumers must at least recognize how much is *not* being accomplished through even the most credible eco-labels.

4 — FOOD

Global Agriculture and Local Institutions

"BOOM TIMES IN PARAGUAY LEAVE MANY BEHIND," PROCLAIMED AN article in the *New York Times* in April 2013. The country's 13 percent rate of economic growth was the highest in the hemisphere. But as the article pointed out, there was an enormous gulf between the expanding market for luxury lofts and the plight of urban garbage pickers. Behind Paraguay's economic growth was a massive expansion of soy production, much of it exported for use in animal feed, but the social benefits of this industry have been scarce. The soy industry contributes little to the tax base, generates few jobs, and has contributed to a highly unequal distribution of land, the major productive asset in an agrarian country. One-third of the population is below the poverty line, while 1 percent controls roughly 77 percent of the arable land. Mechanized soy production has displaced smallholder peasant communities, unleashing a series of violent conflicts, one of which precipitated the collapse of the Paraguayan government in 2012.

For many consumers the politics of food are increasingly engrossing. Food is at once a basic requirement for material subsistence and a powerful symbol of cultural meaning and identity, which has made it a perennial object of protest and political struggle. Conscientious consumers bring numerous concerns into their food purchases, ranging from the environmental effects of industrial agriculture, to the safety of food imports, to the rights of migrant farmworkers. The effects of agri-food globalization on small farmers, who make up the majority of the world's poor, has also attracted a great deal of attention. Critics allege that globalization is driving dispossession of small farmers from land, exacerbating inequality, and forcing the rural poor to migrate to urban areas or other countries. Might concerns among consumers have implications for dispossession and social inequality in places like Paraguay? Or is conscientious food consumption in distant markets, and the standards it supports, too weak to make a difference?

In this chapter we delve into the world of agri-food commodity chains and several attempts to make them fairer and more sustainable. Agriculture is unique among global industries because for most crops large, commercial plantations or corporate farms that rely on wage labor are less common than small, family-owned farms that rely predominantly on their own labor power and sometimes produce partly for their own subsistence. Unlike manufacturing industries, where household craft production occupies small niches, many globally traded commodities, such as coffee and cacao, remain dependent on peasant farming, as does most domestic produce in developing countries. Yet globalization is rapidly spreading corporate forms of organization to agricultural production and distribution around the world. This can create new opportunities for development, but it also places new demands on smallholders and often threatens to exclude them from economic gains.

For this reason the conditions of smallholder farmers must be central to any attempt to evaluate conscientious consumption and the standards it supports. How do standards influence the balance between forms of production that provide meaningful opportunities for smallholders and those that marginalize them? Our examination of fairness and sustainability standards suggests that some are more geared than others toward supporting small farmers' competitiveness. Specifically, we compare the logic and impact of fair trade certification with the increasingly popular "commodity roundtable" approach to certification, as seen in the Roundtable on Responsible Soy, Roundtable on Responsible Palm Oil, and several others. Despite significant flaws and growing concerns about mainstreaming, we find that fair trade can sometimes promote and strengthen alternative production and governance structures at the local level, enhancing small farmers' ability to profit from globalization. In contrast, commodity roundtables have taken dominant—and highly unequal—local structures as given and attempted to regulate them through global scrutiny and auditing. In the process they have abetted the marginalization of smallholders.

We base this argument on an analysis of the rules, constituencies, and documented performance of these systems as well as a close look at the sugar and soy industries in Paraguay. Our research there reveals how local structures of production shape the influence of global standards for fairness and sustainability. In addition, our examination of sugar production helps to balance a literature on fair trade certification that has focused almost exclusively on coffee.[1]

We begin with a look at the global structure of production and consumption in agri-food industries. Although much has been written about the growing power of retailers in the food system, we show that large non-retail companies often retain a great deal of power in these global value chains. The balance of power and the kinds of fairness and sustainability standards that take hold depend in large part on the product. In focusing strongly on the power of global retailers, scholars and practitioners have often overlooked how globalization and standards shape national and subnational power dynamics in both positive and negative ways. We highlight these influences as we describe fair trade certification and the commodity roundtables, and especially as we try to unpack "localized globalisms" in the sugar and soy fields of Paraguay.

THE STRUCTURE OF FOOD CONSUMPTION AND PRODUCTION

Total demand for food in the affluent countries of North America and Europe has stagnated.[2] But food consumption has become highly stratified in tandem with rising income inequality. In the United States most household incomes have been fairly stagnant (or declining with the "great recession" of 2008–2009), and these consumers continue to demand the low-cost, mass-produced food that dominated agri-food markets for most of the twentieth century. Price remains the central dimension of product competition in this part of the market, leading retailers to greatly expand their "private label"

lines to complete with branded items (Burch and Lawrence 2007). In contrast, growing incomes at the top of the distribution have enhanced market
niches where price is less important than quality (Hatanaka, Bain, and Busch
2006; Michel, Cecile, and Vololona 2002; Wilkinson 1997).[3] In addition to
the traditional sense of quality (i.e., more expensive ingredients, more attractive visual appearance), products appeal to consumer identities and lifestyle narratives, and their value derives largely from marketing. Consumer
concern about personal identity (e.g., social status, connoisseurship, group
belonging), convenience, health, environment, and social justice has driven
a great deal of innovation in the food sector. What marketers have dubbed
the LOHAS market segment (lifestyles of health and sustainability) has
brought together identity-based, political, and even spiritual dimensions—as
Monica Emerich (2011) puts it, "tossed together in the same sustainability
salad" (xii).

It is in this context that conscientious consumerism in the food industry
has exploded, as illustrated by the rapid growth of organic food and (to a
lesser extent) fair trade–certified coffee, tea, and other products. (See fig.
2.1. in chapter 2.) Not only have specialized retailers such as Whole Foods
grown, but mainstream grocery stores have greatly expanded their offerings
of organic, eco-labeled, and social-labeled items. It should be no surprise
that retailers are keen to attract and retain the loyalty of affluent consumers
whose spending has continued to grow while that of others has stagnated.

Linking these two poles of food demand in affluent countries is a process
by which products that began as costly luxuries have become, via global
trade, staples of daily consumption.[4] In roughly historical order, examples
include coffee, tea, cocoa, tropical fruit, counter-seasonal/temperate-climate
fruit and vegetables, and farmed seafood. Most recently, traditional products
from abroad, such as the Andean pseudo-grain quinoa, have been marketed
as health foods in the United States and Europe. Food brands and retailers
have boosted their profits by turning niche products into mass consumption
products, taking advantage of low production costs and climatic conditions
in developing countries as well as consumers' tendency to buy far more of
these items when prices go down slightly. "New" agricultural exports such
as seafood, fruits, vegetables, and processed foods now make up 50 percent
of the exports from developing countries, while traditional products like tea,
coffee, cocoa, sugar, and cotton make up a small and shrinking share (Aksoy

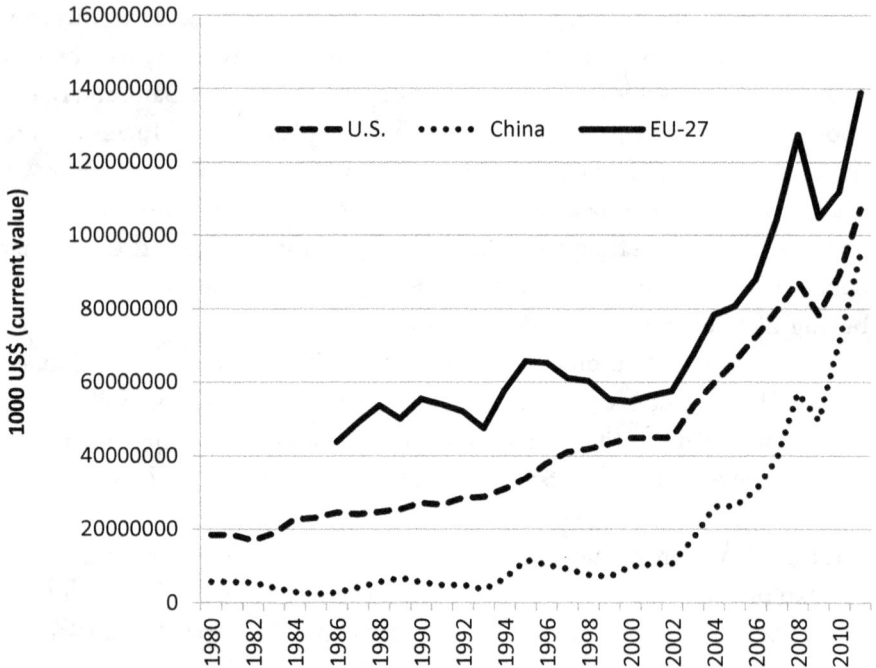

Figure 4.1: Total Agricultural Imports to the US, China, and EU-27, 1980–2010. *Source:* FAOSTAT data.

and Beghin 2004). In spite of stagnant aggregate demand, the United States and the EU have seen increased food imports, driven largely by high-value fruits and vegetables. American companies import these products primarily from Mexico, Canada, and South America (Huang and Huang 2007), while imports to Europe come from a wider array of places, including African, North American, and South American countries.[5]

While aggregate food demand is slowing in affluent countries, it is growing rapidly in developing countries, especially in places such as China, India, and Brazil, with large populations and growing middle classes. Increased incomes have driven rising demand for animal protein and, consequently, for animal feed to permit mass production of pork, chicken, seafood, eggs, and dairy products. The South-South trade networks that have resulted are beginning to diminish the outsized influence of the United States, Europe, and Japan on the global food system (Peine 2013). As shown in figure 4.1, China has rapidly caught up with the United States and the EU as a major importer of agricultural commodities. This growth has been driven almost entirely by raw soy imports, mostly from the United States, Brazil, and Argentina.[6] This is processed in China into animal feed and subsequently products such as pork meat or into edible oils.

Industry Power and the Structure of Agri-Food Value Chains

Given stagnant food demand in affluent countries and growing markets in developing countries, food retailers and manufacturers in Europe and North America have sought growth by merging, cultivating lower-cost suppliers in developing countries, or investing in developing countries to gain access to new markets. This has often led to the concentration of power in particular nodes of global value chains. But the structure of global value chains, and the holders of this power, vary widely in different parts of the multifaceted agri-food sector.

In many parts of the industry, multinational retail companies (e.g., Walmart, Carrefour, Metro) are playing an increasingly important role in co-ordinating global production, potentially at the expense of food manufacturing brands (Burch and Lawrence 2005; Connor and Schiek 1997; Kaufman 2000). Because consumers shop for groceries on a weekly or even daily basis, food is central to the strategies of globalizing retail companies. As shown in table 4.1, the eight largest retailers in the world are food retailers (at least in part), as are thirty-two of the world's top fifty retailers. Most of the world's largest retailers are headquartered in the United States or Western Europe but operate in dozens of countries. Companies like Walmart, Carrefour, Tesco, and Royal Ahold have simultaneously consolidated ownership in their home markets and invested in retail infrastructure abroad (Burch and Lawrence 2007; Reardon and Berdegue 2002; Reardon et al. 2003).

In the United States the market share of the top twenty retailers increased from 39 percent to 65 percent from 1992 to 2011 (James Jr., Hendrickson, and Howard 2013). The effects of multinationalization strategies are also clear in Latin American countries, where the market share of supermarkets has gone from as low as 10 percent in the 1980s to 35–75 percent by 2000. Foreign ownership of supermarkets has also increased, such that by the year 2000 multinational corporations held 43 percent of the supermarket market share in Brazil, 64 percent in Argentina, 72 percent in Mexico, and 93 percent in

Table 4.1. Top Global Retailers

Rank	Company	Country of Origin	2011 Retail Revenue (US$ Millions)	Format	Countries of Operation	Global Market Share*
1	Walmart Stores Inc.	US	446,950	Hypermarket/ Supercenter	28	3.4
2	Carrefour S.A.	France	113,197	Hypermarket/ Supercenter	33	0.8
3	Tesco	UK	101,574	Hypermarket/ Supercenter	13	0.7
4	Metro AG	Germany	92,905	Cash & Carry/ Warehouse	33	—
5	Kroger Co.	US	90,374	Supermarket	1	0.6
6	Costco Wholesale Corp.	US	88,915	Cash & Carry/ Warehouse	9	0.6
7	Schwartz Unternehmens Treuhand	Germany	87, 841	Discount Supermarkets	26	0.6
8	Aldi Einkauf GmbH	Germany	73,375	Discount Supermarkets	17	0.5

Source: Deloitte 2013; Euromonitor 2013.

Guatemala (Reardon and Berdegue 2002). A similar trend is occurring in some parts of Asia and Africa, as multinational companies buy up national and regional supermarket chains. Walmart gained access to fourteen Sub-Saharan African countries by buying a controlling share of the South African retailer Massmart in 2011, and it has made large investments in China as well, including a controlling share of the online grocery retailer Yihaodian.[7]

As supermarket chains have become the dominant gatekeepers to many consumer markets, they have also gained the ability to impose conditions "upstream" in agricultural value chains.[8] This has brought about three types of changes in the governance of global value chains (Reardon et al. 2009; Reardon et al. 2003). First, there has been a shift from public standards for food quality and safety (or sometimes the absence of standards) to private standards imposed by retailers. Second, there has been a shift from agricultural goods being sold through "spot markets" and wholesale outlets toward vertical coordination through supply contracts between buyers and sellers.

Third, there has been a shift from local procurement to regional, national, and global sourcing. Logistics and inventory systems that allow for "just in time" delivery and "traceability" of quality over long distances have facilitated this expansion. The systems and standards that retailers demand, though, are quite costly, and this has sometimes led to a concentration of ownership in food processing and distribution (Martinez 2007). Extensive research exists on the declining viability of small-scale farming as small farmers are outcompeted by larger landowners and agribusiness firms that can meet the scale, quality, investment, and administrative demands of complying with retailers' standards (e.g., Van der Meer 2006).

At the same time, most large retailers center their operations in a single country or a few neighboring countries (Rugman and Girod 2003). Moreover, national regulations, land-use patterns, transport infrastructures, and consumer cultures may preserve a substantial role for traditional distribution systems (wholesale and wet markets) and small-scale ("mom and pop") retail in some developing countries (Harvey 2007; Neilson and Pritchard 2007). As with the European countries analyzed in chapter 1, there is significant national variation in the structure of retailing.

More importantly, and often overlooked, the power of retailers is challenged for many products by the concentration of power and ownership "upstream" in the agri-food value chain. Global food brands (like PepsiCo, Kraft, and Nestlé), agricultural traders (like Archer Daniels Midland [ADM] and Cargill), and input providers (like Monsanto and Syngenta) occupy quite powerful positions, and these companies too have expanded their international reach. Researchers have documented trends toward multinationalization and concentration of ownership in food branding (Bolling and Gehlhar 2005; Wilkinson and Rocha 2009), food processing (in affluent and developing countries alike) (Farina 2002; Wilkinson and Rocha 2009), and trading and logistics activities (Gilbert and ter Wengel 2001; Vorley and Fox 2004). Large-scale land investment by agribusiness and financial companies has created enormous challenges for farmers, who also increasingly find themselves dependent on a few companies that dominate the upstream portions of the agri-food value chain (Amanor 2012; Deininger and Byerlee 2011; Zoomers 2010).

One cannot understand agri-food value chains without attending to concentrated power in both upstream and downstream locations. It appears that where power lies in these value chains depends largely on the features of the product. In particular, we see agri-food value structures as shaped by two key factors: (1) the extent to which crops are sold directly to consumers and (2) the degree of crop perishability. First, when crops have large direct-to-consumer segments, power tends to be concentrated downstream in retailing, branding, and food processing. In contrast, when crops are used primarily as industrial inputs, power tends to be concentrated further upstream, among traders, primary processors, and input suppliers. Second, crop perishability shapes the geographical location of primary processing—that is, whether it is located near farming activities or near final markets—and in turn the boundaries of companies. Highly perishable crops must be processed near the farm, which gives rise to powerful local processing companies that are often integrated "backward" into farming. Crops that are less perishable are more commonly processed near consumer markets, giving rise to large trading companies that are often integrated "forward" into food processing.

Consider what these two factors reveal about crops such as soy, corn, and wheat. They are sold overwhelmingly to industrial processors that transform them into animal feed, food ingredients, and industrial food and chemical inputs. They are the most widely produced and globally traded agricultural products in the world, and they have a low degree of perishability. Retailers play a secondary role in governing these global value chains, but other types of large companies—based in countries with large consumer markets—are extremely important. Companies such as Monsanto, Cargill, and ADM dominate upstream portions of these value chains, while food processing companies such as PepsiCo and Unilever are powerful actors at the other end.

In contrast, for fruits and vegetables that are consumed in fresh form (rather than processed into shelf-stable industrial products), supermarket retailers play a central role, setting the quality and safety standards that producers must meet. The fact that many such products are also highly perishable means they are the least globalized of the agri-food industries. National, regional, and even local companies occupy strategically important positions, in part because the international sourcing that does occur requires close coordination of harvesting, post-harvesting activities (e.g., sorting, washing, treating, packing), and "cool chain" transportation logistics that provide an unbroken chain of refrigeration from the packinghouse to the supermarket.

Of course, these factors do not completely determine the structure of production. Banana and pineapple production are dominated not by retailers but by vertically integrated brands (such as Dole, Chiquita, Del Monte) that own marketing, distribution, packing, and farming operations (Friedland 1994; Frundt 2009). The production of fresh green beans for export to the United States and Europe appears to be compatible with informal smallholder supply networks in Burkina Faso, large-scale corporate production in Zambia, and smallholder cooperatives in Guatemala (Freidberg 2004; Jay and Lundy 2008). To understand this type of variation we must go beyond the characteristics of products to consider historical legacies of developmental strategies as well as national and subnational organizational structures. As we will see, these are important for understanding not only the structure of production but the meaning of standards for fairness and sustainability.

The Local and National Dimensions of Global Value Chains

For much of the twentieth century, governments and experts in developing countries assigned an important but limited role to agricultural development. They sought to harness industrialization as an engine of economic development and social transformation, and they viewed agriculture as the fuel for that engine (Bates 1981; B. Johnston and Mellor 1961). For instance, agriculture could provide cheap food for the urban workforce in order to keep wages low and prop up rates of profit, reinvestment, and economic growth. As development proceeded, agriculture would theoretically play a diminishing role, eventually becoming highly mechanized (Lewis 1954). To use the agricultural sector in this way, many governments created state-owned enterprises, marketing boards, ministries of agriculture, and other institutions to coordinate and set prices for raw materials and food products. Often these institutions had the result of discriminating against small farmers in favor of industry and urban consumers (Bates 1981), even as state support contributed to the growth and modernization of large-scale farmers (Grindle 1986). Some states, such as Taiwan, South Korea, and Japan, supported productivity gains among small farmers but then extracted many of the economic benefits (Kay 2002).

In the latter half of the twentieth century, developing countries largely abandoned these industrial policies and shifted from "taxing" agriculture in these ways to opening it to market forces and promoting it to some degree (Organization for Economic Cooperation and Development 2013). They privatized commodity marketing boards and liberalized price controls. In the debt crises of the 1980s agricultural exports became a source of foreign exchange to pay foreign debts (Raynolds 1994). In the 1990s nontraditional agricultural exports to affluent countries grew rapidly, becoming the leading industries in some regions and leading to a reappraisal of agriculture as an engine of development. Countries like Brazil, Chile, and Thailand have become "new agricultural countries" that form the basis for agri-food global value chains (Friedmann 1991). In many countries in Southeast Asia, Africa, and Latin America, exports of specific products, such as farmed fish and shrimp, fresh-cut flowers, and counter-seasonal vegetables, have come to play an important economic role. In addition, agriculture remains important in driving other forms of economic growth, largely through its linkages to the food processing industry, which accounts for 30–50 percent of the manufacturing sector in low- and lower-middle-income countries (Wilkinson and Rocha 2009).

Diverse national histories of agricultural development and liberalization have left a varied landscape of farms that are being integrated into global value chains. As global markets are refracted through local structures, their implications for social class relations (between agribusiness owners, landowners, and workers, for instance), income distribution, and resource use can vary dramatically. Perhaps most important, the history and structure of land tenure varies greatly across countries, regions, and globalizing agro-industries. Export-oriented farming may take place on plantations owned by traditional elites, on corporate farms owned by diversified agribusinesses, on small family-owned farms, or on a mixture of these forms. Furthermore, it may take place in the context of either land scarcity or abundance. When land is scarce and export booms increase land values, the result is often "land grabbing," wherein investors take advantage of farmers' inability to defend their rights (Berry 2001). Where land is abundant, labor is likely to be scarce, which encourages landowners to either offer higher wages and better conditions or to engage in coercive labor practices.

The distributional consequences of global food markets and quality standards depend largely on factors like the strength of national labor regulation (Aparicio, Ortiz, and Tadeo 2008), unionization of farmworkers (Aparicio,

Ortiz, and Tadeo 2008; Damiani 2003), and the organization of farmers, including the capacities of cooperative organizations (Gomes 2006; Raynolds 2004; Setrini 2011). For example, agricultural regions with strong unions and labor regulation, like Petrolina-Juazeiro in Brazil and Corrientes, Argentina, have gained export competitiveness and standards compliance through a virtuous cycle of productive modernization, skill enhancement, and improved labor relations (Aparicio, Ortiz, and Tadeo 2008; Damiani 2003). In contrast, in regions with weak regulation and labor organizations, competitive strategies often rely on low wages and the informalization of labor relations. For example, the need to comply with quality standards has come at the cost of vulnerable and exploited workers in the citrus industry of Entre Rios, Argentina (Aparicio, Ortiz, and Tadeo 2008); the Mexican tomato industry (Carton de Grammont and Lara Flores 2010); and the South African table fruit industry (Barrientos and Kritzinger 2004). If smallholder organizations are absent or weak, the "upgrading" of quality standards often results in concentrated land ownership, as seen in the Chilean table fruit industry (Carter, Barham, and Mesbah 1996; Gwynne 2003) and the vegetable industry in Kenya (Dolan and Humphrey 2000; Freidberg 2004).

The decline in state management and regulation of agri-food production and the consolidation of private power in the global food system have stimulated the growth of private standards not only for food quality and safety but also for fairness and sustainability, as we will discuss below. The legacies of distinct forms of agricultural development exert a strong influence on the meaning of these standards.

GLOBALIZED LOCALISMS: THE DEVELOPMENT OF RULE-MAKING PROJECTS FOR FAIR AND SUSTAINABLE AGRICULTURE

NGOs, global social movements, and civil society organizations have catalyzed criticism of the global food system as unsustainable and unjust. They have linked the increasingly corporatized global food system described above to a variety of problems: land grabs and the dispossession of local people, deforestation and the degradation of land, overfishing and species depletion, the exploitation of farmworkers, and poisoning by pesticides, to name just a few. At the same time, some segments of consumer demand have shifted toward higher-value niches and nonmaterial qualities of products, as described above. The combination of the two has helped to create a market for standards for fair or sustainable food. That demand for standards has been expressed in two ways.

One path is illustrated by the rise of fair trade certification. In this case, activists have called on retailers, brands, and food service providers to begin carrying and producing certified products. In the early 2000s the NGO Global Exchange campaigned to get Starbucks to stock Fair Trade–certified coffee, and TransFair USA encouraged Green Mountain Coffee Roasters to become a major seller of Fair Trade coffee (Conroy 2007). NGOs have sometimes mobilized conscientious consumers to make their demands heard. Oxfam, for instance, has sponsored campaigns among university students, religious organizations, and social justice activists to demand fair trade products in their schools, workplaces, congregations, and communities in the UK, European countries, Canada, and the United States.

In another path NGOs have mobilized pressure from investors more than from consumers. This has put standards for fairness and sustainability onto the agendas of food companies that are less recognizable to consumers (e.g., Unilever, Cargill) or the corporate parents of well-known outlets (e.g., Darden Restaurants, parent of Red Lobster and Olive Garden). Professionalized NGOs and socially responsible investment groups have essentially lobbied companies to adopt standards without customers even being aware of it. For example, the Interfaith Center on Corporate Responsibility, which represents faith-based institutional investors, sponsored shareholder resolutions in 2013 asking a number of companies (e.g., Darden, Church & Dwight, Kroger, Dean Foods) to adopt standards for sustainable palm oil amid concerns that the expansion of oil palm plantations was driving deforestation (see chapter 3).[9] This kind of behind-the-scenes pressure has been important in spurring corporate participation in "commodity roundtables"—that is, initiatives that certify particular commodities, such as the Roundtable on Sustainable Palm Oil (RSPO), the Roundtable on Responsible Soy (RTRS), and the Global Roundtable for Sustainable Beef (GRSB).

We focus our attention on these two models. There are of course hundreds of other standards for fair and sustainable food, covering issues from organics to the humane treatment of animals. But the fair trade and commodity roundtable models are especially notable for several reasons. First, both types of standards are intended to deal with the global dimensions of food production, consistent with our focus in this book; some other food standards are more domestically oriented. Second, together they capture different parts of the agri-food industry as described above, from well-known brands and retailers to less visible commodity processors and input providers. Both initiatives certify operations and allow for the labeling of products. However, they adopt varying approaches to certification and labeling in response to the distinct value-chain structures of different global agri-food commodities. For direct-to-consumer products with short value chains that are dominated by food retailers and brands—such as coffee, cocoa, tea, and fruit—labeling products as "fair trade" is intended to inform consumer purchases. In contrast, commodity roundtables focus more on supply chain management than on consumer marketing, and they have emerged around industrial commodities such as soy, palm oil, biofuels, and livestock, where traders and primary processors occupy dominant positions in global value chains. Some industries, such as sugar, have large direct-to-consumer and industrial markets and have been targets of both fair trade and "roundtabling." Third, as we will see, these two models also link global standards to local structures of production in different ways.

Fair Trade

As described briefly in chapter 2, fair trade began not as a label or even a consumer movement but as an offshoot of the alternative trading organizations (ATOs) and "solidary trade" networks of the 1960s. Organized coffee producers played an important role in making certification part of the fair trade model in the late 1980s. Finding that the market for sales through ATOs appeared to be saturated, a group of coffee producer organizations in Mexico and Central America, along with the Dutch Christian development organization Solidaridad (Inter-Church Foundation for Action for Latin America), founded the Max Havelaar label, named for the protagonist of an anticolonial Dutch novel. This was a way to market the coffee of small farmer cooperatives in traditional retail outlets (Renard 1999). Around the same time, peace activists in the United States had begun selling "Café Nica" coffee imported from Nicaraguan farmers as an act of solidarity with the Sandinista government (Auld 2014; Rice and McLean 1999). Equal Exchange, the organization that had led this action, soon became the main promoter of fairly traded coffees in the United States. With the collapse of the International Coffee Agreement in 1989–1990 and subsequent volatility in coffee prices, fair trade became a way to guarantee a minimum price for coffee producers (Linton, Liou, and Shaw 2004). The Fairtrade Labelling Organization (FLO) was formed in 1997 to coordinate and oversee a growing number of fair trade labels.

As fair trade certification grew and entered mainstream markets, some charged that the FLO had abandoned the radical potential of fair trade to wrest control of global trade from monopolistic multinational corporations (Fridell 2004). FLO standards did take some structures of the global economy as a given, but at the level of production those standards codified support for cooperative modes of production and collective action among small farmers. In this sense fair trade certification sought to provide an alternative to consolidated control of land and corporate plantation farming.

Fairtrade International (as FLO was renamed in 2011) issues standards for both producer organizations (e.g., cooperatives) and trading enterprises, which allow particular products (e.g., coffee, tea, cocoa, sugar, bananas) to carry its Fairtrade logo. In order to receive certification, producer organizations must be made up primarily of smallholder farmers, engage in business and development planning, and adhere to norms of democratic governance. They must also adopt environmental management practices such as soil and water conservation, integrated pest management, and the safe use of pesticides as well as international labor norms such as freedom of association and bans on discrimination, forced labor, and child labor (Fairtrade International 2011). To sell a product that is to be labeled "Fairtrade," trading enterprises must enter into contracts with producers, provide them with presale financing, and buy the product at a commodity-specific minimum price, plus a "social premium" to be used for producers' collective investments (Fairtrade International 2011). Both parties must meet a variety of product-specific standards as well.[10]

Auditing of compliance with these standards is carried out by a separate organization, FLO-CERT. Most certification systems, including the factory certification programs discussed in chapter 5, the sustainable forestry programs in chapter 3, and the commodity roundtables discussed below, accredit multiple auditing organizations. But the fair trade system has relied on this single auditing organization, which has more than a hundred auditors based in various parts of the world.

Fairtrade International's membership is composed of labeling initiatives in a number of affluent countries and three networks representing more than one thousand producer organizations in Asia, Africa, and Latin America. For most of the organization's history these producer networks contributed only three votes in the organization's general assembly, with the other twenty-one votes going to the labeling organizations. But in 2011 Fairtrade International sought to rectify this imbalance by increasing the producer networks' share to half of the representation in the general assembly (Fairtrade International 2013).

Until recently, Fairtrade International oversaw the application of essentially all fair trade labels found in the markets of North America and Europe. But in 2011 the US-based affiliate, Fair Trade USA (previously called TransFair USA), announced its exit from Fairtrade International. Fair Trade USA's departure was largely due to its desire to certify larger coffee plantations, not just smallholder farms. Fairtrade International had already developed standards that allowed large plantations growing tea, bananas, and cut flowers to be certified, which would allow for increased volumes of certified goods for products that did not have large numbers of preexisting smallholder suppliers. But a shift toward plantation standards in coffee proved too contentious, since it would create direct competition for smallholder cooperatives in fair trade's oldest, most iconic, most traded product. (The power of its original constituents surely helps to explain Fairtrade International's reluctance to expand coffee certification.) In essence the debate over smallholder production and cooperatives pushed fair trade's mainstreaming to a breaking point. Fair Trade USA's exit has challenged not only the meaning of fair trade but the clarity of its labeling as well: consumers in the United States may notice that Fair Trade USA's logo (a person holding a single container, which is a revision of its previous two-container version) is now facing competition from Fairtrade International's logo (resembling a person raising one arm). Furthermore, the rise of newer "direct trade" initiatives that invoke some of the original fair trade rationales further complicates the set of choices consumers face.[11] The future of fair trade is uncertain, but Fairtrade International remains the largest fair trade labeling organization by geographic scope and overall market share, and it is the historical performance of this initiative that we consider in the remainder of this chapter.

Commodity Roundtables

The commodity roundtable approach has a shorter history. It begins in some ways with the 1993 founding of the Forest Stewardship Council, which we discussed in chapter 3. Though unique in several respects, the FSC's construction of a multi-stakeholder initiative to certify a particular commodity inspired later initiatives like the RSPO and RTRS, founded in 2003 and 2006, respectively.[12] The roundtable approach, which brings actors from different parts of the industry together with representatives of NGOs, has become a popular way to certify sustainability for a variety of products, from seafood to biofuels (Ponte 2014).

As opposed to the ostensibly developmental purpose of fair trade, commodity roundtables have had more exclusively regulatory objectives, reflecting the interests of their main NGO constituents. The hope of WWF (previously World Wildlife Fund), a founding member of each of the commodity roundtables, is to curb environmentally damaging practices of companies operating in countries with weak or nonexistent environmental regulation. NGOs, including WWF, had previously looked to national law and international agreements to set environmental standards, but in the 1990s many sought to influence markets more directly and to engage with companies in order to do so. Many NGOs argued that a small number of oligopolistic multinational companies had gained the power to privately enforce production standards throughout the global economy. This power could be leveraged to support environmental standards, they hoped, but it would require some engagement with the very companies that bore responsibility for environmental damage. WWF's work is increasingly aimed at "transforming markets," by "promot[ing] Better Management Practices (BMP), and increas[ing] the supply of certified products through Multi-Stakeholder Engagements such as Roundtables and Dialogues that involve businesses, trade and industry, as well as producers and other NGOs."[13] The RSPO began, in fact, as a partnership between WWF and Unilever, and RTRS began as a partnership between WWF and the Swiss supermarket chain Coop. The membership of commodity roundtables tends to be dominated by the leading global agribusiness companies from different parts of the value chain and a few large NGOs like WWF, Fauna and Flora International, and Conservation International.

The RTRS' agribusiness chamber includes major food processors such as Unilever and Nestlé; input providers including Monsanto and Dow Agro-Sciences; trading companies such as ADM and Cargill; retailers such as Carrefour and Sainsbury; and even energy and financial firms including Royal Dutch Shell and Rabobank. The civil society chamber features large environmental NGOs headquartered in the Global North, including WWF, the Nature Conservancy, Fauna and Flora International, and Solidaridad. Several NGOs based in developing countries participate (e.g., Instituto Ethos from Brazil and Fundación para la Conservación y el Uso Sustentable de los Humedales from Argentina), but domestic organizations advocating for small farmers are not well represented.[14] The "producer" chamber is composed primarily of large corporate farming enterprises, especially in Latin America. This includes Grupo Andrew Maggi, the world's largest soy farming enterprise, with more than 135,000 hectares planted, and Grupo Lucci, which has large farms and processing facilities in Argentina. Several associations of large commercial farmers are also members, as is one organization composed of smallholder farmers, Bijawar Producer Company from India.

Although the commodity roundtables share the FSC's discursive commitment to multi-stakeholder representation (see chapter 3), their governance structures and standard-setting procedures generally privilege the interests of agribusiness over civil society. While the FSC gives those with environmental and social interests in forests two-thirds of the voting power, the RTRS gives two-thirds of the voting power to producers and industry representatives. The RSPO divides representation on its executive board across seven groups, but environmental and social/developmental NGOs comprise only two of the seven (with the other five groups being growers, processors/traders, manufacturers, retailers, and banks/investors) (RSPO 2004). Moreover, researchers have found that commodity roundtables often eschew debate among stakeholders with opposing views and instead structure deliberations around technical questions and expert scientific recommendations. Observing RSPO meetings, Stefano Ponte and Emmanuelle Cheyns (2013) find that roundtables marginalize organizations with "local" knowledge as well as social scientific perspectives that could bring issues such as "migrant work, land conflicts and rights, and the living conditions of people affected by palm oil expansion to the discussion table" (470). Furthermore, the meeting organizers use technology and agenda setting to preclude debates over questions perceived as "too political or controversial such as . . . production models or a common definition of sustainability" (470).

In the RTRS the veto power of agribusiness and the avoidance of polarizing topics has led the organization to adopt flexible and vague standards that lack enforceable provisions (Elgert 2012). For instance, the criteria for certifying soy producers fall into five categories: (1) legal compliance and good business practice, (2) responsible labor conditions, (3) responsible community relations, (4) environmental responsibility, and (5) good agricultural practice. The last two categories are ostensibly the core of the standard, but they often lack specific enforceable criteria, instead providing general principles such as the following: "pollution is minimized and production waste is managed responsibly"; "efforts are made to reduce emissions and increase sequestration of greenhouse gases on the farm"; and "soil quality is maintained or improved and erosion is avoided by good management practices." One of the few specific, enforceable provisions is the banning of polluting and hazardous chemicals listed in the Stockholm and Rotterdam Conventions, multilateral treaties that regulate chemical production and trade.

The weakest provisions of the RTRS standards are those involving social responsibility. Like most multi-stakeholder initiatives, the RTRS includes an array of labor standards, such as those discussed for the apparel industry in chapter 5. But the most serious social impacts of soy farming have little to do with labor exploitation and much to do with the concentration of land assets and income. Mechanized soybean production utilizes vast expanses of land while employing relatively few workers for tasks like tractor driving and the application of chemicals. But soy expansion has often come at the expense of smallholder communities whose cropping and farming practices generate much greater labor demand. The soy industry's greatest threat to social conditions is its potential to exacerbate elevated levels of economic inequality and to dispossess economically and politically weak actors of their livelihoods. The RTRS standards do require producers to demonstrate clearly defined land use rights. But legal regimes for land rights in developing countries are often illegitimate and highly contested, and soy farmers have frequently relied on legal manipulation, corruption, intimidation, and lethal violence to secure and exercise land rights (Hetherington 2011). The RTRS standards ask producers to maintain channels of communication to resolve conflicts with neighboring communities, but they give no guidance about what specific measures must be taken. Moreover, the vagueness of these standards suggests that the roundtable members may be lacking expertise on smallholder, peasant, and indigenous production systems.

Like the mainstreaming of fair trade, the rise of commodity roundtables has provoked controversy. Critics see them as insufficiently stringent, corporate-controlled exercises in greenwashing.[15] Some opponents argue that they are exclusionary because they do not effectively include the voices of small farmers and indigenous populations, especially those opposed to the expansion of large-scale mechanized agriculture.[16] For example, the Southern Brazilian Family Farmworkers' Federation (FETRAF-Sul) participated in early negotiations to draft "social responsibility criteria for soy," but they declined further participation in the RTRS in opposition to the use of genetically modified soy, which they worry contributes to the dominance of input providers like Monsanto. Small farmers and their advocates have held a series of protests against the RTRS, a "counter conference," and campaigns to pressure NGOs to abandon the system (Schouten, Leroy, and Glasbergen 2012).

At the same time, as Stefano Ponte (2014) notes, commodity roundtables compete with more commercially driven organizations that are generally "less democratic, leaner, quicker, and more attuned to industry interests" (2). Competitors to the RTRS, such as the International Sustainability and Carbon Certification (ISCC) system; the ProTerra Certification System; and the Biomass, Biofuels Sustainability Voluntary Scheme (2BSvs), currently have less stringent criteria and smaller market shares than the RTRS (KPMG 2013). In addition, the RTRS found itself competing with national sustainability initiatives after some leading agribusiness groups withdrew their support. The Brazilian Association of Vegetable Oil Industries (ABIOVE), the National Association of Grain Exporters (ANEC), and the Mato Grosso Soybean Producers Association (Aprosoja), which together represent the largest and most powerful actors in Brazil's soy industry, partnered with the Responsible Agribusiness Institute to organize "Soja Plus." This initiative supports compliance among Brazilian companies with federal environmental laws that are less stringent than global sustainability standards (Hospes, Van der Valk, and Mheen-Sluijer 2012). At the same time, these groups supported a successful moratorium on soy expansion in deforested land in Brazil in 2006, demonstrating that the RTRS is not the only relevant reform project. Ponte (2014) suggests that commercial certifications may be gaining the upper hand over commodity roundtables but that criticism of the commodity roundtables has generated pressure for commercial certifiers to be somewhat more responsive and inclusive.

There is potential for both a "ratcheting up" and a "watering down" of soy standards over time. But more important than the standards on paper are the effects of these systems at the point of production. Have commodity roundtables altered how industries operate? Do fair trade standards actually benefit smallholder farmers? How should we understand the meaning of these standards on the ground? It is to these questions that we now turn.

IMPLEMENTING AGRICULTURAL STANDARDS

Both fair trade and the commodity roundtables certify producers that are found to be in compliance with standards. While FLO-CERT is the sole auditor for fair trade certification, the commodity roundtables rely on multiple accredited certifiers, including some that also certify forests (see chapter 3) or factories (see chapter 5).[17] Although both types of initiatives have grown, the share of global trade that is certified remains small. In 2011 the market share of fair trade–certified products was less than 2 percent of global exports, even for the most successful products, such as coffee and bananas. Fair trade tea and sugar account for 0.7 percent and 0.4 percent of global volumes, respectively.[18] The commodity roundtables similarly apply to fairly small portions of global trade. RSPO-certified palm oil now accounts for approximately 15 percent of the global total, but the RTRS' market share is much smaller. Roughly 2 percent of globally traded soy has received sustainability certification of any kind (KPMG 2013). RTRS-certified producers accounted for just 0.3 percent of the land devoted to soy production (as of 2012) and 0.8 percent of soy global soy imports (as of 2011).[19] Furthermore, we suspect that there are serious limits to the growth of roundtable certifications. Demand for responsible soy and palm oil comes primarily from European markets.[20] But the growth in soy production in South America is being driven by demand from Chinese meat producers, and most oil palm plantations in Southeast Asia are selling to markets in India and China.

Even within their small niches, how much difference are these two models of certification making? To evaluate the effects of fair trade, much research focuses on the prices that farmers in the coffee industry receive. Do certified farms receive higher prices than noncertified farms, are price premiums enough to improve farmers' material conditions, and can fair trade certification make global trade viable for smallholder farmers in developing countries? Generally researchers have found that owners of certified farms do receive higher prices for their crops than do those of comparable noncertified farms (Arnould, Plastina, and Ball 2009; Bacon 2005; Barham et al. 2011; Fort and Ruben 2008; Jaffee 2007). However, when world market prices are not depressed, the differences may be negligible (Fort and Ruben 2008). Furthermore, organizations of certified farms are often unable to sell all of their products through certified channels, so only a portion of their members' production receives a price premium (Carranza et al. 2010). In addition, fair trade premiums are often less than premiums for top quality and organic coffee. Thus, what appears to be an effect of fair trade on farmers' incomes can sometimes be a result of higher yields (Barham et al. 2011).

Farms that are certified as both fair trade and organic can typically fetch the highest prices for their coffee, but the ultimate benefits of this are often ambiguous, since farmers must spend more (and sometimes hire casual labor) to meet organic standards and must manage the new administrative burdens of inspection (Jaffee 2007; Mutersbaugh 2002; Wilson 2010). This raises questions about whether coffee production, even with multiple certifications, is profitable. In southern Mexico Bradford Barham and his colleagues (2011) found that household investments in coffee production were far less profitable than investment in child education or migration to areas where nonagricultural work was available. Similarly, in Nicaragua both Christopher Bacon and his colleagues (2008) and Bradley Wilson (2010) found high levels of household debt, poverty, food insecurity, and migration among fair trade–certified farmers, despite positive impacts of fair trade on education and household savings.

Nevertheless, there is evidence that fair trade can support managerial upgrading within farmers cooperatives, supporting activities like grading, sorting, and extension services. These in turn help farmers improve yields, increase quality, diversify crops, and ultimately increase their incomes in ways that are not dependent on the fair trade premium. For instance, Ruerd Ruben and Ricardo Fort (2012) found that fair trade–certified farmers in Peru had greater agricultural assets; more access to credit (via buyers); greater satisfaction with prices, technical assistance, and management services; and more optimism about their future economic prospects than did noncertified farmers. These effects tended to increase with the length of time a farmer had been a member of a fair trade cooperative. Similar effects have been detected through qualitative case studies of fair trade cooperatives in Latin America (Bacon 2005; Calo and Wise 2005; Jaffee 2007; Raynolds, Murray, and Leigh Taylor 2004). Many of fair trade's successes depend on cooperatives that can effectively assist and coordinate farmers in a way that steers them toward higher-value markets and activities. In Latin America cooperative institutions often predated fair trade, originating in state-driven agrarian reform and rural development policies. Importantly, fair trade has provided a key source of revenue and support to cooperative institutions at a time when government support has almost disappeared.

On the other hand, farmer cooperatives generally fail to live up to the democratic ideals that the fair trade system espouses. Fair trade cooperatives often inhabit rural economies with deep histories of inequality and authoritarianism. Elections for cooperative boards of directors are often uncompetitive and dominated by large farmers or other economic elites. Similarly, professional managerial staff can use their educational and social advantages to avoid accountability. Members sometimes have little understanding of the democratic principles of cooperatives and fair trade, and their participation in decision making is often shallow or nonexistent (Setrini 2011; Wilson 2013). Even when cooperatives are not captured or corrupt, intense competition with private agribusiness firms may significantly narrow the space for democratic management.

The auditing and certification model encounters serious limits when it comes to organizational democracy. Even if fair trade certifiers were to collect sufficient data to measure the quality of cooperative governance and incentivize democratic decision making, it is unlikely that this would spur significant democratization. Cooperative governance is bound up with local politics and factional struggle more than with outside incentives.

The commodity roundtables have a shorter track record, but emerging research raises concerns about the implementation of their standards. This is especially the case with social standards pertaining to the use of land, the resolution of land conflicts, and the effects on neighboring communities. In the Indonesian palm oil industry, John McCarthy and his colleagues (2012) found that land deals between the Indonesian government and oil palm plantation developers dispossessed small farmers of their land rights in ways that violated the RSPO's standards for informed consent for land use. The RSPO lacks "capacity to affect micro-processes in upstream production networks" (McCarthy et al. 2012, 565), and the state policies and civil society structures that do shape land use are beyond the RSPO's reach. (As described in chapter 3, similar problems have plagued FSC certification in Indonesia.) Moreover, as Laura Silva-Castañeda (2012) documents, when auditors for the RSPO assess conflicts over land rights, they privilege forms of evidence that companies can provide (e.g., formal permits) and disqualify evidence that indigenous communities provide (e.g., the physical existence of graves and certain trees). As we will see, when it comes to the RTRS in Paraguay, smallholder farmers have also been marginalized in the implementation of standards, despite assurances to the contrary from RTRS and companies that support it.

Comparing the commodity roundtables with fair trade, one can see how the histories and constituents of each are embedded in their standards. Fairtrade (as defined by Fairtrade International standards for most products) privileges a specific way of organizing production: the cooperative (or similar organization of small farmers). Farmer cooperatives fall short of Fairtrade's democratic ideals, but Fairtrade nevertheless provides support for the expansion and institutionalization of cooperative farming in the global economy. In regional economies that are dependent on the export of agricultural commodities, cooperatives can have important distributional, social, and political consequences. They can limit the concentration of land ownership and equalize market access among farmers, for instance. In contrast, commodity roundtables generally endorse practices rather than structures and are agnostic about the organization of production. In so doing, they take as a given structures of production that emerged historically through local processes of exclusion and global concentrations of power. In the case of Paraguay, this means that roundtable standards (wittingly or unwittingly) contribute to the marginalization of smallholders.

LOCALIZED GLOBALISMS: FAIRTRADE SUGAR AND RESPONSIBLE SOY IN PARAGUAY

Paraguay has experienced an extended soy boom over the past two decades. Soy plantings and harvests grew by roughly 40 percent per year on average from 1992 to 2012, making Paraguay the world's sixth-largest producer and fourth-largest exporter of soybeans for much of this period.[21] The government's extremely permissive trade, tax, and land use policies have encouraged the rapid expansion of soy plantations, as had the development of global value chains that link South American production to demand for soy in East Asia and Europe.

Yet smallholder farmers have been losing ground economically and politically. Before the 1990s smallholders had been central figures in government-sponsored land colonization and agricultural development programs. In exchange for loyalty to the authoritarian regime, tens of thousands of farmers received small parcels of land and access to agricultural inputs, credit, and markets. To be sure, smallholders endured severe limits on their rights and were subordinated to political and commercial elites who controlled agricultural policy and trade (Turner 1993). Still, small farmers, especially those in cotton farming, served as the basis for Paraguay's insertion into the global economy (Weisskoff 1992). Then in the 1990s a slump in cotton prices, the spread of the cotton boll weevil, and the withdrawal of government support severely damaged the profitability of small-scale farming. All of this occurred just as the soy boom began to inflate land prices and subject small farmers to unprecedented competitive pressures.

The result has been the extreme inequality mentioned at the beginning of this chapter. Paraguay has abundant productive farmland, high levels of private investment, and rising agricultural outputs, but the share of the population without adequate access to food has risen from 11 percent to 23 percent from 2002 to 2012.[22] Paraguay remains one of the most rural countries in Latin America, but soy expansion has stimulated more migration to urban areas, contributing to unemployment, international migration, and dependence on remittances for income.

Because it is dependent on international soy prices, currency fluctuations, and weather conditions, Paraguay's economic growth has also been extremely volatile, fluctuating from −4 percent to 13.1 percent in 2009 and 2010 and from −1.3 percent to 13 percent in 2012 and 2013. This instability has made it difficult to lay foundations for economic diversification and steadier growth. Moreover, Paraguay does not tax raw soy exports, unlike Argentina, which taxes them at 35 percent or more. Thus, although soy production contributes roughly 20 percent of Paraguay's gross domestic product, it accounts for only 2 percent of tax receipts, most of which are value-added taxes on internal transactions (Borda 2013). The Paraguayan government has made no attempt to harness the windfall profits of the soy industry in order to make public investments to manage vulnerability, diversify the economy, or reduce inequality. The recent construction of soy processing plants by Cargill, ADM, and Louis Dreyfus could reduce the country's dependence on raw soy exports and alter the fiscal scenario, but it will also leave Paraguay's economy dependent on the decisions of a few powerful trading-processing companies.

Fairtrade and Smallholder Farmers in the Sugar Industry

Sugarcane is among the few crops that are viable for smallholder farmers in Paraguay, and expanding their competitiveness in this industry can help to stem the negative effects of soy dependence. In many countries sugarcane is grown on large plantations, but in Paraguay it historically has been grown by small farmers. The sugar industry in Paraguay developed late compared to the rest of Latin America, during the nationally oriented authoritarian developmental period of the twentieth century. Because the market was small and grew slowly, sugar producers had few incentives to increase productivity or modernize their technology. The political economy of sugar in twentieth-century Paraguay was a contest to divide a fixed amount of profits between the sugarcane farmers, a small number of sugar mills, and industrial users and retailers of sugar. A state-appointed commission set prices and distributed production quotas. Sugar mills were given a guaranteed share of the domestic market and thus protected from competition, but they were prevented from investing in their own plantations and obliged to purchase raw materials from small farmers nearby. In turn, small farmers were guaranteed an outlet for their crops but were economically and politically subordinated to a single mill. The result was a stable but technologically backward industry. Compared to Brazil and other countries, sugarcane yields in Paraguay were low—because of limited use of agrochemicals—and sugar mills were small and inefficient. As the economy integrated with the regional and global economy in the 1990s, the Paraguayan government expected that the sugar industry would gradually disappear.

Indeed, although the sugar industry remained partially protected within the Southern Cone Common Market (MERCOSUR), in the 1990s low-cost Argentine and Brazilian sugar regularly flooded Paraguay's market and led to the near collapse of the domestic industry. But at the same time, niche markets for "natural," organic, and fair trade foods were beginning to expand. Importantly, the small scale of Paraguay's sugar mills and the de facto organic production methods of its farmers made it among the world's only locations where it was possible to source organic crystallized sugar produced from smallholder sugarcane.[23]

Companies in Paraguay currently process sugarcane for sugar, molasses, cane liquor, fuel ethanol, and a number of other products (Republic of Paraguay 2011). Fifty-five percent of the sugarcane land that supplies these industries is planted in small and medium plots (less than 50 hectares) by more than twenty thousand farmers (Republic of Paraguay 2008). Currently as many as seven thousand growers have organic certification, and approximately twenty-five hundred have received fair trade certification.[24]

However, the history of authoritarian rural social relations and hierarchical economic relations between farmers and the sugar mills has left many of Paraguay's smallholder farmer organizations poorly prepared to take advantage of fair trade. While at least fifteen producer cooperatives, associations, and committees are active in sugarcane growing, they vary greatly in their managerial capacities and their political independence and representativeness. The gains that small farmers can obtain from participating in global value chains depend in part on the performance of sugar mills. But as we will see, it also depends on the effectiveness of farmers organizations in mediating between pressures for efficiency from sugar mills and demands for improved terms from their members. The case of one mill, Azucarera Paraguaya, and the farmers that supply it illustrates how fair trade certification can contribute to the effectiveness of farmers organizations. This outcome is far from inevitable, but the case points to certain conditions under which conscientious consumption of fair trade products can support meaningful change on the ground.

Azucarera Paraguaya (AZPA) is the largest sugar mill in Paraguay. The family that owns it has modernized management and taken advantage of organic sugar export markets. The company has expanded its plantations and processing capacity, implemented quality and safety standards required for export, expanded ethanol production from sugar by-products, and launched a set of additional agribusiness enterprises. Small farmers are mostly absent from the company's vision of modernization. The mill purchases about half of its raw materials from a roster of more than two thousand farmers, but as an organic sugar purchasing agent put it, "Maintaining small producers is not a priority for AZPA. . . . The owners and their relatives can make much more money with their own production than by externally buying sugarcane, and they have capital to invest."[25] AZPA's commercial manager claimed that sourcing from small farmers is "to help the social environment," but admits that "it isn't better for the company because logistically it is difficult."[26] But demand for fair trade–certified products has allowed smallholder farmers to retain their position. As the purchasing agent put it, "This [the mill's disinterest in small farmers] makes Fairtrade really important and one of the only ways small growers survive—at least with the big mills." The AZPA manager explained that "Fairtrade is a very small niche, even compared to organic. Honestly we do it in order to meet the demands of our clients . . . and will do it as long as they demand. We don't get any benefit."[27]

Fair trade initially generated a divide between winners and losers. One activist grower organized a group of approximately two hundred suppliers from one region into a Fairtrade-certified association. This group received social premium payments and made investments in transport and harvesting equipment that increased their efficiency. But the vast majority of the mill's other suppliers did not have an association or were part of nominal but inactive associations. Many in this latter group found their access to the mill increasingly uncertain as the company expanded its own plantations. This inequality initially led to tensions, but it soon encouraged the formation of three additional fair trade farmers associations among AZPA's suppliers. Apart from the resources that these associations receive directly through fair trade premiums, the associations are able to both represent farmers' collective interests to the mill and invest in improving farming processes in ways that make small farming operations more efficient and responsive to market demands. For AZPA the creation of these associations shifted the supply chain from a set of inefficient individual relationships with sugarcane farmers to a more manageable set of transactions mediated by the associations.

This case illustrates both how fair trade interacts with preexisting institutional structures and how it can help small farmers to effectively participate in global agri-food industries. The very existence of the smallholder sugarcane farms, some of which came to be fair trade certified, is a legacy of Paraguay's path of agricultural development. As demand for fair trade products grew, one group of small farmers was well poised to take advantage of this opportunity, and other groups were soon able to join in by organizing new associations. This is just one of several similar cases in Paraguay (Setrini 2011). Certainly the capacity to form effective, productivity-enhancing associations varies with the local political and economic context and should not be taken for granted. But at least in some circumstances it is clear that fair trade can help smallholder farmers become more viable and serve as a counterweight to the concentration of power in large agribusiness companies. This stands in contrast to the performance of the RTRS.

Responsible Soy and the Limits of Corporate Social Responsibility

As described above, the main social problem associated with soybean production in general and in Paraguay in particular is the displacement of small-scale farming. The RTRS social standards give minimal guidance as to how this problem should be mitigated. But Paraguay's lone RTRS-certified company, Desarrollo Agricola Paraguaya (DAP), has demonstrated a commitment to corporate social responsibility that goes beyond what is required by RTRS. DAP thus provides a most likely case for finding positive impacts of soy standards. However, nearly a decade of experience with this company has demonstrated how the soy industry's production model severely limits the benefits that small farmers receive.

DAP is the Paraguayan subsidiary of NFD Agro, a multinational agribusiness investment group bankrolled by private investors, financial companies, and the World Bank's International Finance Corporation (IFC) (Leperouse 2012). The company purchases and develops agricultural land, which it then sells or uses to grow soy, corn, and sunflower.[28] Beginning in 2005 the company chose to invest heavily in Paraguay, because productive land there can cost 50–75 percent less than in Argentina and Brazil. NFD Agro boasts that land values have appreciated by 30–50 percent in two years, permitting the company to reinvest its substantial profits.[29] Compared to Paraguay's historical reliance on the re-export of imported manufactured goods, companies such as DAP are indeed forcing a particular kind of economic progress. DAP has converted low-productivity grazing land into mechanized farmland for grain and oilseed production, allowing two annual harvests. It has introduced new management systems, such as the outsourcing of production activities to contractors. And it has incorporated Paraguayan agriculture into international business and financial circuits, leading Paraguayan land prices and production practices to converge with those in the United States, Brazil, and Argentina. For instance, it has popularized crop rotation, no-till production methods, genetically modified seeds, agrochemicals such as Roundup, and mechanized planting and harvesting.

For these reasons the leaders of DAP and its parent company view themselves as modernizing and progressive forces. Moreover, DAP has adopted a "triple bottom line" approach, linking economic returns to environmental sustainability and social responsibility. The company has pursued a range of internationally recognizable certifications, including the ISO 14001 environmental management standard, OHSAS 18001 occupational health and safety standard, and RTRS certification for its soy farms.

Yet DAP's operations are fraught with potential for conflict with peasant farmers. As soy producers have monopolized land and other productive assets, traditional subsistence-oriented peasant farming has been threatened. Large landholders and agribusiness corporations often buy land from the beneficiaries of earlier agrarian reform policies, although this technically violates Paraguayan law and results in invalid land titles. Large farms commonly suffer land occupations by organized peasant farmers claiming ownership of the land and contesting the legitimacy of the company's purchase. Some lead to violence, and in June 2012 one such conflict escalated into a national political crisis that precipitated the impeachment of Paraguay's president.[30]

DAP/NFD Agro has interpreted "corporate social responsibility" (CSR) primarily in terms of maintaining good relationships with neighboring communities, which is highly consistent with the RTRS standard. It also appears to follow through in its actions. NFD Agro chose the location of its land acquisitions to minimize the chance of conflict, and as a result it is one of the few companies that has not experienced land occupations. The activities of DAP's full-time sustainability manager have also taken the company well beyond the RTRS requirements. The company has progressively expanded the scope of its social engagements, according to its manager passing through phases of philanthropy, to corporate social responsibility, to the integration of social values into the business model.[31]

In one early program DAP worked with the environmental NGO Fundación Moises Bertoni to address deforestation, poverty, and compliance with environmental laws, but the company's sustainability manager described this "transactional" approach to CSR as unsustainable. Projects like this helped to spread new, more environmentally friendly farming methods to small farmers. However, the gains were lost once the project ended, but commercial and financial barriers to small farmers' viability remained.

DAP then moved toward working directly with small farmers, incorporating them into the company's supply chain and production model. The company offered agricultural inputs and services to small farmers—to be repaid after the harvest—in order to address the scale barriers that small farmers face in selling to a large buyer. However, the capital-intensive model of farming that the company was supporting proved too risky for small farmers. As described by DAP's sustainability manager, in a good year farmers could repay their debts and even expand production, but in a bad year, when climate or price variation reduced earnings, farmers were left with debts they could not repay and the threat of losing their land. An Oxfam report on DAP's projects confirms this problem, citing cases where debts of $US 1,000–2,000 forced farmers to divert productive resources to making interest payments or to default, cutting them off from credit altogether (Guereña and Riquelme 2013). Rather than planting crops and risking further failures, small farmers have often rented their land to large producers, which brings a more secure but smaller income.

Over time, DAP has moved further toward investing in unique structures to support the viability of small farmers. For example, DAP has proposed taking the money that companies usually spend on short-term CSR projects and putting it toward a small farmer investment trust fund. This fund would provide longer-term credit (five years) at below-market rates and technical assistance to implement organic production methods that are less capital-intensive and better suited to small farmers' competitive advantage. In some ways DAP's projects have moved closer to the principles of fair trade, far beyond what is required by the RTRS.

Yet even a company as dedicated to social responsibility as DAP has so far failed to meaningfully contribute to making smallholder farming viable in Paraguay. The problem is, even as the company has provided some support for smallholders, its core business strategy has made it very difficult for smallholder farmers to survive. DAP/NFD is essentially in the business of "land arbitrage"—that is, purchasing cheap land in frontier regions, converting it to productive farmland, and then selling it at a substantial premium. This has internationalized Paraguay's land market, raising land prices even in the most remote and undeveloped regions. In fact, NFD's success in Paraguay has accelerated the purchasing of Paraguayan land by other foreign investors who are less concerned than they used to be about "investment risks" in the country. As cross-border land prices have converged, small farmers have been priced out of the land market and pushed further toward the margins of the agricultural frontier—onto ecologically fragile land, into conflict with other landowners, or into urban and international migration.

In short, DAP/NFD's investments are helping to institutionalize the financial, managerial, political, and physical structures of the soy economy and to foreclose developmental trajectories that are more compatible with smallholder farming and the kinds of alternatives that are emerging in the sugar industry.

This development pattern is damaging not only to economic and social equality but also to economic efficiency. Soy production is an efficient use of land relative to the cattle grazing that it has often replaced, but not relative to the high-value and labor-intensive food crops (fruits and vegetables) that can boost the incomes of well-managed small farms.

CONCLUSION

The globalization of agri-food industries has expanded the choices of consumers in affluent countries and has often lowered the prices they pay. For investors, globalization has brought an opportunity to find financial returns in underutilized economic assets (e.g., farmland) in developing countries. Yet both consumers and investors have sometimes feared that they are complicit in exploitation and environmental degradation perpetrated by global companies and their suppliers in developing countries. In the food and agriculture sector, such concerns are heightened by histories of slavery, colonial exploitation, persistent poverty, and political subjugation of peasant farmers.

As consumers and investors have voiced these concerns and pressured global companies for responses, the result has been the growth of initiatives to certify fairness and sustainability in agri-food value chains. One approach, exemplified by fair trade, seeks to support farmers' livelihoods through the labeling of high-value consumer goods. Another approach, exemplified by the commodity roundtables, focuses on mass commodities that are often at the base of industrial supply chains. Albeit in different ways, both types of initiatives are "market-driven" mechanisms for creating fair and sustainable trade.

However, as this chapter suggests, this view of conscientious food consumption overlooks a key fact: farm-level outcomes are driven in large part by the local political economy of agriculture and nonmarket institutions, not merely by incentives rooted in northern consumer markets. The interactions and struggles of national industry organizations, farmers associations, and government agencies in agricultural exporting countries matter at least as much as the content of standards adopted by global companies and supported by conscientious consumers. This is not to say that global standards are irrelevant. Instead, the key is to consider how standards for fairness and sustainability intersect with the local politics of land tenure and smallholder farmer development. To retain their land, small farmers must be able to keep pace with profitable and efficient global agribusiness firms. At the same time, small farmers are best able to compete when they are organized to demand that companies and governments support their alternative production systems and respect their land claims. When it comes to the politics of food, then, a key question is whether standards for fairness and sustainability enhance the political and economic capacities of small farmers.

One way that fair trade certification matters is in the premium prices that certified farms receive (albeit to varying degrees). But importantly, fair trade also bolsters institutions of market coordination and interest representation (like cooperatives) where they already exist and sometimes supports the creation of such institutions where they do not exist. Farmers can use these institutions to articulate their economic and political interests, adjust to the demands of globalization, and counterbalance the power of large companies as gatekeepers to the global economy. In Paraguay's sugar industry, fair trade stimulated the formation of new associations among largely atomized farmers that are helping them negotiate with a large and expanding sugar mill.

By contrast, the regulatory approach of commodity roundtables does little to support the capacities and rights of small farmers. The RSPO has struggled to address conflicts over land tenure, and the RTRS has largely sidestepped the representation of small farmers, while soy expansion continues to threaten their livelihoods. The RTRS takes as a given the technologies, production structures, financial arrangements, and commercialization practices that favor large-scale agribusiness companies, and it deliberately steers clear of the politics of national development. As we saw in Paraguay, even when a large soy company takes CSR seriously, small farmers remain vulnerable and marginal.

What does this analysis mean for the practice of conscientious consumption? First, it suggests that consumers should not expect great change simply from "voting with their forks." Demand for fair and sustainable food can sometimes spur marginal improvements by companies and sometimes create new opportunities for farmers. But consumer demand is only one of many conditions that must be met in order for significant improvement to occur at the point of production. Many of the other conditions lie beyond the influence of consumer choice—in the domestic political economy of agriculture, for instance. Recall, in addition, that markets in the United States and Europe, where conscientious consumption campaigns have been focused, are becoming less influential in the global agri-food system with the rise of Chinese and other rapidly growing economies. Second, some conscientious food choices are more linked to alternative models of production than are others. Fair trade certification certainly does not guarantee effective, democratic farmers cooperatives, but it does sometimes support such structures, and it brings the organization of production to the fore rather than just nudging companies to use "best practices." That said, recent moves by Fair Trade USA to certify corporate coffee plantations (and large apparel factories, as discussed in chapter 5) suggest that this component of the fair trade model may be dwindling, at least in the US market.

Regardless of the fate of the fair trade model, a third practical point must be kept in mind. If conscientious consumption of food is to significantly alter conditions in agri-food global value chains, then it must be coupled with transnational social movements and revisions to world trade policies that create space for robust domestic agrarian reforms. The political and economic choices of agricultural *producers* should be at least as central to discussions of fair and sustainable food as are the preferences of *consumers*.

5 – APPAREL AND FOOTWEAR

Standards for Sweatshops

ON A SATURDAY AFTERNOON IN MARCH 1911 A FIRE BROKE OUT ON the eighth floor of a garment factory in New York City. The blouses and scrap materials at the Triangle Shirtwaist Factory burned quickly. Workers struggled to get out of the building, blocked by locked doors, flames, and the collapse of the fire escape, and many resorted to jumping. In total 146 people, mostly young women, died. The Triangle fire became the deadliest accident in the American garment industry and inspired a generation of activists, unionists, and reformers.

Eighty-two years later, in 1993, the Kader toy factory in Thailand experienced a similar fire, killing 188 workers, again mostly women. This time activists raised questions about the responsibilities of retailers and brands such as Toys R Us and Hasbro that were sourcing from Kader. In the ensuing years, as the apparel and footwear industry aggressively embraced the supply chain revolution, similar questions began to be asked about the responsibilities of Nike, Walmart, and others. The rise of anti-sweatshop movements in the United States and Europe led most apparel and footwear brands to adopt "codes of conduct" and to promise to better police their suppliers, spawning a growing field of "corporate social responsibility" (CSR).

Mounting questions about these activities' effectiveness became especially acute in 2010–2012, when a series of factory fires in Bangladesh killed nearly two hundred people who had been producing apparel for H&M, Tommy Hilfiger, C&A, Walmart, and others. Then, in Bangladesh in the spring of 2013, the Rana Plaza complex of factories collapsed, killing more than eleven hundred workers—once again, mostly women. This was the worst industrial accident in the history of the garment industry, and it happened despite the codes of conduct and CSR programs of Primark, Benetton, the Children's Place, and other companies that were sourcing there. In the same industrial district, a factory producing sweaters for H&M had collapsed eight years earlier (Miller 2013), but the scrutiny that ensued was clearly not enough.

In this chapter we examine the emergence and influence of voluntary labor standards (codes of conduct, factory auditing, and certification) for apparel and footwear production. As these industrial accidents suggest, despite the rise of CSR and many calls for "ethical fashion," clothing sold in the United States and Europe comes with few meaningful guarantees of decent production. The reason, we argue, stems from a combination of factors—namely, the power of companies in standard-setting initiatives, questionable factory auditing, weak links between companies' compliance and sourcing decisions, and a highly mobile industry that has relentlessly chased low prices at the expense of decent labor conditions. These forms of "unruliness" have greatly limited improvements and undermined certification of "good" factories. Some firms have done little to make their codes of conduct meaningful, but even the brands and retailers that have become known as leaders in the field of CSR, such as Nike, the Gap, and H&M, have often worked at cross-purposes. They have asked suppliers to improve but have continued to push for low prices and quick delivery times and to move in search of them. Promoting "fair" labor in the apparel and footwear industry has mostly meant slapping standards onto existing, highly unequal, structures of production.

Overall, this chapter shows that codes of conduct have regulated the conduct of suppliers, although only marginally and unreliably. But they have not regulated the conduct of brands and retailers themselves, and this is their greatest weakness. We begin by describing the structure of production and consumption, which has fostered the rise of global rule making but also limited its impact. Then, examining the formation of monitoring and certification programs, we show how a range of different programs, serving different constituencies, sought to define rules for "fair" labor. We then examine some marginal impacts of these rules and explain their larger failings by showing how implementation and industry dynamics have remained "unruly." A closer look at factories in China further illustrates how local contexts can generate serious challenges for global rule making. Finally, given these failings, we consider whether some emerging alternative models might provide more meaningful choices for conscientious consumers.

THE STRUCTURE OF PRODUCTION AND CONSUMPTION

American and European (EU-27) households spend an average of $1,700–$1,800 per year on apparel and footwear (US Department of Labor 2013; Eurostat 2009, 182). (In contrast, even with rising consumer expenditures in China, urban households there spend an average of around $260 per year on apparel and footwear [Li & Fung 2012].) Approximately half of the world's exported apparel ends up in the United States or EU countries (and more than this if one counts cross-border trade within the EU).[1] Since the United States and some European countries require the country of origin to be shown on apparel and footwear labels, consumers have been able to wonder, as journalist Kelsey Timmerman (2012) puts it, "Where am I wearing?" The answers to that question have shifted over time. To understand why the global apparel and footwear industry have been mobile, and why they have generated so many concerns about sweatshops and labor rights, a brief sketch of its structure and operation is necessary.

The "Sweating System"

A tendency to "sweat" the workforce—that is, to extract as much as possible through long hours and low pay—is to some degree built into the structure of apparel production. In industries where employers have large fixed costs—

for heavy machinery, for instance—they are generally motivated to invest in workers' productivity. They have already sunk a great deal of money into the machinery, so they need to get as much production from it as possible. As Michael Piore (1997) points out, since apparel production is a labor-intensive activity that cannot easily be mechanized, employers have little reason to maximize hourly productivity, especially if workers are paid by the piece, as they still are in many parts of the garment industry. Employers can simply push workers to put in longer hours when high output is necessary and fewer hours during low seasons. Seasonal swings and rapidly changing fashions can further exacerbate instability, resulting in long, sometimes unpaid, overtime and high-stress working conditions (Anner, Bair, and Blasi 2013; Bonacich and Appelbaum 2000). Footwear production is slightly more mechanized, and textile production (that is, the manufacturing of fabrics) is significantly more so, which means capital investments are greater for these types of firms. Still, the apparel, textile, and footwear sector as a whole is among the most labor-intensive of all industries. Labor costs contribute only 2 to 6 percent of the final retail price of apparel (Collins 2003; Nova and Kline 2014), but employers still compete fiercely over these small differences.

Contracting relationships, rather than vertically integrated production, have long been central to apparel production. Brands and retailers that are familiar to consumers typically do not own the factories where production occurs, instead relying on independent contractors and suppliers, who may themselves subcontract some parts of the job. This feature of the industry is not new. Even when it was primarily nationally or locally based, apparel production was organized through contracting relationships (Bonacich and Appelbaum 2000; Uzzi 1996; Waldinger 1986). But globalization amplified this tendency, as the "branded manufacturers" that did own some of their own factories (e.g., Levi Strauss, Phillips Van Heusen, VF) increasingly shut them down to join the "supply chain revolution" of the 1990s.

Apparel and footwear production is often seen as the prototypical "buyer-driven commodity chain," meaning firms that are closest to consumers (retailers and brands) are the powerful "lead firms," with the power to shape styles, technologies, and prices throughout the supply chain (Gereffi 1994). These lead firms include general retailers that sell "private label" apparel (e.g.,

Walmart, Carrefour, Macy's), specialty apparel retailers (e.g., the Gap, H&M, Zara), "branded manufacturers" (e.g., Levi Strauss, Phillips Van Heusen), and "branded marketers" who focus almost exclusively on design and marketing (e.g., Nike, Liz Claiborne). Growing concentration in the retail sector has put department stores and discount retailers in an especially powerful position (Collins 2003), with the largest discount retailers accounting for most apparel sales in the United States (Appelbaum and Gereffi 1994). In the athletic footwear industry the power of brands such as Nike, Adidas, Puma, and New Balance has not yet been rivaled by footwear retailers.

If suppliers are "captive" to these powerful buyers, one might expect the buyers to be able to force their suppliers to comply with labor standards. As Richard Locke and his colleagues (2009) point out, advocates for fair labor standards have often assumed, incorrectly, that this type of power was likely to bring about factory-level compliance. As some suppliers have grown larger and taken on more complex manufacturing tasks, scholars have questioned whether lead firms are fully in the driver's seat (Gereffi, Humphrey, and Sturgeon 2005) and whether collaborative relationships might have more potential for improving labor conditions (Frenkel and Scott 2002; Locke, Amengual, and Mangla 2009). In footwear manufacturing, Asian transnational manufacturing companies (e.g., Ching Luh, Pou Chen/Yue Yuen) have become larger and more powerful, and some apparel manufacturing companies (e.g., Luen Thai and the massive sourcing firm Li & Fung) are following suit (Appelbaum 2008).

Nevertheless, the degree of inequality between brands and retailers on one hand and the factories that supply them on the other remains stark, especially in the apparel industry. Retailers and brands continue to capture an outsized share of the profits from global production, and they are often able to nimbly shift their orders between suppliers and locations to drive down prices. This becomes clear when looking at the prices that manufacturers receive. Even when factories have "upgraded" their manufacturing capacities, the prices they can command has often *fallen* (Schrank 2004). Based on calculations made by Mark Anner and his colleagues (2013), the real unit price of men's and boy's cotton trousers from the top four exporting countries (China, Mexico, Honduras, and Bangladesh) declined between 2000 and 2010, and the unit price of all apparel imported into the United States fell by almost half between 1989 and 2010. In addition, the rise of "fast fashion" discount retailers, such as H&M and Forever 21, has meant that factories are under pressure not just to sell at low prices but also to adapt to frequent changes in orders and short turnaround times. These pressures have left little room for significant improvement in labor conditions.

Gender and Geography in the Making of the Global Apparel Industry

When one says "workers" in the apparel and footwear industry, more often than not this means women, especially young women. Young women have long been the preferred workers in labor-intensive manufacturing industries (e.g., apparel and electronics), in large part because managers expect them to be docile and willing to work for low wages (Cowie 1999). As apparel and footwear production globalized, it gravitated especially to places where patriarchy was strong—first South Korea, then Indonesia—where young women from rural areas were expected to be "good daughters," saving for their dowries and sending money home to their families (Enloe 2000). But beyond simply taking advantage of gender inequality, companies have often fostered gendered images of workers. As Jane Collins (2003) puts it, "Managers in the apparel industry have historically relied on gendered ideologies of sewing work to devalue women's skill and lower their wages" (16). Leslie Salzinger (2003) goes further, showing how shop floor relations in Mexican maquiladoras *produce* particular notions of femininity. When production demands have outstripped the supply of women who are willing to work for low wages, apparel firms have proven willing to employ men (Ross 2004), but apparel production has continued to be viewed—and paid—as low-wage, feminized work.

Government policy has also played an important role in the globalization of apparel and footwear production. As Ellen Israel Rosen (2002) has shown, US military and foreign policy interests during the Cold War shaped the first wave of globalization, taking apparel (and later footwear) production to Asia—first to Japan, then to Hong Kong, Taiwan, and South Korea—as a buffer against left-wing parties and the specter of communism. In the 1980s, US trade policy began to strongly promote apparel production in Central America and the Caribbean. Many manufacturers and specialty retailers shifted from domestic production to this region, taking advantage of wages that were less than fifty cents per hour in Guatemala and El Salvador, sixty to seventy-five cents per hour in Honduras and the Dominican Republic to eighty-eight cents per hour in Mexico at the beginning of the 1990s (Bonacich and Waller 1994). For European firms, production in Eastern Europe and North Africa played a similar role (Gereffi 1999).

Discount retailers had long had extensive ties to suppliers in Taiwan and Hong Kong, but by the late 1980s they were increasingly sourcing from mainland China as well (Cheng and Gereffi 1994). Korean, Taiwanese, and Hong Kong–based owners of apparel factories were also investing in the Philippines, Indonesia, and Thailand, which soon became key sourcing destinations for global brands (Bonacich and Waller 1994). Apparel industries in Southeast Asia, Central America, and Eastern Europe soon found themselves in heavy competition with factories in China and Vietnam. As of the early 1990s labor costs in China were well below those in most Southeast Asian countries (Yang, Chen, and Monarch 2010), and by 1994 mainland China had become the world's top apparel exporter.[2]

Trade policy also kept the industry geographically dispersed, as opposed to gravitating to just a few countries. The Multi-Fiber Arrangement (MFA), a set of trade agreements originating in the 1970s, limited the extent of apparel and textile imports to the United States, Canada, and European countries that could come from any single country. Exporting country governments received negotiated quotas for imports to these markets, which they could then distribute to firms. As a result, even as China became a major apparel exporter, it was limited by its quota allotment. The MFA fostered the growth of garment factories in Lesotho, Mauritius, and other hinterland locations that had enough infrastructure to take advantage of their quota allotments. Ultimately, however, the MFA was judged to be inconsistent with the growing project to promote free trade, under the auspices of the General Agreement on Tariffs and Trade (and soon the World Trade Organization). The MFA began to be phased out in 1995 and the final set of quotas was eliminated in 2005.

In the post-MFA period China's apparel exports have continued to grow and the small hinterland industries have declined. But the industry did not gravitate entirely to China, in part because wages there began to rise. With rising wages in China and a wave of strikes in Vietnam, apparel production in places such as Indonesia and Honduras continued to be competitive. But brands and retailers have increasingly looked to South Asia as the next key location. Low tariff treatment for the European market made Bangladesh especially attractive for European firms, helping the value of Bangladesh's apparel exports to increase by 294 percent from 2000 to 2011 and its share of total world apparel exports to increase by a whopping 713 percent between 1990 and 2011. Less dramatically, India's share increased by 49 percent and Pakistan's by 17 percent from 1990 to 2011.[3]

In contrast, Thailand's share declined by 42 percent from 1990 to 2011. In Mexico and Indonesia apparel exports grew in the 1990s but then declined— sharply in Mexico (by 74 percent from 2000 to 2011) and more modestly in Indonesia (by 18 percent from 2000 to 2011). China's apparel exports continued to grow, and Indonesia remained competitive because wages were rising much more slowly there than in the coastal regions of China. But monthly minimum wages of $120–$140 in the main manufacturing regions of China and Indonesia in 2010 were far higher than in Bangladesh, where the monthly minimum wage stood at $43, even after a substantial increase in response to workers' protests.[4]

Wages are not the only factor that makes a particular country attractive or unattractive to global apparel brands. Brands also consider factors such as labor productivity, whether suppliers can deliver the appropriate quality and quantity quickly and reliably, and how tariff rates (which may vary by country and product) will shape their final costs. Governments in developing countries have sought to attract international orders by building export-processing zones (EPZs) with improved infrastructure, favorable tax treatment, and sometimes exemptions from national law. Still, enough governments have been competing in this way that labor costs have often been decisive in shifting apparel production from one frontier to another.

This networked, stratified, global, and quite mobile system of production has hovered over, and often haunted, calls for "corporate social responsibility" and "ethical fashion." Large parts of the global apparel and footwear industry are geared toward serving American and European consumers, and as described in chapter 2, some nontrivial portion of these consumers does care about labor conditions. But this does not mean that conscientious consumerism has transformed apparel and footwear production, as the rest of this chapter will show.

GLOBALIZED LOCALISMS: THE DEVELOPMENT
OF GLOBAL RULE-MAKING PROJECTS

Anti-Sweatshop Activism and Corporate Responses

Inequalities and exploitation in the global apparel industry might have remained largely hidden were it not for the rise of a new anti-sweatshop movement. The Triangle Shirtwaist Fire provoked an earlier wave of anti-sweatshop activism, union organizing, and state-building in the United States (see Stein 1977). Yet this mid-twentieth-century "social compact" began to break down as US-based apparel companies found new opportunities to move abroad (Esbenshade 2004). With apparel production becoming more globalized, and work in domestic garment districts becoming more precarious, activists from unions and from religious, immigrant rights, and human rights organizations began building a new anti-sweatshop movement in the 1990s. They focused to some degree on US government trade policy, which had facilitated the migration of the industry (e.g., Krupat 1997), but they quickly seized on the strategy of "naming and shaming" well-known brands and retailers.

In early campaigns, immigrant rights activists named and shamed fashion designers such as Jessica McClintock for using domestic sweatshops (Louie 2001). UNITE (the Union of Needletrades, Industrial, and Textile Employees) and the National Labor Committee (NLC) were central to a number of campaigns that followed. Starting in 1995 the two cooperated on a campaign targeting the Gap, among others (JC Penney, Eddie Bauer, and Target), over the repression of union organizing at the Mandarin apparel factory in El Salvador. Walmart and Nike soon became the top recipients of the sweatshop stigma, mostly due to exposés of child labor, harsh treatment, and poverty-level wages in Asia. On college campuses in the United States, students affiliated with United Students Against Sweatshops rallied against collegiate licensing deals that made universities complicit in labor rights abuses. In Europe the federated Clean Clothes Campaign used a mixed "oppose and propose" strategy to press firms such as H&M, Adidas, Karstadt-Quelle, and Carrefour to take responsibility for labor conditions in their supply chains (Ascoly, Oldenziel, and Zeldenrust 2001; Bair and Palpacuer 2012). With the exception of a boycott against child labor in Bangladesh, activists rarely called for outright boycotts, but they did seek to demonstrate that consumers, investors, and business partners would not remain silent. As the NLC's Charles Kernaghan said of the Gap campaign, "[We are] not calling a boycott, but we want the Gap to get the message" (qtd. in Tosh 1995). In total, in the United States more than 25 percent of large lead firms in the apparel and footwear industry were targeted in anti-sweatshop campaigns between 1993 and 2000, and many faced persistent pressure (Bartley and Child 2014).

Anti-sweatshop campaigns catalyzed an array of rule-making projects as companies, NGOs, and unions vied to define the responsibilities of lead firms and the meaning of fair labor conditions. Initially, when faced with sweatshop accusations, brands and retailers minimized their responsibilities, emphasizing that they did not directly own the factories or that apparently shocking stories were not what they seemed. Walmart's CEO infamously replied, "The pictures you showed mean nothing to me," when confronted with images of child laborers in a Bangladeshi factory (qtd. in Ramey and Barrett 1996, 10). But as anti-sweatshop pressure mounted, companies began to accept at least a limited responsibility for improving conditions in their supply chains. After years of such pressure, Nike's CEO admitted that the company "has become synonymous with slave wages, forced overtime and arbitrary abuse" (qtd. in Cushman 1998). Brands were beginning to accept an *ethical* responsibility for their supply chains, but they have fiercely resisted the idea that they might have a *legal* responsibility for their supply chains (Bonacich and Appelbaum 2000; Shamir 2004).

Levi Strauss, Nike, Reebok, and the Gap were among the first companies to adopt "codes of conduct" for their suppliers, but by the end of the 1990s the vast majority of large lead firms in the apparel and footwear industry had followed. Companies targeted by anti-sweatshop campaigns were hoping, as one industry advisor put it, to "put a muzzle on these watchdog groups" (Rolnick 1997), but even those that had so far largely flown under the radar (e.g., Jones Apparel, Talbots, and VF—maker of Lee, Wrangler, Jansport, and many other brands) quickly adopted codes in hopes of preempting campaigns or protecting their reputations (US Department of Labor 1996).

Codes of conduct (sometimes known as ethical sourcing policies) typically ask suppliers to eliminate child or forced labor, to ensure that working conditions are safe, that workers receive at least the legal minimum wage, and that working hours are kept within a given standard (often sixty hours per week). Many codes also ask suppliers to respect workers' freedom of associa-tion—that is, their right to join unions—and invoke conventions developed by the International Labor Organization (ILO).

At first lead firms adopted these rules without taking serious steps to en-force them. Some asked quality control personnel to also check compliance with labor standards, while others sent poorly trained external auditors to the factories. Nike initially used auditors from Ernst & Young and Pricewater-houseCoopers, who were poorly suited to gather accurate information from young migrant workers or to assess health and safety conditions (O'Rourke 1997, 2002). Labor rights groups called for "independent monitoring" of fac-tories by impartial, well-trained observers, especially local NGOs that could gather information through off-site interviews with workers.

The fight over independent monitoring played out in large part through the construction of larger organizations to coordinate rule making and audit-ing. With activists arguing that companies should not be trusted to police themselves and with companies looking to lend credibility to their standards and protect their reputations, there were demands on both sides of the aisle for greater oversight. However, there were quite different views of what this should entail, and the highly contentious debates that ensued would ulti-mately lead to several different types of programs in the United States and Europe, each with different core constituencies. In other words, a number of different globalized localisms have sought to define "ethical" apparel.

Beyond Self-Policing? The Struggle over
Monitoring and Certification Initiatives

Three main types of initiatives, defined largely by their core constituencies, have sought to define and oversee fair labor standards in the apparel and footwear industries. First, there are initiatives founded by coalitions of large brands and other stakeholders (e.g., NGOs and sometimes unions), such as the Fair Labor Association (FLA), Social Accountability International (SAI), and Ethical Trading Initiative (ETI). In various ways these initia-tives sought to help brands improve conditions in their suppliers' factories and to uphold the brands' substantial investments in their corporate images. Because industry outsiders were involved to some degree in their creation, these initiatives adopted rules that pushed slightly beyond standard practices in the industry. This made many brands and especially retailers reluctant to join (Bartley 2009). Second, charging that these initiatives were too lax, NGOs and unions played more central roles in creating initiatives such as the Worker Rights Consortium (WRC) and Fair Wear Foundation (FWF). These set higher standards, with a particular emphasis on the rights of workers, not just their "protection." Unlike others, these initiatives conduct their own monitoring and investigation, but they operate on a small scale within particular market niches. Third, industry associations sponsored their own programs—namely, the Business Social Compliance Initiative in Europe and the Worldwide Responsible Accredited Production program in the United States—that attracted a larger swath of corporate participants, including those with lower brand investments. They developed baseline standards with little input from industry outsiders. In addition, rather than being focused on protecting brand reputations, these initiatives have sought to give their members information about the compliance profiles of suppliers. As we describe below, these three models unfolded dynamically over time, with the first set of programs—that is, those negotiated with some "multi-stakeholder" input—emerging first.

Brand Protection and the Rise of Voluntary Initiatives

President Clinton's convening of the Apparel Industry Partnership in 1996 marked the beginning of a struggle to define the responsibilities of American brands and retailers. In the wake of the Kathie Lee Gifford scandal, in which child laborers in Honduras were found to be producing her line of children's clothing, the Clinton administration called together a group of representatives from apparel and footwear brands, NGOs, and unions. Early talk of a "no sweat" label quickly fell by the wayside amid companies' resistance to the "knotty issues" this would entail (Ramey 1996). For their part, labor rights advocates were reluctant to grant a simple endorsement of companies in a complex and largely nonunionized industry. The group did develop an overarching code of conduct, but disagreement quickly surfaced, especially over whether a "living wage" should be required and the meaning of "freedom of association" in places where unions were legally restricted (e.g., China).

The disagreements intensified as the Apparel Industry Partnership spawned the Fair Labor Association (FLA) to oversee compliance with this code. Several smaller companies had already left the partnership, leaving mainly large, brand-sensitive firms (e.g., Nike, Reebok, Liz Claiborne, and Phillips Van Heusen). UNITE and the Interfaith Center for Corporate Responsibility dropped out when the FLA was announced, charging that its monitoring amounted to "the fox guarding the henhouse" (Benjamin 1999). With a depleted set of NGOs, FLA leaders recruited universities, which were facing student protest. By 2001 FLA had begun its program of having accredited monitors visit a sample of member companies' factories. It did not certify factories or produce a consumer label, but it did lend its approval to the compliance programs of members, befitting these companies' interest in a form of "reputation protection" that would not overshadow their own brand images.

In the UK a somewhat similar organization, the Ethical Trading Initiative, was being formed, again with government support and appealing primarily to image-sensitive firms. But in this case labor unions and NGOs such as Oxfam and Women Working Worldwide were more influential, shaping many of the standards that would become the ETI "base code" (Schaller 2007). It garnered some participation by apparel companies such as Marks & Spencer and Levi Strauss, but the ETI also addressed a wider array of products, including tea, wine, and cosmetics.

Another brand-NGO coalition produced an initiative called Social Accountability International, to certify particular factories. The Council on Economic Priorities, a New York–based nonprofit focused on socially responsible investment and consumption, teamed up with fashion brand Eileen Fisher, German catalog retailer Otto Versand, Toys R Us, the auditing firm SGS, and several others to produce the SA8000 standard for factory certification. A representative of the International Textile, Garment, and Leather Workers Federation also supported the standard, but its US affiliate, UNITE, saw SA8000 as no better than the corporate-dominated FLA. The number of SA8000 facilities worldwide rose from eight in 1998 to more than one hundred in 2001 and to nearly three thousand in 2012. There is no product label, but factories can advertise their certification, and lead firms that support SAI, including the Gap, Timberland, and Tchibo, can advertise that involvement to consumers and, perhaps more importantly, to audiences in the socially responsible investment community.

These three organizations—FLA, ETI, and SAI—make frequent references to ILO conventions and ask companies to promote "best practices" for labor conditions in their supply chains. While the FLA largely ignored the conundrum of freedom of association in countries where independent unions were prohibited, ETI and SAI called for factory managers to support or allow "parallel means" of worker representation, such as worker committees. On the other hand, these programs did not require dramatic changes in the organization of production. Lead firms could produce more or less wherever they wanted and continue to demand low prices from their suppliers so long as they pushed for marginal improvements in working conditions. As we will see, this has greatly limited the impact of standards.

Advocates and Trade Associations Respond

Labor rights activists challenged "checklist monitoring" and corporate-dominated initiatives by developing their own programs. Some groups that had exited the FLA joined with student anti-sweatshop activists and sympathetic scholars to create the Worker Rights Consortium (WRC), which focused on collegiate-licensed apparel. Enrolling universities as opposed to companies as its members, the WRC adopted a "fire alarm" model (McCubbins and Schwartz 1984), in which complaints from workers would trigger investigations by the WRC, drawing on local experts. Rather than "credentialing companies" and their claims of responsibility, the WRC would, as one developer put it, "credential workers" and their claims about injustice.[5] Having successfully recruited a critical mass of colleges and universities, the WRC quickly became an important player in identifying violations of labor rights, especially those involving the repression of independent union organizing.

In Europe the Dutch affiliate of the Clean Clothes Campaign (CCC) was the key architect of the Fair Wear Foundation (Bair and Palpacuer 2012; O'Rourke 2003). Unlike the WRC, the FWF initially cooperated with industry, but the CCC's insistence on substantive verification of factory conditions by well-qualified local groups led the representatives of large apparel retailers to leave the project (Fransen 2011). Some smaller apparel brands remained, though, making the FWF a somewhat unusual program: a "multi-stakeholder initiative," in which the balance of power tilts toward nonindustry groups, including NGOs and unions.

On the other side of the aisle, apparel industry associations developed their own alternatives. The American Apparel and Footwear Association, whose members accounted for the vast majority of garments sold in the United States, created a shared code of conduct and a factory certification program: the Worldwide Responsible Accredited Production (WRAP) program.[6] WRAP became formally independent of the trade association, but its personnel continued to have strong ties to the industry. At first glance WRAP's standards appear similar to others, but they tend to offer greater flexibility. For instance, WRAP allows for exceptions to the standard regarding maximum days of work when "required to meet urgent business needs." By setting a basic standard to which many factories can be certified, WRAP sought to provide assurances that would be useful for the less visible, but still large, lead firms in the apparel industry. As one developer put it, "We believe Nike has to be able to stand up and say 'Nike stands for this and Nike is this and that.' At VF, we don't need to do that, because nobody knows who VF is. But what we need to do is to be able to tell Walmart, 'You can buy from us and [be] confident about this stuff, because we're buying your product in factories that have been certified.'"[7]

The Business Social Compliance Initiative (BSCI) is the main industry-driven initiative in Europe. It was founded by the Foreign Trade Association, a group of retailers, brands, and other importers in consumer products industries. The BSCI's formation was fueled in part by the exit of Dutch companies from the Fair Wear Foundation (Fransen 2011) and by the collapse of a nascent partnership between companies, unions, and NGOs in Sweden (Egels-Zandén and Wahlqvist 2007). Although it was unions and NGOs that dropped out of coalitions in the United States, it was companies that did so in Europe. Like WRAP, BSCI's goal is to coordinate auditing so that results from a single BSCI-approved audit of a given factory can be available to all member companies (Egels-Zandén and Wahlqvist 2007). It relies on auditors that have been accredited to grant SA8000 certification, but BSCI does not actually certify factories, and its expectations for factories are somewhat lower than the SA8000 standard. If a factory does not show improvement, BSCI "encourage[s] participants to reconsider their relations with that producer," but it does not require them to do so.[8] BSCI has become the main compliance initiative for European companies, including mega-retailers such as Metro (Germany), E. Leclerc (France), and El Corte Ingles (Spain), specialty apparel retailers (e.g., KappAhl, Esprit), and numerous other brands.

THE IMPLEMENTATION OF RULES

Evaluating Codes of Conduct

Codes of conduct and factory auditing/certification initiatives have certainly not transformed the apparel and footwear industries. Existing evidence suggests that they have had some meaningful but narrow effects on working conditions and the management of human resources. But the rights of workers have been less affected, and even on the issues where codes tend to be most meaningful, standards in many parts of the industry remain criminally low in an absolute sense.

Researchers generally have found that codes of conduct, and the auditing thereof, have led to some improvement in workplace health and safety (Barrientos and Smith 2006; Mamic 2004). For instance, looking at toy manufacturers in China, Niklas Egels-Zandén (2014) found that scrutiny from buyers led factory managers to provide health and safety education to workers. Examining the apparel industry in Bangladesh, Faisal Z. Ahmed and his colleagues (2014) suggest that despite a repressive political environment for workers, supply chain scrutiny has made factory managers slightly more sensitive to "worker welfare." In the athletic footwear factories of Southeast Asia and China, the toxin Toluene had been widely used as a glue, but scrutiny from Nike, Reebok, Adidas, and New Balance have made it far less common. Officially it has been phased out, "except when it's not," as one compliance official for a major brand put it, admitting that it often works better than substitutes.[9]

Scrutiny from auditors and brands has also reduced, though not eliminated, the incidence of especially harsh, abusive treatment of workers. Early exposés showed managers screaming insults at workers or using physical punishment to induce greater productivity. In 1996 managers at a footwear factory in Vietnam producing for Nike ordered workers to run around the factory in sweltering heat as punishment, leading some of them to faint

(Herbert 1997). Over time and with prodding from its buyers, the company that owned this factory, Pou Chen/Yue Yuen, has embraced a gentler and more formalized model of human resource management. Visiting a Yue Yuen factory more recently, we found an internal compliance staff with little tolerance for abusive supervisors, as well as a "counseling room," hotline, and "worker welfare committee" for workers to lodge complaints.[10] Such reforms are often cosmetic and rarely give real voice to workers. But they suggest that codes of conduct have shifted at least the first tier of suppliers to global brands away from intimidation as a management strategy.

On the other hand, improvements are certainly not guaranteed. Even brands that have audited suppliers closely have not necessarily spurred progress. Nike developed one of the most sophisticated auditing programs in the industry, but the vast majority of its suppliers' factories—roughly 80 percent—failed to improve from 2001 to 2004, and some actually experienced a decline in their overall compliance rating (Locke, Qin, and Brause 2007). While codes of conduct have sometimes increased compliance with minimum wage standards and reduced arbitrary pay deductions (Barrientos and Smith 2006), one can still find suppliers to major brands paying below the legal minimum (e.g., Worker Rights Consortium 2013b). Furthermore, in many apparel-exporting countries the value of garment workers' wages has *decreased* during the period that codes of conduct have been in place. In a recent study of fifteen major exporting countries, research found that in nine of these countries, the local purchasing power of prevailing wages declined from 2001 to 2013 (Worker Rights Consortium 2013a).[11]

When it comes to the rights and empowerment of workers, codes of conduct have had scattered and short-lived impacts at best. Industry-driven programs (e.g., WRAP and BSCI) have shown little interest in making respect for labor rights a necessary ingredient of socially responsible production. But even multi-stakeholder initiatives have largely failed as guarantors of labor rights. In their evaluation of ETI, Stephanie Barrientos and Sally Smith (2006) found that codes of conduct had made a difference for health and safety at work but essentially no difference when it came to workers' empowerment. Retaliation against union supporters was common in many of the sites they studied, and "codes have done little to address this" (30). Codes "have had some superficial impacts on discrimination [in employment]. But they have had no impact on underlying patterns of employment based on gender, ethnicity, caste and religion" (30). In Cambodia the Better Work Program, sponsored by the International Labor Organization and International Finance Corporation (IFC) has worked to help factories comply with labor standards set by foreign buyers. It has resulted in a number of improvements in working conditions (Brown, Dehejia, and Robertson 2013), but outside the factory insurgent labor unions in the Cambodian garment industry have faced repression, as seen in the 2004 assassination of union leader Chea Vichea (Hughes 2007) and the 2014 police shooting of striking garment workers (BBC 2014).

In a few apparel and footwear factories, grassroots unions have effectively used the "brand boomerang" strategy to counteract resistance and repression from factory managers and local governments. In the best-known cases, independent unions at the Kukdong factory in Mexico and BJ&B factory in the Dominican Republic successfully gained collective bargaining rights after international campaigns led Nike to intervene in support (Anner and Evans 2004; Ross 2006). In another case, Liz Claiborne and the FLA played positive roles in preserving space for an independent union at the Choishin factory in Guatemala (Rodríguez-Garavito 2005; US/LEAP 2003). But the success of these campaigns depended on a rare confluence of factors *in addition* to codes of conduct—namely, grassroots organizing, strong cross-border activist networks, and leverage from trade agreements (Rodríguez-Garavito 2005; Seidman 2007; US/LEAP 2003). Furthermore, a number of factories in which unions gained recognition by "leveraging" codes of conduct later shut down, including BJ&B, Choishin, and factories where unions had gained ground in Indonesia, Thailand, and Sri Lanka (Egels-Zandén and Bartley 2014; Evans 2010).[12]

Recent industrial accidents (such as those mentioned at the beginning of this chapter) have provided a brutal reminder that even though occupational health and safety conditions have sometimes improved, serious threats have not been eliminated. In 2012 an apparel factory in Pakistan that had just been approved for SA8000 certification caught fire, killing nearly 300 workers who were trapped behind locked emergency exits and barred windows (Walsh and Greenhouse 2012). In Bangladesh a series of factory fires from 2010 to 2012 killed several hundred people in factories producing for—and audited by—Tommy Hilfiger, Walmart, C&A, and others. At one of these factories, Tazreen Fashions, auditors for BSCI and Walmart had noted problems, but the factory was still producing for a BSCI member (C&A) and as a subcontractor for Walmart (among others) when a fire killed 112 workers (Theuws et al. 2013). Sadly, the scale of these disasters paled in comparison to the 2013 collapse of the Rana Plaza building in Bangladesh, where more than 1,100 workers died. Factories within this complex were producing for British retailers Primark, Benetton, and others, and for Walmart just prior to the disaster (Greenhouse 2013). BSCI auditors, who had visited factories in Rana Plaza, were left in the awkward position of explaining that "audits do not include building construction or integrity."[13] In short, after nearly two decades of codes of conduct, factory auditing, and a variety of related projects, the global apparel industry bears strong resemblances to the period prior to the anti-sweatshop movement—and even to the period of the Triangle Shirtwaist fire.

Explaining the Limited Progress: The Persistence of Unruliness

The rise of codes of conduct would appear to make the apparel industry increasingly rule-governed. Rather than feigning ignorance or looking the other way, lead firms were beginning to present factory managers with long lists of what they could and could not do and sending auditors to police their behavior. Yet in many ways the implementation process and the industry have proven quite unruly. Specifically, three forms of unruliness help to explain why rule-making projects have had such a limited impact in this industry.

First, the auditors who were supposed to police factories in many cases turned out to be of poor quality or even corrupt. Early critics of "checklist monitoring" argued that factory auditing should be done by skilled observers who could gather trustworthy information from workers—by taking the time to conduct off-site interviews, for instance (Esbenshade 2004; Labor Rights in China 1999; O'Rourke 2002). Some specialized and dedicated nonprofit monitoring organizations did emerge (e.g., Verité in the United States, Impactt in the UK, Coverco in Guatemala). But as factory auditing became more common, the larger, lower-priced auditors (e.g., generalist firms with office around the world, such as Intertek, Bureau Veritas, SGS, and TÜV) came to dominate the market. In effect, factory auditing became commoditized—that is, treated as a low-cost, highly substitutable good—

rather than becoming a profession. Specialized and nonprofit monitors still perform some audits and trainings, but the large generalist firms do most of the auditing for BSCI, SA8000, and WRAP, in addition to being hired by individual firms.

Despite oversight from accreditation bodies, the auditors from these firms have earned a reputation for being inexperienced, overstretched, and willing to turn a blind eye to problems when necessary to please factory managers. According to an auditor for one of the large firms in Vietnam, auditors are offered bribes by roughly 30 percent of factory managers, and others offer dinners and accommodations to try to curry favor.[14] Auditors have also been caught tipping off factory managers about the timing of a supposedly unannounced audit.[15] In China an undercover investigation found rampant corruption in Bureau Veritas' factory auditing, including extortion by auditors and bribery by consultants who had been hired to guarantee that the factory would pass (China Labor Watch 2009).

The problems of factory auditing have become widely apparent over time. Exposés in *Business Week* and the *Financial Times* have shown how factory managers, especially in China, offer bribes, keep falsified records of wages and working hours, and coach workers to give the "correct" answer to auditors (*Business Week* 2006; Foster and Harney 2005). Practitioners have long recognized the cat-and-mouse game that even honest and dedicated auditors get trapped in: auditors chase the elusive "real" data, managers offer suspicious or partial records, and workers parrot answers that auditors suspect are coached. In response to these problems, some rule-making projects have lost faith in factory auditing. The ETI declared a "growing crisis in ethical trade auditing" (Ethical Trading Initiative 2006), and the FLA soon moved away from its original monitoring model, calling it an "inadequate tool to create sustainable change in working conditions," in order to instead emphasize learning and "capacity-building" at the factory level (Fair Labor Association 2007).

Second, rule-making projects have done little to alter the sourcing practices of lead firms, which are a root cause of many factory-level problems. Even imperfect auditing can identify problems, but this does not mean they are necessarily resolved. Lead firms have demanded that suppliers comply with codes of conduct, but their sourcing priorities—low prices and fast delivery—send quite different messages. To the standard criteria of "quality, delivery, and price" that brands and retailers use to place their orders, "compliance," in theory, has been added. But as one brand representative put it, "We both know that's bullshit."[16] Some brands and retailers have well-staffed and well-meaning compliance departments, but these departments rarely have the power to shape the decisions of the production/sourcing departments. As assessors for ETI found, "Some suppliers believe one standard is operated by buyers who make commercial demands which require certain labor practices (such as long overtime). Another standard is operated by code of conduct managers, who deem the same practices as non-compliance" (Barrientos and Howell 2006, 9). In a study of one large brand at the forefront of CSR efforts, researchers found that more than half of the company's current suppliers had *not* been approved by the company's compliance department (with non-approval rates of over 85 percent in South Asia and East Asia). As these researchers put it:

> While sourcing departments continue to squeeze factories on price, compress lead times, and demand high-quality standards, compliance officers visit the factories and document the problems but do little to change the root causes underlying poor working conditions. [One] auditor reported that "if [the sourcing department] has already sold the sample before I set foot in the factory, I know that we will give them business no matter what." (Locke, Amengual, and Mangla 2009, 335)

In this situation the compliance efforts of brands and retailers are at worst an exercise in futility and at best akin to janitorial work. The role of compliance staff is to clean things up—that is, to spur minor improvements in factories that can produce the right product for the right price—rather than to identify factories with decent working conditions. For factories, improvements that raised costs or made it more difficult to produce large volumes in short time periods would certainly mean a severe risk of losing business.

Relatedly, factory managers often use subcontracting to meet deadlines and control costs, and brands' scrutiny rarely reaches these second- and third-tier suppliers. Tazreen Fashions, the site of a deadly factory fire in Bangladesh, had actually been dropped as a first-tier supplier for Walmart, but it was continuing to work as a subcontractor, supposedly unbeknownst to Walmart officials. It is the complexity and poor scrutiny of subcontracting that has allowed the implementation of fair labor standards to coexist with especially harsh practices such as the resurgence of bonded labor schemes in the Indian garment industry (SOMO 2012). The Gap earned a reputation as a leader in the monitoring of its suppliers, but when journalists exposed bonded child labor at one of its Indian subcontractors, brand's staff pleaded ignorance (McDougall 2007).

A third source of unruliness is the apparel industry's geographical mobility. Lead firms have been quite willing—and able—to move their orders from one location to another to keep costs low. This has meant not just the decline of apparel manufacturing within affluent countries but also a series of rapid shifts from one set of developing countries to another. Places where labor conditions are improving typically have been abandoned for new locations. As described above, unions in Indonesia, the Dominican Republic, and Thailand have gained ground in some factories, only to see those factories, and often those countries, lose orders. In addition, researchers have shown that when brands and factory managers cooperate over long periods of time, they *can* improve working conditions (Frenkel and Scott 2002; Locke, Amengual, and Mangla 2009). But the mobility of the industry undermines these types of slow improvements. In essence, lead firms must restart their compliance efforts as they move to new locations.

It is not just mobility in the abstract that limits improvements; it is also the industry's gravitation toward places with shoddy infrastructure and regulation that is poorly enforced or intended to constrain workers' rights. Consider two countries where apparel exports have risen, Bangladesh and Pakistan. In Bangladesh the rapid buildup in the apparel industry came at the expense of building safety, because entrepreneurs built multistory factories, which are known to be hazardous. "It was designed as an apartment building, and now it's a factory," said one of the few engineering inspectors working there (qtd. in Srivastava and Shannon 2013, 2). As of the mid-2000s the Bangladeshi government employed just seventeen engineering inspectors to cover the entire economy (Miller 2013, 141). Furthermore, the political context in Bangladesh has privileged garment factory owners and marginalized their workers (Ahmed, Greenleaf, and Sacks 2014). In Pakistan government labor inspection has been dramatically scaled back (US Department of Labor 2012), and in some regions inspectors cannot check a factory within its first year of operation or without the cooperation of the owner (International Labor Organization 2011, 369).

It is in large part because of the industry's migration to these locations that apparel production continues to be plagued by factory fires, industrial accidents, bonded labor, and other extreme conditions. Based on the industry's history, some of these conditions could be improved over time, but that would likely be followed by a shift to new destinations. In this sense, severe forms of exploitation are built into the unruly logic of the global apparel industry, and rule-making projects have done little to alter that.

Admittedly, some companies and initiatives have gone further than others to temper the forms of unruliness discussed above. Alternative rule-making projects such as the WRC and Fair Wear Foundation have been all too aware of how sourcing practices and industry mobility matter, since these factors have undercut many of their projects. The FLA and ETI have tempered their expectations of auditing, shifting instead to a focus on capacity building at the factory level. SAI has launched several projects emphasizing dialogue and capacity building, although they have also allowed SA8000 certification to expand under questionable circumstances. A few brands, such as Marks & Spencer and Nike, have done more than others to link compliance and sourcing decisions. But these projects have a great deal to prove, since "capability-building" projects have sometimes been quite thin, as the next chapter will discuss.

LOCALIZED GLOBALISMS: RULES AND RIGHTS IN CHINA

Even with the growth of production in Bangladesh, China remains the world's top apparel exporter by far, accounting for 37 percent of total world clothing exports in 2010.[17] China also holds particular challenges for the implementation of codes of conduct: factories are staffed by migrant workers from rural areas who lack rights to government services in the cities where they work and are often marginalized in a country where the urban-rural divide is strong. Guarantees of freedom of association are difficult if not impossible to square with the government's restrictions on labor organization. In looking more closely at the implementation of voluntary labor standards in China, we focus on two key issues: how rules regarding freedom of association have been interpreted and how attempts to certify the best factories have fared.

The Problem of Freedom of Association

Most codes of conduct, monitoring, and certification initiatives ask suppliers to respect workers' freedom of association, including their rights to form unions and engage in collective bargaining. But the Chinese government limits union activity to the official, state-endorsed All China Federation of Trade Unions (ACFTU). ACFTU officials are closely tied to the state, and factory-level representatives are usually selected by union officials and factory management. More than "management unions" elsewhere, ACFTU unions have served as a means for the state to control workers (E. Friedman 2013). Even while emphasizing regional variation in ACFTU autonomy, Mingwei Liu (2010) concludes that "because the Party-State supports the unions with the aim of regaining control over society rather than protecting worker rights per se, too much dependence on the Party-State may cause the unions to act completely in the Party-State's interests and thus become its tool for the maintenance of social stability" (50). Outside of the ACFTU there are some NGOs focused on supporting migrant workers, but they are in a highly precarious position. Authorities can (and do) revoke NGOs' registrations or harass their leaders if they come to close to "sensitive" issues, and even those NGOs that are able to find a space where they can do meaningful work must constantly and cautiously manage their relationships (Chang, Ngok, and Zhuang 2010).

How, then, can companies and standard-setting initiatives implement rules calling for freedom of association in China? Companies have most commonly addressed this contradiction by simply ignoring it—that is, by overlooking restrictions on unions and associations of workers in China. In a few telling cases, companies have sought other ways around the problem. The most ambitious effort was taken by Reebok in the early 2000s. In two footwear factories in South China, Reebok sponsored elections whereby employees could select their own ACFTU representatives. Although this experiment began with a great deal of promise, and representatives were elected, it ended with reprisals from factory management and ACFTU officials, infighting among representatives, and mixed signals from Reebok (A. Chan 2009; Yu 2008b). Subsequent union leaders were not elected, and conditions in one of these factories got significantly worse over time (P. Lee

2007). What began as a groundbreaking experiment ended as a reminder that collective representation could not be created out of thin air, especially in China.

While they do not go as far as elected union officials, ETI and SAI call for "parallel means" of worker representation where union rights are restricted. In addition, some brands have promoted "worker welfare" or "health and safety" committees as ways of giving Chinese workers some voice. However, evidence of sustained and empowered worker committees is scant. In one case that has often been celebrated, an active worker committee was formed in a factory producing for Timberland (Center for International Private Enterprise and Social Accountability International 2009; Huang 2008; Huang and Guo 2006). But attempts to locate this committee in 2010 revealed that the factory had lost its orders from Timberland, as well as the manager who had supported the committee. In SA8000-certified factories, committees may be extremely rudimentary, dominated by management, or completely absent. As one certification practitioner admitted, "Auditors don't really understand the purpose of the committee," going on to explain that they often simply ask managers if there is a worker representative.[18] Adidas' compliance staff has facilitated the election of worker committees at several of its key supplier factories in China, but a meeting with one such committee revealed that its role was quite limited—weighing in on the food in the factory canteen and activities in the dormitory, for instance.[19]

In contrast, outside of channels provided by brands, Chinese migrant workers have sometimes been quite demanding. Through a wave of strikes they have engaged in a version of what Eric Hobsbawm (1952) called "collective bargaining by riot." Strikes surged in the late 1990s and early 2000s, initially among urban workers in state-owned enterprises. But it was not long before migrant workers in export-oriented industries were waging strikes as well (Lee 2007; Silver and Zhang 2009). Most take the form of quick "wildcat" strikes in response to delayed wages or other immediate grievances, but in a handful of cases striking workers have demanded rights, not just compensation (Butollo and ten Brink 2012; E. Friedman 2013). The kind of formalized worker representation promoted by apparel and footwear brands is a far cry from this kind of grassroots mobilization. When asked if a worker with a more activist orientation would be allowed to be elected to the committee, one brand's compliance expert answered, "If it was a strike leader? Almost surely not."[20]

Certifying Factories in China

While rule-making projects have proven ineffective in promoting freedom of association in China, they have been more successful in formalizing factory management systems. Often this takes the form of what Ngai-Ling Sum and Ngai Pun (2005) call the "institutionalization of paperwork," whereby a supplier subject to a buyer's code of conduct develops "elaborate managerial and audit/documentation systems to defend the [factory] against charges of infringing the code" (197). Most of the managerial changes that this entails are little more than window-dressing, but there do seem to be differences between Chinese factories that are subject to buyers' scrutiny and those that are not. For instance, examining codes of conduct in two apparel factories in China, Ngai Pun (2005) found "no cases of 'bonding' workers by requiring deposits of money from them when they are hired. Nor did either company keep workers' identity cards, which other enterprises in China often do to prevent them from quitting. Disciplinary penalties were replaced by a system of rewards and compensation" (108).

As the most credible factory certification effort, one might expect the SA8000 standard to be applied only to those factories with superior management systems, where even if workers voices are muted their treatment should be above average. But a closer look at SA8000 certification in China reveals that there is wide variability among SA8000-certified factories, in large part because of lax auditing. As discussed above, falsified records and careless, sometimes corrupted auditing had become common in China, including among auditors accredited to grant SA8000 certification. By some accounts, managers facing an all-or-nothing audit for certification are especially likely to hide the true information, since failing would lead to the loss of business.[21] Practitioners within China suggest that both the international accreditors and SAI "have not really been thinking about the challenges here."[22] As a result, as one brand representative put it, "some factories are getting certified by just hiring a consultant to get them certified."[23] In addition, certification audits might be scheduled at a particularly low point in the production season (to meet working-hour standards) or with enough advance notice to temporarily improve workplace conditions.[24] Factory certification in China boomed in the mid-2000s, but oversight was weak, leaving practitioners uncertain as to how many certified factories are truly above and below the standard.[25]

Interviews with several workers (conducted outside factories) suggest that some SA8000-certified apparel factories in South China are indeed above average. One apparel factory producing for Nike and a Chinese brand appears to have reduced working hours while also offering wages that are comparable to or slightly above those in other factories in the area. But this is not always the case. At another certified factory in the same area, this one producing for Billabong and other brands, working hours remained well above the legal limit and the SA8000 standard.[26] Some SA8000-certified factories have turned out to have working conditions that were well below average. In one certified home furnishings factory a follow-up visit revealed child labor, as well as horrendous health and safety conditions, such as workers making candles by hand over dangerous, primitive gasoline-bottle stoves.[27] The variation in SA8000-certified factories has meant that when certified and noncertified factories are compared, the average differences are often negligible (see Bartley and Zhang forthcoming).

In sum, as global rules have been put into practice in China, they have often become watered down, whether to accommodate the authoritarian political environment or because of weak oversight of auditing. As the failed experiments with worker representation suggest, there was no quick fix for labor rights when the local context did not support it. And as the growth of SA8000 illustrates, simple assurances about "good" factories and "responsible" production of apparel and footwear are, although not outright shams, not reliable indicators. Even though wages have increased over time in China's major manufacturing areas, tellingly, these changes have little to do with codes of conduct, factory auditing, or certification. Instead, as a large body of research is finding, wage increases have been driven by strikes, the tightening of labor markets, and the strengthening of Chinese labor law (see Kuruvilla, Lee, and Gallagher 2011). Domestic factors, it turns out, have been more important than global standards in bringing about marginal improvements in the apparel and footwear factories of China.

IN SEARCH OF ALTERNATIVES: DOMESTIC PRODUCTION, UNIONIZED FACTORIES, AND FAIR TRADE

The limitations of codes of conduct and factory auditing/certification may rightly leave conscientious consumers looking for alternatives. Furthermore, while the projects described above are mainly focused on labor conditions in the final manufacturing process, there are also reasons to be concerned about conditions further upstream in the supply chain—from water pollution and worker poisoning in the manufacturing and dyeing of textiles in China and India to forced labor in the cotton fields of Uzbekistan. Perhaps some emerging models of production in the apparel industry can provide more opportunities for conscientious consumers.

As labor costs have risen in China, some apparel manufacturers have partially "re-shored" production to the United States and UK (Bishop 2011). Fashion designers and upscale brands such as Eileen Fisher and Brooks Brothers have been able to allow consumers to bear the increased costs of manufacturing in domestic garment districts. But some other attempts to return to domestic production, particularly in mass-market goods, have foundered. The department store Dillards, for instance, quickly abandoned its re-shoring project, and the Pennsylvania company that was supplying it soon went out of business (Clifford 2013; A. Friedman 2012). While a "Made in the USA" label on apparel does suggest higher wages and a decreased chance of serious safety hazards (e.g., factory fires), it is hardly a guarantee of ideal working conditions. Immigrant workers in domestic garment districts in New York, Los Angeles, and elsewhere are often in a precarious position and have been subject to below-minimum wages, unpaid overtime, and retaliation against unionization efforts (Bonacich and Appelbaum 2000; Ross 2004). Some unionized apparel factories remain, but many of these shut down in the late 1990s.

The most prominent effort to promote domestic production has come from American Apparel, a vertically integrated retailer and manufacturer with a factory in Los Angeles. The company pays factory workers above the minimum wage and offers health insurance. It has at various points portrayed itself as "sweatshop free," although it has recently focused its marketing on a "Made in Los Angeles" identity, as well as sexually provocative advertisements that many have charged with being porn-inspired and misogynistic. The company's recently ousted CEO has also been charged with sexual harassment by a number of retail employees and has engaged in a number of explicit acts in the workplace. Despite its occasional attempts to claim a moral high ground, the company has also proven hostile to unions, fighting vigorously against early attempts to organize its manufacturing workers (Brooks 2007). Overall, American Apparel's manufacturing process does differ from most of the industry in some respects, but its antiunion stance and regressive gender politics have made labor rights advocates extremely reluctant to endorse the company.

An alternative model that takes rights more seriously is the Alta Gracia factory in the Dominican Republic, where unionized workers earn a living wage making T-shirts primarily for the collegiate market. The story of Alta Gracia begins with the failure of the BJ&B factory in the same location, which produced baseball caps for Nike and Reebok. In the late 1990s anti-sweatshop activists in the United States exposed management abuse of BJ&B workers and repression of their efforts to form a union. With support from campaigns targeting Nike and investigation by the WRC, BJ&B workers successfully formed a union and engaged in collective bargaining in 2003 (Ross 2006). But this victory was short-lived. Within several years the Korean company that owned the factory and many of its buyers were shifting to factories in Vietnam, Bangladesh, and other Asian countries. The BJ&B workforce shrank to one-fifth of its previous size, and in 2007 the factory shut down (Clean Clothes Campaign 2007; Nova and Kline 2014).[28]

Out of the rubble of the BJ&B campaign, the WRC brokered an agreement with Knights Apparel, a US-based apparel company, to open the Alta Gracia factory at this location. Knights Apparel was a major manufacturer of collegiate-licensed apparel but did not have a strong brand image, and its CEO had developed a personal interest in social responsibility (Kline 2010). The factory opened in 2010, hiring some former BJ&B workers. It paid a living wage as calculated by the WRC and local experts—$115 per week, roughly three times higher than the legal minimum wage or the prevailing wage in the apparel industry in that region; and workers got cushioned ergonomic chairs rather than the commonly used metal stools (Kline 2010). Most notably, management had agreed to negotiate with a union, which workers quickly organized. The factory has navigated several production challenges and has succeeded in getting its products into university bookstores, as well as selling through the bulk wholesaler Ethixmerch. As of 2013 it had survived but was not yet turning a profit (Northam 2013).

Alta Gracia is only one small factory. The conditions that facilitated this project, including the prior unionization efforts and broader reforms in Dominican labor standards (Schrank 2013), make it difficult to replicate elsewhere. Nevertheless, it demonstrates that it is possible to produce apparel in developing countries *and* respect labor rights. Although labor rights activists have been reluctant to follow organic and fair trade advocates in seeking to build markets, the Alta Gracia project may be changing that (Nova and Kline 2014:274).

Finally, as seen in previous chapters, consumers of coffee, flowers, sugar, and chocolate have turned to fair trade certification as an alternative to the mainstream industry. Some cotton farms in developing countries are also part of the fair trade system (Bassett 2010), and apparel brands have begun to sell clothes made of fair trade–certified cotton. Note, however, that using fair trade cotton has no implications for the manufacturing process, despite what advertisements might imply. There is not yet a process in place to certify an entire fair trade garment, but Fair Trade USA has recently been working on one. Their system would certify both cotton producers and sewing operations so that a full garment could be labeled as Fair Trade. The challenges of adapting the fair trade model to wage earners in manufacturing operations are substantial, especially in a rapidly changing, highly mobile industry like apparel (Maquila Solidarity Network 2006). Nevertheless, Fair Trade USA pushed forward with a pilot project for garment manufacturing (as it has with other extensions of the fair trade model, as described in chapter 4). It appears that Fair Trade manufacturing will take certification to the SA8000 standard as its baseline while also adding a premium of up to 10 percent of the factory price of the item, which is to be distributed to a "Fair Trade committee" of workers (Fair Trade USA 2012). It does not appear that a union will be required for a factory to be certified. Overall, it is too soon to say how meaningful of an alternative Fair Trade apparel might provide, but our examination of worker committees and SA8000 certification should raise questions about whether they can provide a solid foundation for real alternatives. On the other hand, while the initiatives described above have focused narrowly on labor conditions in manufacturing, the fair trade model at least has the virtue of taking account of conditions further upstream in the supply chain, as in cotton farming.

The *Guardian* newspaper's "Ethical Fashion Directory" is a telling indicator of the state of alternative production models in the apparel industry. Reflecting the proliferation of green consumer assurances, it shows items made with organic cotton, sustainable fabrics, and recycled and vegan materials. But when it comes to labor standards, the offerings are slim. It shows a handful of brands with at least some products that are labeled "Made in the UK," and it shows a much larger number of brands that use fair trade cotton. But as one looks further into these companies' manufacturing processes, guarantees about working conditions are either absent or quite similar to the assurances about codes and auditing that are given by mainstream companies. Even in the UK, the bastion of conscientious consumerism, the search for ethical fashion remains confusing.

CONCLUSION

On the heels of "green" consumer movements, anti-sweatshop activists sought to add "fair labor" to the list of conscientious consumers' concerns. They "named and shamed" well-known brands and urged consumers in affluent countries to act in solidarity with apparel and footwear workers elsewhere. There is no doubt that anti-sweatshop activists succeeded in getting the attention of companies and consumers. But the rule-making projects that emerged have largely failed to alter the logic of the industry or offer meaningful alternatives to consumers.

In large part this is because of the constituencies that had the most power in those projects. Large, high-profile brands were able to steer monitoring and certification initiatives (FLA, SAI, and to a lesser extent ETI) to approaches that did not require dramatic changes in their operations, even though the involvement of nonindustry groups pushed these firms a bit further than their competitors. This push was absent in programs sponsored by industry associations (WRAP and BSCI), which have lower standards and weaker enforcement. All of these initiatives have relied on auditing practices that, while variable, have often been quite shoddy. Unions and NGOs did take the lead in some smaller projects (the WRC and FWF) that have become key voices pushing for stringent enforcement and serious remediation of problems. But their scope of influence is small.

Aside from these programs, some brands and retailers have developed significant internal compliance programs. But to a striking extent, the activities of compliance personnel have been decoupled from the companies' sourcing programs, where low prices and quick delivery—and geographical mobility in search of these—have remained the priorities. In short, there has been a proliferation of rules for fair labor conditions, but the industry has remained unruly in many respects.

So what is a conscientious consumer to do? Consumers' desires to identify "good" and "bad" companies runs into the problem that the leading apparel brands and retailers are more similar than different when it comes to labor conditions. Even those with sophisticated compliance programs operate within a highly competitive, mobile, and unequal structure of production. The desire to push product prices down and to spend on marketing, design, and distribution has remained powerful. Conscientious consumers might seek to reward firms that are likely to be slightly better than average (such as those that participate in the ETI, FLA, or SAI), but the magnitude of this difference must be kept in mind. One can look for alternative models of production, although as we have seen, domestic production and fair trade assurances are not necessarily reliable indicators of decent labor conditions in the apparel industry. One can seek to build collective consumer power in support of stringent standards, as university students have for the WRC. But concerned citizen-consumers must also look for other ways of promoting global labor standards, such as supporting trade policy that allows for the strengthening of labor rights and opposing trade policy that ignores or undermines labor regulation.

Some recent initiatives in the apparel industry suggest some tentative movement toward new approaches. First, the ILO-IFC Better Work program seeks to help factories in a given country to meet buyers' codes of conduct and domestic legal requirements while still remaining competitive. Perhaps most importantly it seeks to bridge the gap between voluntary rule making and government labor inspection in developing countries. Originating from the project in Cambodia mentioned above, Better Work programs have been launched in Vietnam, Indonesia, Haiti, Jordan, Nicaragua, and Lesotho.

Unlike the Cambodian program, these offshoots are not backed by trade agreements (which make Cambodian garments' access to the United States dependent on improvement in labor conditions), and even in Cambodia repression of trade unions continued. Still, Better Work has the virtue of at least recognizing that governments must be part of any path toward decent work.

Second, in the wake of industrial accidents in Bangladesh, international labor rights advocates have convinced some lead firms to sign on to a binding Accord on Fire and Building Safety in Bangladesh. Signatory companies agree to support a new safety inspection and remediation program headed by international experts and to stop buying from factories that refuse to participate in the program.[29] The number of signatory companies increased after the Rana Plaza collapse, reaching 140 by early 2014. These include European retailers and brands including Primark, Marks & Spencer, Carrefour, Kik, H&M, Adidas, and Benetton, as well as Philips Van Heusen, Abercrombie and Fitch, and eight other American companies. In contrast, many other American firms (including the Gap, Walmart, Target, and VF) have refused to accept a binding obligation, organizing a voluntary program on Bangladesh instead. The binding Bangladesh accord represents an intriguing model, although the baseline level of safety in Bangladesh remains well below many other apparel-producing countries. In another interesting move, the Walt Disney Company ultimately decided that Bangladesh (along with Pakistan, Belarus, Ecuador, and Venezuela) was too risky for its licensed apparel and toys to be produced there—a controversial but notable decision, since brands have rarely been willing to constrain their geographical choices.

These new approaches have some potential to improve on the failings of voluntary codes of conduct and checklist factory auditing. Still, unless the mobility and price sensitivity of the apparel industry is tamed to some degree, rules will give way to unruliness. Perhaps if conscientious consumption can translate into greater political engagement, especially with issues of trade policy and global labor regulation, the history of the apparel industry will not be doomed to repeat itself once more.

6 — ELECTRONICS

The Hidden Costs of Computing

Any committed foodie will wax lyrical about the value of provenance—the integrity of the food, the care and craft behind creating it. How long, then, before this middle-class preoccupation with quality, traceability and plain goodness of the things we buy extends into technology? We suspend our ethics when Apple launches a new phone. That unboxing is a virgin moment, as if the phone morphed inside the box from the tiny sparkling seed implanted by Jonathan Ive. Slide your finger through the *Designed In California* seal and your phone takes its first breath.
—Jemima Kiss, "The Real Price of an iPhone 5" (2012)

IN EARLY 2012 THE *NEW YORK TIMES* RAN THE FIRST OF A SERIES OF articles outlining health, safety, and working conditions in Apple's Asian supply chain (Duhigg and Barboza 2012).[1] This was not the first time poor conditions at Apple's partners were reported. Labor rights and student groups in the United States and Hong Kong had been publicizing exploitation in the electronics industry for nearly a decade, and a string of suicides in 2010 by employees of Foxconn, a key Apple supplier in China, captured international attention (e.g., Dean and Tsai 2010). But the *Times* coverage was by far the most extensive exposé of Apple's supply chain.

At the time, Apple had the largest stock market capitalization in the world, $550 billion. Under the previous reign of CEO and cofounder Steve Jobs, Apple had mostly avoided responding to complaints of poor working conditions. Jobs had commented in 2010, "I actually think Apple does one of the best jobs of any companies in our industry, and maybe in any industry, of understanding the working conditions in our supply chain" (qtd. in Duhigg and Barboza 2012). Yet the *Times* article highlighted repeated instances of employees at Apple's suppliers working twelve-hour days, six days per week, being ordered to use poisonous chemicals to clean iPad surfaces, or living with twenty people in a three-room apartment. A deadly explosion inside a factory in Chengdu, China, in 2011 seemed less idiosyncratic as the *Times* unearthed recurrent problems in worker health and safety.

While the series focused on Apple, it did not leave other global electronics giants, such as Hewlett-Packard (HP), IBM, Nokia, and Sony, unscathed. The *Times'* findings, while perhaps not surprising to scholars and activists (Ferus-Comelo 2008; Smith, Sonnenfeld, and Pellow 2006), increased public attention to the ethically precarious foundations of an industry that is adored almost universally—by consumers for its technological innovation, by investors for its high profitability, and by policy makers in developing countries for fueling economic development and technology transfer.

The electronics industry is very dynamic, on almost every dimension more so than the other industries discussed in this book.[2] It is large, global, and rapidly expanding. Manufacturers of consumer electronics and information and communications technology (ICT) had revenues of more than $3.6 trillion in 2012, a figure that is projected to grow even more with the burgeoning "Internet of Things" market (that is, the network of connected devices) (MacGillivray, Turner, and Lund 2013). The industry's leading companies have strong management, well-capitalized balance sheets, substantial cash flows, and deep technological and innovative capacities.

Why, then, have these companies struggled with accusations of exploitation in their supply chains? If they can introduce complex new products to diverse global markets every four to six months, why can they not manage to ensure fair conditions of production? Furthermore, the challenges in electronics extend beyond working conditions to environmental hazards and the use of "conflict minerals." Certainly the problem cannot be constrained resources, a justification broadly seen in industries with low profit margins and strong pressures for price reduction (like many parts of the apparel industry, as analyzed in chapter 5). Moreover, while most electronics production occurs in newly industrializing Asian economies such as China and Thailand, these are not weak states incapable of enforcing standards. They actively manage complex economic agendas and volatile political environments. While lower-technology industries (e.g., apparel) can threaten to exit a country if labor costs and regulations increase, electronics manufacturers have relatively high fixed capital investments, which makes relocation costly. Why, then, do these states not enforce their own labor laws, particularly in an industry that is well resourced enough to meet them and not itching to leave?

In this chapter we consider why working conditions in the electronics industry have been so difficult to improve. The answer, we argue, has much to do with the structure of consumption and production. Consumers' seemingly insatiable desires for the latest technology have supported a system of production that can deliver on these demands but does so by demanding an extreme degree of flexibility by production workers. Given the interest of newly industrializing countries in development and technology transfer, the organization of work and its lack of regulation have also been shaped by the policies of governments. Electronics manufacturers have developed some rules for themselves, in the form of company-specific codes of conduct and the Electronic Industry Citizenship Coalition. As we show, these standards are not especially stringent and are often watered down in the auditing process. However, the fundamental problem is not in these self-regulatory standards, but rather in a system of production that pushes directly against what these standards call for.

As the case of Apple illustrates, major electronics brands are being pushed to take labor standards more seriously, but the results are quite ambiguous. After years of downplaying their responsibilities, Apple responded to the *New York Times* series by asking the Fair Labor Association to audit its suppliers (Duhigg and Wingfield 2012). Labor groups protested that the FLA is biased to brands—as discussed in the previous chapter—but Apple's turn to an outside organization is certainly notable for a company that has long relished its privacy. Apple's decision may have been influenced by fears of a diminishing corporate reputation, but one thing is certain: it was not driven, directly at least, by the phenomenon that motivates this book—conscientious consumption. The electronics industry has faced few organized boycotts and until very recently almost no efforts to offer "alternative," ethically made products. Observers have often wondered if Apple will be the "new Nike," referring to the extended anti-sweatshop pressure against that company. Yet as an Apple executive told the *New York Times,* "You can either manufacture in comfortable, worker-friendly factories, or you can reinvent the product every year, and make it better and faster and cheaper, which requires factories that seem harsh by American standards. . . . And right now, customers care more about a new iPhone than working conditions in China" (Duhigg and Barboza 2012). What is it about the electronics industry, with all of its distinct characteristics—technology, innovation, profitability, size—that subjects it to the same intractable problems that observers thought belong only to lower-technology, labor-intensive industries such as footwear and apparel?

THE GLOBAL ELECTRONICS INDUSTRY: THE STRUCTURE OF PRODUCTION AND CONSUMPTION

Like many other industries discussed in this book, the electronics industry is composed of a complex, disaggregated global network of companies for manufacturing and a relatively small number of dominant national retailers for distribution. Yet consumption and production are tightly linked through a fascinating system of information gathering, "pull-based" ordering, and rapid assembly. In the following section we describe this architecture, how it came to be, and how governments have sought to harness it for economic development.

Retail Concentration, Technological Advance, and a New Production Architecture

Beginning in the late 1980s retail markets in the United States and Europe underwent rapid consolidation, especially with the rise of "big box" retailers such as Best Buy and Walmart in the United States and Dixon's and Media Markt in Europe. By the mid-2000s the market share of the four largest retailers in the United States and most European countries was well above 50 percent. Even with an oligopolistic retail structure, the electronics industry has continued to evolve rapidly. Amazon.com has become the fourth-largest retailer of consumer electronics in the United States (Smith and Wolf 2011). Adoption rates for consumer technology and e-commerce have soared over the past decade. The smartphone has now outpaced all previous technological innovations in the speed of achieving mainstream use (DeGusta 2012). In developing countries, globalization and market liberalization have opened up substantial new markets, creating hundreds of millions of new electronics consumers and hundreds of new competitors to established American and European brands.

In this highly dynamic context, electronics brands introduce new models to remain differentiated. This is especially important in fiercely competitive and "winner take all" markets such as those for smartphone operating systems (Schilling 2002). Apple has shortened the average time between new iPhone/iPad rollouts from more than a year in 2008 to just four months in 2012. Samsung reduced its new product rollout time to just ninety-one days in 2013 (Marketwatch 2013). The leading firms, including IBM, Nokia, Motorola, Apple, and HP, have been able to accomplish these shorter cycles by shifting from vertically integrated production structures to outsourced manufacturing, concentrating their own competencies on nonproduction activities (e.g., design, marketing, and research and development) (Gereffi, Humphrey, and Sturgeon 2005; Sturgeon 2002; Sturgeon and Lester 2002). Beginning in the 1990s and accelerating into the 2000s, these firms divested their manufacturing and production facilities to leading contract manufacturers, including Taiwanese companies such as Hon Hai Precision Industries (better known as Foxconn) and Quanta and US-based companies such as Flextronics and Jabil.

This shift from vertical integration to horizontal global value chains was hastened by three factors. Globalization facilitated cross-border production, and "financialization" encouraged large firms to shed manufacturing to focus on their "core competencies" (Davis 2009). But it was the third factor—rapid technological advance—that most facilitated the remaking of the industry's production architecture and accelerated its growth. Earlier generations of computing equipment were sold as integrated products with closed systems. IBM historically delivered mainframe computers that used proprietary software and hardware. Minicomputer makers such as Digital Equipment Corporation (DEC) and Wang followed a similar path, using proprietary operating systems and peripherals that locked customers into the same manufacturer's product family for many years. Manufacturers privileged reliability over new technologies given their hold on customers, and companies chose to be vertically integrated in order to ensure their systems remained stable. Most leading firms in the 1970s maintained their own "wafer fabs" (semiconductor wafer fabrication factories), while almost no computer companies do so today.

IBM's decision in 1982 to enter the personal computer (PC) market ended this era. It introduced standardized product architectures and interfaces by breaking the PC into a series of tasks that could be easily codified into distinct modules. Because of this, components and subsystems could be designed independently but expected to function as part of the larger product (Baldwin and Clark 2009). Transparent product standards allowed component and peripheral manufacturers to develop new products, such as hard disk drives and monitors, without having to rely on the larger companies for product integration. Perhaps most importantly, this "modularity" enabled new entrants into product markets. Cisco and other startups never had to build manufacturing plants. Instead they were able to rely upon this nascent group of contract manufacturers for all of their production needs. If a company such as Dell chose to assemble its own product, it still completely outsourced all component manufacturing.

Competition and the Global Division of Labor

Modularity allowed electronics companies to introduce new products faster and more broadly, but they soon learned that this was a double-edged sword, since new products hastily came into competition and sometimes failed. By integrating modular components into novel products, firms could reduce costs and increase selection, but so could their competitors. Product markets quickly became "commoditized"—that is, markets in which products were almost indistinguishable—as competitors imitated one another's innovations. A common operating system reduced switching costs for consumers, driving retail prices down and pushing manufacturers to reduce costs.

In addition to lower profit margins, electronics firms faced the challenge of managing "network effects"—in other words, the need to have many users before the benefits of a technology can be fully realized. Electronics equipment often requires a period of gestation before an accumulation of users begins to make further purchases almost inevitable. For consumers, network effects mean there are incentives to join with a rapidly expanding set of users, which in turn increases the network's power and utility, creating a virtuous circle (Katz and Shapiro 1994). VCRs, fax machines, and, more recently, location-based smartphone applications have all grown via network effects.

For electronics companies, building a technology platform that enables network effects is highly rewarding but also increasingly challenging. On one hand, once consumers experience the benefits of a network, they become resistant to switching product families. On the other hand, the potentially cascading gain or loss of customers due to network effects means companies constantly develop new products out of fear that competitors will steal their current users. As Annabelle Gawer and Michael Cusumano (2002) put it, "The balance of power among component providers is tenuous because continuous innovation on components can alter the drivers of demand. As a result, positions of leadership, whether technical or market-share leadership, are in a constant state of challenge" (3). Research in Motion's Blackberry network moved quickly toward obsolescence as the company struggled to match Apple's iPhone, despite repeated new product offerings. Rapid advances in technology compound the threat of obsolescence. According to one Dell executive, "Inventory has the shelf life of lettuce" (qtd. in Catholic Agency for Overseas Development 2004). Companies must be extremely careful to minimize inventory of finished products, because as Tim Cook, the current CEO of Apple, is fond of saying, "Nobody wants to buy sour milk" (Satariano and Burrows 2011).

Electronics companies divide their innovative and productive labor to meet this challenge. Research and development (R&D) expenditures amount to 8–10 percent of revenues, higher than any other global industry (Jaruzelski, Loehr, and Holman 2013). Electronics brands focus on R&D, design, and marketing, leaving manufacturing and industrial engineering to their component suppliers and contract manufacturers. Given this new division of labor, contract manufacturers have grown rapidly. By 2008 the leading contract manufacturers had plants in dozens of countries. Most manufacturing takes place in Asia, with significant activity in Mexico and Eastern Europe as well (New Venture Research Corporation 2009). We estimate that roughly 70 percent of global electronics manufacturing currently takes place in East and Southeast Asia, much of it in China. Apple may promote the "Designed in California" tagline, but "Made in China" is commonly in the fine print.

A small number of international buyers and suppliers control much of the electronics market. Since consumer-facing brands still control the industry's product definition, design, and innovation trajectories, they are able to capture most of the profits from new technologies and high-end markets (Sturgeon 2002). Breaking down the production and sale of Apple products, Kenneth Kraemer and his colleagues (2011) found that Apple captures close to 60 percent of an iPhone's retail price. Material, component, and labor costs constitute roughly 27 percent of the price, leaving just 15 percent for every other participant in this global value chain. For some products Apple's share is even higher (Clark, Kraemer, and Dedrick 2009).

There is evidence that large contract manufacturers such as Foxconn and Flextronics may be catching up with lead firms such as Apple, Dell, and HP in terms of revenue and employment. Moreover, some large and diverse contract manufacturers (e.g., Acer, which had revenues of $14.7 billion in 2012) have successfully established their own computer hardware brands. Yet much of the profit continues to be captured by branded lead firms rather than the contract manufacturers responsible for production. In 2009, a year after the financial crash, the electronics industry's top five contract manufacturers lost a total of $4.4 billion. This may not seem surprising, except that the large brands had the opposite result. That same year, the total net income for the five largest lead firms was $37.8 billion.[3]

Building on the Korean Model: Why Developmental States Privilege Electronics

The new division of labor in the electronics industry has been greatly facilitated by the success of electronics companies in Japan and South Korea, with support from the state, in the 1980s and 1990s. Newly industrializing countries, particularly in Asian countries such as China, Thailand, Malaysia, and the Philippines, have sought to reproduce that success by aggressively court-ing electronics companies. Their idea is that "developmental states" can help firms with low capabilities (e.g., assemblers) to eventually "move up the value chain," where profits and technological capacities are much higher. Drawing on the success of the Korean developmental state (see Amsden 1989), policy makers have repeatedly sought to construct the right set of conditions for firms to adopt imported technology and then advance it while absorbing unemployed or displaced workers. As scholars of "industrial upgrading" have argued, firms may start on the bottom rung of technological tasks and then work their way up to increasingly complex activities, gaining experience, higher profitability, and diversification as they go (Gereffi, Humphrey, and Sturgeon 2005). For governments of developing countries, electronics pro-duction also brings the potential spillover benefits in the form of R&D and management training.

Policy makers often point to the Korean company Samsung as proof that mastering a technology platform allows firms to embark on new, higher-value activities in other industries. Samsung shifted from consumer electron-ics assembly to very large-scale integrated-circuit (VLSI) manufacturing (Kim 1997), helping it to eventually become a major electronics brand. Thus, by subsidizing electronics suppliers, policy makers expect local firms to move from absorption of foreign technology, to mastery, and finally on to product definition and design (Ohno 2009).

Governments in Southeast Asia and China aggressively courted contract manufacturers, offering tax holidays, building ports, and setting up free-trade zones that eliminated import duties on intermediates. Firms were also attracted by abundant labor, low wages, and perhaps most importantly, flexible labor markets, which governments constructed or maintained. For-eign firms were typically sorted by common language, ethnic networks, or both: American semiconductor manufacturers set up operations in English-speaking Malaysia in the late 1970s, and Taiwanese firms moved into south China ten years later. By 2009 exports of consumer electronics and informa-tion technology (IT) equipment were exceeding 30 percent of total exports in some countries (World Bank 2009). Given its importance in economic development plans, the industry typically maintains very strong relations with the state.

The Hidden Costs: Labor Conditions, Environmental
Damage, and "Conflict Minerals"

Leading electronics brands have been quite effective at standardizing tech-nologies and assembly practices (Lüthje 2002; Sturgeon 2002), but manag-ing labor standards has been more problematic. As contract manufacturing expanded, NGOs exposed low pay for production workers, deductions for performance and discipline, and exposure to hazardous materials (Catholic Agency for Overseas Development 2004; Good Electronics 2009; Schipper and de Haan 2007). Scholars followed with detailed research on working conditions in electronics plants, pollution from electronics manufacturing, and the problem of toxic e-waste (i.e., toxic substances like mercury, cad-mium, and arsenic in discarded or recycled electronics) (Smith, Sonnenfeld, and Pellow 2006). As has become especially clear in China, the rapid growth of export-oriented manufacturing has left serious environmental scars (see Streets et al. 2006).

Workers in electronics assembly factories are typically in-country or for-eign migrants who have been subject to high recruitment fees they must pay to the labor agencies that matched them with their jobs (Catholic Agency for Overseas Development 2004; Chan and Peyer 2008). Often, these agents would hold the workers' passports until the fees—sometimes amounting to a year's worth of base pay—were paid. As production quantities have increased, contract manufacturers have drawn on greater numbers of con-tingent workers. This not only limits the payment of benefits, but as we will see, it is also crucial in allowing companies to hire and fire employees rapidly in response to volatility in demand. Intentionally or not, reliance on contin-gent workers also pushed migrant workers into the informal economy, where immigration enforcement was weak and contract agencies could maintain a reserve supply of abundant and flexible labor (Locke and Samel 2012).

This combination of intermittent low-skilled assembly work and large numbers of contingent or migrant workers exacerbated existing problems, including excess working hours, no benefits, and negligent safety practices. A wave of suicides at Foxconn's onsite dormitories in 2010 brought the plight of migrant workers in the electronics industry to international attention (Inter-faith Center on Corporate Responsibility 2010). The suicides may be linked in several ways to the organization of work in the electronics industry. The first suicide, in July 2009, was committed by an employee accused of facilitating a leak of secret design information. A Foxconn human resources (HR) manager described what happened:

> When Sun Danyong, 25 years old, was held responsible for losing one of the iPhone 4 prototypes, he jumped from the 12th floor to his death. Not only the short delivery deadline but also Apple's secretive culture and business approach, centered on creating great surprise in the market and thereby adding sales value to its products, have sent extreme pressure all the way down to its Chinese suppliers and workers. (qtd. in Chan, Pun, and Selden 2013, 107)

Second, as a wave of suicides unfolded in 2010, many observers saw this as reflecting the high pressure, dehumanizing work hours, and tight discipline imposed on ordinary production workers (Chan, Pun, and Selden 2013).

Of course, many migrant workers in China and elsewhere seek to maximize their earnings by working large numbers of overtime hours. Because overtime pay is often calculated only on the sixth and seventh days of work, a preference for working through the weekend is not uncommon. Managers and migrant workers may have their interests aligned when it comes to long hours of work, but this position is in tension with the arguments of NGOs, scholars, and other employees that hours must be restricted in order to prevent work from being dehumanizing. The hope of limiting working hours as a way to promote decent work in the electronics industry has repeatedly crashed against a system of production that demands the flexibility to work very long (or short) hours.

In addition to problems in the manufacturing process, electronics brands have been forced to consider the sources of the minerals that are used in components. NGOs such as Global Witness and the Enough Project have publicized the use of "conflict minerals" in the production of smartphones and other electronics (Khan 2013; Lezhnev and Hellmuth 2012). Referred to as 3TG, conflict minerals are tantalum, tin, tungsten, and gold. Tantalum is used in capacitors, which store energy; tungsten is used in wires; tin is used for soldering; and gold is used for component connections. These minerals are frequently mined through forced labor in zones of extreme conflict in central Africa, then smuggled out of the country to Asian smelters for refinement, generating significant revenues for local armed militias. In the Democratic Republic of the Congo (DRC) and Central African Republic, powerful militias have been able to force children into dangerous mines, buy arms with mineral proceeds, and then force the same children into battle zones (Banco 2011).

The United Nations has joined NGOs in calling on the electronics industry to end the trade in conflict minerals, and there does appear to be some change afoot in this part of the industry's operations. Electronics brands have begun to audit 3TG smelters to trace their sources, and the Electronics Industry Citizenship Coalition has called on its members to mandate that only approved suppliers are used. Because alternative sources of the 3TG are available, public concern has had some impact in delinking electronics from violent conflicts in Central Africa. In 2012 the Enough Project reported that a sufficient number of leading electronics companies had made enough progress in identifying their sources of 3TG that the amount earned by militias since 2010 had shrunk by 65 percent (Lezhnev and Hellmuth 2012). Furthermore, a little-known provision of the Dodd-Frank Wall Street Reform and Consumer Protection Act, which was passed in 2010, requires publicly traded companies to trace and disclose the sources of 3TG in their products (KPMG 2011). Still, identifying the origin of minerals and stopping their transshipment is difficult, since the companies that are subject to this law and to public pressure buy ready-made components. In addition, minerals from conflict zones may be blended with ore from other countries before shipment.[4]

Might the steps that have been taken on conflict minerals bode well for reform of labor conditions in the global electronics industry? To answer this question we turn to our analysis of the origins and effects of rule-making projects for fair labor in electronics production. As we will see, electronics brands have struggled to comply with the very standards they have created for themselves.

GLOBALIZED LOCALISMS: THE DEVELOPMENT OF GLOBAL RULE-MAKING PROJECTS

While consumers in the United States and Europe began hearing about sweatshops in apparel and footwear manufacturing in the mid-1990s, most remained blissfully unaware of the hidden costs of computing. By the early 2000s NGOs were publicizing poor working conditions in electronics, and electronics companies soon began to adopt standards for their supply chains. But neither the activism nor the corporate responses generated the kind of public debates that have surrounded the other products examined in this book. Rule-making projects in the global electronics industry have been limited in their interaction with nonindustry stakeholders and in their impacts at the point of production.

NGOs and Socially Responsible Investors: Voices in the Wilderness?

A 2004 report from the Catholic Agency for Overseas Development (CAFOD), titled "Clean Up Your Computer," was among the first to highlight labor rights abuses in the global electronics industry. Building on "naming and shaming" campaigns in the apparel and footwear industry, the report focused on the supply chains of HP, IBM, and Dell. It documented discrimination against pregnant women, abusive management styles, subminimum wages, and health hazards in the electronics factories of Mexico and China (Catholic Agency for Overseas Development 2004; Raj-Reichert 2011). The Dutch NGO Stichting Onderzoek Multinationale Ondernemingen (SOMO) has since become a major player in highlighting labor rights abuses in the electronics industry. It coordinates the "Make IT Fair" campaign to inform European consumers about the conditions under which their mobile phones and laptops are manufactured, and it hosts the Good Electronics network, which provides research to socially responsible investors. Closer to the point of production, Hong Kong—based SACOM (Students and Scholars Against Corporate Misbehavior) and other groups have used undercover investigations to document overwork, underpayment, and serious safety hazards (including dangerous exposure to benzene, hexane, and aluminum dust) (see, e.g., Chan and Peyer 2008).

Some socially responsible investors have pushed electronics companies to change. For instance, the Interfaith Center on Corporate Responsibility (ICCR) successfully lobbied Apple to adopt a code of conduct, eventually leading it to join the Electronic Industry Citizenship Coalition as well.[5] The most significant outcome of NGOs' and investors' efforts has been increased transparency in some parts of the industry. Apple and HP now publish lists of their top suppliers, making it easier for researchers and activists to assess improvements in their supply chains. Still, unlike the anti-sweatshop movement in the apparel industry, there have been few sustained social movement campaigns targeting electronics brands, and it was not until the *New York*

Times flexed its investigative muscle and broad distribution that Apple felt significant pressure. Even as conscientious consumption has become popular, consumers have mainly focused on product features and quality when selecting electronics.

Advent of the Electronic Industry Citizenship Coalition

Very soon after the CAFOD report, HP, IBM, and Dell joined together with five contract manufacturers (Celestica, Flextronics, Jabil, Sanmina SCI, and Solectron) to form the Electronic Industry Citizenship Coalition (EICC). While voluntary initiatives in other industries have often been organized at least in part by NGOs, the EICC was created by the industry for the industry, without outside help. By the end of 2008 the initiative had grown to forty-five member companies, including most well-known brands (e.g., Apple, Intel, Lenovo, Microsoft, Sony, Samsung), a key retailer (Best Buy), and additional contract manufacturers (e.g., Foxconn, Pegatron/Asus) (EICC 2009). By 2012 the organization had grown to seventy-eight member companies, representing $1.7 trillion in revenue. In perhaps a measure of the industry's power, no other stakeholders have taken on roles in the EICC since the organization's founding. As Luc Fransen and Thomas Conzelmann (forthcoming) show, concerns about electronic waste and environmental damage eventually led the EICC to propose that NGOs might join in an advisory-only role, but NGOs have declined to accept this marginal, token position.

The EICC developed an industry-wide code of conduct, which currently focuses on five dimensions: (1) labor (e.g., banning forced labor and child labor, limiting working hours), (2) health and safety (e.g., controlling workers' exposure to hazardous materials, promoting emergency preparedness), (3) environment (e.g., pollution reduction, monitoring of emissions, acquisition of necessary permits), (4) ethics (e.g., against bribery and for intellectual property rights), and (5) management systems (e.g., to systematize risk assessment, training, and corporate social responsibility).[6] Consistent with the lack of involvement of nonindustry groups, the EICC code covers a wide terrain but is not as demanding as the codes of "multi-stakeholder" initiatives in other industries. As Fransen and Conzelmann (forthcoming) put it, "Compared to labor standards in clothing, the social part of EICC's standards is arguably lax. There is neither reference to ILO standards nor to living wage requirements, and soft language on rights of association" (17). The content of the EICC code is consistent with our claim in the introduction that industry-initiated programs tend to promote "best practices" rather than alternative production practices. As we will see, the dynamics of the electronics industry have often frustrated even the achievement of best practices.

In addition to its code, the EICC has sought to facilitate efficient auditing of labor and environmental conditions in electronics supply chains. In partnership with GeSi, a European group of ICT companies interested in sustainability, EICC developed a self-assessment questionnaire for suppliers that serves as the basis for auditing and evaluation of improvement. Critics have questioned this "non-rigorous process of self-regulation," since, as one NGO representative noted, "managers can lie on the forms" (interview with Good Electronics Network member, qtd. in Raj-Reichert 2012). Unlike most initiatives discussed elsewhere in this book, the EICC has relied largely on member companies themselves to conduct or arrange factory auditing. The coalition also asks brands' first-tier suppliers (e.g., Foxconn or Flextronics) to be responsible for training and auditing second-tier suppliers (i.e., factories making processor chips and other inputs) (Raj-Reichert 2011).

There have been some shifts toward external auditing, however. Since 2010 EICC has added a "Validated Audit Process" by which key suppliers are audited by providers that have been approved by the International Register of Certificated Auditors (IRCA), an oversight body for management systems auditing. These audit results are intended to be sharable among EICC members, in hope that pooling information can further enhance the efficiency of industry compliance efforts. In addition, while most EICC members have relied heavily on their own internal compliance programs (Satariano and Burrows 2012), Apple's recent turn to the FLA and HP's recent participation in Social Accountability International suggest that the electronics industry may be inching toward broader engagement with nonindustry actors and the kinds of initiatives discussed in chapter 5.

Global rule making for electronics, then, has been accomplished largely by companies themselves, although they have drawn on existing management system standards for occupational health and safety (i.e., OHSAS 18001) and have been nudged by NGO pressure and media attention to seek greater credibility for their self-regulatory program. The early results of EICC's own assessments also illustrated that there was much room for improvement. A

2008 survey of EICC companies found that 90 percent saw long working hours—in excess of sixty hours per week—as a continuing challenge. Most (59 percent) also mentioned concerns about wages and benefits, such as withholding or deductions from pay for disciplinary punishment. Fewer were concerned about occupational safety and hazardous substances (33 percent and 30 percent respectively), but 60 percent saw emergency preparedness as a problem (EICC 2009). In the sections below, we go further in assessing the auditing done by EICC member companies and the extent to which progress has been made.

IMPLEMENTING RULES: CHALLENGES AND IMPACTS FOR HEWLETT-PACKARD

To understand the implementation of rules for fair and sustainable electronics manufacturing, one of us (Samel) and a fellow group of researchers from the Massachusetts Institute of Technology (MIT) studied a company that has both reasons and resources to comply with standards, Hewlett-Packard.[7] This study of HP's global supply chain is one of very few that have had access to audit results and corporate practices over time, and it has offered a number of insights into how rules are interpreted and implemented on the ground.

At the time of the study (2009), HP ranked ninth on the Fortune 500 list of the United States' top firms by revenue and thirty-second globally, having surpassed the industry's long-time leader, IBM. The company has a large and complex supply chain, which allowed it to ship more than forty-eight million PCs and fifty-two million printers that year (Ward et al., 2010). HP also has a strong corporate culture, reflected in a set of norms known as "The HP Way." Handed down from the firm's founders, "The HP Way" stresses not only factors such as technical contributions, corporate performance, and trust but also the question of "Are the communities in which we operate stronger and the lives of our employees better than they would be without us?" (Collins and Packard 2005, iv). HP has been lauded by various ranking systems: *Newsweek* ranked HP first in its Green Rankings in 2009; *Corporate Responsibility* magazine rated it the best corporate citizen in 2010, and *Fortune* has named it first in social responsibility in the computer industry. HP publishes an annual CSR report and has a board-level committee to oversee the company's global citizenship.

Consistent with this culture, HP employees became early advocates for labor standards. Well before the public exposure of poor working conditions and the formation of the EICC, HP engineers who were supervising the shift of company-owned printer-manufacturing facilities from the United States to overseas were struck by the lack of labor standards on their visits. During one trip they took multiple photographs surreptitiously, which they assembled into an album and distributed internally to provoke a reaction.[8] In response, the company developed its first supplier code of conduct in 2002. As noted above, it was a founder of the EICC and one of the few electronics companies to publicly disclose a list of suppliers. HP has its own internal department to monitor compliance with its code of conduct and group of in-region auditors with engineering backgrounds to oversee audits and work with suppliers. Given HP's resources and commitments, one might expect it to effectively monitor and improve conditions in its supply chain. However, the pitfalls have been substantial.

The Audit Process: Consistency and Biases

HP's social auditors are not full-time auditors but rather members of the company's Global Procurement Services division, based in regional offices around the world. Yet unlike auditors in other industries, they have industrial engineering backgrounds, extensive plant experience, and broad understandings of process engineering. First-time supplier audits usually take two days and make broad use of document reviews, manager interviews, worker interviews, and production line observation. All audits are scheduled in advance, which may give suppliers time to prepare their facilities and coach their employees. Yet this is just one reason why auditing is not as clear-cut as it may initially seem.

Another challenge is that significant violations to one auditor may not seem as egregious to another. Production practices that violate the EICC code are scored as either major or minor violations/nonconformances. Major nonconformances represent systemic issues, including "significant failure in the management system" and "failure of an organization to verify its compliance to applicable laws and regulations."[9] Such major violations may include the employment of underage workers, forced labor, excessive working hours, and safety hazards that pose immediate or serious danger. In contrast, a minor violation is "typically an isolated or random incident" (Locke et al. 2012). Yet consistent with other observations in this book (see especially chapter 3), in practice the line between major and minor violations can be fuzzy and unreliable. Interviews with auditors revealed that they often struggle with the decision between major and minor violations. Furthermore, the MIT team's examination of audit reports found that some violations that were categorized as minor reflected much larger systemic problems in basic working conditions.[10]

For example, one audit report stated that "a tour of the site found that the emergency exits in the manufacturing area are locked."[11] In another factory the auditors noted wage problems: "the performance bonus is [below standards] and the transportation allowance is zero, resulting in a total less than the basic wage requirement . . . and is inconsistent with the information HR management provided to HP auditor."[12] Despite signifying fundamental problems, both of these observations were noted as minor violations. This suggests that the auditing process is biased toward minor violations and assurances of compliance rather than findings of noncompliance.

In addition, auditors rely heavily on documentation of management *processes,* increasing the chances of finding compliance when there may still be behavioral violations. For instance, HP's audits reveal significant improvement in eliminating discrimination in hiring. The rate of compliance increased by 25 percent from the initial to final audit.[13] Yet with no measure for assessing discriminatory *practices,* auditors relied on whether there were explicit, discriminatory statements in hiring advertisements. Initially they found such statements. As one audit reported, "Upon review of [the facility's] recruitment advertisement, it was discovered that it specified age (17–23), height (female: +1.53m; male: +1.65m), vision requirements and colorblind is prohibited."[14] Indeed, gender, age, and height requirements are commonly used in Chinese labor markets (Kuhn and Shen 2013). Yet in a subsequent audit the facility was judged to be compliant with nondiscrimination rules because "the facility has a nondiscrimination policy in place and no discriminatory requirement was found in the recruitment advertisements."[15] But, of course, removing discriminatory language from recruitment materials is different from stopping discrimination. Factories may still discriminate in favor of young women and against older workers or those who are expected to be less docile. One HR manager explained her preference for female workers by explaining that "twenty-year-old men are mischievous."[16] In the factory found to be in compliance, 90 percent of workers were women, which the company claimed was "due to the major production lines needing to have detailed work done by hand."[17] These observations suggest that auditors have difficulty assessing employment discrimination through document review or worker interviews.[18]

Improvement over Time?

Notwithstanding significant efforts by HP and the EICC, analysis of HP's audit reports from 2004 to 2008 reveals persistent problems. At the end of this period nearly 60 percent of audited facilities, including those with follow-up or periodic audits, had routine workweeks longer than sixty hours per week. In 40 percent of the plants, emergency planning, training, and evacuation procedures were poor or nonexistent. Finally, 32.5 percent of audited firms had some troubles with their management of hazardous materials, and 30.2 percent had wage and benefit problems, such as failing to meet the legal minimum or failing to pay the required premium for overtime work.

When these top four violations are examined by year of audit, a clearer picture of improvement (or the lack thereof) begins to emerge. If "best practices" are being promoted by HP and EICC, then we would expect factories to demonstrate improvement over time. However, the rate of audit failure in these four areas tended to increase over time (from 2004 to 2008), with some improvements in wage and benefit requirements occurring more recently. In addition, as factories are subject to more auditing, we might expect to see improvements, whether because of policing, learning, or both. But here too, except when it came to wages and benefits, violations increased. Violations of working-hour limits became especially problematic, occurring at nearly twice the rate of the next most common violation, emergency preparedness (67 percent vs. 35 percent).

It has become clear to many scholars and practitioners that factory auditing mainly generates superficial attempts to "pass" auditors' checklists (as described in the apparel industry in chapter 5). In response, many have argued that lead firms can and should help their suppliers gain deeper capabilities to make their operations both more ethical and more productive (Locke, Amengual, and Mangla 2009; Locke et al. 2007; Sabel 2007). Such capabilities include technical know-how, effective management systems, and inter-viewing/communication skills. Electronics firms, including HP, have initi-ated "capability-building" programs to enhance their management skills and remedy whatever organizational deficiencies might be causing poor working conditions. HP has not only led such initiatives; it has also trained its first-tier suppliers to provide auditing and training deeper into the supply chain.

One of HP's capability-building programs, the Focused Improvement Sup-plier Initiative (FISI), trained hundreds of participants from two electronics-producing regions of China, starting in 2006. The project addressed issues such as overtime reduction, worker-management communication channels, and the implementation of new Chinese labor regulations. By working with managers this project sought to develop management systems to support compliance with EICC standards, responding to the complaint that buyers are more interested in pushing the costs of compliance onto suppliers than in helping them develop systems to ensure future success.

Yet the results of this program have been ambiguous. The twenty-four FISI-participant companies showed modestly improved compliance in the labor and health and safety sections of subsequent audits. But a control group of nonparticipants improved in roughly equal measure.[19] On environmental compliance, FISI participants actually declined slightly over time.

With all of its resources, commitment to CSR, and capability-building programs, why could Hewlett-Packard not improve? Furthermore, if HP could not improve, can we expect improvement from other, less wealthy companies? In the next section we shed light on these questions by looking more closely at one type of violation and the specific industry practices that have made it highly resistant to change.

LOCALIZED GLOBALISMS: WORKING HOURS IN APPLE'S AND HP'S EAST AND SOUTHEAST ASIAN SUPPLIERS

Working hours are the only EICC code item where a specific, substantive standard is stipulated: "A workweek should not be more than 60 hours per week, including overtime, except in emergency or unusual situations." Yet employees in the electronics industry frequently work far more than this. Seventy- to eighty-hour weeks are common, and having onsite dormitories means workers can be woken up to start production in the middle of the night when production schedules demand it (Duhigg and Bradsher 2012). NGOs and scholars regularly cite working-hour violations as a highly significant, recurring issue, often assigning blame to brands (Chan, Pun, and Selden 2013; Good Electronics 2009; Level Works 2006; Verite 2004). As Jenny Chan and her colleagues (2013) put it, "At the workplace level, very short delivery times imposed by Apple and other multinational corporations make it difficult for suppliers to comply with legal overtime limits" (111). Brands' executives do not necessarily disagree. In a 2008 survey an extraordinary 90 percent of EICC members admitted that excessive working hours are their major ongoing challenge (EICC 2009).

An examination of HP's working-hour violations by region reveals the most frequent violations, more than 83 percent, occur in Chinese plants. This is consistent with other research on Chinese labor issues (Pun 2005; Yu 2008a). Apple has not fared any better. While Apple has just started to cooperate with outside researchers (Heisler 2013), a review of their "Supplier Responsibility" reports demonstrates problems similar to those at HP. Sixty percent of Apple's audited facilities had excess working-hour problems in 2010, and this percentage did not improve in 2011. In 2012 the Apple Supplier Responsibility report explicitly discussed this persistent problem: "We continue to address excessive working hours, and this has been a challenge throughout the history of our program. While this problem is not unique to Apple, we continue to fight it." Eliminating excessive working hours is not an insignificant undertaking, since as the FLA report on Apple pointed out, monthly overtime hours would need to be reduced from an average of eighty to thirty-six in order to strictly comply with Chinese labor law (Fair Labor Association 2012).

How can one explain the persistence of excessive working hours in the electronics industry? It would be tempting to look for explanations from within the factories, perhaps focusing on the productivity of workers, their desire to maximize income, or the harsh militaristic styles of production managers. While there can be a tendency to "look for the keys under the lamppost," the shared problems of HP and Apple point in a different direction. We argue that practices further afield—particularly, where design, product development, and consumer purchasing occur—cascade powerfully at the point of production. In the context of highly dynamic consumer and retail markets, brands' strategies have produced a very particular architecture of production and organization of work.[20]

Consumer Markets, Production Practices, and Their Cascading Effects

The electronics industry has become increasingly dependent on fast-moving consumer markets. Since the advent of the personal computer, the industry evolved from being primarily a supplier to companies and governments to being dependent on consumer markets. Consumer markets breed "disruptive innovation" and encourage firms to advance the technological frontier while reducing costs in order to prevent "disruption from below" (Christensen 1997). To maximize market share over short product life cycles, retailers engage in constant promotions to drive down selling prices. With an average product life cycle of eight months, prices may drop as often as every two months. This price erosion, along with the need to carry a broad product assortment, means retailers have no appetite for large inventories. Instead they opt for frequent shipments to meet consumer demand (Leinbach and Bowen, 2004). Of course, brands and retailers do not want to find themselves out of stock if a product is successful, since consumers may choose a competitor if their own product is no longer available.

This balancing act is complicated by the concentration of electronics retailing. As noted earlier, the top four companies in the European and US consumer electronics and computer retail distribution channels control most of the market—more than 50 percent in Europe and closer to 75 percent in the United States. Their market power allows retailers to maintain their own profit margins and force price reductions on brands as products move through their life cycles. Retailers also seek to differentiate products to minimize comparison shopping, which is facilitated by the Internet. This means that brands often make small changes to the functionality of products to disguise similarities between the offerings of rival retailers. This thin differentiation of products leads to a constant parade of new product introductions, punctuated by rapid phase-outs. In 2010 HP maintained more than two thousand different SKUs (stock-keeping units) for laser printers, more than fifteen thousand for servers and storage equipment, and more than eight million possible configure-to-order combinations in its desktop and notebook product lines (Ward et al. 2010).

These practices create great uncertainty within the industry. Buffeted by rapidly changing technology, volatile consumer demand, and powerful retail customers, electronics brands seek to optimize supply chain management practices to remain competitive. In research conducted by Riikka Kaipia and her colleagues (2006) on demand and production volatility in the production of a major European mobile phone brand, it was determined that even with a relatively linear increase in demand in stores, equipment manufacturers faced extreme volatility in demand. They had to cope with production changes of up to 80 percent on a week-by-week basis. They would hold their inventory and ship it on an as-needed basis, but often only after wholesale prices had already dropped. Kaipia and her fellow researchers present this dynamic as a classic bullwhip effect, where fluctuations become progressively amplified throughout the supply chain. The consequences of this bullwhip effect, including excess inventories and late deliveries, can add to costs and weaken companies' reputations.

The electronics industry has sought to manage these supply chain challenges through three broad strategic responses: (1) modular product design, (2) production of buffer inventories of intermediates, and (3) postponement of final assembly until signaled by "pull-based" ordering systems. First, products (computers, printers, and mobile phones) are designed with standardized, substitutable components that can be assembled when necessary into common modules. Second, these components and modules, known as "intermediates," have separate production schedules, which allows for the buildup of buffer inventories. These can be reallocated across different products during final assembly depending on consumer demand at the moment. Finally, assembly of finished goods is postponed until accurate demand signals are available. This triggering of orders is known as "pull-based" ordering due to the dependence on consumer demand, as measured by point-of-sales data, to release orders into a production system. Thus, if one model of phone does not sell well, the components ordered for it may be used in other phones. However, once a phone is built, it must be sold at an acceptable price or, if not, heavily discounted to clear the inventory—the "sour milk" in Apple CEO Tim Cook's terminology (Satariano and Burrows, 2011). In the contemporary electronics industry, final products have significantly higher costs than just the sum of their parts because of the threat of rapid obsolescence. Yet postponement reduces the risks of holding unsold finished goods.

Although these practices mitigate risks for brands and retailers, they create volatility in the manufacturing process and, we argue, generate many of the labor problems that have plagued HP, Apple, and others. A by-product of pull-based systems is that demand volatility is magnified at the final point of assembly. As brands postpone final assembly for as long as possible, production volumes exhibit period spikes of 300–500 percent over baseline levels. This is further amplified by new product introductions that require large ramp-ups and by the difficulty of projecting whether a product will be successful. Brands and suppliers recognize the need to plan for volatility, and HP has sought to optimize capacities in this area by encouraging its supply chain professions to publish their research in scholarly journals. But even with this effort, the bullwhip can sting. During the introduction of new HP ink jet printer, adjusted low and high forecasts varied as much as 250 percent, amounting to a difference of five hundred thousand units. For a factory, going from the bottom end of this forecast to the top would require the hiring of roughly eight thousand additional employees within one to two months, most of whom would need to be released three to four months later as the product's short life cycle ended (Locke and Samel 2012).

From the Dynamics of Production to the Factory Floor

In the MIT study of factories in Southeast Asia (in Malaysia, Thailand, and Singapore) that are suppliers for HP, the vast majority had working-hour violations in 2007.[21] Closer analysis reveals that all of the violations occurred in plants with high unit volumes and a relatively small mix of different products. In interviews, managers often cited the management of working hours as the most significant problem they face. They all employed large numbers of short-term "agency" or contract workers to smooth production. These workers, who are overwhelmingly migrants, routinely exceeded 60 percent of a plant's total workforce.

Volatility in manufacturing is not new; it has a long history in an array of industries (see Katz and Sabel 1985). But it is being managed in a unique way in today's electronics industry. Here, manufacturing processes are an odd amalgam of "lean production" principles and traditional Taylorist work practices. Originating in the early twentieth century and named after its main proponent, Frederick Winslow Taylor, Taylorism—or "scientific management" of the work process—splits manufacturing into many small, standardized, repeatable, and meticulously timed tasks. In electronics, pull-based ordering and the postponement of final assembly demand a high degree of flexibility and adaptation, as plants need to scale up and down quickly. In principle, automation might help to manage volatility, but this approach would run the same risk that mass producers in an earlier era faced: that capital-intensive equipment is underutilized when orders are low. Thus, contract manufacturers combine lean manufacturing techniques with large-scale hand assembly and a Taylorist division of labor, both reminiscent of a bygone era. This style of work is common not only in the factories in the MIT study but also in electronics plants throughout East and Southeast Asia, and it is especially pronounced in plants with high-volume, low-variety production schedules (Lüthje 2002; McKay 2006). In his study of electronics plants in the Philippines, Steven McKay (2006) found that companies staffed their Taylorist workplaces by taking advantage of segmented labor markets, and especially by hiring young women who were marginalized in local labor markets and willing to work for low wages.

Nearly all of the Southeast Asian manufacturers in the MIT study used conveyer assembly lines, in which operators are fixed in place and the product travels past them. Each assembly station involved work tasks of between twenty and thirty seconds. Depending upon the sophistication of the product, lines consisted of eighty to two hundred workers and could be altered rapidly to meet demand. Most managers were aware of alternative "cell assembly" options, and one plant used both approaches when possible. But roughly 95 percent of employees worked on conveyor assembly lines. Plant managers explained that this Taylorist form of work organization permits very short training periods for new operators, further contributing to their ability to expand and contract production quickly. Furthermore, the vast majority of engineers in these factories were process engineers, focused on maximizing efficiency in the assembly line.

Their strategy for maximizing efficiency depends heavily on the flexible use of labor. Firms periodically hire and shed large numbers of contingent workers, largely drawn from the ranks of migrants from other parts of the country (in Thailand and China) or other countries (in Malaysia and Singapore). Employee turnover at these plants is high, and mobility between factories is facilitated by the common work organization of conveyor assembly. Most assembly line operators are women migrant workers, hired on two-year contracts. Because of volatility, factories break their labor contracts on a regular basis (Bormann, Krishnan, and Neuner 2010; Good Electronics 2009).

But adding and shedding new workers on a large scale is costly and difficult, so managers must also squeeze more hours out of their existing workers and cut their hours when production declines. Research on Apple's main supplier in China, Foxconn, helps to put this problem in perspective. As one senior Foxconn official explained,

> When a company like Apple or Dell needs to ramp up production by 20 percent for a new product launch, Foxconn has two choices: hire more workers or give the workers you already have more hours. When demand is very high, it's very difficult to hire 20 percent more people. Especially when you have a million workers—that would mean hiring 200,000 people at once. (qtd. in Chan, Pun, and Selden 2013, 108)

As this suggests, the system that promotes extreme working hours is not unique to HP's suppliers. Indeed, the managers interviewed in the MIT study indicated that their organization of work—conveyer assembly and rapid scaling up and down—was independent of any specific brand that they were working with. Furthermore, they explained that their usual schedule of two twelve-hour shifts often had to be expanded from five to six or seven days per week to meet production deadlines. For their part, migrant workers in East and Southeast Asia often seek to maximize their earnings by working overtime whenever possible.[22]

Given this architecture of production, contract manufacturers' main way of staying profitable is to squeeze as much as possible out of the work process, leading to an interlinked set of labor problems—namely, excessive working hours and reliance on contingent workers. This architecture of production limits brands' and manufacturers' inventory risks, but it also limits the opportunity for contract manufacturers to take other paths to profitability (Clark, Kraemer, and Dedrick 2009). It is clear that there is a deep contradiction between the idea of limiting working hours, along with the standards that HP and Apple have adopted on this, and the structure and dynamics of electronics production.

State Support for Industrial Development (Not Labor Laws)

As discussed earlier, since electronics factories are more difficult to move than are apparel factories, we might expect governments to play a role in limiting working hours. Workweeks of seventy to eighty hours exceed not only the standards of EICC and major electronics brands but also the standards of labor law throughout East and Southeast Asia. Many scholars and practitioners have argued that private, voluntary standards are needed precisely because governments do not have the capacity to enforce their own labor laws (e.g., Sabel, O'Rourke, and Fung 2000). Yet others have argued that private initiatives must be complemented by government action (Locke 2013; Weil 2004) and that some states have developed the capacity for effective enforcement (Piore and Schrank 2008; Schrank 2013).

Notably, however, our research on the electronics industry suggests that excessive working hours persist in factories operating in both strong and weak regulatory environments. For example, in Singapore, a country with strong regulatory institutions and high wages, excessive working hours were readily observed in local electronics assemblers (Locke and Samel, 2012). This finding is not surprising given that Singapore has historically used a foreign-worker levy scheme to facilitate the availability of significant numbers of foreign migrant workers at lower wages. Like migrant workers elsewhere, low wages and available hours create ample incentive for excess overtime. In nominally weaker states, government officials have regular access to electronics plants and thus arguably access to information regarding labor practices. For example, Malaysian and Thai policy makers routinely visit plants to discuss ways of cooperating in order to enhance compliance with national labor laws and the EICC. Yet these plants manifest repeated violations.

As it turns out, growing their electronics industry, not regulating it, motivates policy makers in emerging economies. To support the industry a range of different types of governments have converged in support of flexible labor markets. As McKay (2006) argues, firms have often convinced local officials in the Philippines to suppress labor organizing, which, they argued, would reduce competitiveness because of higher wages, workers who are less compliant, and the threat of disruption. Reflecting on this dynamic, McKay

sheds light on how developmental states come to promote flexibility at the
cost of labor standards:

> When I began this research, I was struck by what seems to me a great potential for devel-
> oping country workers to organize collectively in one of the world's leading industries.
> The industry, after all, consists of high-profile multinationals, sensitive to disruption that
> employs nearly all permanent workers. But I soon found that the firms—and their ac-
> complices in the Philippine state—recognize this potential far more clearly than workers,
> and accordingly take active steps to head off potential collective worker action both inside
> and outside the plants. (226)

This approach, however, may have negative unintended consequences for
developmental states. In the Penang, Malaysia, semiconductor cluster, successful local firms were able to use flexible labor markets to increase their
profits. But their management routines discouraged technological upgrading, which was the stated objective of the government's support for the industry (Samel 2012). In the absence of clear developmental benefits, there might
be rationales for governments to move away from active support for highly
flexible labor markets and perhaps even to tighten labor market regulations.
The Chinese government has begun to do this in the Pearl River Delta region,
where it has encouraged rising wages and more aggressively enforced regulations in order to encourage industrial upgrading (Oster 2011). Whether this
could occur in other countries that host electronics manufacturing remains
to be seen.

CONCLUSION

While the other industries highlighted in this book are also large, none are
as fast-moving and dynamic as electronics. The investments both brands
and manufacturers have made in building the capacity to introduce new
technology at a scale of millions of units makes change incredibly difficult
to bring about. The architecture of electronics production, honed by decades
of growing competition and shrinking product life cycles, has created a system of work organization that appears to be both exploitative and resistant
to change.

Where does this leave conscientious consumers who care about labor conditions in global industries? It is relatively unreflective consumer demand,
for rapidly changing new devices, that has fueled the existing system. As

the Jemima Kiss quote at the beginning of this chapter implies, provenance does not appear to be an important purchasing consideration for electronics, especially when contrasted with performance, network effects, design, and technological innovation. Yet attention to "conflict minerals" has fueled some change in the electronics industry, so perhaps a wave of consumer concern could also transform labor conditions in manufacturing. For the most part, our analysis suggests that the current system of production will be quite resistant to change. It is "locked in" by the dominant system of innovation and retailing.

Yet there are several avenues worth considering. First, arguably, some brands should be more capable of improving conditions than others. Apple, for instance, is the market leader, sells a relatively small assortment of products, and owns its own retail stores, giving it better control of inventory planning. Apple's recent engagement with the FLA and labor standards scholars suggests that the company has abandoned its earlier strategy of largely ignoring its critics. But it is not yet evident if the company's new commitments will lead to sustainable changes, particularly as Apple faces threats to its platform leadership.

Second, there is a small movement, led by a Dutch social enterprise, to produce a phone that is both free of conflict minerals and produced under fair working conditions. The company promotes the product, appropriately named the Fairphone, as being made by workers who are paid fair wages and as offering an open "future-ready" design so that it can be updated rather than replaced.[23] The initial production runs will be small—just 25,000 phones in an industry that sold 1.75 billion phones in a single year (Gartner 2013). The availability of Google's Android operating system, a competitor to Apple's iOS platform, enables this effort. Without a technologically sophisticated offering, it is doubtful that "alternative" electronics could gain any traction. Yet even if it meets this condition, Fairphone acknowledges it faces challenges in production. For example, because its production occurs on only one or two lines of a much larger factory, Fairphone is reluctant to offer higher wages to just a small group of workers. Instead it will place funds in a welfare account that can be distributed to all workers in this factory.[24] This is far from perfect, but it is an improvement. The more important questions are how often consumers will insist on new models and how big the company's volume will be. If production remains small and model development is infrequent, then perhaps a fair device is possible. But if scale or speed increases substantially, then Fairphone will find it challenging to remain true to its founding ideals.

A third avenue involves changes in the relationship between developmental states and the electronics industry. As described above, the high expectations of states have sometimes been met with the reality of limits on technological spillovers and industrial upgrading of electronics assemblers. This may give NGOs and conscientious consumers a new ally: the host country governments. As we have seen, leading brands have been able to push market uncertainty down to the employees at final assembly. In addition to poor working conditions, this has also restrained skill and capability building among local firms (Samel 2012). Governments may push back against this regime by tightening labor markets; allowing wages to rise; and enforcing laws on wages, hours of work, and industrial pollution. While the active involvement of the state in reducing labor market flexibility is nascent, it may be the best hope that conscientious consumers have for bringing about robust improvement in the electronics industry.

CONCLUSION

Beyond Conscientious Consumerism

IS "SHOPPING WITH A CONSCIENCE" A PROMISING OR PAINFULLY wrongheaded way to bring about social change? Debates over this question have been vibrant and often heated. But to date they have rarely been informed by research on the implementation of standards in global industries. Celebrants and critics have argued about the politics of conscientious consumerism, but they have left the work of figuring out what lies "behind the label" to other sets of scholars, or ignored it entirely. Our goal has been to mobilize a wide range of evidence to bridge this gap. We have documented patterns in conscientious consumer behavior, proposed an interpretation of it, and developed a series of case studies of global industries, helping to answer the question of whether standards created to please (or appease) conscientious consumers actually make a difference "on the ground." In this chapter we briefly take stock of our findings, identify some overarching patterns in the case studies, and discuss what we see as useful paths forward for both conscientious consumers and scholars of conscientious consumption.

We began our analyses by examining patterns of boycotting and buycotting by European and American consumers. Among other implications, these analyses challenged the image of conscientious consumerism as a fully individualized identity project of "sovereign" consumers. It is true that individuals who prioritize post-materialist values and have a strong sense of personal political efficacy are more likely than others to be conscientious consumers. But a variety of social structures also matter—from gender, income, and social class to cross-national economic opportunity structures.

This rough sketch of consumers then led us to a deeper interpretation of consumer behavior and its sociopolitical implications. Our interpretation, as developed in chapter 2, emphasized that consumer demand for "alternative" products is often, though not always, bound up with self-interest and perceived private benefits (e.g., improved health or energy cost savings). Furthermore, we argued, conscientious consumerism can take self-serving, exclusionary, antiegalitarian, and counterproductive forms. The ideology of conscientious consumerism, which glosses over all of this to paint a rosy picture of shopping to save the world, must be rejected. Yet practices of conscientious consumption, if divorced from this ideology, might still be useful in promoting fairness and sustainability. There is evidence to suggest that individuals can sometimes act as hybrid citizen-consumers who make conscientious consumption part of a repertoire of political engagement.

In part 2 we looked more closely at standards for fairness and sustainability in four global industries. Notably, the standards covered here do not have obvious private benefits for consumers, so an analysis of their emergence and effectiveness is especially important. Our four case studies do not capture the full gamut of conscientious consumption, but they have allowed us to explore a wide range of issues and locations. Moreover, all four industries make products that consumers use literally every day—clothing, electronics, wood and paper, and food. Even if one just considered sugar and soy, it would be difficult to get through a day without consuming them in one form or another.

Consistent with our approach (as outlined in the introduction), these case studies showed that local sites of implementation are not "empty spaces" that merely receive global standards; they are rich social orders, where global standards layer onto preexisting systems of power, inequality, and governance. Whether looking at the problem of freedom of association in China, agrarian histories in Paraguay, or contentious forest boundaries in Indonesia, it should be clear that national and local circumstances cannot be ignored if one wants to go "behind the label." In addition, the standards that have arisen in these industries vary in their stringency and independence, but it takes more than simple designations of "greenwash" or "fairwash" to understand them. Reasonably credible labels have often fallen short of their goals, and initiatives led by companies and industry associations have increasingly used at least some external auditing to check compliance rather than merely asserting it through public relations campaigns.

This tour of four global industries has taken us across a wide swath of terrain not only in terms of production locations in Asia and South America but also in terms of the array of products, rule-making initiatives, dynamics of implementation, and countervailing trends. Table C1 summarizes some of the key features of our four industry cases. The rough characterizations in this table assist in integrating information and comparing cases, although they are not meant to replace the more nuanced findings in the chapters.

Looking at the making of wood and paper products in chapter 3, we saw how the FSC became the most credible certifier of the world's forests and labeler of sustainable forest products, despite initially low levels of consumer demand. The FSC found enough support from retailers, foundations, and governments to survive competition with an industry-based competitor. But this has not been sufficient to halt deforestation. The FSC label has grown in the marketplace, especially on paper products. But certification at the forest level has been messier than the label implies, and it has often been incapable of preserving endangered ecosystems and ensuring the rights of forest-dwelling communities.

One reason for the limited impact of forest certification is that forests are being converted to agricultural uses. In chapter 4 we unpacked the structure of agri-food value chains and honed in on two models of standard setting in this industry: the commodity roundtables (like RTRS and RSPO) and fair trade. Looking closely at sugar and soy production in Paraguay, we argued that fair trade certification, despite some shortcomings (and some recent drift away from its original rationale), can help smallholder farmers upgrade their capacities and increase their competitiveness. The commodity roundtable approach, in contrast, may promote CSR in the agribusiness industry

Table C1. Key Features of Four Industries

	Wood and paper	Food	Apparel and footwear	Electronics
Products emphasized in chapters	Sawn wood and plywood, furniture, wood pulp, paper (office paper, books, magazines/catalogs, paperboard packaging)	Sugar, soy (input for production of pork, chicken, beef, oils, various processed foods)	Clothing (mass-market, high-fashion, university-licensed), athletic footwear	Smartphones, personal computers, monitors and TVs, printers
Key actors in GVCs (most powerful firms bolded)	**Home improvement and furniture retailers** **Pulp and paper manufacturers** Furniture manufacturers Lumber manufacturers Timber traders Logging companies	**Super- and hyper-market retailers** **Food manufacturing brands** **Agribusiness firms (processors and input-suppliers)** Smallholder farmers	**General and specialty apparel retailers** **Branded manufacturers and branded marketers** Sourcing companies Contract manufacturers	**Big box retailers** **Electronics and computer brands** Contract manufacturers/assemblers Manufacturers of "intermediates"
Focal problems of rule-making projects	Environmental degradation, deforestation, rights of forest-dwelling communities	Livelihoods of smallholder farmers, environmental degradation, rights of communities	Exploitation of workers	Exploitation of workers, conflict minerals, health and safety hazards
Central rule-making initiatives (and their initiators)	FSC (NGO-retail coalition) PEFC (industry associations)	Fair trade (NGOs) Commodity roundtables: RTRS and RSPO (manufacturer-NGO coalitions)	FLA, SAI, ETI (varied brand coalitions) WRAP, BSCI (industry associations) WRC, FWF (NGOs)	EICC (brands) Firm-specific CSR programs

On-product labels?	Yes	Yes	No	No
Extent of conscientious consumption	Modest	Substantial (fair trade)	Modest	Very little
Impacts of production standards	Varied (strict but uneven)	Limited (commodity roundtables) Significant (fair trade)	Limited (marginal and unreliable)	Limited (persistent problems)
Reasons for persistent unruliness	Conversion to agriculture, illegal logging	Rapid expansion	High mobility, price pressure, poor auditing	Short product cycles, high demand for flexibility

but ends up marginalizing small farmers and ignoring alternative models of production.

Turning from food to clothing, we examined the rise and limited effects of codes of conduct, factory auditing, and certification in the apparel and footwear industry. Chapter 5 illustrated not only the role of different constituencies in driving different rule-making projects, but it also vividly illustrated the puzzle of rules: after almost two decades of rule making and auditing, apparel production is still quite unruly, as seen in its mobility and in recent deadly accidents. Anti-sweatshop campaigns awakened consumers to global labor exploitation, but the improvements that have occurred have been small or offset by the industry's movement to new locations.

In chapter 6 we examined how similar concerns about labor conditions have arisen in the global electronics industry, especially in the past several years. In this industry, conscientious consumption has been slow to emerge, and unreflective consumerism has fueled a dynamic system of production that demands highly flexible labor markets and sometimes extremely long working hours. This industry seemingly has the resources, and perhaps even some of the will, to improve conditions. But despite some progress in tracking "conflict minerals," the industry has remained stuck in an architecture of production that impedes significant progress on labor standards in the assembly process.

Across all of these industries, we have seen that the impacts of production standards are less than their backers claim. Simple images of "sweat-free" factories, fair distributions of profit, and sustainable resource use bear little resemblance to the sites of production that we have studied. That said, it would be wrong to conclude that nothing has changed. Indeed, each chapter points out some progress that has been made and some ways in which voluntary standards have contributed. But even the most credible standards are not guaranteed to improve production conditions. Their effects depend on a number of other circumstances, from local institutional arrangements to particular structures of production. In addition, even the most credible voluntary standards are essentially powerless to affect larger trajectories of economic development, such as the conversion of forests to agricultural land, the rise of large-scale, mechanized soy production, or the globetrotting character of the apparel industry.

Our case studies also suggest that consumer markets must be seen as part of the problem, not just a potential solution. Despite the growth of conscientious consumption, there is a great deal of unreflective consumerism behind the exploitation of workers and environments around the world. This is clearest in the electronics industry, where consumers' taste for ever newer products fuels the short product life cycles (to avoid the "sour milk" problem) and rapid churning of styles. It is striking how rarely conscientious consumers have questioned the consequences for workers. The same individuals who demand organic food and fair trade coffee are often all too eager to scoop up the next smartphone.

REVISITING THE ROUGH GUIDE

With these comparative cases in mind, we can revisit the "rough guide" developed in our introductory chapter. There we suggested that one could understand conscientious consumption and production projects by focusing on four factors: (1) global-local linkages (globalized localisms and localized globalisms), (2) the "puzzle of rules," (3) constituencies behind standards, and (4) structures of consumption and production. Each of these factors has been illustrated explicitly in the four main chapters in part 2. Recall from our analysis of agri-food production, for instance, how domestic political histories and local institutional structures have created distinct "localized globalisms" in the global value chains for sugar and soy. More broadly, "globalized localisms" have fueled the proliferation of standards for fair and sustainable food, as illustrated by the globalization of fair trade out of earlier local attempts to support farming cooperatives in particular countries.

When it comes to the "puzzle of rules"—that is, the simultaneous explosion of rules and unruliness—recall the analysis of the apparel industry, where a variety of rule-making projects has arisen but where the industry nevertheless remains footloose in search of low wages. Similar stories of unruliness, although with less geographical mobility, characterize the rapid scaling up and down in electronics, the rise of illegal logging networks, and the expansionary logic of commodity agriculture.

Perhaps our most basic point is that standards, labels, and other assurances arise from the priorities of particular constituencies. Recall the example of the apparel and footwear sector, where some rule-making projects are tailored to the interests of heavily branded firms, others spring from the needs of their less branded competitors, and still others represent labor rights activists' attempts to set a high bar for compliance. This is a fragmented field of rule making (Fransen and Conzelmann forthcoming), and it is fragmented in large part by competing interests, not just multiple approaches. In the forest products industry, competition is largely between the FSC and PEFC, with the former being largely a coalition of NGOs and retailers and the latter being a coalition of timber manufacturers and landowners. It is tempting to view the proliferation of eco-labels and social labels as simply reflecting a diversity of opinions about what sustainability and fairness mean. But it is crucial to remember that these opinions are rooted in particular interests and agendas. Our point is not to entirely dismiss initiatives that serve industry interests. Programs like the EICC in electronics, BSCI in apparel, and PEFC in timber can sometimes foster small improvements to the existing system of production. But they have shown no capacity to push firms to significantly alter their production methods, and this is not terribly surprising given their origins.

Turning to structures of consumption and production, our case studies provide several new insights. Most fundamentally, while the discourse of conscientious consumerism imagines changes being made through "the global market," our case studies show that markets are structured differently across industries, and that global industries intersect with varied national and subnational political arrangements. Even the features of products, such as the perishability of food, can influence which companies are susceptible to consumer pressure and what kinds of standards emerge. In addition, our case studies reinforce and to some degree revise ideas about industry concentration and global value chains, as we discuss below.

The Contradiction of Concentrated Retailing

First, it is clear that NGOs seeking to make rules for global industries want to leverage the power of large, well-known lead firms in global value chains. We have seen how social movement campaigns or media exposés of Nike, Apple, The Home Depot, and Starbucks, among others, led them to develop or support standards for their suppliers. Naming and shaming well-known firms has certainly attracted public attention to labor and environmental problems, and in some cases it has been used to "make a market" for independently certified products. Large, well-known lead firms and global standard setting would appear to go hand in hand, then. In addition, as the analyses in chapter 1 showed, when a country's retailing structure is concentrated (featuring a small number of large supermarkets/hypermarkets), consumers are more likely to engage in boycotting and buycotting than when retailing is fragmented among many smaller stores. Here again it would appear that mega-retailing and conscientious consumption are highly compatible.

But our case studies suggest that this is not the entire story. There is what might be dubbed the "contradiction of retail concentration." While facilitating product certification and conscientious consumption in some ways, the concentrated power of large retailers also puts downward pressure on prices in global value chains and poses risks for the independence and integrity of certification initiatives. In the apparel industry, Walmart, Kmart/Sears, Target, and Tesco are certainly not alone in pushing down clothing prices, but their scale allows their decisions to ripple broadly, and their sourcing and pricing strategies are what many others in the industry have imitated. In furniture retailing, IKEA's power to demand low prices from manufacturers is similar to Walmart's, and both companies put low prices at the center of their strategy, even though they also both support FSC certification. In electronics, mega-retailers like Best Buy, MediaMarkt, and, more recently, Amazon.com can press brands for lower prices, indirectly facilitating the rapid introduction of new models to forestall falling prices. If low prices were consistent with fair and sustainable production, there would be no problem. But in various ways our case studies have illustrated how intense pressure for low prices (and quick deliveries) leaves suppliers with little space to meet demands for fairness and sustainability.

Furthermore, working with large retailers may allow independent certification initiatives to build their market share, as seen in the mainstreaming of fair trade and FSC certification, but it can also make them more dependent on corporate supporters and lead to a watering down of standards. By some accounts, dependence on large companies is what lies behind fair trade's drift away from smallholder cooperatives, especially the recent moves by Fair Trade USA described in chapter 4 (see Jaffee 2012). As our analysis of the FSC shows, mainstreaming does not necessarily eviscerate stringent standards, but it does require some compromise. Furthermore, when large retailers do support independent certification initiatives, they often end up capturing part of a price premium that conscientious consumers assume goes directly to producers, workers, or communities (see Stecklow and White 2004). The contradiction of concentrated retailing does not have a simple solution, but we hope that both practitioners and future researchers will consider whether in particular situations the benefits of hitching conscientious consumption to large retailers and brands are worth the costs.

Complexity and Buyer-Drivenness of Global Value Chains

In addition, our case studies have illustrated how the complexity of global value chains has muted the effects of production standards. Subcontracting remains common in the apparel industry, yet subcontractors rarely receive the scrutiny that first-tier suppliers do. As evidenced by scandals involving Walmart and the Gap, lead firms may not even fully know where their products are being made, although it is sometimes hard to tell the difference between real and feigned ignorance of subcontracting. In some parts of the timber industry, complex and often illegal timber trading networks have made it difficult for companies like IKEA and JYSK to even trace the sources of raw materials, much less ensure that those sources are sustainable. In electronics, the shift from integrated systems to modular production enabled complex supply chains and the kind of fast competition that demands ultra-flexible labor markets. Some global value chains are simpler, such as those for coffee, some types of lumber, and fresh fruit and vegetables, and this has made it somewhat easier to enforce standards for these products. But it turns out that even products that would appear to have simple links from producer to consumer are increasingly being made by breaking the global value chain into smaller segments so that lead firms can find the lowest-cost providers at each node. For instance, fish are being farmed in Latin America, frozen and shipped to China to be filleted, and then frozen and shipped to grocery stores and restaurants in the United States (see Stringer et al. 2011). The perishability of food puts some limits on this process, so food production will never be as "modularized" as electronics, but the trends in this direction are striking.

Relatedly, our case studies reveal that there has been a partial convergence of global industries on something roughly akin to the "buyer-driven" model of global value chains, seen especially in the growing power of large retailers. But there is significant variation *within* the four industries we have discussed. Recall from chapter 4 that supermarkets have become quite powerful in the production of fresh fruit and vegetables, but for processed foods, manufacturers, processors, and even input providers can be the lead firms. Recall from chapter 3 that retailers have become powerful in the production of lumber and furniture, but they are less powerful in the pulp and paper industry, where large manufacturers remain dominant (even though they are challenged by retailers such as Staples).

In addition, though, it does not appear that global value chains need to be strongly buyer-driven in order for standards for fairness and sustainability of some sort to take hold. The commodity roundtables (e.g., RTRS and RSPO) are mainly geared toward food processors and input suppliers; unlike fair trade, they have not staked their claims on support from retailers and consumers. In the forestry arena the FSC was able to make headway into the pulp and paper industry, although it had to alter its approach to labeling to do so (creating "FSC Mix" and "FSC Recyled" labels). The "buyer-driven" designation has been a powerful conceptual tool for practitioners and scholars of global standards, but the specialized literature on global value chains has moved on to a more elaborate typology of governance structures (e.g., Gereffi et al. 2005). Our case studies show some convergence but also the importance of fine-grained distinctions between global value chains. On the other hand, we suspect that typologies of coordination in global value chains, whether crude or elaborate, are unlikely to determine the shape of rule-making projects for fairness and sustainability. Industry structure is an important variable, but rule-making projects are varied, dynamic, and shaped by a variety of historical and political processes.

LOOKING FORWARD: THREE REMAINING QUESTIONS

When does supporting fairness and sustainability mean promoting alternative models of production?

In many instances, projects to promote fairness and sustainability take the form of standards that are applied to existing structures of production, no matter how unequal or exploitative they are. This is true of most initiatives in the apparel and electronics industries (e.g., FLA, SAI, ETI, BSCI, EICC), the commodity roundtables (RTRS and RSPO), and, in many parts of the world, forest certification (e.g., PEFC and much FSC certification). The best hope from these initiatives is that they can spur managerial improvements: factories can become somewhat safer and more humane, farms can become less destructive to land and more charitable toward local people, and timber harvesting can become less disruptive of local ecosystems.

In contrast, some projects explicitly promote alternative models of production, equating fairness and sustainability with democratically managed cooperatives, community-based forestry operations, or factories organized by independent labor unions. As we have shown, projects of this type invariably originate outside the industry, from NGOs and activists. Standards to support these models are "in the market but not of it," as Peter Leigh Taylor (2005) put it. Fair trade is the clearest example of this sort of standard, even though it (especially Fair Trade USA) has partially drifted away from its original commitment to cooperatives. The origins of the FSC lie in part in attempts to promote community-based forestry projects, and the FSC has certified some community forestry operations in addition to mainstream industrial operations. In the apparel industry, rule making took off primarily without endorsing an alternative production model, yet recently the WRC has supported alternatives such as the unionized Alta Gracia factory in the Dominican Republic. In the electronics industry the recently developed Fairphone project seeks to provide an alternative, although it is not entirely separate from the mainstream production architecture.

Apart from noting that they require support from industry outsiders, what more can be said about the promotion, and possible consumption, of alternative production models? First, our case studies suggest that the likelihood of viable alternatives depends on the characteristics of the industry in at least two ways. To start, there must be a niche that is not being filled by dominant firms. Interestingly, there are theoretical reasons to believe that it is when large, generalist firms dominate a market that the viability of smaller specialists increases.[1] Second, the resource and technical requirements for making the project must be relatively low in order for industry outsiders to be able to construct viable alternatives. We suspect this is one reason that alternative production models are more prominent in agriculture and forestry than in manufacturing. Especially in the case of electronics, resource and technological requirements mean that Fairphone entrepreneurs have to rely on the existing production architecture (i.e., using standard inputs and an assembly factory in China).

Third, however, we should not view the emergence of alternatives only in terms of industry structures. History matters. Alternative production models are not formed out of thin air. They need decades of prior institution building to become viable in global markets. In some ways the consumption of alternatives is made possible by what Marc Schneiberg (2007), in a different context, called the "flotsam and jetsam . . . of abandoned or partly realized institutional projects" (70). Recall that fair trade certification has been able to support cooperatives because of decades of land reform and local organizing projects that came before. Community-based forestry has a similar, though not unblemished, history (see Agrawal 2005). The recent development of the Alta Gracia rested on years of activism at the BJ&B factory in the same location and on larger labor reforms in the Dominican Republic. In some circumstances, conscientious consumption can support alternative forms of production, but those circumstances should not be taken for granted.

Fourth, conscientious consumers should remember that there are serious business risks involved in departing from dominant industry structures. Alternative models for apparel and electronics will have to abandon "fast fashion"/"fast electronics" in order to improve labor conditions, for instance. If conscientious consumers want to support such alternatives, they must provide not merely a premium price but some patience as well, which may mean missing out on the latest fashions and technologies. A "slow goods" movement, akin to the "slow food" movement, may ultimately be required for alternative production models to gain traction.

How can researchers go further in unpacking
conscientious consumption in global industries?

Many questions remain about consumer behavior, production standards, and the connections between them. We hope that researchers can extend our approach to further assess the accomplishments and limits of conscientious consumption. We see three types of tasks as especially important.

To begin, there are additional questions to be asked about consumers. To go beyond the existing survey evidence on boycotting and buycotting, researchers need richer, more nuanced data on what these activities mean to consumers. For instance, boycotting may mean simply avoiding one product and choosing an easy substitute, or it may mean participating in a long-term and costly effort as part of a social movement. Overall, scholars should build more holistic portraits of consumers, putting their occasional conscientiousness about fairness and sustainability in the context of their larger understandings of "morals and markets" (see Fourcade and Healy 2007). More nuanced data—whether through in-depth interviews or more sophisticated survey designs—can also help to identify the conditions under which consumers attach explicitly political, ethical, or mainly self-serving meanings to their purchases, extending or testing our interpretation in chapter 2. Examining consumers outside of Europe and the United States is also important, especially for extending the analysis of how political, economic, and cultural contexts shape conscientious consumption. Remember, however, that evidence based on surveys and interviews has serious limits if one wants to assess consumer behavior. The field experiments described in chapter 2 have provided important findings, and they deserve to be extended into other markets, products, and issues.

Ultimately research on individual consumers can go only so far before it runs into two other crucial types of questions. First, how significant are diffuse consumer tastes and preferences in structuring markets? Scholars have rightly emphasized that organized consumer demand is more powerful than diffuse preferences (Seidman 2007) and have rightly criticized "naïve aggregationist" views of consumer markets (Willis and Schor 2012). But this does not eliminate the possibility that shifts in consumer tastes could in some ways alter industry operations, even though they are not guaranteed to do so. Mass consumer tastes have shaped earlier trajectories of industrialization (see Sabel and Zeitlin 1985) as well as both the rise and decline of the tobacco industry (see Brown et al. 1999; Schudson 1984), so it is worth inquiring into mechanisms by which they might subtly influence global industries.

A focus on consumers also runs into questions about the effectiveness of standards that they might support. After all, consumers can rarely observe the social and environmental implications of a product directly. There is a great need for well-structured research to enrich the kinds of analyses in our industry case studies. We believe that the most promising research designs will be comparative. They may involve comparing similar firms that are and are not subject to scrutiny/standards. They may involve comparing the implementation of standards in different industries, as we have begun to do. Or they may involve comparing the implementation of the same standards in different places. Researchers have begun to take up these tasks, but getting solid evidence on implementation takes great time and effort, so there is much work left to be done. As our case studies have illustrated, private, voluntary rules are not implemented in a vacuum, so we would encourage researchers to take public/state regulation seriously as well. Much can be learned, for instance, by comparing the implementation of public and private regulation on the same issue in a given location (see Amengual 2010).

Taking governments seriously also means doing a better job of linking research on labor and environmental standards with research on development. Our case studies have referenced the role of developmental states, but many questions remain about how government policy and trajectories of industrial innovation influence conditions at the point of production and whether they might accomplish some of the fairness and sustainability goals that have caught the attention of conscientious consumers. Often the priorities of developmental states and transnational corporations are in alignment—for flexible labor markets, rapid scaling up of exports, and containment of popular disruption (e.g., strikes and agrarian movements), for instance. But sometimes governments realize they are getting less than they bargained for, and they begin to adopt reforms that do not serve the needs of transnational corporations. In other words, corporations' desire for "one big market" governed by a logic of neoliberalism may push up against divergent goals from governments in developing countries. As discussed in chapter 6, governments that promoted electronics and the flexible labor markets it required have sometimes begun to question the lack of spillover benefits and to shift toward a tightening of labor markets. To the extent that global industries have heavy investments in a particular place, due to sunk costs or natural resource endowments, such reforms may be promising. Research on the space for developmental states to be strong regulatory states is crucial if we are to move past the impasses of voluntary standards.

What does it mean to shift from an ideology of conscientious
consumerism to a repertoire that includes conscientious consumption?

Finally, it is important to return to our point in chapter 2 in light of the material that has followed. In that chapter we argued that the ideology of conscientious consumerism is vapid and regressive but that specific practices of conscientious consumption might be meaningful and progressive if treated as part of a repertoire of political engagement. Our industry case studies have identified a few positive effects of conscientious consumption, and we hope they can help readers to identify more and less meaningful labels and assurances. Enthusiastic consumers can also consult a growing set of consumer guides, including Goodguide.com's product ratings and *Consumer Reports'* "Greener Choices" guide to food labels. But it is crucial to remember that these guides rely heavily on companies' and labels' *procedures.* Information on their performance is extremely sparse. For some products, consumer guides can make inferences about sustainability based on the species and location of production, as does the Seafood Watch guide produced by the Monterey Bay Aquarium, though the growing complexity of the seafood trade has made a once simple guide increasingly byzantine.

Notwithstanding variation in the impacts of production standards, our case studies have highlighted the need for other approaches, since even the best voluntary standards and assurances make relatively small dents in global industries. These other approaches have included binding as opposed to voluntary agreements, strong local social movements, and reinvigorated governmental regulation. As we argued in our chapter on food, fair trade certification can sometimes be one ingredient for the improvement of smallholders' capacities, but many of the other ingredients come not from consumers but from the domestic political context. Or, as seen in our analysis of deforestation, what neither the FSC nor the RSPO have been able to do is to engage in land-use planning and authoritatively enforce land rights; these tasks require governmental action. In the apparel and electronics industries, some of what private rule-making projects have struggled to do is being accomplished by worker militance and government reform in the coastal areas of China.

So how can conscientious consumers build a repertoire of political engagement that would recognize and support nonconsumerist solutions? There is no easy answer to this question. In fact, the first step may be to recognize that significant social change comes from long-term, hard-fought social movements, supported by sympathetic outsiders but led by committed grassroots activists. In some cases conscientious consumers can become those activists, and in others they can support such movements by contributing to local civil society organizations or well-networked NGOs.

As for other things that citizen-consumers can do to build their repertoires of engagement, we suggest the following: when confronted with concerns about a product's social or environmental implications, do not simply look for an alternative in the market; instead, use the opportunity to find out what policy choices are available to deal with the underlying problem. For instance, one could respond to industrial accidents in the apparel industry by searching for sweat-free clothing. (One could also give preference to companies that have signed the binding Bangladesh Accord on Fire and Building Safety, which might be more productive.) But one should also inquire into how trade policy can be made more supportive of labor rights (as opposed to treating labor standards merely as barriers to trade, as the WTO has done) and make this part of one's political priorities. To take another example, in coming to terms with deforestation's role in exacerbating global warming, one should not simply look for FSC-certified paper and RSPO-certified snacks. One should look for local and national policies that reduce the main causes of global warming—that is, the burning of fossil fuels—and policies that support stronger governance of the world's forests.

In short, a simple narrative about shopping for alternatives has been all too consuming for many scholars and citizens. Romanticized ideologies of conscientious consumerism are harmful. Romanticized images of fair and sustainable products are inaccurate. But hardheaded engagement with the politics of globalization is essential, and perhaps products can be an entry point for that kind of engagement.

APPENDIX

Table A1. Description of Individual-Level Variables

Variable	Mean	(SD)	Description
Dependent variables			
Buycott	0.29	(0.45)	Bought products for political, ethical, or environmental reasons in last 12 months (dummy): 1=yes; 0=no
Boycott	0.18	(0.38)	Boycotted products in the last 12 months (dummy): 1=yes; 0=no
Independent variables			
Female	0.52	(0.50)	Gender (dummy): female=1, male =0
Age	47.15	(17.75)	Age of respondents in years
Education level			Respondents' level of education
primary	0.38	(0.49)	No formal education/primary education
secondary	0.41	(0.49)	Completed secondary education
post-secondary	0.21	(0.41)	Completed post-secondary education
Relative equivalence income			Equivalence household income (new OECD scale) relative to average national household income
less than 50%	0.17	(0.38)	Respondents living in households with equivalence income of less than 50% of average national household income
50–80%	0.22	(0.41)	Respondents living in households with equivalence income of between 50 and 80% of average national household income
80–120%	0.22	(0.41)	Respondents living in households with equivalence income of between 80 and 120% of average national household income
more than 120%	0.22	(0.42)	Respondents living in households with equivalence income of more than 120% of average national household income
missing value	0.18	(0.38)	Respondents did not report household income

Social class		Erickson & Goldthorpe (1992) class scheme.
Higher salariat occupations	0.30 (0.46)	Service class 1 & 2 (Large employers, higher- and lower-grade professionals)
Higher-grade white-collar occupations	0.09 (0.29)	Intermediate occupations
Self-employed, small business owners, farmers	0.10 (0.30)	Self-employed, small employers, and farmers
Higher-grade and supervisory blue-collar occ.	0.20 (0.40)	Lower supervisory and lower technical occupations
Lower-grade white-collar occ.	0.10 (0.31)	Lower services, sales, and clerical occupations
Lower-grade blue-collar occ. & unskilled	0.17 (.38)	Routine occupations
Generalized trust	5.08 (2.46)	Respondents' assessment whether most people can be trusted: coded 1 to 10 (10=most people can be trusted)
Interest in politics	0.51 (0.50)	Respondents' interest in politics (dummy): 1=very or quite interested; 0=hardly or not at all interested)
Trust in political institutions	0 (1.00)	Factor of respondents' trust in political institutions (parliament, legal system, police). (Eigen value: 2.65; all factor loadings higher than 0.75.)
Post-materialism (Self-transcendence values [in Schwartz values scale])	0 (1.00)	Factor score of the following variables: a) Important that people are treated equally and have equal opportunities b) Important to understand different people c) Important to help people and care for others' well-being d) Important to be loyal to friends and devote to people close e) Important to care for nature and environment

Source: European Social Survey, Round 1 Data (2002). N = 26,981 respondents, 19 countries.

Table A2. Description of Country-Level Variables

Variable	Mean	(SD)	Description	Source(s)
Affluence	84.4	(5.7)	100 minus the share of household expenditure spent on food relative to all other expenditure	1999 Household Budget Survey (Eurostat 2010)
Retailing structures	96.41	(88.07)	The average number of small retailers (that is, fewer than 10 employees) for an average from 1999 to 2001 standardized by population size	Structural Business Statistics Database (Eurostat 2009b)
Label supply	0.00	(0.82)	The national supply with eco-, organic, and Fair Trade–labeled goods in the year 2001 measured as the share of organic farmland of all farmland, the number of products with an EU or national eco-label, and the number of retail outlets for fair trade products per country	Willer and Toralf 2004, 118–119; Eurostat, 2009c; Global Ecolabeling Network 2003; Kern et al., 2001;Krier 2001
Statism	0.58	(0.51)	Dummy variable, where 1 indicates "statist" and 0 "societal authority"	Jepperson 2002; Schofer and Fourcade-Gourinchas 2001
Social movement organizations	5.80	(6.74)	Share of people within a country who are members in a peace, human rights, or environmental movement organization	European Value Study (EVS) of 1999/ 2000 (EVS 2011)
Generalized trust	36.75	(17.64)	Share of respondents per country who report that "most people can be trusted"	EVS 2011
Post-materialism	15.76	(6.33)	Share of post-materialists within a country	Inglehart four-question index (EVS 2011)

Table A3. Values of Country–Level Variables

Country	Affluence	Retailing structures	Label supply	Statism	Soc. Movement Orgs.	Generalized trust	Post–materialism
Austria	86.6	53.48	1.44	1	4.64	33.43	28.81
Belgium	86.7	107.56	-0.51	1	7.60	29.22	23.42
Czech Republic	76.8	48.14	0.19	1	2.90	24.55	10.05
Denmark	86.9	54.14	1.28	0	6.00	66.53	16.08
Finland	85.8	24.03	1.19	0	3.98	57.44	11.01
France	84.6	68.09	-0.69	1	1.24	21.35	17.68
Germany	88.9	27.38	0.54	1	0.92	37.53	14.80
Great Britain	89.5	56.73	-0.31	0	1.53	28.85	21.96
Greece	83.4	252.01	-0.88	1	6.71	23.73	16.73
Hungary	75.0	106.23	-0.25	1	0.87	22.35	2.33
Ireland	84.3	48.75	-0.82	0	2.53	35.99	13.07
Netherlands	89.5	66.05	0.01	0	24.09	60.08	22.20
Norway	88.3	23.96	0.55	0	10.88	65.30	11.24
Poland	67.5	84.78	-0.97	1	0.67	18.41	7.07
Portugal	81.3	280.63	-0.78	1	0.93	12.31	10.90
Spain	81.7	318.47	-0.59	1	1.92	36.25	17.21
Sweden	84.6	73.45	1.01	0	9.66	66.32	22.15
Switzerland	89.9	107.56	0.54	0	21.46	36.96	16.77

Table A4. Individual-Level Coefficients from Multilevel
Logistic Regression Models, ESS

Variable	Model 1		Model 2	
	Buycotting		Boycotting	
Constant	−2.70***	(0.21)	−3.31***	(0.23)
Female	0.51***	(0.03)	0.31***	(0.04)
Age	0.02**	(0.01)	0.02***	(0.01)
Age^2	−0.00***	(0.00)	−0.00***	(0.00)
Education level (Ref.: primary education)				
Secondary education	0.45***	(0.04)	0.34***	(0.05)
Post-secondary education	0.82***	(0.05)	0.58***	(0.06)
Social class (Ref.: low blue coll.& unskilled)				
Higher salariat	0.47***	(0.06)	0.35***	(0.06)
Higher-grade white-collar occ.	0.44***	(0.06)	0.27***	(0.07)
Self-emp./small business, farmers	0.33***	(0.07)	0.31***	(0.08)
Higher-grade/supervisory blue-collar	0.27***	(0.06)	0.15*	(0.07)
Lower-grade white-collar occ.	0.25***	(0.06)	0.17*	(0.07)
Relative equivalence income (Ref.: 80–12%)				
less than 50%	−0.16**	(0.05)	−0.10	(0.06)
50–80%	−0.02	(0.04)	−0.08	(0.05)
More than 120%	0.16***	(0.04)	0.06	(0.05)
Missing value	−0.15**	(0.05)	−0.04	(0.06)
Interest in politics	0.50***	(0.04)	0.57***	(0.04)
Trust in political institutions	−0.01	(0.02)	−0.19***	(0.02)
Political efficacy	0.27***	(0.02)	0.32***	(0.02)
Generalized trust	0.13***	(0.02)	0.04+	(0.02)
Self-transcendence values	0.68***	(0.03)	0.55***	(0.03)
Intercept residual variance	0.462	(0.15)	0.554	(0.18)
r_{Deviance}	3643.15***		2114.18***	

Note: Unstandardized regression coefficients, Standard errors in parentheses;
Significance levels: $+ p < 0.10$, $* p < 0.05$, $** p < 0.01$, $*** p < 0.001$.
N=26,981 individuals; 19 countries

Table A5. Individual-Level Coefficients from Multilevel Logistic Regression Models, ESS, and CID

Variable	Model 1		Model 2	
	Buycotting		Boycotting	
Constant	−2.88***	(0.18)	−3.27***	(0.19)
Female	0.48***	(0.03)	0.25***	(0.03)
Age	0.04**	(0.00)	0.03***	(0.00)
Age^2	−0.00***	(0.00)	−0.00***	(0.00)
Education level (Ref.: primary education)				
Secondary education	0.61***	(0.03)	0.46***	(0.04)
Post-secondary education	1.22***	(0.04)	0.94***	(0.04)
Interest in politics	0.79***	(0.03)	0.89***	(0.03)
Trust in political institutions	−0.01	(0.01)	−0.20***	(0.02)
Generalized trust	0.21***	(0.02)	0.13***	(0.02)
Intercept residual variance	0.462	(0.15)	0.554	(0.18)
$r_{Deviance}$	3643.15***		2114.18***	

Note: Unstandardized regression coefficients, Standard errors in parentheses;
Significance levels: $+ p < 0.10$, $* p < 0.05$, $** p < 0.01$, $*** p < 0.001$.
N= 39,768 individuals; 23 countries

Table A6. Country-Level Coefficients from Multilevel Logistic Regression Models, ESS

Variable	Model 3		Model 4		Model 5		Model 6		Model 7		Model 8	
	Buycotting		Boycotting		Buycotting		Boycotting		Buycotting		Boycotting	
Constant	−2.70***	(0.16)	−3.31***	(0.19)	−2.70***	(0.16)	−3.31***	(0.19)	−3.00***	(0.34)	−3.46***	(0.36)
Economic Opp. Structure												
Affluence	0.05**	(0.02)	0.08***	(0.02)	0.06**	(0.02)	0.11***	(0.02)	0.04+	(0.02)	0.07**	(0.03)
Fragmented retailing structure	−0.02+	(0.00)	−0.03+	(0.00)	−0.02*	(0.00)	−0.03*	(0.00)	−0.02+	(0.00)	−0.02	(0.00)
Supply labeled products	0.29*	(0.15)			0.40**	(0.14)			0.20	(0.17)		
Political Opp. Structure												
Statism					−1.54*	(0.74)	−1.43+	(0.85)				
Social Movement Orgs.					0.00	(0.02)	−0.01	(0.02)				
Cultural Opp. Structure												
Post-materialism									0.01	(0.02)	0.01	(0.02)
Generalised Trust									0.01	(0.01)	0.00	(0.01)
Intercept residual variance	0.158	(0.05)	0.237	(0.08)	0.127	(0.04)	0.197	(0.07)	0.150	(0.05)	0.234	(0.08)
$r_{Deviance}$	3663.15***		2110.81***		3667.06***		2114.18***		3664.18***		2111.09***	

Note: Micro-level coefficients are not reported. Standard errors in parentheses.

Significance levels: + $p < 0.10$, * $p < 0.05$, ** $p < 0.01$, *** $p < 0.001$.

N=26,981 individuals, 19 countries

NOTES

1. Ecolabel Index, http://www.ecolabelindex.com.

2. Different initiatives use different versions of the term "fair trade." Throughout this book, we use the generic, lowercase version ("fair trade") when referring to the concept or model in general. When referring specifically to certification by Fair Trade USA (previously known as TransFair USA), we follow that initiative (and many researchers in North America) in capitalizing the term ("Fair Trade"). When referring to certification by Fairtrade International (previously known as the Fairtrade Labeling Organization), we follow that initiative (and many researchers in Europe) in combining the terms ("Fairtrade").

3. Whether a "best in class" or "continuous improvement" model is more central depends in large part on whether the founding constituency of firms seeks to gain a competitive advantage over other companies (in which case the first model is preferable) or seeks to spread the costs of improving industry practice broadly across firms (in which case the second is more attractive) (see Auld [2014] for an analysis of this sort).

4. Furthermore, even within a single initiative there may be a wide range of standards covering environmental issues, labor rights, community rights, and more. As we discuss in the conclusion, it seems that not all standards are implemented equally.

1. THE MAKING OF CONSCIENTIOUS CONSUMERS

1. This is the most recent and highest-quality data available. More information can be found at the European Social Survey website (http://www.europeansocialsurvey.org) and at the Inter-University Consortium for Political and Social Research (http://doi.org/10.3886 /ICPSR04607.v1). Our operationalization of the data as well as the statistical models are described in the appendix.

2. See figure 1.3 for the list of countries.

3. These questions are widely used in survey research, having become the backbone of much writing on "political consumerism." Some support for the validity of the measure, at the aggregate level at least, is provided by the following: at the country level there is a strong correlation (Pearson's $r = 0.804$) between the rate of buycotting and per capita spending on organic food (Koos 2012).

4. Researchers have proposed a variety of explanations for conscientious consumption choices. These mostly focus on motivations and beliefs, and we see our emphasis on opportunities as an important corrective to the voluntarism of much of the research literature.

5. We used hierarchical logistic regression models that allow us to account for the nested structure of the data (individuals within countries).

6. Denmark is the leading country with more than $200 per capita spent on organic food in 2010 (Willer and Kilcher 2012). Sweden ($116), Germany ($99), the United States ($82), and France ($74) are following. People in the UK are second to last in Europe, with $43 spent on organic food in 2010, followed by Spain ($27). Belgium and the Netherlands assume a middle ground, with a bit more than $50 per person spent on organic food.

7. This is just a small sampling of the criticism of the fair trade system. Critics have raised numerous questions about who is able to get into the system at all, whether premiums actually reach farmers, and whether the system undermines self-sufficiency or distorts market forces. In chapter 4 we provide a closer look at fair trade certification in agriculture. Our research there suggests that the fair trade model can be effective, but whether it actually is depends crucially on local circumstances.

8. These results reflect average predicted probabilities based on our analyses of ESS data.

9. Overall, researchers have tended to find rather mixed results regarding trust in institutions (e.g., Goul Andersen and Tobiasen 2004; Stolle et al. 2005; Strømsnes (2005).

10. Scholars of political engagement have distinguished between *external political efficacy,* which has to do with the perceived responsiveness of the political system, and *internal political efficacy,* which refers to individuals' sense of personal competence (Craig et al. 1990).

11. See Smith (2014) for a new approach to comparisons of this sort.

12. Our results in this section come only from the European sample. All models control for the individual factors discussed above. The result tables can be found in the appendix.

13. One might also consider states' roles in governing conscientious consumption itself. In some countries the state has played a vital role in initiating eco-labels in cooperation with NGOs—for instance, the US state label for organic food (USDA organic)—and state involvement in labeling is believed to positively affect conscientious consumption (Crespi and Marette 2005). The reason for this is that states often have a higher claim to legitimacy as regulatory agents and also have more resources than private NGOs to promote and control the label and sanction "greenwashing." The empirical results for state involvement are rather mixed. While Sebastian Koos (2011) does not find any support for the impact of state labeling across a large set of European countries, Carsten Daugbjerg and Kim Mannemar Sønderskov (2012) show in a comparison of the United States, UK, Sweden, and Denmark, that state labeling seems to have a positive impact on market development.

14. To be sure, supply and demand co-evolve, and it is difficult to disentangle them. But keep in mind that our measure of supply is focused on particular types of products, while our measure of conscientious consumption is broad-based.

15. Although one might argue that this is due to the high correlation between post-materialism and affluence, both measures used here are not strongly correlated.

16. A similar pattern can also be observed for boycott behavior. Note that we do not have evidence for this kind of interaction between post-materialism and income at the individual level.

2. THE DILEMMAS OF CONSCIENTIOUS CONSUMERISM

1. Based on information from RESOLVE (2012) and www.ecolabelindex.com.

2. The countries are Belgium, Denmark, France, Germany, Netherlands, Spain, Sweden, and the United Kingdom.

3. Larger percentages said they had done these things at least once in the past year, but the gaps remain, with around 25 percent more students saying they had bought an organic item than saying they had bought something for political, environmental, or ethical reasons.

4. This research focuses on the United States (Dickson 2001; Lourerio and Lotade 2005), Europe (De Pelsmacker, Driesen, and Rayp 2005), and Australia and Hong Kong (Auger et al. 2003, 2008). The type of premium analyzed varies by study, which makes comparisons difficult. In fact, several studies do not estimate the size of premium that consumers would be willing to pay. Instead they use the analysis of the relative value that respondents place on product attributes in their survey/experiment to extrapolate the likelihood of future purchasing decisions. For instance, Pat Auger and his colleagues (2003) claim that "the average consumer in our sample is quite willing to pay a significant percentage of the value of the product for specific ethical features" (299). However, they analyze "purchase intentions," not actual purchases of products in real market settings.

5. See Arnot et al. (2006) on willingness to pay (WTP) for Fair Trade–labeled coffee in a university coffee store, Hiscox and Smyth (2006) for WTP for luxury home goods with an ethical production label, and Hiscox et al. (2011) for WTP premiums on Fair Trade coffee beans on eBay.

6. The label specifically said "A Fair Price to Support Fair Trade."

7. The label for the control condition read "Support Fair Trade."

8. Those who had boycotted in the past year scored about a half a point lower than others on a five-point scale of agreement with that statement, controlling for political views and a number of other factors.

3. WOOD AND PAPER PRODUCTS

1. This estimate is based on our analysis of FAOStat data, available at http://faostat.fao.org.

2. See Dauvergne and Lister (2011) for much more on these companies.

3. IKEA's enormous scale has led it to invest in its own factories to produce particleboard and some of them to manufacture furniture. IKEA has also led the way in pushing some of the costs of production onto consumers themselves (the "prosumer" model), who must assemble the furniture sold in flat packs.

4. Some companies (e.g., International Paper and Weyerhaeuser) have been selling off their timber holdings in recent years, while others (e.g., Stora Enso) continue to expand their own timber plantations (Stringer 2006).

5. Interview with NGO representative, United States, March 8, 2004.

6. Interview with NGO representative, United States, March 17, 2004.

7. Interview with FSC founder, United States, July 22, 2002.

8. Interview with retail executive, United States, March 24, 2004.

9. Interview with auditor, Beijing, July 14, 2011; interview with auditor, Beijing, March 14, 2014; analysis of public summaries of audit reports.

10. The EU Timber Regulation requires companies that introduce timber products into the European market to exercise "due diligence" in ensuring legality in their supply chains.

The Lacey Act uses a somewhat similar standard of "due care" and puts sellers of wood products at risk of having products seized if they can be traced to illegal logging operations. See Bartley 2014b for more information.

11. Interview with auditor, Jakarta, September 20, 2010.

12. They found, for instance, that "though the details [of a corrective action related to Reduced Impact Logging (RIL), a more sustainable harvesting method] have been addressed there were issues beyond the scope of the specific focus of this verification audit that need to be noted," and they went on to describe further weaknesses in the RIL system (SmartWood 2008c, 3–4).

13. Interview with forestry researcher, Bogor, June 30, 2008; interview with NGO representative, Jakarta, September 21, 2010.

4. FOOD

1. We do also discuss the evidence regarding fair trade and organic certification of coffee, referencing a growing body of work that interested readers can consult. There is also some research on fair trade flowers, found, for instance, in Lyon and Moberg (2010) and Dolan (2007).

2. Three factors account for the stagnation of food demand in affluent countries. First, as household incomes rise, demand for food does not rise proportionally, meaning that, over time, continued economic growth drives smaller and smaller increases in total food demand. Second, affluent countries exhibit low and declining rates of population growth. Third, the rate of economic growth in affluent countries has also gradually declined, limiting demand growth in general.

3. Between 1989 and 2007 the total personal consumption expenditures of the top 5 percent of income earners in the United States grew at a rate of 5.2 percent versus 2.8 percent for the rest of the US population. Since the 2007 recession the consumption behavior of the wealthy has strongly diverged from the rest of households. While consumption collapsed among the bottom 95 percent of earners, it held steady and then rebounded with the renewed income growth in the top 5 percent. See Cynamon and Fazzari 2014.

4. This dynamic has been central to the international economy since its very birth. Sidney Mintz (1985) describes how sugar's transformation from a luxury of European royalty to a staple food of the industrial proletariat depended on the establishment of sugar-producing colonies in the Caribbean that were at once a source of cheap sugar and a market for cheap industrial goods.

5. According to the European Commission, Turkey, the United States, South Africa, and Chile accounted for approximately 40 percent of imports to the EU-27 in 2011. http://ec.europa.eu/agriculture/statistics/trade/2011.

6. According to the UN Food and Agriculture Organization's statistical database (FAOSTAT), 98 percent of China's raw soy imports come from these three countries. http://faostat3.fao.org/faostat-gateway/go/to/download/T/TM/E.

7. Reuters, "Walmart Plans More Stores and E-Commerce in China," *New York Times* online, October 24, 2013 (http://www.nytimes.com/2013/10/25/business/international/wal-marts-china-plan-to-focus-on-e-commerce.html)"; "Walmart Global eCommerce Completes Increased Investment In Yihaodian," Walmart.com, October 26, 2012 (http://news.walmart.com/news-archive/2012/10/26/walmart-global-ecommerce-completes-increased-investment-in-yihaodian.)

8. Observers of the US food system assert that firms exert market power and distort supply markets even when their market shares are as low as 20 percent (James, Hendrickson, and Howard 2013).

9. The US Forum for Sustainable and Responsible Investment (US SIF), CERES, and other socially responsible investment funds and portfolio management organizations play a similar role.

10. Currently Fairtrade International maintains commodity-specific certification standards for cocoa, coffee, tea, sugar, vegetables, fresh fruit, preserved fruits and vegetables, cereals, herbs and spices, oilseeds, nuts, honey, cotton, and flowers and plants, as well as sports balls, gold, and timber.

11. The U.S. market had previously been dominated by TransFair USA'S black-and-white containers label.

12. The FSC also inspired the Marine Stewardship Council, which in some respects was copied quite directly from the FSC, except that its architects wanted to avoid the "psychotic democracy" that had slowed the FSC's growth (see Auld 2014).

13. "Transforming Markets," WWF Global, http://wwf.panda.org/what_we_do/how_we_work/businesses/transforming_markets.

14. Basic information on the members is available through the RTRS website, www.responsiblesoy.org.

15. GM Freeze, http://www.gmfreeze.org/publications/briefings/131.

16. Corporate Europe Observatory, http://corporateeurope.org/agribusiness/2008/06/round-table-ir-responsible-soy; GM Freeze, http://www.gmfreeze.org/news-releases/32.

17. For example, Control Union Certification is accredited to certify for the RTRS, RSPO, and FSC. Various branches of the global firm SGS are accredited to certify for the RTRS, FSC, and SAI.

18. Fairtrade International Annual Report, FAOSTAT.

19. Three countries—Argentina, Brazil, and Paraguay—account for 93 percent of the certified area and 95 percent of certified soy volumes. Calculated using production data from FAOSTAT (http://faostat3.fao.org/faostat-gateway/go/to/download/Q/QC/E) and the RTRS (http://www.responsiblesoy.org/index.php?option=com_content&view=article&id=297&Itemid=181&lang=es).

20. Nearly half of the RTRS' members are drawn from European countries. Dutch agro-industries have committed to making all soy used in the Netherlands RTRS-certified in the future, and similar pledges have been made in Belgium and the UK.

21. FAOSTAT Country Rankings by Commodity, http://faostat3.fao.org/faostat-gateway/go/to/browse/rankings/countries_by_commodity/E.

22. FAOSTAT Food Security Statistics, http://faostat3.fao.org/faostat-gateway/go/to/download/D/FS/E.

23. As the government began promoting ethanol as a fuel, this provided a second outlet to support smallholder sugarcane production.

24. These are estimates given by the sugar industry association and the Paraguayan Fairtrade Producers' Federation.

25. Interview with purchasing company representative, July 10, 2009.

26. Interview with company representative, July 13, 2009.

27. Interview with purchasing company representative, July 10, 2009.

28. After recent land sales, DAP manages 11,350 hectares in five properties in the department of San Pedro and an additional 7,000 hectares of rented land elsewhere in Paraguay.

29. NF Developers, http://www.nfdevelopers.com/NFD_Agro_eng.htm.

30. Gustavo Setrini and Lucas Arce, "Paraguay's Impeached Democracy," Project Syndicate, July 9, 2012, http://www.project-syndicate.org/commentary/paraguay-s-impeached-democracy.

31. Interview with company manager, February 15, 2013.

5. APPAREL AND FOOTWEAR

1. Based on our calculations from WTO trade data, www.wto.org/english/res_e/statis_e/statis_e.htm.

2. Based on WTO data.

3. Based on our calculations from WTO data.

4. The footwear industry has also been mobile, but at a slower pace, due to the larger capital investments necessary. In 1994 Reebok's annual report disclosed that its footwear was made primarily in China (29 percent), Indonesia (28 percent), Thailand (14 percent), and South Korea (9 percent). By the time the 2000 report was released, South Korea had fallen off of the list, and China's share had risen to 48 percent, with Indonesia and Thailand holding roughly steady.

5. Phone interview with union representative, July 8, 2002.

6. The association was previously known as the American Apparel Manufacturers' Association, and WRAP initially stood for Worldwide Responsible Apparel Production.

7. Interview with auditor and consultant, New York, July 17, 2002.

8. "Monitoring: Assessing the Level of Compliance," Business Social Compliance Initiative, http://www.bsci-intl.org/our-work/monitoring.

9. Interview with brand representative, Shenzhen, October 15, 2010.

10. Visit to factory in Dongguan, China, November 4, 2010.

11. The value of wages increased in China, Haiti, Vietnam, Indonesia, India, and Peru, but they declined in Bangladesh, Cambodia, the Dominican Republic, El Salvador, Guatemala, Honduras, Mexico, the Philippines, and Thailand.

12. Some of these were slated to become part of the WRC's "Designated Supplier Program," which was derailed not only by opposition from the FLA but also by the dearth of qualified factories.

13. "Statement on the Rana Plaza Building Collapse," Business Social Compliance Initiative, April 30, 2013, https://bsci-intl.org/news-events/statement-rana-plaza-building-collapse-bangladesh.

14. Interview with auditor, Ho Chi Minh City, May 28, 2007.

15. Interview with retail compliance official, Hong Kong, May 22, 2007.

16. Interview with brand representative, Shenzhen, October 15, 2010.

17. WTO data.

18. Interview with certification practitioner, Shenzhen, November 12, 2010.

19. Interview with committee representatives, Dongguan, November 4, 2010.

20. Interview with compliance official, Dongguan, November 4. 2010.

21. Interview with auditor, Guangzhou, October 26, 2010.

22. Interview with certification practitioner, Shenzhen, December 11, 2010.

23. Interview with compliance official, Shanghai, July 13, 2011.

24. Interview with certification practitioner, Shenzhen, November 12, 2010.

25. Interview with certification practitioner, Beijing, December 8, 2010.

26. These findings are based on a small number of interviews conducted by two Chinese research assistants outside two SA8000-certified factories in the Guangzhou area in the fall of 2010.

27. Interview with certification practitioner, Shenzhen, December 11, 2010.

28. Similar fates would befall some of the other unionized factories to be included in the WRC's Designated Suppliers Program, creating further challenges for the organization's attempt to promote an alternative model.

29. See "Accord on Fire and Building Safety in Bangladesh," May 13, 2013, http://www .bangladeshaccord.org/wp-content/uploads/2013/10/the_accord.pdf.

6. ELECTRONICS

1. The newspaper was awarded the 2013 Pulitzer prize for explanatory reporting for this series, titled "The iEconomy," which ran throughout 2012. See "The iEconomy," Business Day, *International New York Times,* http://www.nytimes.com/interactive/business/ieconomy .html?_r=0.

2. We use the term "electronics industry" to describe the population of firms that actively produce or manage the production of computers, computer peripherals, communications equipment, and similar electronic products. While these hardware firms may engage in other diversified technology services, a core aspect of their business focuses on the production of physical computer hardware. Lead firms in this industry almost always classify themselves within North American Industry Classification System (NAICS) codes for "Electronic Computer Manufacturing" (334111) and "Other Computer Peripheral Manufacturing" (334119).

3. These figures are based on our calculations derived from industry reports produced by IBISWorld, March 2010, http://www.ibisworld.com.

4. In addition, the tendency to equate conflict-free with DRC-free has frustrated legitimate mine owners there. As the DRC's ambassador to the United States stated, "The private sector has been obliged to lay off people because they are not allowed to export. We really need to find a quick solution, otherwise this God-given potential that God put in the DRC might truly turn into some sort of curse" (qtd. in Banco 2011).

5. Asset manager Boston Common has posted a history of social investors' discussions with Apple, which outlines the long duration of their involvement: "Boston Common Engages Apple Inc.," Boston Common Asset Management, http://www.bostoncommonasset.com /news/press/apple-engagement.php.

6. The EICC code has been revised several times. The current version is available at "Code of Conduct," Electronic Industry Citizenship Coalition, http://www.eicc.info /documents/CodeofConduct3ovs4oFINAL.pdf.

7. This study has yielded a number of articles and working papers (e.g., Locke, Distelhorst, Pal, and Samel 2012; Locke, Rissing, and Pal 2013; Locke and Samel 2012). We have integrated insights from several of these studies into our own framework. In this section we draw especially from Locke et al. (2012).

8. Telephone interview with HP senior manager, March 2009.

9. Hewlett-Packard Social and Environmental Reporting Audit Process Manual, 5th ed., May 11, 2007, provided to research team.

10. See Locke et al. (2012) for a full analysis of HP's audit results.

11. Audit #447, Mainland China, 2005.

12. Audit #504, Taiwan, 2008.

13. Assertions about improvement rates are based on the 135 facilities audited more than once. Improvement is measured by comparing the percentage of compliant facilities at their initial audits with the percentage compliant in their final audits.

14. Audit #149, Mainland China, 2005.

15. Audit #150, Mainland China, 2007.

16. Interview with HR manager, China, 2009.

17. Audit #38, Mainland China, 2007.

18. There is variation, however. During MIT researchers' observation of one audit in Mainland China, auditors demonstrated awareness of this and attempted to use other techniques to reduce discriminatory hiring. They discussed the current gender ratio with management, praising them for making progress toward gender balance since the last audit and encouraging them to continue working on it.

19. The capability program participants also had, on average, more time between their initial and final audits to address violations. The average time between first and final audits was two years eight months in the capability-building group and two years two months for the control group. See Locke et al. (2012) for a fuller analysis of capability-building programs.

20. This section draws on another paper resulting from the MIT study (Locke and Samel 2012). HP's characteristics are reported as of 2009, the time of the study.

21. While this section draws on research conducted in HP's suppliers' Southeast Asian plants, the MIT study did find similar behavior in Chinese plants as well.

22. Interviews with HR managers, Johor Bahru, Malaysia, June 2009 and Penang, Malaysia, August 2011. Overtime is calculated on a weekly rather than a daily basis, which thus requires working weekends to earn premium pay.

23. Fairphone, fairphone.com, accessed January 17, 2014.

24. "Criticism in a Blog—What Do You Think about This?" Fairphone.com, https://fairphone.zendesk.com/hc/communities/public/questions/200680086-Criticism-in-a-blog-what-do-you-think-about-this-.

CONCLUSION

1. Carrol and Swaminathan (2000) develop this idea of resource partitioning through a study of the microbrewing movement.

REFERENCES

Agrawal, Arun. 2005. *Environmentality: Technologies of Government and the Making of Subjects.* Durham, NC: Duke University Press.

Ahmed, Faisal Z., Anne Greenleaf, and Audrey Sacks. 2014. "The Paradox of Export Growth in Areas of Weak Governance: The Case of the Ready-Made Garment Sector in Bangladesh." *World Development* 56:258–71.

Aksoy, M. Ataman, and John C. Beghin. 2004. *Global Agricultural Trade and Developing Countries.* Washington, DC: World Bank Publications.

Alam, Julhas. 2013. "Dozens Hurt in Bangladesh Garment Factory Protest." Associated Press. November 12. http://bigstory.ap.org/article/bangladesh-violence-closes-100-garment-factories.

Almond, Gabriel A., and Sidney Verba. 1989. *The Civic Culture: Political Attitudes and Democracy in Five Nations.* Boston: Little, Brown.

Amanor, Kojo Sebastian. 2012. "Global Resource Grabs, Agribusiness Concentration, and the Smallholder: Two West African Case Studies." *Journal of Peasant Studies* 39, no. 3–4:731–49.

Amengual, Matthew. 2010. "Complementary Labor Regulation: The Uncoordinated Combination of State and Private Regulators in the Dominican Republic." *World Development* 38, no. 3:405–14.

Amsden, Alice H. 1989. *Asia's Next Giant: South Korea and Late Industrialization.* New York: Oxford University Press.

Anderson, Roy C., and Eric N. Hansen. 2004. "Determining Consumer Preferences for Eco-labeled Forest Products: An Experimental Approach." *Journal of Forestry* 102, no. 4:28–32.

Anner, Mark, Jennifer Bair, and Jeremy Blasi. 2013. "Towards Joint Liability in Global Supply Chains: Addressing the Root Causes of Labor Violations in International Subcontracting Networks." *Journal of Comparative Labor Law and Policy* 35, no.1:1–44

Anner, Mark, and Peter Evans. 2004. "Building Bridges across a Double Divide: Alliances between US and Latin American Labour and NGOs." *Development in Practice* 14, no. 1/2:34–47.

Aparicio, Susana, Sutti Ortiz, and Nidia Tadeo. 2008. "Have Private Supermarket Norms Benefited Laborers? Lemon and Sweet Citrus Production in Argentina." *Globalizations* 5, no. 2:167–81.

Appelbaum, Richard P. 2008. "Giant Transnational Contractors in East Asia: Emergent Trends in Global Supply Chains." *Competition and Change* 12, no. 1:69–87.

Appelbaum, Richard P., and Gary Gereffi. 1994. "Power and Profits in the Apparel Commodity Chain." In *Global Production: The Apparel Industry in the Pacific Rim,* edited by Edna Bonacich, Lucie Cheng, Norma Chinchilla, Nora Hamilton, and Paul Ong, 42–62. Philadelphia: Temple University Press.

Arndorfer, Veronika A., and Ulf Liebe. 2013. "Consumer Behavior in Moral Markets: On the Relevance of Identity, Justice Beliefs, Social Norms, Status, and Trust in Ethical Consumption." *European Sociological Review* 29, no. 6:1251–65.

Arnot, Chris, Peter C. Boxall, and Sean B. Cash. 2006. "Do Ethical Consumers Care about Price? A Revealed Preference Analysis of Fair Trade Coffee Purchases." *Canadian Journal of Agricultural Economics/Revue canadienne d'agroeconomie* 54, no. 4:555–65.

Arnould, Eric J., Alejandro Plastina, and Dwayne Ball. 2009. "Does Fair Trade Deliver on Its Core Value Proposition? Effects on Income, Educational Attainment, and Health in Three Countries." *Journal of Public Policy and Marketing* 28, no. 2:186–201.

Ascoly, Nina, Joris Oldenziel, and Ineke Zeldenrust. 2001. "Overview of Recent Developments on Monitoring and Verification in the Garment and Sportswear Industry in Europe." Report published by SOMO: Centre for Research on Multinational Corporations, Amsterdam.

Auger, Pat, Paul Burke, Timothy M. Devinney, and Jordan J. Louviere. 2003. "What Will Consumers Pay for Social Product Features?" *Journal of Business Ethics* 42, no. 3:281–304.

Auger, Pat, Timothy M. Devinney, Jordan J. Louviere, and Paul F. Burke. 2008. "Do Social Product Features Have Value to Consumers?" *International Journal of Research in Marketing* 25, no. 3:183–91.

Auld, Graeme. 2014. *Constructing Private Governance: The Rise and Evolution of Forest, Coffee, and Fisheries Certification.* New Haven, CT: Yale University Press.

Auld, Graeme, Lars H. Gulbrandsen, and Constance L. McDermott. 2008. "Certification Schemes and the Impacts on Forests and Forestry." *Annual Review of Environment and Resources* 33:187–211.

Bacon, Christopher. 2005. "Confronting the Coffee Crisis: Can Fair Trade, Organic, and Specialty Coffees Reduce Small-Scale Farmer Vulnerability in Northern Nicaragua?" *World Development* 33, no. 3:497–511.

Bacon, Christopher M., V. Ernesto Mendez, María Eugenia Flores Gómez, Douglas Stuart, and Sandro Raúl Díaz Flores. 2008. "Are Sustainable Coffee Certifications Enough to Secure Farmer Livelihoods? The Millenium Development Goals and Nicaragua's Fair Trade Cooperatives." *Globalizations* 5, no. 2:259–74.

Bair, Jennifer, ed. 2008. *Frontiers of Commodity Chain Research.* Stanford, CA: Stanford University Press.

Bair, Jennifer, and Florence Palpacuer. 2012. "From Varieties of Capitalism to Varieties of Activism: The Antisweatshop Movement in Comparative Perspective." *Social Problems* 59, no. 4:522–43.

Baldwin, Carliss, and Kim Clark. 2009. "Managing in an Age of Modularity." In *Managing in the Modular Age: Architectures, Networks, and Organizations,* edited by Raghu Garud, Arun Kumaraswamy, and Richard Langlois, 149–60. Malden, MA: Blackwell.

Balsiger, Philip. 2010. "Making Political Consumers: The Tactical Action Repertoire of a Campaign for Clean Clothes." *Social Movement Studies: Journal of Social, Cultural and Political Protest* 9, no. 3:311–29.

Banco, Erin. 2011. "Is Your Cell Phone Fueling Civil War in Congo?" *Atlantic,* July 11. http://www.theatlantic.com/international/archive/2011/07/is-your-cell-phone-fueling-civil-war-in-congo/241663.

Barham, Bradford L., Mercedez Callenes, Seth Gitter, Jessa Lewis, and Jeremy Weber. 2011. "Fair Trade/Organic Coffee, Rural Livelihoods, and the 'Agrarian Question': Southern Mexican Coffee Families in Transition." *World Development* 39, no. 1:134–45.

Barnett, Clive, Paul Cloke, Nick Clarke, and Alice Malpass. 2005. "Consuming Ethics: Articulating the Subjects and Spaces of Ethical Consumption." *Antipode* 37, no. 1:23–45.

Barr, Christopher. 2001. "Banking on Sustainability: Structural Adjustment and Forestry Reform in Post Suharto Indonesia." Report published by the Center for International Forestry Research (CIFOR), Bogor, Indoneisa.

Barrientos, Stephanie, and Jude Howell. 2006. "ETI Impact Assessment: Findings and Recommendations from a Scoping Study Carried Out in China." Report issued by the Ethical Trading Initiative, London. http://www.ethicaltrade.org/sites/default/files/resources/Impact%20assessment%202f%20China.pdf.

Barrientos, Stephanie, and Andrienetta Kritzinger. 2004. "Squaring the Circle: Global Production and the Informalization of Work in South African Fruit Exports." *Journal of International Development* 16, no. 1:81–92.

Barrientos, Stephanie, and S. Smith. 2006. "The ETI Code of Labour Practice: Do Workers Really Benefit?" Impact assessment report issued by the Ethical Trading Initiative, London. http://www.ethicaltrade.org/resources/key-eti-resources/eti-impact-assessment-report-summary.

Barrientos, Stephanie, and Sally Smith. 2007. "Mainstreaming Fair Trade in Global Production Networks." In *Fair Trade: The Challenges of Transforming Globalization*, edited by L. Raynolds, D. Murray, and J. Wilkinson, 103–21. New York: Routledge.

Bartley, Tim. 2005. "Corporate Accountability and the Privatization of Labor Standards: Struggles over Codes of Conduct in the Apparel Industry." *Research in Political Sociology* 12:211–44.

———. 2007a. "How Foundations Shape Social Movements: The Construction of an Organizational Field and the Rise of Forest Certification." *Social Problems* 54, no. 3:229–55.

———. 2007b. "Institutional Emergence in an Era of Globalization: The Rise of Transnational Private Regulation of Labor and Environmental Conditions." *American Journal of Sociology* 113, no. 2:297–351.

———. 2009. "Standards for Sweatshops: The Power and Limits of Club Theory for Explaining Voluntary Labor Standards Programs." In *Voluntary Programs: A Club Theory Perspective*, edited by Aseem Prakash and Matthew Potoski, 107–132. Cambridge, MA: MIT Press.

———. 2011. "Transnational Governance as the Layering of Rules: Intersections of Public and Private Standards." *Theoretical Inquiries in Law* 12, no. 2:25–51.

———. 2012. "How Certification Matters: Examining Mechanisms of Influence." In "Toward Sustainability: The Roles and Limits of Certification. Steering Committee of the State-of-Knowledge Assessment of Standards and Certification," Appendix C. Report issued by RESOLVE, Inc. Washington, DC.

———. 2014a. "Global Production and the Puzzle of Rules." In *Framing the Global,* edited by Hilary Kahn, 229–52. Bloomington: Indiana University Press.

———. 2014b. "Transnational Governance and the Re-centered State: Sustainability or Legality?" *Regulation and Governance* 8, no. 1:93–109.

Bartley, Tim, and Curtis Child. 2014. "Shaming the Corporation: The Social Production of Targets and the Anti-Sweatshop Movement." *American Sociological Review* 79, no. 4:653–679.

Bartley, Tim, and Shawna Smith. 2010. "Communities of Practice as Cause and Consequence of Transnational Governance: The Evolution of Social and Environmental Certification."

In *Transnational Communities: Shaping Global Economic Governance,* edited by Marie-Laure Djelic and Sigrid Quack, 347–74. Cambridge: Cambridge University Press.

Bartley, Tim, and Lu Zhang. Forthcoming. "China and Global Labor Standards: Making Sense of Factory Certification." In *The Dragon's Learning Curve: Global Governance and China,* edited by Scott Kennedy. New York: Routledge.

Bassett, Thomas J. 2010. "Slim Pickings: Fairtrade Cotton in West Africa." *Geoforum* 41, no. 1:44–55.

Bates, Robert H. 1981. *States and Markets in Tropical Africa: The Political Basis of Agricultural Policy.* Berkeley: University of California Press.

Baumol, William J., Wallace E. Oates, and Sue A. Blackman. 1979. *Economics, Environmental Policy, and the Quality of Life.* Englewood Cliffs, NJ: Prentice Hall.

BBC. 2014. "Cambodia Garment Workers Killed in Clashes with Police." *BBC News.* January 3. http://www.bbc.com/news/world-asia-25585054.

Beck, Ulrich. 1994. "The Reinvention of Politics: Towards a Theory of Reflexive Modernization." In *Reflexive Modernization: Politics, Tradition and Aesthetics in the Modern Social Order,* edited by Ulrich Beck, Anthony Giddens, and Scott Lash, 1–55. Cambridge: Polity Press.

———. 1997. *The Reinvention of Politics: Rethinking Modernity in the Global Science Order.* Oxford: Polity Press.

———. 2000. *What Is Globalisation?* Cambridge: Cambridge University Press.

Beder, Sharon. 2001. "Greenwashing." In *International Encyclopedia of Environmental Politics,* edited by John Barry and Gene Frankland, 253–55. New York: Routledge.

Beers, David, and Catherine Capellaro. 1991. "Greenwash!" *Mother Jones.* March–April, 38–43.

Benford, Robert D., and David A Snow. 2000. "Framing Processes and Social Movements: An Overview and Assesment." *Annual Review of Sociology* 26:611–39.

Benjamin, Medea. 1999. "What's Fair about the Fair Labor Association? Putting the Fox in Charge." *Against the Current,* March-April. http://www.solidarity-us.org/site/node/1739.

Berry, Albert. 2001. "When Do Agricultural Exports Help the Rural Poor? A Political-Economy Approach." *Oxford Development Studies* 29, no. 2:125–44.

Bishop, Margaret L. 2011. "Reshoring Garment Production: China to the United States—The Tipping Point." Report distributed by Margaret L. Bishop, New York: Fashion Institute of Technology. http://www.seams.org/PDFs/Margaret%20Bishop%20Presentation.pdf.

Blaser, Juergen, Alastair Sarre, Duncan Poore, and Steven Johnson. 2011. "Status of Tropical Forest Management 2011." Report issued by the ITTO Technical Series No. 38, International Tropical Timber Organization, Yokohama, Japan.

Bolling, Chris, and Mark Gehlhar. 2005. "Global Food Manufacturing Reorients to Meet New Demands." In *New Directions in Global Food Markets,* edited by A. Regmi and M. Gehlhar, 62–73. Agriculture Information Bulletin 74. USDA. Washington, DC.

Boltanski, Luc, and Laurent Thévenot. 2006. *On Justification: Economies of Worth.* Princeton, NJ: Princeton University Press.

Bolzendahl, Catherine, and Sigrun Olafsdottir. 2008. "Gender Group Interest or Gender Ideology? Understanding U.S. Support for Family Policy in a Comparative Perspective." *Sociological Perspectives* 51, no. 2:281–304.

Bonacich, Edna, and Richard P. Appelbaum. 2000. *Behind the Label: Inequality in the Los Angeles Apparel Industry.* Berkeley: University of California Press.

Bonacich, Edna, and David V. Waller. 1994. "Mapping a Global Industry: Apparel Production in the Pacific Rim Triangle." In *Global Production: The Apparel Industry in the Pacific Rim,* edited by Edna Bonacich, Lucie Cheng, Norma Chinchilla, Nora Hamilton, and Paul Ong, 21–41. Philadelphia: Temple University Press.

Borda, Dionisio. 2013. "El auge de la soja y sus derivaciones." *Economía y Sociedad* 6:21–30.

Bormann, Sarah, Pathma Krishnan, and Monika E. Neuner. 2010. "Migration in a Digital Age: Migrant Workers in the Malaysian Electronics Sector." Report published by World Economy, Ecology, and Development (WEED), Berlin, Germany. http://electronicswatch .org/migration-in-a-digital-age_3542.pdf.

Borneo Initiative. 2014. "The Borneo Initiative: Large Scale Forest Certification in Indonesia." http://www.theborneoinitiative.org/client/borneo/uploads/factsheets/2014_en _flyer_tbi_web.pdf.

Börzel, Tanja A., and Thomas Risse. 2010. "Governance without a State: Can It Work?" *Regulation and Governance* 4, no. 2:113–34.

Bourdieu, Pierre. 1984. *Distinction: A Social Critique of the Judgement of Taste.* Translated by Richard Nice. Cambridge: Harvard University Press.

Bowles, Samuel, and Herbert Gintis. 2012 [1986]. *Democracy and Capitalism: Property, Community, and the Contradictions of Modern Social Thought.* New York: Routledge.

Brady, Henry E., Sidney Verba, and Kay Lehman Schlozman. 1995. "Beyond SES: A Resource Model of Political Participation." *American Political Science Review* 89, no. 2:271–94.

Brooks, Ethel C. 2007. *Unraveling the Garment Industry: Transnational Organizing and Women's Work.* Minneapolis: University of Minnesota Press.

Brown, A. Blake, William M. Snell, and Kelly H. Tiller. 1999. "The Changing Political Environment for Tobacco: Implications for Southern Tobacco Farmers, Rural Economies, Taxpayers, and Consumers." *Journal of Agricultural and Applied Economics* 31, no. 2: 291–308.

Brown, Drusilla, Rajeev Dehejia, and Raymond Robertson. 2013. "Regulations, Monitoring, and Working Conditions: Evidence from Better Factories Cambodia and Better Work Vietnam." Working paper, Tufts University. http://users.nber.org/~rdehejia/papers/Brown _Dehejia_Robertson_RDW.pdf.

Bryant, Raymond, Michael Goodman, and Michael Redclift. 2008. "Spaces of Intention as Exclusionary Practice: Exploring Ethical Limits to 'Alternative' Sustainable Consumption." Environment, Politics, and Development Working Paper Series, Department of Geography, King's College, London. http://www.kcl.ac.uk/sspp/departments/geography /research/epd/BryantetalWP4.pdf.

Brysk, Alison. 2005. *Human Rights and Private Wrongs: Constructing Global Civil Society.* New York: Routledge.

Burch, David, and Geoffrey Lawrence. 2007. "Supermarkets' Own Brands, Supply Chains, and the Transformation of the Agri-Food System." In *Supermarkets and Agri-Food Supply Chains: Transformations in the Production and Consumption of Foods,* edited by David Burch and Geoffrey Lawrence, 89–105. Northampton, MA: Edward Elgar.

———, eds. 2007. *Supermarkets and Agri-Food Supply Chains: Transformations in the Production and Consumption of Foods.* Northampton, MA: Edward Elgar.

Business Week. 2006. "Secrets, Lies, and Sweatshops." *Business Week.* November 27, 50–58.

Butollo, Florian, and Tobias ten Brink. 2012. "Challenging the Atomization of Discontent: Patterns of Migrant-Worker Protest in China during the Series of Strikes in 2010." *Critical Asian Studies* 44, no. 3:419–40.

Calo, Muriel, and Timothy A. Wise. 2005. "Revaluing Peasant Coffee Production: Organic and Fair Trade Markets in Mexico." Report issued by the Global Development and Environment Institute, Tufts University, Medford, MA. http://ase.tufts.edu/gdae/pubs/rp /RevaluingCoffee05.pdf.

Cao, Xiaozhi, Xiufang Sun, and Ivan Eastin. 2014. "Chinese Era." In *The Global Forest Sector,* edited by Eric Hansen, Rajat Panwar, and Richard Vlosky, 151–84. Boca Raton, FL: CRC Press.

Caplan, Jeremy. 2005. "Paper War: Environmentalists Take on Victoria's Secret for Mailing More Than 1 Million Catalogs a Day." *Time,* December 19, B1.

Carlson, Kimberly M., Lisa M. Curran, Dessy Ratnasari, Alice M. Pittman, Britaldo S. Soares-Filho, Gregory P. Asner, Simon N. Trigg, David A. Gaveau, Deborah Lawrence, and Hermann O. Rodrigues. 2012. "Committed Carbon Emissions, Deforestation, and Community Land Conversion from Oil Palm Plantation Expansion in West Kalimantan, Indonesia." *Proceedings of the National Academy of Sciences* 109, no. 19:7559–64.

Carlton, Jim. 2000. "Against the Grain: How Home Depot and Activists Joined to Cut Logging Abuse—If a Tree Falls in the Forest, the Small, Powerful FSC Wants to Have Its Say." *Wall Street Journal,* September 26, A1.

Carranza, Cecilia, Laura Trujillo, Carlos Guadarrama-Zugasti, Antonio Cordon, and Angel Mendoza. 2010. "Effects of Fair Trade and Organic Certifications on Small-Scale Coffee Farmer Households in Central America and Mexico." *Renewable Agriculture and Food Systems* 25, no. 3:236–51.

Carroll, Glenn R., and Anand Swaminathan. 2000. "Why the Microbrewery Movement? Organizational Dynamics of Resource Partitioning in the U.S. Brewing Industry." *American Journal of Sociology* 106, no. 3:715–62.

Carter, Michael R., Bradford L. Barham, and Dina Mesbah. 1996. "Agricultural Export Booms and the Rural Poor in Chile, Guatemala, and Paraguay." *Latin American Research Review* 31, no. 1:33–65.

Carton de Grammont, Hubert, and Sara Lara Flores. 2010. "Productive Restructuring and 'Standardization' in Mexican Horticulture: Consequences for Labour." *Journal of Agrarian Change* 10, no. 2:228–50.

Casadesus-Masanell, Ramon, Michael Crooke, Forest Reinhardt, and Vishal Vasishth. 2009. "Households' Willingness to Pay for 'Green' Goods: Evidence from Patagonia's Introduction of Organic Cotton Sportswear." *Journal of Economics and Management Strategy* 18, no. 1:203–33.

Cashore, Benjamin, Graeme Auld, and Deanna Newsom. 2004. *Governing through Markets: Forest Certification and the Emergence of Non-State Authority.* New Haven, CT: Yale University Press.

Cashore, Benjamin, Fred Gale, Errol Meidinger, and Deanna Newsom. 2006. "Forest Certification in Developing and Transitioning Countries." *Environment* 48, no. 9:6–25.

Catholic Agency for Overseas Development (CAFOD). 2004. "Clean Up Your Computer: Working Conditions in the Electronics Sector." Report issued by CAFOD, London. http://www.catholiclabor.org/gen-art/cafod-computers.pdf.

Caulfield, John. 2001. "Few Can Afford to Remain Green over Eco-friendly Wood." *National Home Center News* 27, no. 15:1–2.

Center for International Private Enterprise, and Social Accountability International. 2009. "From Words to Action: A Business Case for Implementing Workplace Standards." Report issued by the Center for International Private Enterprise and Social Accountability International, New York. http://www.cipe.org/publications/papers/pdf/SAI.pdf.

Cerutti, Paolo Omar, Luca Tacconi, Robert Nasi, and Guillaume Lescuye. 2011. "Legal vs. Certified Timber: Preliminary Impacts of Forest Certification in Cameroon." *Forest Policy and Economics* 13:184–90.

Chan, Anita. 2009. "Challenges and Possibilities for Democratic Grassroots Union Elections in China: A Case Study of Two Factory-Level Elections and Their Aftermath." *Labor Studies Journal* 34, no. 3:293–317.

Chan, Cheris Shun-ching. 2009. "Creating a Market in the Presence of Cultural Resistance: The Case of Life Insurance in China." *Theory and Society* 38, no. 3:271–305.

Chan, Jenny, and Chantal Peyer. 2008. "High Tech—No Rights? One Year Follow-Up Report on the Working Conditions in the Electronic Hardware Sector in China." Report issued by Students and Scholars Against Corporate Misbeavior (SACOM), Hong Kong. http://sacom.hk/wp-content/uploads/2008/07/report-high-tech-no-rights-may2008.pdf.

Chan, Jenny, Ngai Pun, and Mark Selden. 2013. "The Politics of Global Production: Apple, Foxconn, and China's New Working Class." *New Technology, Work, and Employment* 28, no. 2:100–15.

Chang, Joseph Y. S., Kinglun Ngok, and Wenjia Zhuang. 2010. "The Survival and Development Space for China's Labor NGOs: Informal Politics and Its Uncertainty." *Asian Survey* 50, no. 6:1082–106.

Cheng, Lucie, and Gary Gereffi. 1994. "U.S. Retailers and Asian Garment Production." In *Global Production: The Apparel Industry in the Pacific Rim,* edited by Edna Bonacich, Lucie Cheng, Norma Chinchilla, Nora Hamilton, and Paul Ong, 63–79. Philadelphia: Temple University Press.

China Labor Watch. 2009. "Corrupt Audits Damage Worker Rights: A Case Analysis of Corruption in Bureau Veritas Factory Audits." Report issued by China Labor Watch, New York. http://www.chinalaborwatch.org/upfile/2009_12_9/2009bvcorruption1209.pdf.

Christensen, Clay M. 1997. *The Innovator's Dilemma: When New Technologies Cause Great Firms to Fail.* Boston: Harvard Business Press.

Clark, Gregory, Kenneth L. Kraemer, and Jason Dedrick. 2009. "Who Captures Value in a Global Innovation Network? The Case of Apple's iPod." *Communications of the ACM* 52, no. 3:140–44.

Clarke, Nick, Clive Barnett, Paul Cloke, and Alice Malpass. 2007. "The Political Rationalities of Fair-Trade Consumption in the United Kingdom." *Politics and Society* 35, no. 4:583–607.

Clarke, Roger, Stephen Davies, Paul Dobson, and Michael Waterson. 2002. *Buyer Power and Competition in European Food Retailing.* Cheltenham: Edward Elgar Publishing.

Clean Clothes Campaign. 2007. "Sportswear Workers in the Dominican Republic Need Your Support." Report issued by the Clean Clothes Campaign, Amsterdam. http://digitalcommons.ilr.cornell.edu/globaldocs/114.

Clifford, Stephanie. 2013. "That 'Made in U.S.A.' Premium." *New York Times,* November 30.

Colchester, Marcus, Martua Sirait, and Boedhi Wijardjo. 2003. "Obstacles and Possibilities: The Application of FSC Principles 2 and 3 in Indonesia." Report published by Wahana Lingkungan Hidup Indonesia (WAHLI), Aliansi Masyarakat Adat Nusantara (AMAN), and the Rainforest Foundation. http://www.forestpeoples.org/sites/fpp/files/publication/2010/08/indonesiaobstaclesandpossibilitieso3eng_1.pdf.

Collett, Jessica L., and Omar Lizardo. 2009. "A Power-Control Theory of Gender and Religiosity." *Journal for the Scientific Study of Religion* 48, no. 2:213–31.

Collins, Jane L. 2003. *Threads: Gender, Labor, and Power in the Global Apparel Industry.* Chicago: University of Chicago Press.

Collins, Jim, and David Packard. 2005. "Foreword to the HP Way." In *The HP Way,* edited by David Kirby and Karen Lewis, xi–xviii. New York: Harper Collins.

Connolly, John, and Andrea Prothero. 2008. "Green Consumption Life: Politics, Risk and Contradictions." *Journal of Consumer Culture* 8, no. 1:117–45.

Connor, John M., and William A. Schiek. 1997. *Food Processing: An Industrial Powerhouse in Transition.* New York: John Wiley and Sons.

Conroy, Michael E. 2007. *Branded!: How the Certification Revolution Is Transforming Global Corporations.* Gabriola Island, BC, Canada: New Society Publishers.

Copeland, Lauren. 2014. "Value Change and Political Action: Postmaterialism, Political Consumerism, and Political Participation." *American Politics Research* 42, no. 2:257–82.

Coslovsky, Salo V. 2011. "Relational Regulation in the Brazilian Ministério Publico: The Organizational Basis of Regulatory Responsiveness." *Regulation and Governance* 5, no. 1:70–89.

Cowie, Jefferson. 1999. *Capital Moves: RCA's Seventy-Year Quest for Cheap Labor.* New York: New Press.

Craig, Stephen C., Richard G. Niemi, and Glenn E. Silver. 1990. "Political Efficacy and Trust: A Report on the NES Pilot Study Items." *Political Behaviour* 12, no. 3:289–314.

Crespi, John M., and Stéphan Marette. 2005. "Eco-labelling Economics: Is Public Involvement Necessary?" In *Environment, Information, and Consumer Behaviour,* edited by Signe Krarup and Clifford S. Russell, 93–109. Cheltenham, UK: Edward Elgar Publishing.

Cushman, John H., Jr. 1998. "Nike Pledges to End Child Labor and Apply U.S. Rules Abroad," *New York Times,* May 13, D1, D5.

Cynamon, Barry Z., and Steven M. Fazzari. 2014. "Inequality, the Great Recession, and Slow Recovery." Working paper, available at http://ssrn.com/abstract=2205524 or http://dx.doi.org/10.2139/ssrn.2205524.

Dalton, Russell J. 2008. "Citizenship Norms and the Expansion of Political Participation." *Political Studies* 56, no. 1:76–98.

Damiani, Octavio. 2003. "Effects on Employment, Wages, and Labor Standards of Non-Traditional Export Crops in Northeast Brazil." *Latin American Research Review* 38, no. 1:83–112.

Dara, Mech, and Alex Willemyns. 2014. "As Garment Sector Strikes Loom, Soldiers Watch over Factories." *Cambodia Daily.* February 27. http://www.cambodiadaily.com/archives/as-garment-sector-strikes-loom-soldiers-watch-over-factories-53275.

Daugbjerg, Carsten, and Kim Mannemar Sønderskov. 2012. "Environmental Policy Performance Revisited: Designing Effective Policies for Green Markets." *Political Studies* 60:399–418.

Dauvergne, Peter, and Jane Lister. 2011. *Timber.* Malden, MA: Polity Press.

———. 2012. "Big Brand Sustainability: Governance Prospects and Environmental Limits." *Global Environmental Change* 22, no. 1:36–45.

David, Paul A. 1985. "Clio and the Economics of QWERTY." *American Economic Review* 75, no. 2:332–37.

Davis, Gerald F. 2009. *Managed by the Markets: How Finance Re-Shaped America.* New York: Oxford University Press.

De Pelsmacker, Patrick, Liesbeth Driesen, and Glenn Rayp. 2005. "Do Consumers Care about Ethics? Willingness to Pay for Fair-Trade Coffee." *Journal of Consumer Affairs* 39, no. 2:363–85.

De Pelsmacker, Patrick, and Wim Janssens. 2007. "A Model for Fair Trade Buying Behaviour: The Role of Perceived Quantity and Quality of Information and of Product-Specific Attitudes." *Journal of Business Ethics* 75:361–80.

Dean, Jason, and Ting-I. Tsai. 2010. "Suicides Spark Inquiries." *Wall Street Journal,* May 27, B1, B7.

DeGusta, M. 2012. "Are Smart Phones Spreading Faster than Any Technology in Human History?" *MIT Technology Review,* May 9. http://www.technologyreview.com/news/427787 /are-smart-phones-spreading-faster-than-any-technology-in-human-history.

Deloitte LLP. 2013. "Global Powers of Retailing 2013: Retail Beyond." Report issued by Deloitte Global Services Limited, London. http://www.deloitte.com/assets/Dcom-Kenya /Local%20Assets/Documents/CB_Global-Powers-of-Retailing-2014.pdf.

Deininger, Klaus, and Derek Byerlee. 2011. "Rising Global Interest in Farmland: Can It Yield Sustainable and Equitable Benefits?" Report issued by the World Bank, Washington, DC. http://siteresources.worldbank.org/DEC/Resources/Rising-Global-Interest-in-Farmland .pdf.

Dickson, Marsha A. 2001. "Utility of No Sweat Labels for Apparel Consumers: Profiling Label Users and Predicting Their Purchases." *Journal of Consumer Affairs* 35, no. 1:96–119.

Diekmann, Andreas, and Peter Preisendörfer. 2003. "Green and Greenback. The Behavioural Effects of Environmental Attitudes in Low-Cost and High-Cost Situations." *Rationality and Society* 15, no. 4:441–72.

DiMaggio, Paul. 1992. "Cultural Boundaries and Structural Change: The Extension of the High Culture Model to Theater, Opera, and the Dance, 1900–1940." In *Cultivating Differences: Symbolic Boundaries and the Making of Inequality,* edited by Michèle Lamont and Marcel Fournier, 21–57. Chicago: University of Chicago Press.

Djelic, Marie-Laure, and Kerstin Sahlin-Andersson, eds. 2006. *Transnational Governance: Institutional Dynamics of Regulation.* New York: Cambridge University Press.

Doane, Deborah. 2005. "The Myth of CSR." *Stanford Social Innovation Review* 3, no. 3:22–29.

Dolan, Catherine S., and John Humphrey. 2000. "Governance and Trade in Fresh Vegetables: The Impact of UK Supermarkets on the African Horticulture Industry." *Journal of Development Studies* 37, no. 2:147–76.

Dolan, Catherine S. 2007. "Market Affections: Moral Encounters with Kenyan Fairtrade Flowers." *Ethnos* 72, no. 2:239–61.

Donovan, Richard. 1990. Memo of December 2, 1990. Personal archives of FSC organizer.

———. 2001. "A Perspective on the Perum Perhutani Certification Suspension." Report issued by the Rainforest Alliance, New York. http://www.rainforest-alliance.org/news/2001 /perhutani-perspective.html.

Duhigg, Charles, and David Barboza. 2012. "Apple's iPad and the Human Costs for Workers in China." *New York Times,* January 25, A1.

Duhigg, Charles, and Keith Bradsher. 2012. "Apple, America, and a Squeezed Middle Class." *New York Times,* January 21, A1.

Duhigg, Charles, and Nick Wingfield. 2012. "Apple Asks Outside Group to Inspect Factories." *New York Times Bits Blog,* February 14. http://bits.blogs.nytimes.com/2012/02/14/daily -report-apple-asks-outside-group-to-inspect-factories.

DuPuis, E. Melanie. 2000. "Not in My Body: BGH and the Rise of Organic Milk." *Agriculture and Human Values* 17, no. 3:285–95.

Durkheim, Emile. 1898 [1995]. *The Elementary Forms of Religious Life.* New York: Free Press.

Ebeling, Johannes, and Maï Yasué. 2009. "The Effectiveness of Market-Based Conservation in the Tropics: Forest Certification in Ecuador and Bolivia." *Journal of Environmental Management* 90, no. 2:1145–53.

Ecological Trading Company. 1990. Letter of July 1990. Personal archives of a member of the Certification Working Group.

Edwards, David P., Trond H. Larsen, Teegan D. S. Docherty, Felicity A. Ansell, Wayne W. Hsu, Mia A. Derhé, Keith C. Hamer, and David S. Wilcove. 2011. "Degraded Lands Worth Protecting: The Biological Importance of Southeast Asia's Repeatedly Logged Forests." *Proceedings of the Royal Society B: Biological Sciences* 278, no. 1702:82–90.

Edwards, Michael, and David Hulme. 1996. *Beyond the Magic Bullet: NGO Performance and Accountability in the Post–Cold War World.* West Hartford, CT: Kumarian Press.

Egels-Zandén, Niklas. 2014. "Revisiting Supplier Compliance with MNC Codes of Conduct: Recoupling Policy and Practice at Chinese Toy Suppliers." *Journal of Business Ethics* 119, no. 1:59–75.

Egels-Zandén, Niklas, and Tim Bartley. 2014. "Can Unions Leverage Corporate Social Responsibility? Contestation, Negotiation, and Re-Coupling in the Indonesian Apparel and Footwear Industry." Working paper, Department of Sociology, Ohio State University.

Egels-Zandén, Niklas, and Evelina Wahlqvist. 2007. "Post-Partnership Strategies for Defining Corporate Responsibility: The Business Social Compliance Initiative." *Journal of Business Ethics* 70, no. 2:175–89.

EICC. 2009. "Electronic Industry Citizenship Coalition: 2008 Annual Report." Report issued by the Electronic Industry Citizenship Coalition, Alexandria, VA.

Ekawati, Arti. 2009. "New Rule to Add Indonesian Timber Revenues to Government Coffers." *Jakarta Globe.* July 28. http://thejakartaglobe.beritasatu.com/archive/new-rule-to-add-indonesian-timber-revenues-to-government-coffers/320541.

Elgert, Laureen. 2012. "Certified Discourse? The Politics of Developing Soy Certification Standards." *Geoforum* 43, no. 2:295–304.

Elliott, Chris. 2000. *Forest Certification from a Policy Network Perspective.* Jakarta: Center for International Forestry Research (CIFOR).

Elliott, Kimberly Ann, and Richard B. Freeman. 2003. *Can Labor Standards Improve under Globalization?* Washington, DC: Institute for International Economics.

Elson, Dominic. 2011. "An Economic Case for Tenure Reform in Indonesia's Forests." Washington, DC: Rights and Resources Initiative. http://www.rightsandresources.org/wp-content/uploads/2014/01/elson_brief_final.pdf.

Emerich, Monica M. 2011. *The Gospel of Sustainability: Media, Market, and LOHAS.* Champaign: University of Illinois Press.

Enloe, Cynthia. 2000. "Daughters and Generals in the Politics of the Globalized Sneaker." In *Rethinking Globalization: Corporate Transnationalism to Local Interventions,* edited by Preet S. Aulakh and Michale G. Schechter, 238–48. London: Macmillan.

Erikson, Robert, and John H. Goldthorpe. 1992. *The Constant Flux: A Study of Class Mobility in Industrial Societies.* Oxford: Clarendon Press.

Esbenshade, Jill. 2004. *Monitoring Sweatshops: Workers, Consumers, and the Global Apparel Industry.* Philadelphia: Temple University Press.

Espach, Ralph H. 2009. *Private Environmental Regimes in Developing Countries: Globally Sown, Locally Grown.* New York: Palgrave Macmillan.

Ethical Trading Initiative. 2006. "Getting Smarter at Auditing: Tackling the Growing Crisis in Ethical Trade Auditing." Report issued by the Ethical Trading Initiative, London. www.eti2.org.uk/Z/lib/2006/11/smart-audit/eti-smarter-auditing-2006.pdf.

Euromonitor. 2013. "Tesco PLC in Retailing." Report from Passport database, prepared by Euromonitor International, London.

European Social Survey. 2002. ESS Round 1 Data. Data file edition 6.3., distributed by Norwegian Social Science Data Services.

European Tissue Symposium. 2008. "Facts and Figures on Tissue." European Tissue Symposium, Brussels, Belgium. http://www.europeantissue.com/facts-studies/fact-and-figures.

European Values Survey. 2011. European Values Study, 1981–2008. Longitudinal Data File. GESIS Data Archive, Cologne. ZA4804 Data File Version 2.0.0, DOI:10.4232/1.11005.

Eurostat. 2009a. "Consumers in Europe." Report issued by the Office for Official Publications of the European Communities, European Commission, Luxembourg. http://epp.eurostat .ec.europa.eu/cache/ITY_OFFPUB/KS-DY-09-001/EN/KS-DY-09-001-EN.PDF.

———. 2009b. "Structural Business Statistics." Report issued by the Office for Official Publications of the European Communities, European Commission, Luxembourg. http://epp .eurostat.ec.europa.eu/portal/page/portal/european_business/data/database, December 8.

———. 2009c. "Eco-label Awards by Products." Report issued by the Office for Official Publications of the European Communities, European Commission, Luxembourg. http://epp .eurostat.ec.europa.eu/portal/page/portal/eurostat/home, December 10.

———. 2010. "Consumption Expenditure of Private Households." Report issued by the Office for Official Publications of the European Communities, European Commission, Luxembourg. http://epp.eurostat.ec.europa.eu/portal/page/portal/eurostat/home, January 15.

Evans, Peter. 1997. "The Eclipse of the State? Reflections on Stateness in an Era of Globalization." *World Politics* 50:62–87.

———. 2010. "Is It Labor's Turn to Globalize? Twenty-First-Century Opportunities and Strategic Responses." *Global Labour Journal* 1, no. 3:352–79.

Fair Labor Association. 2007. "FLA 3.0—Toward Sustainable Compliance." Report issued by the Fair Labor Association, Washington, DC. http://www.fairlabor.org/about/fla_30 _-_toward_sustainable_compliance.

———. 2012. "Fair Labor Association Secures Commitment to Limit Worker Hours." Press release issued by the Fair Labor Association, Washington, DC. http://www.fairlabor.org /blog/entry/fair-labor-association-secures-commitment-limit-workers-hours-protect-pay -apples-largest.

Fair Trade Foundation. 2013. "Facts, Figures & Resources." Report issued by the Fair Trade Foundation, London. http://www.fairtrade.org.uk/press_office/facts_figures.aspx.

Fair Trade USA. 2012. "A Bold Experiment in Ethical Clothing: Fair Trade Certified Apparel and Linens Pilot Lessons Learned 2010–2012." Report issued by Fair Trade USA, Oakland, CA. http://fairtradeusa.org/sites/default/files/Apparel%20Pilot%20Report.pdf.

Fairtrade International. 2011. "Fairtrade Standard for Small Producer Organizations." Report issued by Fairtrade International, Bonn, Germany.

———. 2013. "Annual Report: Unlocking the Power." Report issued by Fairtrade International, Bonn, Germany.

Farina, Elizabeth MMQ. 2002. "Consolidation, Multinationalisation, and Competition in Brazil: Impacts on Horticulture and Dairy Products Systems." *Development Policy Review* 20, no. 4:441–57.

Feenstra, Robert C. 1998. "Integration of Trade and Disintegration of Production in the Global Economy." *Journal of Economic Perspectives* 12, no. 4:31–50.

Ferrer, Mariona, and Marta Fraile. 2006. "Exploring the Social Determinants of Political Consumerism in Western Europe." Working Paper 57, Universidad Autónoma de Madrid. Departamento de Ciencia Política y Relaciones Internacionales, Madrid.

Ferus-Comelo, A. 2008. "Mission Impossible? Raising Labor Standards in the ICT Sector." *Labor Studies Journal* 33, no. 2:141–62.

FLO. 2005. "Fairtrade Annual Report 2003/04." Report issued by the Fairtrade Labelling Organization International, Bonn.

———. 2006. "Fairtrade Annual Report 2004/05." Report issued by the Fairtrade Labelling Organization International, Bonn.

———. 2007. "Fairtrade Annual Report 2005/06." Report issued by the Fairtrade Labelling Organization International, Bonn.

———. 2008. "Fairtrade Annual Report 2006/07." Report issued by the Fairtrade Labelling Organization International, Bonn.

———. 2009. "Fairtrade Annual Report 2007/08." Report issued by the Fairtrade Labelling Organization International, Bonn.

———. 2010. "Fairtrade Annual Report 2008/09." Report issued by the Fairtrade Labelling Organization International, Bonn.

———. 2011. "Fairtrade Annual Report 2009/010." Report issued by the Fairtrade Labelling Organization International, Bonn.

Food and Agriculture Organization (FAO). 2006. "Global Forest Resources Assessment 2005." Report issued by the Food and Agriculture Organization of the United Nations, Rome.

———. 2010. "Global Forest Resources Assessment 2010." Report issued by the Food and Agriculture Organization of the United Nations, Rome.

Forest Stewardship Council. 2001. "List of Forest Management Certificates, January 31, 2001." Report issued by the Forest Stewardship Council, Bonn.

———. 2013. "FSC Market Info Pack 2013." Report issued by the Forest Stewardship Council. Bonn. http://ic.fsc.org/download.market-info-pack-2012.414.htm.

Fort, Ricardo, and Ruerd Ruben. 2008. "The Impact of Fair Trade Certification on Coffee Producers in Peru." In *The Impact of Fair Trade,* edited by Ruerd Ruben, 75–98. Wageningen, Netherlands: Wageningen Academic Publishers.

Foster, Lauren, and Alexandra Harney. 2005. "Doctored Records on Working Hours and Pay Are Causing Problems for Consumer Multinationals as They Source More of Their Goods in Asia." *Financial Times,* April 22. http://www.ft.com/intl/cms/s/0/203674f2-b2cd-11d9 -bcc6-00000e2511c8.html#axzz3IhN3MCyT.

Fourcade, Marion, and Kieran Healy. 2007. "Moral Views of Market Society." *Annual Review of Sociology* 33:285–311.

Frank, Dana. 2000. *Buy American: The Untold Story of Economic Nationalism.* Boston: Beacon Press.

Frank, David John, Ann Hironaka, and Evan Schofer. 2000. "The Nation-State and the Natural Environment over the Twentieth Century." *American Sociological Review* 65:96–116.

Frank, Robert H. 2010. *Luxury Fever: Weighing the Cost of Excess.* Princeton, NJ: Princeton University Press.

Fransen, Luc. 2011. "Why Do Private Governance Organizations Not Converge? A Political–Institutional Analysis of Transnational Labor Standards Regulation." *Governance* 24, no. 2:359–87.

Fransen, Luc, and Thomas Conzelmann. Forthcoming. "Fragmented or Cohesive Transnational Private Regulation of Sustainability Standards? A Comparative Study." *Regulation and Governance* (early view, DOI: 10.1111/rego.12055).

Freidberg, Susanne. 2004. *French Beans and Food Scares: Culture and Commerce in an Anxious Age.* New York: Oxford University Press.

Frenkel, Stephen J., and Duncan Scott. 2002. "Compliance, Collaboration, and Codes of Labor Practice: The Adidas Connection." *California Management Review* 45, no. 1:29–49.

Fridell, Gavin. 2004. "The Fair Trade Network in Historical Perspective." *Canadian Journal of Development Studies/Revue canadienne d'études du développement* 25, no. 3:411–28.

Friedland, Lewis A., Hernando Rojas, and Leticia Bode. 2012. "Consuming Ourselves to Dearth Escalating Inequality and Public Opinion." *ANNALS of the American Academy of Political and Social Science* 644, no. 1:280–93.

Friedland, William H. 1994. "The Global Fresh Fruit and Vegetable System: An Industrial Organization Analysis." In *The Global Restructuring of Agro-food Systems,* edited by Philip McMichael, 173–89. Ithaca, NY: Cornell University Press.

Friedman, Arthur. 2012. "Fessler USA, Made in America Proponent, Closing Down." *Women's Wear Daily,* November 5, 23–24.

Friedman, Eli. 2013. "Insurgency and Institutionalization: The Polanyian Countermovement and Chinese Labor Politics." *Theory and Society* 42, no. 3:295–327.

Friedmann, Harriet. 1991. "Changes in the International Division of Labor: Agri-Food Complexes and Export Agriculture." *Towards a New Political Economy of Agriculture,* edited by William H. Friedland, Lawrence Busch, Frederick H. Buttel, and Alan Rudy, 65–93. Boulder, CO: Westview.

Frundt, Henry J. 2009. *Fair Bananas!: Farmers, Workers, and Consumers Strive to Change an Industry.* Tucson: University of Arizona Press.

Gartner Inc. 2013. "Gartner Says Worldwide Mobile Phone Sales Declined 1.7 Percent in 2012." Press release issued by Gartner, Egham, UK. http://www.gartner.com/newsroom /id/2335616.

Gawer, Annabelle, and Michael A. Cusumano. 2002. *Platform Leadership.* Boston: Harvard Business School Press.

Gellert, Paul. 2005. "The Shifting Natures of "Development": Growth, Crisis, and Recovery in Indonesia's Forests." *World Development* 33, no. 8:1345–64.

Gerber, Julien-François. 2011. "Conflicts over Industrial Tree Plantations in the South: Who, How, and Why?" *Global Environmental Change* 21, no. 1:165–76.

Gereffi, Gary. 1994. "The Organization of Buyer-Driven Global Commodity Chains: How U.S. Retailers Shape Overseas Production Networks." In *Commodity Chains and Global Capitalism,* edited by Gary Gereffi and Miguel Korzeniewicz, 95–122. Westport, CT: Praeger.

———. 1999. "International Trade and Industrial Upgrading in the Apparel Commodity Chain." *Journal of International Economics* 48, no. 1:37–70.

Gereffi, Gary, Ronie Garcia-Johnson, and Erika Sasser. 2001. "The NGO-Industrial Complex." *Foreign Policy* (July/August):56–65.

Gereffi, Gary, John Humphrey, and Timothy Sturgeon. 2005. "The Governance of Global Value Chains." *Review of International Political Economy* 12, no. 1:78–104.

Gilbert, C. L., and J. ter Wengel. 2001. "The Production and Marketing of Primary Commodities." In "Commodities and Development at the Turn of the Millennium," 21–62. Report issued by Common Fund for Commodities, Amsterdam.

Gomes, Raquel. 2006. "Upgrading without Exclusion: Lessons from SMEs in Fresh Fruit Producing Clusters in Brazil." In *Upgrading to Compete: Global Value Chains, Clusters, and SMEs in Latin America,* edited by Carlo Pietrobelli and Roberta Rabellotti, 71–107. Washington, DC: Inter-American Development Bank.

Good Electronics. 2009. "Reset: Corporate Social Responsibility in the Global Electronics Supply Chain." Report issued by the Good Electronics MVO Platform, Amsterdam. http://goodelectronics.org/publications-en/Publication_3248.

Goodman, Michael K., Damian Maye, and Lewis Holloway. 2010. "Ethical Foodscapes? Premises, Promises, and Possibilities." *Environment and Planning. A* 42, no. 8:1782–96.

Goul Andersen, Jørgen, and Mette Tobiasen. 2004. "Who Are These Political Consumers Anyway? Survey Evidence from Denmark." In *Politics, Products, and Markets,* edited by Michele Micheletti, Andreas Follesdal, and Dietlind Stolle, 203–21. Brunswick, London: Transaction Publishers.

Gray, Margaret. 2014. *Labor and the Locavore: The Making of a Comprehensive Food Ethic.* Berkeley: University of California Press.

Greenhouse, Steven. 2013. "U.S. Retailers Decline to Aid Factory Victims in Bangladesh." *New York Times,* November 22, 17.

Greenpeace. 1992. "The Greenpeace Book of Greenwash." Washington, DC: Greenpeace. Available at http://research.greenpeaceusa.org/?a=view&d=4588.

2011. "Stolen Future: Conflicts and Logging in the Congo's Rainforests—The Case of Danzer." Report issued by Greenpeace International, Amsterdam. http://www.greenpeace.org/international/Global/international/publications/forests/2011/stolen%20future.pdf.

Grimes, Kimberly M. 2000. "Democratizing International Production and Trade. North American Alternative Trading Organizations." In *Artisans and Cooperatives: Developing Alternate Trade for the Global Economy,* edited by Kimberly M. Grimes and Barbara L. Milgram, 11–24. Tucson: University of Arizona Press.

Grindle, Merilee Serrill. 1986. *State and Countryside: Development Policy and Agrarian Politics in Latin America.* Baltimore: Johns Hopkins University Press.

Grunert, Klaus G., Allan Baadsgard, Hanne Hartvig Larsen, and Tage Koed Madsen. 1996. *Market Orientation in Food and Agriculture.* Dordrecht: Kluwer Academic Publishers.

Guagnano, Gregory A. 2001. "Altruism and Market-Like Behavior: An Analysis of Willingness to Pay for Recycled Paper Products." *Population and Environment* 22, no. 4:425–38.

Guereña, Arantxa, and Quintín Riquelme. 2013. "The Soy Mirage: The Limits of Corporate Social Responsibility—The Case of the Company Desarrollo Agrícola del Paraguay." Report issued by Oxfam International, Oxford, UK. http://www.oxfam.org/sites/www.oxfam.org/files/rr-soy-mirage-corporate-social-responsibility-paraguay-290813-en.pdf.

Guido, Gianluigi, ed. 2009. *Behind Ethical Consumption: Purchasing Motives and Marketing Strategies for Organic Food Products, Non-GMOs, Bio-Fuels.* Bern, Switzerland: Peter Lang.

Guido, Gianluigi, Giovanni Pino, and M. Irene Prete. 2009. "Effects of Attitude and Personal Values on the Purchase Intention of Genetically Modified Food Products." In *Behind Ethical Consumption,* edited by Gianluigi Guido, 95–118. Oxford: Peter Lang Publishing Group in association with GSE Research.

Gulbrandsen, Lars H. 2010. *Transnational Environmental Governance: The Emergence and Effects of the Certification of Forests and Fisheries.* Northampton, MA: Edward Elgar Publishing.

Gullison, R. E. 2003. "Does Forest Certification Conserve Biodiversity?" *Oryx* 37, no. 2:153–65.

Guthman, Julie. 2004. *Agrarian Dreams: The Paradox of Organic Farming in California.* Berkeley: University of California Press.

———. 2007a. "Can't Stomach It: How Michael Pollan et al. Made Me Want to Eat Cheetos." *Gastronomica: The Journal of Food and Culture* 7, no. 3:75–79.

———. 2007b. "The Polanyian Way? Voluntary Food Labels as Neoliberal Governance." *Antipode* 39, no. 3:456–78.

———. 2008. "'If They Only Knew': Color Blindness and Universalism in California Alternative Food Institutions." *Professional Geographer* 60, no. 3:387–97.

Gwynne, Robert N. 2003. "Transnational Capitalism and Local Transformation in Chile." *Tijdschrift voor Economische en Sociale Geografie* 94, no. 3:310–21.

Hainmueller, Jens, and Michael Hiscox. 2012. "The Socially Conscious Consumer? Field Experimental Tests of Consumer Support for Fair Labor Standards." Working paper, Social Science Research Network. http://ssrn.com/abstract=2062435.

Hainmueller, Jens, Michael Hiscox, and Sandra Sequeira. 2011. "Consumer Demand for the Fair Trade Label: Evidence from a Field Experiment." Working paper, Social Science Research Network. http://ssrn.com/abstract=1801942.

Halliday, Terence C., and Bruce G. Carruthers. 2009. *Bankrupt: Global Lawmaking and Systemic Financial Crisis.* Stanford, CA: Stanford University Press.

Hannan, Michael T., and John Freeman. 1989. *Organizational Ecology.* Cambridge, MA: Harvard University Press.

Harvey, Mark. 2007. "The Rise of Supermarkets and Asymmetries of Economic Power." *Supermarkets and Agri-Food Supply Chains: Transformations in the Production and Consumption of Foods,* edited by David Burch and Geoffrey Lawrence, 51–68. Northampton, MA: Edward Elgar Publishing.

Hatanaka, Maki, Carmen Bain, and Lawrence Busch. 2006. "Differentiated Standardization, Standardized Differentiation: The Complexity of the Global Agrifood System." *Research in Rural Sociology and Development* 12:39–68.

Heisler, Yoni. 2013. "Apple Creates Academic Advisory Board to Oversee Its Supplier Responsibility Program." *TUAW—The Unofficial Apple Weblog.* July 28. http://www.tuaw.com/2013/07/27/apple-creates-academic-advisory-board-to-oversee-its-supplier-re.

Herbert, Bob. 1997. "Brutality in Vietnam." *New York Times,* March 28. http://www.nytimes.com/1997/03/28/opinion/brutality-in-vietnam.html.

Hertel, Shareen, Lyle Scruggs, and C. Patrick Heidkamp. 2009. "Human Rights and Public Opinion: From Attitudes to Action." *Political Science Quarterly* 124, no. 3:443–59.

Hetherington, Kregg. 2011. *Guerrilla Auditors: The Politics of Transparency in Neoliberal Paraguay.* Durham, NC: Duke University Press.

Hinrichs, Clare, and Kathy S. Kremer. 2002. "Social Inclusion in a Midwest Local Food System Project." *Journal of Poverty* 6, no. 1:65–90.

Hiscox, Michael, Michael Broukhim, and Claire Litwin. 2011. "Consumer Demand for Fair Trade: New Evidence from a Field Experiment Using Ebay Auctions of Fresh Roasted Coffee." Working paper, Social Science Research Network. http://ssrn.com/abstract=1811783.

Hiscox, Michael J., and Nicholas F. B. Smyth. 2006. "Is There Consumer Demand for Fair Labor Standards? Evidence from a Field Experiment." Working paper, Social Science Research Network. http://ssrn.com/abstract=1820642.

Hobsbawm, Eric J. 1952. "The Machine Breakers." *Past and Present* 1:57–70.

Holzer, Boris. 2006. "Political Consumerism between Individual Choice and Collective Action: Social Movements, Role Mobilization, and Signalling." *International Journal of Consumer Studies* 30, no. 5:406–15.

———. 2007. "Framing the Corporation: Royal Dutch/Shell and Human Right Woes in Nigeria." *Journal of Consumer Policy* 30, no. 3:281–301.

Holzman, David C. 2012. "Organic Food Conclusions Don't Tell the Whole Story." *Environmental Health Perspectives* 120, no. 12:a458.

Hospes, Otto, Olga van der Valk, and J. Mheen-Sluijer. 2012. "Parallel Development of Five Partnerships to Promote Sustainable Soy in Brazil: Solution or Part of Wicked Problems." *International Food and Agribusiness Management Review* 15, no. B: 39–62.

Huang, Sophia Wu, and Kuo S. Huang. 2007. "Increased US Imports of Fresh Fruits and Vegetables." Report issued by the U.S. Department of Agriculture, Economic Research Service. http://www.ers.usda.gov/media/187841/fts32801_1_.pdf.

Huang, Yan. 2008. "Labor Solidarity in Contract Manufacturing: The Staff Committee Experiment in Xinda Company as an Example." *Chinese Journal of Sociology* 28, no. 4:20–33.

Huang, Yan, and Weiqing Guo. 2006. "The Transnational Network and Labor Rights in China." *China Rights Forum* 3:57–62.

Hughes, Caroline. 2007. "Transnational Networks, International Organizations and Political Participation in Cambodia: Human Rights, Labour Rights and Common Rights." *Democratization* 14, no. 5:834–52.

Hughner, Renée Shaw, Pierre McDonagh, Andrea Prothero, J. Shultz Clifford, and Julie Stanton. 2007. "Who Are Organic Food Consumers? A Compilation and Review of Why People Purchase Organic Food." *Journal of Consumer Behaviour* 6:1–17.

Human Rights Watch. 2006. "Too High a Price: The Human Rights Cost of the Indonesian Military's Economic Activities." Report issued by Human Rights Watch, New York. http://www.hrw.org/reports/2006/06/20/too-high-price.

Humphries, Shoana, Richard P. Vlosky, and Douglas Carter. 2001. "Certified Wood Products Merchants in the United States: A Comparison between 1995 and 1998." *Forest Products Journal* 51, no. 6:32–38.

Inglehart, Ronald. 1990. *Culture Shift in Advanced Industrial Society.* Princeton, NJ: Princeton University Press.

———. 1997. *Modernization and Postmodernization: Cultural, Economic, and Political Change in 43 Societies.* Princeton, NJ: Princeton University Press.

Interfaith Center on Corporate Responsibility. 2010. "Investor Statement Regarding Suicides and Working Conditions at Electronics Manufacturing Facilities." Report issued by the Interfaith Center on Corporate Responsibility, New York. http://www.bostoncommonasset.com/news/documents/InvestorStatementonWorkingConditionsJuly212010.pdf.

International Labor Organization. 2011. "Report of the Committee of Experts on the Application of Conventions and Recommendations." Report issued by the International Labor Organization, Geneva, Switzerland.

Jacobsen, Eivind, and Arne Dulsrud. 2007. "Will Consumers Save the World? The Framing of Political Consumerism." *Journal of Agricultural and Environmental Ethics* 20:469–82.

Jaffee, Daniel. 2007. *Brewing Justice: Fair Trade Coffee, Sustainability, and Survival.* Berkeley: University of California Press.

———. 2012. "Weak Coffee: Certification and Co-Optation in the Fair Trade Movement." *Social Problems* 59, no. 1:94–116.

James, Harvey S., Jr., Mary K. Hendrickson, and Philip H. Howard. 2013. "Networks, Power, and Dependency in the Agrifood Industry." In *The Ethics and Economics of Agrifood Competition,* edited by Harvey S. James Jr., 99–126. New York: Springer.

Jaruzelski, Barry, John Loehr, and Richard Holman. 2013. "The Global Innovation 1000: Navigating the Digital Future." *Strategy+Business Magazine* 73:2–14. http://www.strategyand

.pwc.com/media/file/Strategyand_2013-Global-Innovation-1000-Study-Navigating-the-Digital-Future.pdf.

Jay, Jason, and Mark Lundy. 2008. "The Juan Francisco Project Costco and CIAT's Exploration of Guatemalan Green Beans." In "Innovations for Healthy Value Chains." Report issued by the MIT Sustainable Food Lab, Cambridge, MA. http://sustainablefood.org/images/stories/pdf/hvcn%20innovations%20master%20document%20v15.pdf.

Jepperson, Ronald L. 2002. "Political Modernities: Disentangling Two Underlying Dimensions of Institutional Differentiation." *Sociological Theory* 20, no. 1:61–85.

Johnston, Bruce F., and John W. Mellor. 1961. "The Role of Agriculture in Economic Development." *American Economic Review* 51, no. 4:566–93.

Johnston, Josée. 2008. "The Citizen-Consumer Hybrid: Ideological Tensions and the Case of Whole Foods Market." *Theory and Society* 37, no. 3:229–70.

Johnston, Josée, and Lauren Baker. 2005. "Eating Outside the Box: Foodshare's Good Food Box and the Challenge of Scale." *Agriculture and Human Values* 22, no. 3:313–25.

Johnston, Josée, and Michelle Szabo. 2011. "Reflexivity and the Whole Foods Market Consumer: The Lived Experience of Shopping for Change." *Agriculture and Human Values* 28, no. 3:303–319.

Johnston, Josée, Michelle Szabo, and Alexandra Rodney. 2011. "Good Food, Good People: Understanding the Cultural Repertoire of Ethical Eating." *Journal of Consumer Culture* 11, no. 3:293–318.

Journal of Forestry. 1993. "Certifying Sustainable Forest Products: A Roundtable Discussion." *Journal of Forestry* 91, no. 11:33–38.

Kaipia, Riikka, Hille Korhonen, and Helena Hartiala. 2006. "Planning Nervousness in a Demand Supply Network: An Empirical Study." *International Journal of Logistics Management* 17, no. 1:95–113.

Katz, Harry, and Charles Sabel. 1985. "Industrial Relations and Industrial Adjustment in the Car Industry." *Industrial Relations: A Journal of Economy and Society* 24, no. 3:295–315.

Katz, Michael L., and Carl Shapiro. 1994. "Systems Competition and Network Effects." *Journal of Economic Perspectives* 8:93–93.

Kaufman, Phil R. 2000. "Consolidation in Food Retailing: Prospects for Consumers and Grocery Suppliers." *Agricultural Outlook* 273:18–22.

Kay, Cristóbal. 2002. "Why East Asia Overtook Latin America: Agrarian Reform, Industrialisation and Development." *Third World Quarterly* 23, no. 6:1073–1102.

Keck, Margaret, and Kathryn Sikkink. 1998. *Activists beyond Borders: Trans-National Advocacy Networks in International Politics.* Ithaca, NY: Cornell University Press.

Kern, Kristine, Ingrid Kissling-Näf, Ute Landmann, Corine Mauch and Tina Löffelsend. 2001. "Policy Convergence and Policy Diffusion by Governmental and Non-Governmental Institutions: An International Comparison of Eco-Labeling Systems." *WZB Discussion Paper FS II 01-305*: 66 p.

Khan, Wasima. 2013. "Toward Electronics Free of Conflict Minerals." *Huffington Post.* October 28. http://www.huffingtonpost.com/student-reporter/towards-electronics-free_b_4171929.html.

Kim, L. 1997. "The Dynamics of Samsung's Technological Learning in Semiconductors." *California Management Review* 39, no. 3:86–100.

Kinderman, Daniel. 2012. "'Free Us Up So We Can Be Responsible!' The Co-Evolution of Corporate Social Responsibility and Neo-Liberalism in the UK, 1977–2010." *Socio-Economic Review* 10, no. 1:29–57.

Kiss, Jemima. 2012. "The Real Price of an iPhone 5: Life in the Foxconn Factory." *Guardian*, September 13. http://www.theguardian.com/technology/2012/sep/13/cost-iphone-5 -foxconn-factory.

Klein, Naomi. 1999. *No Logo: Taking Aim at the Brand Bullies*. New York: Picador.

Kline, John M. 2010. "Alta Gracia: Branding Decent Work Conditions." Report for the Kalmanovitz Initiative for Labor and the Working Poor. Karl F. Landegger Program in International Business Diplomacy, Georgetown University. https://georgetown.app.box.com/s /wntf7bah81s1vbbg6ar3.

Klooster, Dan. 2006. "Environmental Certification of Forests in Mexico: The Political Ecology of a Nongovernmental Market Intervention." *Annals of the Association of American Geographers* 96, no. 3:541–65.

———. 2010. "Standardizing Sustainable Development? The Forest Stewardship Council's Plantation Policy Review Process as Neoliberal Environmental Governance." *Geoforum* 41, no. 1:117–29.

Koh, Lian Pin, and David S. Wilcove. 2008. "Is Oil Palm Agriculture Really Destroying Tropical Biodiversity?" *Conservation Letters* 1, no. 2:60–64.

Kollert, Walter, and Peter Lagan. 2007. "Do Certified Tropical Logs Fetch a Market Premium? A Comparative Price Analysis from Sabah, Malaysia." *Forest Policy and Economics* 9, no. 7:862–68.

Koos, Sebastian. 2011. "Varieties of Environmental Labelling, Market Structures, and Sustainable Consumption across Europe: A Comparative Analysis of Organizational and Market Supply Determinants of Environmental-Labelled Goods." *Journal of Consumer Policy* 34, no. 1:127–51.

———. 2012. "What Drives Political Consumption in Europe? A Multi-Level Analysis on Individual Characteristics, Opportunity Structures, and Globalization." *Acta Sociologica* 55, no. 1:37–57.

KPMG. 2011. "Conflict Minerals Provisions of Dodd-Frank." Report issued by KPMG, New York. http://www.kpmg.com/Global/en/IssuesAndInsights/ArticlesPublications /Documents/dodd-frank-conflict-minerals.pdf.

———. 2013. "Sustainable Insight: A Roadmap to Responsible Soy." Report issued by KPMG, New York. https://www.kpmg.com/Global/en/IssuesAndInsights/ArticlesPublications /sustainable-insight/Documents/roadmap-responsible-soy-v2.pdf.

Kraemer, Kenneth L., Greg Linden, and Jason Dedrick. 2011. "Capturing Value in Global Networks: Apple's iPad and iPhone." Working paper, University of California, Irvine; University of California, Berkeley; and Syracuse University, New York. http://pcic.merage.uci .edu/papers/2011/value_iPad_iPhone.pdf.

Krier, Jean-Marie. 2001. "Fair Trade in Europe 2001. Facts and Figures on the Fair Trade Sector in 18 European Countries." Report issued by the European Fair Trade Organization, Maastricht, Netherlands. http://www.european-fair-trade-association.org/efta/Doc /FT-E-2001.pdf.

Krippner, Greta. 2007. "The Making of US Monetary Policy: Central Bank Transparency and the Neoliberal Dilemma." *Theory and Society* 36, no. 6:477–513.

Krupat, Kitty. 1997. "From War Zone to Free Trade Zone: A History of the National Labor Committee." In *No Sweat: Fashion, Free Trade, and the Rights of Garment Workers*, edited by Andrew Ross, 51–77. New York: Verso.

Kuhn, Peter, and Kailing Shen. 2013. "Gender Discrimination in Job Ads: Evidence from China." *Quarterly Journal of Economics* 128, no. 1:287–336.

Kumar, Nirmalya, and Jan-Benedict E. M. Steenkamp. 2007. *Private Label Strategy: How to Meet the Store Brand Challenge.* Boston: Harvard Business Press.

Kuruvilla, Sarosh, Ching Kwan Lee, and Mary E. Gallagher, eds. 2011. *From Iron Rice Bowl to Informalization: Markets, Workers, and the State in a Changing China.* Ithaca, NY: Cornell University Press.

Labor Rights in China (LARIC). 1999. *No Illusions: Against the Global Cosmetic SA8000.* Report issued by Labor Rights in China, Hong Kong. http://www.lancaster.ac.uk/fass/law/intlaw/ibuslaw/docs/noillusions.doc.

Lamont, Michèle. 1992. *Money, Morals, and Manners: The Culture of the French and the American Upper-Middle Class.* Chicago: University of Chicago Press.

Lawson, Sam, and Larry MacFaul. 2010. "Illegal Logging and Related Trade." Report issued by Chatham House, London. http://www.chathamhouse.org/sites/files/chathamhouse/public/Research/Energy,%20Environment%20and%20Development/0710bp_illegal logging.pdf.

Lee, Ching Kwan. 2007. *Against the Law: Labor Protests in China's Rustbelt and Sunbelt.* Berkeley: University of California Press.

Lee, Peter. 2007. "Reebok's Chinese Trade Union Experiment: Five Years On." Report issued by China Labor News Translations. http://www.clntranslations.org/file_download/19.

Leinbach, Thomas R., and John T. Bowen. 2004. "Air Cargo Services and the Electronics Industry in Southeast Asia." *Journal of Economic Geography* 4, no. 3:299–321.

Leperouse, Philippe de. 2012. "Case Studies on Private Investment in Farmland and Agricultural Infrastructure." Report issued by Highquest Partners, Danvers, MA. http://www.landandpoverty.com/agenda/pdfs/paper/de_laperouse_paper.pdf.

Level Works. 2006. "Wages, Benefits, and Work Hours in the Peoples Republic of China." Report issued by Level Works Limited, San Francisco.

Levitz, Jennifer. 2012. "Tissue Rolls to Mill's Rescue." *Wall Street Journal,* February 16. http://online.wsj.com/articles/SB10001424052970204062704577222942113965390.

Lewis, W. Arthur. 1954. "Economic Development with Unlimited Supplies of Labour." *Manchester School* 22, no. 2:139–91.

Lezhnev, Sasha, and Alex Hellmuth. 2012. "Taking Conflict out of Consumer Gadgets." Report issued by The Enough Project, Washington, DC. http://www.enoughproject.org/files/CorporateRankings2012.pdf.

Li & Fung Research Centre. 2012. "China's Apparel Market, 2012." Report issued by Li & Fung Research Centre, Hong Kong. http://www.funggroup.com/eng/knowledge/research/industry_series21.pdf.

Li, Tania Murray. 2010. "Indigeneity, Capitalism, and the Management of Dispossession." *Current Anthropology* 51, no. 3:385–414.

Linden, Eugene. 1989. "Torching the Amazon: Can the Rain Forest Be Saved?" *Time,* September 18.

Linton, April, Cindy C. Liou, and Kelly A. Shaw. 2004. "A Taste of Trade Justice: Marketing Global Social Responsibility via Fair Trade Coffee." *Globalizations* 1, no. 2:223–46.

Liu, Mingwei. 2010. "Union Organizing in China: Still a Monolithic Labor Movement?" *Industrial and Labor Relations Review* 64, no. 1:30–52.

Locke, Richard, Matthew Amengual, and Akshay Mangla. 2009. "Virtue out of Necessity? Compliance, Commitment, and the Improvement of Labor Conditions in Global Supply Chains." *Politics and Society* 37, no. 3:319–51.

Locke, Richard M. 2013. *The Promise and Limits of Private Power: Promoting Labor Standards in a Global Economy*. New York: Cambridge University Press.

Locke, Richard M., Greg Distelhorst, Timea Pal, and Hiram M. Samel. 2012. "Production Goes Global, Standards Stay Local: Private Labor Regulation in the Global Electronics Industry." Working paper, Social Science Research Network. http://ssrn.com/abstract =1978908.

Locke, Richard M., Thomas Kochan, Monica Romis, and Fei Qin. 2007. "Beyond Corporate Codes of Conduct: Work Organization and Labour Standards at Nike's Suppliers." *International Labour Review* 146, no. 1–2:21–40.

Locke, Richard M., Ben A. Rissing, and Timea Pal. 2013. "Complements or Substitutes? Private Codes, State Regulation, and the Enforcement of Labour Standards in Global Supply Chains." *British Journal of Industrial Relations* 51, no. 3:519–52.

Locke, Richard M., and Hiram M. Samel. 2012. "Looking in the Wrong Places? Labor Standards and Upstream Business Practices in the Global Electronics Industry." Working paper, Social Science Research Network. http://ssrn.com/abstract=2102634.

Locke, Richard, Fei Qin, and Alberto Brause. 2007. "Does Monitoring Improve Labor Standards? Lessons from Nike." *Industrial and Labor Relations Review* 61, no. 1:3–31.

Louie, Miriam Ching Yoon. 2001. *Sweatshop Warriors: Immigrant Women Take on the Global Factory*. Cambridge, MA: South End Press.

Loureiro, Maria L., and Justus Lotade. 2005. "Do Fair Trade and Eco-Labels in Coffee Wake Up the Consumer Conscience?" *Ecological Economics* 53, no. 1:129–38.

Lüthje, Boy. 2002. "Electronics Contract Manufacturing: Global Production and the International Division of Labor in the Age of the Internet." *Industry and Innovation* 9, no. 3:227–47.

Lyon, Sarah, and Mark Moberg, eds. 2010. *Fair Trade and Social Justice: Global Ethnographies*. New York: NYU Press.

Macedo, Stephen, Yvette Alex-Assensoh, Jeffrey M. Berry, Michael Brintnall, David E. Campbell, Luis Ricardo Fraga, Archon Fung, et al. 2005. *Democracy at Risk: How Political Choices Undermine Citizen Participation and What We Can Do about It*. Washington, DC: Brookings Institution Press.

MacGillivray, Carrie, Vernon Turner, and Denise Lund. 2013. "Worldwide Internet of Things (IoT) 2013–2020 Forecast: Billions of Things, Trillions of Dollars." Report issued by the International Data Corporation (IDC), Framingham, MA. http://www.idc.com/getdoc .jsp?containerId=243661.

Malets, Olga. 2011. "From Transnational Voluntary Standards to Local Practices: A Case Study of Forest Certification in Russia." Working paper, Max-Planck-Institut für Gesellschaftsforschung, MPIfG Discussion Paper 11/7, Cologne, Germany.

———. 2013. "The Translation of Transnational Voluntary Standards into Practices: Civil Society and the Forest Stewardship Council in Russia." *Journal of Civil Society* 9, no. 3:300–24.

Mamic, Ivanka. 2004. *Implementing Codes of Conduct: How Businesses Manage Social Performance in Global Supply Chains*. Sheffield, UK: Greenleaf Publishing.

Maniates, Michael F. 2001. "Individualization: Plant a Tree, Buy a Bike, Save the World?" *Global Environmental Politics* 1, no. 3:31–52.

———. 2013. "Teaching for Turbulence." In *State of the World 2013: Is Sustainability Still Possible?*, edited by Worldwatch Institute, 255–268. Washington, DC: Island Press.

Maniates, Michael, and John M. Meyer. 2010. *The Environmental Politics of Sacrifice*. Cambridge, MA: MIT Press.

Maquila Solidarity Network. 2006. "Is Fair Trade a Good Fit for the Garment Industry?" MSN Discussion Paper. http://en.maquilasolidarity.org/en/node/215.

Marketwatch. 2013. "iPhones and Other Portables Suffering from 'Device Exhaustion,' Analyst Says." *Wall Street Journal MarketWatch Blog.* http://blogs.marketwatch.com/thetell/2013/08/20/iphones-and-other-portables-suffering-from-device-exhaustion-analyst-says.

Martinelli, Enzo. 1998. "Fair Trade in Europe: Facts and Figures on the Fair Trade Sector in 16 European Countries." Report issued by the European Fair Trade Association, Maastricht, Netherlands.

Martinez, Stephen W. 2007. "The US Food Marketing System: Recent Developments, 1997–2006." Report issued by the United States Department of Agriculture, Economic Research Service. http://www.ers.usda.gov/media/196925/err42_1_.pdf.

Marymount University Center for Ethical Concerns. 1999. "The Consumer and Sweatshops." Report issued by Marymount University, Arlington, VA. www.marymount.edu/news/garmentstudy.

Mayer, Frederick, and Gary Gereffi. 2010. "Regulation and Economic Globalization: Prospects and Limits of Private Governance." *Business and Politics* 12, no. 3:1–27.

McAdam, Doug. 1982. *Political Process and the Development of Black Insurgency, 1930–1970.* Chicago: University of Chicago Press.

McAllister, Lesley K., Benjamin Van Rooij, and Robert A. Kagan. 2010. "Reorienting Regulation: Pollution Enforcement in Industrializing Countries." *Law and Policy* 32, no. 1:1–13.

McCarthy, John F., Piers Gillespie, and Zahari Zen. 2012. "Swimming Upstream: Local Indonesian Production Networks in 'Globalized' Palm Oil Production." *World Development* 40, no. 3:555–69.

McCarthy, John F., and Rob A. Cramb. 2009. "Policy Narratives, Landholder Engagement, and Oil Palm Expansion on the Malaysian and Indonesian Frontiers." *Geographical Journal* 175, no. 2:112–23.

McCubbins, Matthew D., and Thomas Schwartz. 1984. "Congressional Oversight Overlooked: Police Patrols versus Fire Alarms." *American Journal of Political Science* 28, no. 1:165–79.

McDermott, Constance, and Benjamin Cashore. 2009. "Forestry Driver Mapping Project: Global and US Trade Report." Report issued by the Global Institute for Sustainable Forestry, Yale University. http://environment.yale.edu/gisf/files/Forestry_Driver_Mapping_Project_Report_012.pdf.

McDougall, Dan. 2007. "Indian 'Slave' Children Found Making Low-Cost Clothes Destined for Gap." *Observer,* October 27. http://www.theguardian.com/world/2007/oct/28/ethicalbusiness.retail.

McKay, Steven C. 2006. *Satanic Mills or Silicon Islands? The Politics of High-Tech Production in the Philippines.* Ithaca, NY: Cornell University Press.

McNichol, Jason. 2006. "Transnational NGO Certification Programs as New Regulatory Forms: Lessons from the Forestry Sector." In *Transnational Governance: Institutional Dynamics of Regulation,* edited by Marie-Laure Djelic and Kerstin Sahlin-Andersson, 349–74. New York: Cambridge University Press.

Meidinger, Errol E. 2003. "Forest Certification as a Global Civil Society Regulatory Institution." In *The Social and Political Dimensions of Forest Certification,* edited by Errol Meidinger, Chris Elliot, and Gerhard Oesten, 265–89. Remagen-Oberwinter, Germany: Forstbuch.

Merry, Sally Engle. 2006. *Human Rights and Gender Violence: Translating International Law into Local Justice.* Chicago: University of Chicago Press.

Meyer, John M., John Boli, George M. Thomas, and Francisco O. Ramirez. 1997. "World Society and the Nation State." *American Journal of Sociology* 103:144–81.

Michel, Callon, Meadel Cecile, and Raberharisoa Vololona. 2002. "The Economy of Qualities." *Economy and Society* 31, no. 2:194–217.

Micheletti, Michele. 2003. *Political Virtue and Shopping: Individuals, Consumerism, and Collective Action.* New York: Palgrave Macmillan.

Miller, Doug. 2013. *Last Nightshift in Savar: The Story of Spectrum Sweater Factory Collapse:* Pembrokeshire, Wales: McNidder and Grace.

Mintz, Sidney W. 1985. *Sweetness and Power.* New York: Penguin Books.

Molnar, Augusta. 2003. "Forest Certification and Communities: Looking Forward to the Next Decade." Report issued by Forest Trends, Washington, DC. http://www.forest -trends.org/documents/files/doc_126.pdf.

Moog, Sandra, Steffen Böhm, and André Spicer. 2014. "The Limits of Multi-Stakeholder Governance Forums: The Crisis of the Forest Stewardship Council." *Journal of Business Ethics* (advance access).

Mutersbaugh, Tad. 2002. "The Number Is the Beast: A Political Economy of Organic-Coffee Certification and Producer Unionism." *Environment and Planning A* 34, no. 7:1165–84.

Nannestad, Peter. 2008. "What Have We Learned about Generalized Trust, if Anything?" *Annual Review of Political Science* 11:413–36.

Nebel, Gustav, Lincoln Quevedo, Jette Bredahl Jacobsen, and Finn Helles. 2005. "Development and Economic Significance of Forest Certification: The Case of FSC in Bolivia." *Forest Policy and Economics* 7:175–86.

Neilson, Jeffrey, and Bill Pritchard. 2007. "10. The Final Frontier? The Global Roll-Out of the Retail Revolution in India." In *Supermarkets and Agri-Food Supply Chains: Transformations in the Production and Consumption of Foods,* edited by David Burch and Geoffrey Lawrence, 219–35. Northampton, MA: Edward Elgar Publishing.

Neilson, Lisa. 2010. "Boycott or Buycott? Understanding Political Consumerism." *Journal of Consumer Behaviour* 9, no. 3:214–27.

Neilson, Lisa A., and Pamela Paxton. 2010. "Social Capital and Political Consumerism: A Multilevel Analysis." *Social Problems* 57, no. 1:5–24.

New Venture Research Corporation. 2009. "The Worldwide Electronics Manufacturing Market." Report issued by the New Venture Research Corporation, Nevada City, California. http://www.home.agilent.com/upload/cmc_upload/All/Worldwide_Market_and _Trends_for_Electronics_Manufacturing_Services_09Oct08.pdf?&cc=GB&lc=eng.

Newsom, Deanna, and Daphne Hewitt. 2005. "The Global Impacts of SmartWood Certification." White paper issued by the Rainforest Alliance, New York. http://teebforbusiness .earthmind.net/files/The_Global_Impacts_of_SmartWood_Certification.pdf.

Nicholls, Alex, and Charlotte Opal. 2005. *Fair Trade: Market-Driven Ethical Consumption.* London: Sage Publications.

Norris, Pippa. 2002. *Democratic Phoenix. Reinventing Political Activism.* Cambridge, UK: Cambridge University Press.

Northam, Jackie. 2013. "Can This Dominican Factory Pay Good Wages and Make a Profit?" National Public Radio News, June 20. http://www.npr.org/templates/transcript /transcript.php?storyId=193491766.

Nova, Scott. 2011. "P.R. Coup." *Boston Review,* November 17.

Nova, Scott, and John M. Kline. 2014. "Social Labeling and Supply Chain Reform: The Designated Supplier Program and the Alta Gracia Label." In *Workers' Rights and Labor Compli-*

ance in Global Supply Chains: Is a Social Label the Answer?, edited by Jennifer Bair, Marsha A. Dickson, and Doug Miller, 262–81. New York: Routledge.

Nussbaum, Ruth, and Markku Simula. 2004. "Forest Certification: A Review of Impacts and Assessment Frameworks." The Forests Dialogue: Yale University School of Forestry and Environmental Studies. http://www.proforest.net/objects/publications/tfd-forest-certification-executive-summary.pdf.

O'Connor, Clare. 2013. "New App Lets You Boycott Koch Brothers, Monsanto and More by Scanning Your Shopping Cart." Forbes, May 14. http://www.forbes.com/sites/clareoconnor/2013/05/14/new-app-lets-you-boycott-koch-brothers-monsanto-and-more-by-scanning-your-shopping-cart.

O'Rourke, Dara. 1997. "Smoke from a Hired Gun: A Critique of Nike's Labor and Environmental Auditing in Vietnam as Performed by Ernst & Young." Transnational Resource and Action Center, San Francisco. http://nature.berkeley.edu/orourke/PDF/smoke.pdf.

———. 2002. "Monitoring the Monitors: A Critique of Corporate Third-Party Labor Monitoring." In Corporate Responsibility and Labour Rights: Codes of Conduct in the Global Economy, edited by Rhys Jenkins, Ruth Pearson, and Gill Seyfang, 196–208. London: Earthscan.

———. 2003. "Outsourcing Regulation: Analyzing Non-governmental Systems of Labor Standards and Monitoring." Policy Studies Journal 31:1–29.

———. 2011. "Citizen Consumer." Boston Review, November 17.

Obach, Brian K., and Kathleen Tobin. 2013. "Civic Agriculture and Community Engagement." Agriculture and Human Values 31, no.2:307–322.

Organization for Economic Cooperation and Development (OECD). 2013. Agricultural Policy Monitoring and Evaluation 2013: OECD Countries and Emerging Economies. Paris: OECD Publishing.

Ohno, K. 2009. The Middle Income Trap: Implications for Industrialization Strategies in East Asia and Africa. Tokyo: GRIPS Development Forum, National Graduate Institute for Policy Studies. http://www.grips.ac.jp/forum/pdf09/MIT.pdf.

Organic Trade Association. 2011. "OTA Industry Statistics and Projected Growth." Report issued by the Organic Trade Association. http://www.ota.com/organic/mt/business.html.

Oster, Shai. 2011. "China's Rising Wages Propel U.S. Prices." Wall Street Journal, May 9. http://online.wsj.com/articles/SB10001424052748703849204576302972415758878.

Overdevest, Christine. 2010. "Comparing Forest Certification Schemes: The Case of Ratcheting Standards in the Forest Sector." Socio-Economic Review 8, no. 1:47–76.

Oxfam. 2013. "History of Oxfam." http://www.oxfam.org.uk/what-we-do/about-us/history-of-oxfam.

Ozanne, Lucie K., and Richard P. Vlosky. 1997. "Willingness to Pay for Environmentally Certified Wood Products: A Consumer Perspective." Forest Products Journal 47, no. 6:39–48.

———. 2003. "Certification from the U.S. Consumer Perspective: A Comparison from 1995 and 2000." Forest Products Journal 53, no. 3:13–21.

Ozcaglar-Toulouse, Nil, Edward Shiu, and Deirdre Shaw. 2006. "In Search of Fair Trade: Ethical Consumer Decision Making in France." International Journal of Consumer Studies 30, no. 5:502–14.

Pakulski, Jan, and Malcolm Waters. 1996. The Death of Class. London: Sage.

Peine, Emelie K. 2013. "Trading on Pork and Beans: Agribusiness and the Construction of the Brazil-China-Soy-Pork Commodity Complex." In The Ethics and Economics of Agrifood Competition, edited by Harvey S. James Jr., 188–202. New York: Springer.

Peluso, Nancy Lee. 1992. *Rich Forests, Poor People: Resource Control and Resistance in Java.* Berkeley: University of California Press.

Piore, Michael. 1997. "The Economics of the Sweatshop." In *No Sweat: Fashion, Free Trade and the Rights of Garment Workers,* edited by Andrew Ross, 135–42. New York: Verso.

Piore, Michael, and Andrew Schrank. 2008. "Toward Managed Flexibility: The Revival of Labour Inspection in the Latin World." *International Labour Review* 147:1–23.

Ponte, Stefano. 2008. "Greener Than Thou: The Political Economy of Fish Ecolabeling and Its Local Manifestations in South Africa." *World Development* 36, no. 1:159–75.

———. 2014. "'Roundtabling' Sustainability: Lessons from the Biofuel Industry." *Geoforum* 54:261–72.

Ponte, Stefano, and Emmanuelle Cheyns. 2013. "Voluntary Standards, Expert Knowledge, and the Governance of Sustainability Networks." *Global Networks* 13, no. 4:459–77.

Porter, Michael E., and Mark R. Kramer. 2006. "Strategy and Society: The Link between Competitive Advantage and Corporate Social Responsibility." *Harvard Business Review* 84, no. 12:78–92.

Potoski, Matthew, and Aseem Prakash. 2009. "A Club Theory Approach to Voluntary Programs." In *Voluntary Programs: A Club Theory Perspective,* edited by Matthew Potoski and Aseem Prakash, 17–40. Cambridge: MIT Press.

Prasad, Monica, Howard Kimeldorf, Rachel Meyer, and Ian Robinson. 2004. "Consumers of the World Unite: A Market-Based Response to Sweatshops." *Labor Studies Journal* 29, no. 3:57–79.

Pun, Ngai. 2005. "Global Production, Company Codes of Conduct, and Labor Conditions in China: A Case Study of Two Factories." *China Journal* 54:101–13.

Putnam, Robert D. 2001. *Bowling Alone: The Collapse and Revival of American Community.* New York: Simon and Schuster.

Putnam, Robert D., Robert Leonardi, and Raffaella Y. Nanetti. 1994. *Making Democracy Work: Civic Traditions in Modern Italy.* Princeton, NJ: Princeton University Press.

Rainforest Foundation. 2002. *Trading in Credibility: The Myth and Reality of the Forest Stewardship Council.* London: Rainforest Foundation.

Raj-Reichert, Gale. 2011. "The Electronic Industry Code of Conduct: Private Governance in a Competitive and Contested Global Production Network." *Competition and Change* 15, no. 3:221–38.

———. 2012. "Safeguarding Labour in Distant Factories: Health and Safety Governance in an Electronics Global Production Network." *Geoforum* 44:23–31.

Ramey, Joanna. 1996. "10 Makers, Retailers Sign On for Clinton's Anti-Sweatshop Panel." In *Women's Wear Daily,* August 5, 1–2.

Ramey, Joanna, and Joyce Barrett. 1996. "Apparel's Ethics Dilemma." *Women's Wear Daily,* March 18, 10–13.

Rao, Hayagreeva. 1998. "Caveat Emptor: The Construction of Nonprofit Consumer Watchdog Organizations." *American Journal of Sociology* 103:912–61.

Raschke, Markus. 2009. *Fairer Handel. Engagement für eine gerechte Weltwirtschaft.* Ostfildern, Germany: Matthias-Grünewald-Verlag.

Raynolds, Laura T. 1994. "The Restructuring of Third World Agro-Exports: Changing Production Relations in the Dominican Republic." In *The Global Restructuring of Agro-Food Systems,* edited by Philip McMichael, 214–237. Ithaca, NY: Cornell University Press.

———. 2004. "The Globalization of Organic Agro-Food Networks." *World Development* 32, no. 5:725–43.

Raynolds, Laura T., Douglas Murray, and Peter Leigh Taylor. 2004. "Fair Trade Coffee: Building Producer Capacity via Global Networks." *Journal of International Development* 16, no. 8:1109–121.

Reardon, Thomas, Christopher B. Barrett, Julio A. Berdegué, and Johan F. M. Swinnen. 2009. "Agrifood Industry Transformation and Small Farmers in Developing Countries." *World Development* 37, no. 11:1717–27.

Reardon, Thomas, and Julio A. Berdegue. 2002. "The Rapid Rise of Supermarkets in Latin America: Challenges and Opportunities for Development." *Development Policy Review* 20, no. 4:371–88.

Reardon, Thomas, C. Peter Timmer, Christopher B. Barrett, and Julio Berdegue. 2003. "The Rise of Supermarkets in Africa, Asia, and Latin America." *American Journal of Agricultural Economics* 85, no. 5:1140–46.

Reich, Robert B. 2008. *Supercapitalism: The Transformation of Business, Democracy, and Everyday Life*. New York: Random House.

———. 2005. "Don't Blame Wal-Mart." *New York Times,* February 28. http://www.nytimes.com/2005/02/28/opinion/28reich.html?hp.

Renard, Marie-Christine. 1999. *Los intersticios de la globalización*. Mexico City: Centre Français d'Études Mexicaines et Centraméricaines.

Republic of Paraguay. 2008. "National Agricultural Census." Report issued by the Government of the Republic of Paraguay.

———. 2011. "National Agricultural Census." Report issued by the Government of the Republic of Paraguay.

RESOLVE. 2012. "Toward Sustainability: The Roles and Limits of Certification." Report issued by the Steering Committee of the State-of-Knowledge Assessment of Standards and Certification. Washington, DC: RESOLVE.

Rice, Paul D., and Jennifer McLean. 1999. "Sustainable Coffee at the Crossroads." White paper prepared for the Consumer's Choice Council, Washington, DC. http://www.greenbeanery.ca/bean/documents/sustainableCoffee.pdf.

Richter, Toralf, and Susanne Padel. 2005. "The European Market for Organic Foods." In *The World of Organic Agriculture: Statistics and Emerging Trends,* edited by Helga Willer and Minou Yussefi, 107–21. Bonn: International Federation of Organic Agriculture Movements (IFOAM).

Rodríguez-Garavito, César A. 2005. "Global Governance and Labor Rights: Codes of Conduct and Anti-Sweatshop Struggles in Global Apparel Factories in Mexico and Guatemala." *Politics and Society* 33, no. 2:203–33.

Rodrik, Dani. 2011. *The Globalization Paradox*. New York: W. W. Norton.

Rolnick, Alan L. 1997. "Muzzling the Offshore Watchdogs." *Bobbin,* February, 72–73.

Rose, Nikolas. 2000. "Government and Control." *British Journal of Criminology* 40:321–39.

Rosen, Ellen Israel. 2002. *Making Sweatshops: The Globalization of the U.S. Apparel Industry*. Berkeley: University of California Press.

Ross, Robert J. S. 2004. *Slaves to Fashion: Poverty and Abuse in the New Sweatshops*. Ann Arbor: University of Michigan Press.

———. 2006. "A Tale of Two Factories: Successful Resistance to Sweatshops and the Limits of Firefighting." *Labor Studies Journal* 30, no. 4:65–85.

Roth, Louise Marie, and Jeffrey C. Kroll. 2007. "Risky Business: Assessing Risk Preference Explanations for Gender Differences in Religiosity." *American Sociological Review* 72, no. 2:205–20.

Roundtable on Sustainable Palm Oil (RSPO). 2004. "RSPO By-laws." Report issued by RSPO. http://www.rspo.org/file/RSPO%20By-laws.pdf.

Ruben, Ruerd, and Ricardo Fort. 2012. "The Impact of Fair Trade Certification for Coffee Farmers in Peru." *World Development* 40, no. 3:570–82.

Rugman, Alan, and Stéphane Girod. 2003. "Retail Multinationals and Globalization: The Evidence Is Regional." *European Management Journal* 21, no. 1:24–37.

Ruslandi, Oscar Venter, and Francis E. Putz. 2011. "Overestimating Conservation Costs in Southeast Asia." *Frontiers in Ecology and the Environment* 9:542–44.

Sabel, Charles. 2007. "Rolling Rule Labor Standards: Why Their Time Has Come, and Why We Should Be Glad of It." In *Protecting Labour Rights as Human Rights: Present and Future of International Supervision,* edited by George P. Politakis, 257–73. Geneva: International Labor Organization (ILO).

Sabel, Charles, Dara O'Rourke, and Archon Fung. 2000. "Ratcheting Labor Standards: Regulation for Continuous Improvement in the Global Workplace." Working paper, Social Science Research Network. http://ssrn.com/abstract=253833.

Sabel, Charles, and Jonathan Zeitlin. 1985. "Historical Alternatives to Mass Production: Politics, Markets, and Technology in Nineteenth-Century Industrialization." *Past and Present* 108:133–76.

Salzinger, Leslie. 2003. *Genders in Production: Making Workers in Mexico's Global Factories.* Berkeley: University of California Press.

Samel, Hiram M. 2012. "Upgrading under Volatility in a Global Economy." Social Science Research Network. http://ssrn.com/abstract=2102643.

Sandıkcı, Özlem, and Ahmet Ekici. 2009. "Politically Motivated Brand Rejection." *Journal of Business Research* 62, no. 2:208–17.

Santos, Boaventura de Sousa. 2006. "Globalizations." *Theory, Culture, and Society* 23:393–99.

Santos, Boaventura de Sousa, and César A. Rodríguez Garavito. 2005. "Law, Politics, and the Subaltern in Counter-Hegemonic Globalization." In *Law and Globalization from Below,* edited by Boaventura de Sousa Santos and César A. Rodríguez Garavito, 1–26. New York: Cambridge University Press.

Sassatelli, Roberta. 2007. *Consumer Culture: History, Theory, and Politics.* Los Angeles: Sage Publications.

Satariano, Adam, and Peter Burrows. 2011. "Apple's Supply-Chain Secret? Hoard Lasers." *BusinessWeek,* November 3. http://www.businessweek.com/magazine/apples-supplychain-secret-hoard-lasers-11032011.html.

———. 2012. "No Company Follows Apple's Expanded China Factory Audits." *Bloomberg News,* February 26. http://www.bloomberg.com/news/2012-02-27/no-company-follows-apple-allowing-expanded-china-audits-amid-abuses-tech.html.

Schaer, Burkhard. 2009. "The Organic Market in Europe: Trends and Challenges." In *The World of Organic Agriculture: Statistics and Emerging Trends 2009,* edited by Helga Willer and Lukas Kilcher, 164–67. Bonn: International Federation of Organic Agriculture Movements (IFOAM).

Schaller, Susanne. 2007. "The Democratic Legitimacy of Private Governance: An Analysis of the Ethical Trading Initiative." Working paper, University of Duisburg-Essen, Institutfür Entwicklungund Frieden (INEF) Report 91. http://inef.uni-due.de/cms/files/report91.pdf.

Schilling, Melissa A. 2002. "Technology Success and Failure in Winner-Take-All Markets: The Impact of Learning Orientation, Timing, and Network Externalities." *Academy of Management Journal* 45, no. 2:387–98.

Schipper, Irene, and Esther de Haan. 2007. "Hard (Disk) Labour: Research Report on Labour Conditions in the Thai Electronics Sector." Report issued by the Stichting Onderzoek Multinationale Ondernemingen (SOMO), Amsterdam. http://somo.nl/html/paginas/pdf /Hard_disk_labour_NL.pdf.

Schneiberg, Marc. 2007. "What's on the Path? Path Dependence, Organizational Diversity and the Problem of Institutional Change in the US Economy, 1900–1950." *Socio-Economic Review* 5, no. 1:47–80.

Schofer, Evan, and Marion Fourcade-Gourinchas. 2001. "The Structural Contexts of Civic Engagement: Voluntary Association Membership in Comparative Perspective." *American Sociological Review* 66, no. 6:806–828.

Schouten, Greetje, Pieter Leroy, and Pieter Glasbergen. 2012. "On the Deliberative Capacity of Private Multi-Stakeholder Governance: The Roundtables on Responsible Soy and Sustainable Palm Oil." *Ecological Economics* 83:42–50.

Schrank, Andrew. 2004. "Ready-to-Wear Development? Foreign Investment, Technology Transfer, and Learning by Watching in the Apparel Trade." *Social Forces* 83, no. 1:123–56.

———. 2013. "From Disguised Protectionism to Rewarding Regulation: The Impact of Trade-Related Labor Standards in the Dominican Republic." *Regulation and Governance* 7, no. 3:299–320.

Schudson, Michael. 1984. *Advertising, the Uneasy Persuasion*. New York: Basic Books.

———. 2007. "Citizens, Consumers, and the Good Society." *ANNALS of the American Academy of Political and Social Science* 611, no. 1:236–49.

Schulze, Mark, James Grogan, and Edson Vidal. 2008. "Forest Certification in Amazonia: Standards Matter." *Oryx* 42, no. 2:229–39.

Schurman, Rachel, and William Munro. 2009. "Targeting Capital: A Cultural Economy Approach to Understanding the Efficacy of Two Anti-Genetic Engineering Movements." *American Journal of Sociology* 115, no. 1:155–202.

Scott, Allen. 2006. "The Changing Global Geography of Low-Technology, Labor-Intensive Industry: Clothing, Footwear, and Furniture." *World Development* 34, no. 9:1517–36.

Seidman, Gay. 2007. *Beyond the Boycott: Labor Rights, Human Rights and Transnational Activism*. New York: Russell Sage Foundation/ASA Rose Series.

Setrini, Gustavo. 2011. "Global Niche Markets and Local Development: Clientelism and Fairtrade Farmer Organizations in Paraguay's Sugar Industry." PhD Dissertation. Massachusetts Institute of Technology.

Seyfang, Gill. 2005. "Shopping for Sustainability: Can Sustainable Consumption Promote Ecological Citizenship?" *Environmental Politics* 14, no. 2:290–306.

———. 2006. "Ecological Citizenship and Sustainable Consumption: Examining Local Organic Food Networks." *Journal of Rural Studies* 22, no. 4:383–95.

———. 2009. *The New Economics of Sustainable Consumption. Seeds of Change*. Houndmills, UK: Palgrave Macmillan.

Shamir, Ronen. 2004. "Between Self-Regulation and the Alien Tort Claims Act: On the Contested Concept of Corporate Social Responsibility." *Law and Society Review* 38, no. 4:635–64.

———. 2008. "The Age of Responsibilization: On Market-Embedded Morality." *Economy and Society* 37, no. 1:1–19.

Shaw, Deirdre. 2005. "Modelling Consumer Decision Making in Fair Trade." In *The Ethical Consumer*, edited by Rob Harrison, Terry Newholm, and Deirdre Shaw, 137–53. London: Sage Publications.

Silva-Castañeda, Laura. 2012. "A Forest of Evidence: Third-Party Certification and Multiple Forms of Proof—A Case Study of Oil Palm Plantations in Indonesia." *Agriculture and Human Values* 29, no. 3:361–70.

Silver, Beverly, and Lu Zhang. 2009. "China as an Emerging Epicenter of World Labor Unrest." In *China and the Transformation of Global Capitalism*, edited by Ho-fung Hung, 175–87. Baltimore: Johns Hopkins University Press.

Sklar, Kathryn Kish. 1998. "The Consumers' White Label Campaign of the National Consumers' League, 1898–1918." In *Getting and Spending: European and American Consumer Societies in the Twentieth Century*, edited by Susan Strasser, Charles McGovern, and Matthias Judt, 17–36. New York: Cambridge University Press.

SmartWood. 2006a. "Forest Management 2006 CAR Verification Audit Report for PT Intracawood Manufacturing." Report issued by SmartWood. Richmond, Vermont.

———. 2006b. "SmartWood Certification Assessment Report for PT Intracawood Manufacturing." Report issued by SmartWood. Richmond, Vermont.

———. 2008a. "Corrective Action Request Verification Report (Nov. 18): PT. INTRACAWOOD MANUFACTURING." Report issued by SmartWood. Richmond, Vermont.

———. 2008b. "Forest Management 2008 Annual Audit Report for PT Intracawood Manufacturing." Report issued by SmartWood. Richmond, Vermont.

———. 2008c. "Forest Management 2008 CAR Verification Audit Report for PT. Intracawood Manufacturing." Report issued by SmartWood. Richmond, Vermont.

———. 2012. "Forest Management Certification Reassessment 2011 Report for PT. Intracawood Manufacturing." Report issued by SmartWood. Richmond, Vermont.

Smith, N. Craig. 1990. *Morality and the Market*. London: Routledge.

Smith, Steve, and Alan Wolf. 2011. "Amazon's Gain Is Brick and Mortar's Pain in CE Share Shift." *Consumer Electronic News*. http://www.twice.com/news/retail/amazons-gain-brick-and-mortars-pain-ce-share-shift/5364.

Smith, Shawna N. 2014. "Trajectories of Equality: Fair Employment in the US, Great Britain, and Canada." PhD Dissertation. Indiana University.

Smith, Ted, David Sonnenfeld, and David N. Pellow. 2006. *Challenging the Chip: Labor Rights and Environmental Justice in the Global Electronics Industry*. Philadelphia: Temple University Press.

SOMO. 2012. "Bonded (Child) Labour in the South Indian Garment Industry." Report issued by the Stichting Onderzoek Multinationale Ondernemingen (SOMO), Amsterdam. http://somo.nl/publications-en/Publication_3818.

Sønderskov, Kim Mannemar. 2009. "Different Goods, Different Effects: Exploring the Effects of Generalized Social Trust in Large-N Collective Action." *Public Choice* 14, no. 1:145–60.

Southerton, Dale, Heather Chappells, and Bas Van Vliet, eds. 2004. *Sustainable Consumption: The Implications of Changing Infrastructures of Provision*. Cheltenham, UK: Edward Elgar Publishing.

Srivastava, Mehul, and Sarah Shannon. 2013. "A Bangladesh Factory Inspector's Grueling Day in the Life." *Bloomberg Businessweek*, May 30. http://www.businessweek.com/articles/2013-05-30/a-bangladesh-factory-inspectors-grueling-day-in-the-life.

Starr, Martha A. 2009. "The Social Economics of Ethical Consumption. Theoretical Considerations and Empirical Evidence." *Journal of Socio-Economics* 38:916–25.

Stecklow, Steve, and Erin White. 2004. "What Price Virtue? At Some Retailers, 'Fair Trade' Carries a Very High Cost." *Wall Street Journal*, June 8. http://online.wsj.com/articles/SB108664921254731069.

Stein, Leon, ed. 1977. *Out of the Sweatshop: The Struggle for Industrial Democracy.* New York: Quadrangle/New York Times Book Co.

Stokes, Ruth. 2013. "Activism for Busy People Part I: Ethical Consumption." *Ecologist* November 9. http://www.theecologist.org/green_green_living/2149420/activism_for _busy_people_part_i_ethical_consumption.html.

Stolle, Dietlind, Marc Hooghe, and Michele Micheletti. 2005. "Politics in the Supermarket: Political Consumerism as a Form of Political Participation." *International Political Science Review* 26, no. 3:245–69.

Stolle, Dietlind, and Michele Micheletti. 2013. *Political Consumerism: Global Responsibility in Action.* Cambridge: Cambridge University Press.

Streeck, Wolfgang. 2009. *Re-Forming Capitalism: Institutional Change in the German Political Economy.* Oxford: Oxford University Press.

Streets, David G., Carolyne Yu, Michael H. Bergin, Xuemei Wang, and Gregory R. Carmichael. 2006. "Modeling Study of Air Pollution Due to the Manufacture of Export Goods in China's Pearl River Delta." *Environmental Science and Technology* 40, no. 7:2099–107.

Stringer, Christina. 2006. "Forest Certification and Changing Global Commodity Chains." *Journal of Economic Geography* 6:701–22.

Stringer, Christina, Glenn Simmons, and Eugene Rees. 2011. "Shifting Post-Production Patterns: Exploring Changes in New Zealand's Seafood Processing Industry." *New Zealand Geographer* 67, no. 3:161–73.

Strømsnes, Kristin. 2005. "Political Consumption in Norway: Who, Why—and Does It Have Any Effect?" In *Political Consumerism: Its Motivations, Power, and Conditions in the Nordic Countries and Elsewhere,* edited by Magnus Boström, Andreas Føllesdal, Mikael Klintman, Michele Micheletti, and Mads P. Sørensen, 165–81. Copenhagen: Nordic Council of Ministers.

Sturgeon, Timothy. 2002. "Modular Production Networks: A New American Model of Industrial Organization." *Industrial and Corporate Change* 11, no. 3:451–96.

Sturgeon, Timothy, and Richard Lester. 2002. "The New Global Supply Base: New Challenges for Local Suppliers in East Asia." Cambridge, MA: MIT Industrial Performance Center.

Sum, Ngai-Ling, and Ngai Pun. 2005. "Globalization and Paradoxes of Ethical Transnational Production: Code of Conduct in a Chinese Workplace." *Competition and Change* 9, no. 2:181–200.

Sunderer, Georg, and Jörg Rössel. 2012. "Morality or Economic Interest? The Impact of Moral Motives and Economic Factors on the Purchase of Fair Traded Groceries." *International Journal of Consumer Studies* 36, no. 2:244–50.

Szasz, Andrew. 2007. *Shopping Our Way to Safety: How We Changed from Protecting the Environment to Protecting Ourselves.* Minneapolis: University of Minnesota Press.

Tacconi, Luca, Krystof Obidzinski, and Ferdinandus Agung. 2004. *Learning Lessons to Promote Forest Certification and Control Illegal Logging in Indonesia.* Bogor, Indonesia: Center for International Forestry Research.

Taylor, J. Gary, and Patricia J. Scharlin. 2004. *Smart Alliance: How a Global Corporation and Environmental Activists Transformed a Tarnished Brand.* New Haven, CT: Yale University Press.

Taylor, Peter Leigh. 2005. "In the Market but Not of It: Fair Trade Coffee and Forest Stewardship Council Certification as Market-Based Social Change." *World Development* 33, no. 1:129–47.

Teisl, Mario F., Brian Roe, and Robert L. Hicks. 2002. "Can Eco-Labels Tune a Market? Evidence from Dolphin-Safe Labeling." *Journal of Environmental Economics and Management* 43, no. 3:339–59.

Terragni, Laura, and Unni Kjærnes. 2005. "Ethical Consumption in Norway: Why Is It So Low?" In *Political Consumerism: Its Motivations, Power, and Conditions in the Nordic Countries and Elsewhere,* edited by Magnus Boström, Andreas Føllesdal, Mikael Klintman, Michele Micheletti, and Mads P. Sørensen, 471–85. Copenhagen: Nordic Council of Ministers.

Theuws, Martje, Mariette van Huijstee, Pauline Overeem, Jos van Seters, and Tessel Pauli. 2013. "Fatal Fashion: Analysis of Recent Factory Fires in Pakistan and Bangladesh." Report issued by the Centre for Research on Multinational Corporations (SOMO) and Clean Clothes Campaign, Amsterdam. http://somo.nl/publications-en/Publication_3943.

Timmerman, Kelsey. 2012. *Where Am I Wearing: A Global Tour to the Countries, Factories, and People That Make Our Clothes.* New York: Wiley.

Tollefson, Chris, Fred Gale, and David Haley. 2008. *Setting the Standard: Certification, Governance, and the Forest Stewardship Council.* Vancouver: University of British Columbia Press.

Tosh, Mark. 1995. "N.Y. Gap Unit Picketed over El Salvador Pullout." *Women's Wear Daily,* December 4, 24.

Transfair USA. 2009. "Transfair USA Almanac 2009." Report issued by Transfair USA, Oakland, CA.

Turner, Brian. 1993. *Community Politics and Peasant-State Relations in Paraguay.* Lanham, MD: University Press of America.

Tysiachniouk, Maria S. 2012. *Transnational Governance through Private Authority: The Case of the Forest Stewardship Council Certification in Russia.* Wageningen, Netherlands: Wageningen Academic Publishers.

US Department of Labor. 1996. "The Apparel Industry and Codes of Conduct: A Solution to the International Child Labor Problem?" Report issued by the US Department of Labor, Bureau of International Affairs, Washington, DC.

———. 2012. "Pakistan: 2012 Findings on the Worst Forms of Child Labor." Report issued by the US Department of Labor, Bureau of International Affairs, Washington, DC. http://www.dol.gov/ilab/reports/child-labor/pakistan.htm#_ENREF_14.

———. 2013. "Economic News Release: Consumer Expenditures, 2012." Report issued by the US Department of Labor, Bureau of Labor Statistics, Washington, DC. http://www.bls.gov/news.release/cesan.nro.htm.

US Environmental Protection Agency. 2002. "ENERGY STAR and Other Voluntary Programs 2001 Annual Report." Report issued by the US Environmental Protection Agency, Washington, DC.

———. 2010. "ENERGY STAR and Other Climate Protection Partnerships 2009 Annual Report." Report issued by the US Environmental Protection Agency, Washington, DC.

University of Maryland. 2000. "Americans on Globalization: A Study of Public Attitudes." Report issued by the Program on International Policy Attitudes (PIPA), University of Maryland. http://www.pipa.org/OnlineReports/Globalization/AmericansGlobalization_Maroo/AmericansGlobalization_Maroo_rpt.pdf.

Upton, Christopher, and Stephen Bass. 1996. *The Forest Certification Handbook.* Delray Beach, FL: St. Lucie Press.

United States Labor Education in the Americas Project (USLEAP). 2003. "Guatemala Surprise." *USLEAP newsletter,* July 1. http://www.usleap.org/guatemala-surprise.

Uzzi, Brian. 1996. "The Sources and Consequences of Embeddedness for the Economic Performance of Organizations: The Network Effect." *American Sociological Review* 61, no. 4:674–98.

Van der Meer, Cornelis L. J. 2006. "Exclusion of Small-Scale Farmers from Coordinated Supply Chains: Market Failure, Policy Failure, or Just Economies of Scale?" In *Agro-food Chains and Networks for Development*, edited by Ruerd Ruben, Maja Slingerland, and Hans Nijhoff, 209–218. Amsterdam: Springer.

Varul, Mathias. 2009. "Ethical Selving in Cultural Contexts: Fairtrade Consumption as an Everyday Ethical Practice in the UK and Germany." *International Journal of Consumer Studies* 33, no. 2:183–89.

Veblen, Thorstein. 1949 [1899]. *A Theory of the Leisure Class*. London: Allen & Unwin.

Verba, Sidney, Kay Schlozman, and Henry E. Brady. 1995. *Voice and Equality: Civic Voluntarism in American Politics*. Cambridge, MA: Harvard University Press.

Verité. 2004. "Excessive Overtime in Chinese Supplier Factories." Report issued by Verité, Amherst, MA. http://verite.org/sites/default/files/images/Excessive_Overtime_in _Chinese_Factories.pdf.

Vermeir, Iris, and Wim Verbeke. 2006. "Sustainable Food Consumption: Exploring the Consumer 'Attitude–Behavioral Intention' Gap." *Journal of Agricultural and Environmental Ethics* 19, no. 2:169–94.

Vogel, David. 2005. *The Market for Virtue: The Potential and Limits of Corporate Social Responsibility*. New York: Brookings Institution Press.

Vorley, Bill, and Tom Fox. 2004. "Global Food Chains—Constraints and Opportunities for Smallholders." Paris: Organisation for Economic Co-operation and Development, the DAC Network on Poverty Reduction.

Waldinger, Roger D. 1986. *Through the Eye of the Needle: Immigrants and Enterprise in New York's Garment Trades*. New York: New York University Press.

Walsh, Bryan. 2009. "A Delicate Undertaking: You Can Save Virgin Forests by Using Recycled Toilet Paper. But How Hard Is It to Make The Switch?" *Time* online. http://content .time.com/time/magazine/article/0,9171,1904127,00.html.

Walsh, Declan, and Steven Greenhouse. 2012. "Certified Safe, a Factory in Karachi Still Quickly Burned." *New York Times*, December 7. http://www.nytimes.com/2012/12/08 /world/asia/pakistan-factory-fire-shows-flaws-in-monitoring.html?smid=pl-share.

Ward, Julie, Bin Zhang; Shailendra Jain; Chris Fry; Thomas Olavson; Holger Mishal, Jason Amaral, et al. 2010. "HP Transforms Product Portfolio Management with Operations Research." *Interfaces* 40, no. 1:17–32.

Weil, David. 2004. "Public Enforcement/Private Monitoring: Evaluating a New Approach to Regulating the Minimum Wage." *Industrial and Labor Relations Review* 58, no. 2:238–57.

Weisskoff, Richard. 1992. "The Paraguayan Agro-Export Model of Development." *World Development* 20, no. 10:1531–40.

Wilkinson, John. 1997. "A New Paradigm for Economic Analysis? Recent Convergences in French Social Science and an Exploration of the Convention Theory Approach with a Consideration of Its Application to the Analysis of the Agrofood System." *International Journal of Human Resource Management* 26, no. 3:335–39.

Wilkinson, John, and Rudi Rocha. 2009. "The Agro-Processing Sector: Empirical Overview, Recent Trends, and Development Impacts." In *Agro-Industries for Development*, edited by Carlos A. da Silva, Doyle Baker, Andrew W. Shepherd, Chakib Jenane, and Sergio Miranda-da-Cruz, 46–91, Rome: Food and Agriculture Organization.

Willer, Helga, and Lukas Kilcher, eds. 2009. *The World of Organic Agriculture: Statistics and Emerging Trends, 2009.* Bonn: International Federation of Organic Agriculture Movements (IFOAM).

——. 2012. *The World of Organic Agriculture: Statistics and Emerging Trends, 2012.* Bonn: Research Institute of Organic Agriculture.

Willer, Helga, and Richter Toralf. 2004. "Europe." In *The World of Organic Agriculture Statistics and Emerging Trends, 2004,* edited by Helga Willer and Minou Yussefi, 93–121. Bonn: International Federation of Organic Agriculture Movements (IFOAM).

Willer, Helga, and Minou Yussefi, eds. 2007. *The World of Organic Agriculture: Statistics and Emerging Trends 2007.* Bonn: International Federation of Organic Agriculture Movements.

Williams, Christine. 2006. *Inside Toyland: Working, Shopping, and Social Inequality* Berkeley: University of California Press.

Willis, Margaret M., and Juliet B. Schor. 2012. "Does Changing a Light Bulb Lead to Changing the World? Political Action and the Conscious Consumer." *ANNALS of the American Academy of Political and Social Science* 644, no. 1:160–90.

Wilson, Bradley. 2013. "Delivering the Goods: Fair Trade, Solidarity, and the Moral Economy of the Coffee Contract in Nicaragua." *Human Organization* 72, no. 3:177–87.

——. 2010. "Indebted to Fair Trade? Coffee and Crisis in Nicaragua." *Geoforum* 41, no. 1:84–92.

Wolfe, Allis Rosenberg. 1975. " Women, Consumerism, and the National Consumers' League in the Progressive Era, 1900–1923." *Labor History* 16, no. 3:378–92.

Worker Rights Consortium. 2013a. "Global Wage Trends for Apparel Workers, 2001–2011." Report issued by the Center for American Progress, Just Jobs, and Worker Rights Consortium, Washington, DC. http://www.americanprogress.org/wp-content/uploads/2013/07/RealWageStudy-3.pdf.

——. 2013b. "Stealing from the Poor: Wage Theft in the Haitian Apparel Industry." Report issued by the Worker Rights Consortium, Washington, DC. http://www.workersrights.org/freports/WRC%20Haiti%20Minimum%20Wage%20Report%2010%2015%2013.pdf.

World Bank. 2009. "East Asia and Pacific Update: Battling the Forces of Global Production." Report issued by the World Bank, Washington, DC. https://openknowledge.worldbank.org/bitstream/handle/10986/14684/48138.pdf?sequence=1.

Wright, Tom, and Jim Carlton. 2007. "FSC's 'Green' Label for Wood Products Gets Growing Pains." *Wall Street Journal,* October 30. http://online.wsj.com/articles/SB119368082115675124.

WWF. 1994 [1991]. "Truth or Trickery: Timber Labelling Past and Future." Report issued by WWF-UK, London.

WWF European Forest Programme. 2005. "The Effects of FSC-Certification in Estonia, Germany, Latvia, Russia, Sweden and the United Kingdom: An Analysis of Corrective Action Requests." Report issued by WWF-International. http://wwf.panda.org/?18510/The-effects-of-FSC-Certification-in-Estonia-Germany-Latvia-Russia-Sweden-and-the-UK-Summary-report-country-reports.

Xiao, Chenyang, and Aaron M. McCright. 2014. "Gender Differences in Environmental Concern: Revisiting the Institutional Trust Hypothesis in the USA." *Environment and Behavior* 46, no. 2:241–263.

Yang, Dennis Tao, Vivian Weijia Chen, and Ryan Monarch. 2010. "Rising Wages: Has China Lost Its Global Labor Advantage?" *Pacific Economic Review* 15, no. 4:482–504.

Yu, Xiaomin. 2008a. "Impacts of Corporate Code of Conduct on Labor Standards: A Case Study of Reebok's Athletic Footwear Supplier Factory in China." *Journal of Business Ethics* 81, no. 3:513–29.

———. 2008b. "Workplace Democracy in China's Foreign-Funded Enterprises: A Multilevel Case Study of Employee Representation." *Economic and Industrial Democracy* 29, no. 2:274–300.

Zadek, Simon, P. Pruzan, and R. Evans. 1997. *Building Corporate AccountAbility: Emerging Practices of Social and Ethical Accounting, Auditing, and Reporting.* London: Earthscan.

Zanoli, Raffaele, and Simona Naspetti. 2002. "Consumer Motivations in the Purchase of Organic Food: A Means-End Approach." *British Food Journal* 104, no. 8:643–53.

Zelizer, Viviana. 2013. *Economic Lives: How Culture Shapes the Economy.* Princeton, NJ: Princeton University Press.

Zoomers, Annelies. 2010. "Globalisation and the Foreignisation of Space: Seven Processes Driving the Current Global Land Grab." *Journal of Peasant Studies* 37, no. 2:429–47.

INDEX

ACFTU (All China Federation of Trade Unions), 169–70

affluence, 44, 53–54, 57–58, *58*, 115, 143

Africa, 90, 99, 118, 122, 189–90. *See also individual country names*

agrarian reform: commodity roundtables in, 124–25, 128–32, 140–43; Fair Trade in, 124–28, 137–40; implementing, 132–35; in sugar and soy, 135–43

agriculture: activism about, 7–8; alternative production in, 220–21; certification standards in, 132–35; commodity roundtables in, 128–31; CSR in, 140–43, 211, 214; in deforestation, 103, 211; fair trade certification in, 32, 113–14, 124–32, 133–34, 137–45, 211; globalization of, 113, 114–15; government institutions and policy in, 121–22; imports, 116, *116*; markets in, 114–15, 122, 145; rule-making projects in, 123–32; unions in, 122–23; wage labor in, 113, 122

agri-food global value chains: alternative production in, 113–14, 144–45; criticisms of, 123–24; fair trade sugar in, 139–40; fairness and sustainability in, 143–44; local and national dimensions of, 121–23; structure of, 117–21

Alta Gracia, 174–75, 220, 221

alternative production: in agri-food, 113–14, 144–45, 220–21; in apparel/footwear, 173–76, 177, 219–20; consumer support for, 63, 69; in electronics, 193, 207–208, 219–20, 221; in wood and paper, 101–102

Amazon rain forest, 7, 85

American Apparel, 173–74

American Apparel and Footwear Association, 160

American consumers: and apparel, 60–61, 148; and electronics, 182–83; in the fair trade market, 66; and food, 114–17; individual beliefs in behavior of, 44–47; organics consumption by, *63*; social structures in behavior of, 47–51; and wood and paper, 86, 88–89, 96

American Forest and Paper Association, 93

antiegalitarianism, 62, 210

anti-GMO activism, 24, 25

anti-sweatshop activism, 6, 32–33, 146–47, 154–56, 159–60, 176, 214

apparel and footwear industry: alternative production in, 173–76, 177, 219–20; auditing in the, 146–47, 156, 161–62, 168, 176, 214; certification in, 20, 29–30, 156–61, 171–72, 175–77, 214; Chinese government reforming, 224; codes of conduct in, 32–33, 147–48, 161–68, 214; CSR in, 4, 147; domestic production of, 173–74; factory fires in, 33, 146–47, 163–64, 168; gender in, 151–52; geographic mobility in, 151–53, 167, 178, 215, 240n4; industry associations, 147, 160–61, 162–63; key features of, *212–13*; labor productivity in, 148–49, 153; labor standards in, 147–48, 150, 155, 156–61, 166–67, 175–77; organic, 65; production and consumption in, 148–54, 177; retail, 7, 149–50, 152, 154–55, 156–57, 159–60, 166, 217; rules and unruliness in, 29–30, 161–68, 176–77, 214,

215; subcontracting in, 218; "sweat-free" markets, 60–61; sweatshops in, 148–51; working conditions in, 167–68, 178

Apparel Industry Partnership, 157–58

Apple Inc., 99, 179–83, 185, 186, 191–92, 199–206, 207, 216

Argentina, 117, 123, 129

Asia, 90, 151, 181, 186–87. *See also individual country names*

Asia Pacific Resources International (APRIL), 102

Asia Pulp and Paper (APP), 102

ATOs (Alternative Trading Organizations), 42, 125

"attitude-behavior gap," 66

auditing: in apparel/footwear, 147, 156–57, 161–62, 168, 176, 214; for certification, 20; in China, 171–72, 242n18; in commodity roundtables, 135; corruption in, 164–65; in electronics, 98–100, 102, 193, 195–98; in forest certification, 98–99, 107–108

Australia, 96

Azucarera Paruguaya (AZPA), 138–39

Banana Republic, 67–68

B&Q stores, 6, 85, 90, 92, 94–95

Bangladesh, 147, 153, 154, 161, 167, 178

Beck, Ulrich, 17, 40, 49

beef consumption, 7, 81

"best in class" model, 26–27, 235n3

best practices, 20, 100, 145, 159, 192–93, 197

Better Management Practices, 128

big box retailers, 90, 182–83

biodiversity, 64, 85, 102, 109

Biomass, Biofuels, Sustainability Voluntary Scheme, 131–32

BJ&B, 174, 221

Bolivia, 99, 102

boomerang effect, 14–15

Bourdieu, Pierre, 48–49, 72

boycotting: alternatives to, 86, 92; child labor, 154; in concentrated retailing, 217; as conscientious consumerism, 38, 210; cross-national differences in, 51–53, 52; defined, 30–31; of electronics, 182; individual patterns of, 44–47, 59; limits of, 76; political, 17, 46, 53–54, 78–79; social structures

in, 47–51, 53, 210; surveying, 38–39, 222; of tropical timber, 85, 105

Brazil: agri-food in, 116, 117, 122–23, 131–32; land rights in, 22; wood industry in, 85, 87–88, 89, 99

BSCI (Business Social Compliance Initiative), 7, 160–61, 163–64, 165, 216

"buy American" campaigns, 73

buycotting: affluence in, 58; in concentrated retailing, 217; as conscientious consumerism, 38, 210; cross-national differences in, 51–53, 52; defined, 30–31; individual patterns of, 44–47, 59; limits of, 76; political, 46, 53–54, 78–79; post-materialism in, 58; social meaning of, 61; social structures in, 47–51, 53, 210; surveying, 38–39, 222

buyer-driven commodity chains, 10–11, 89, 149–50, 218–19

Cambodia, 22, 104, 163, 177–78

Canada, 77–78, 87–88, 93, 95

Canadian Standards Association, 93

capability-building programs, 168, 198, 242n19

Cargill, 7, 120, 137

Caribbean, 151–52

Carrefour, 117, 129

Catholic Agency for Overseas Development, 191

Central African Republic, 189–90

Central America, 125, 151–52

certification: in agri-food, 130–35; of apparel/footwear, 20, 156–61; independent initiatives in, 217; in labeling, 20–21; trust in, 46–47; of wood and paper, 86, 96–97, 101–102, 110. *See also* commodity roundtable approach; fair trade certification; FSC (Forest Stewardship Council); Marine Stewardship Council; SA8000

child labor, 154–55, 189–90

Chile, 122, 123

China: agricultural imports, 116–17, 116; apparel and footwear industry in, 152–53, 161, 168–72; auditing in, 242n18; corruption of auditors in, 165; electronics industry in, 181, 186, 187, 198, 199; forestry and timber in, 87, 89, 90, 99, 100; freedom of association in, 168–71, 210–11; government regulation in, 206; migrant workers in, 189; reform by, 224

CID (Citizenship, Involvement, Democracy) Survey, 38–39, 233

citizen-consumers, 16–18, 93, 210, 225. *See also* political consumerism

civil society organizations, 53, 123–24, 129, 135, 224–25

class distinction, 49, 71, 72, 82

Clean Clothes Campaign (CCC), 54, 154, 159

clothing. *See* apparel and footwear industry

Coastal Rainforest Coalition, 95

codes of conduct: in apparel and footwear, 32–33, 147–48, 155–56, 157, 161–69, 171, 177, 214; in electronics, 181, 192–93, 194–98; as fair/greenwash, 18–19; freedom of association in, 156, 159, 169; in supply chains, 11, 155–56

coffee, fair trade–certified, 4, 37–38, 42–43, 65–66, 68–69, 115, 124–27, 133

colonialism, 43, 88

commodities, 113, 116–17, 122, 124–32

commodity roundtable approach: to agriculture, 32, 113–14, 124–25, 128–32; in alternative production, 214, 219–20; CSR promoted by, 140–43, 211, 214; implementation of standards in, 134–35; and land rights, 144–45

community relations, 106–107, 130

concentrated retailing, 182–83, 216–18

conflict minerals, 6, 33, 181, 189–90, 207–208, 214

Congo. *See* Democratic Republic of the Congo

conscientious consumerism, defined, 3, 5

constraints on consumerism, 4, 47–51

consumer demand: for alternative production, 63, 69, 210; for certified forest products, 86–87, 94, 95–96, 109, 211; for eco-labels, 65; for electronics, 200–201, 206–207; for fair and sustainable food, 68, 123–24, 145; in markets, 222

Consumer Reports (USA), 9, 224

consumers: and certified forest products, 96, 109; characteristics of, 39–40, 44–47, 57–58, 59, 228–29, 232, 233; empowerment

of, 16–18; guides for, 9, 224; tastes and preferences of, 17–18, 222. *See also* American consumers; European consumers

"continuous improvement" model, 26, 235n3

contract manufacturers, 149, 183, 185–86, 188–90

cooperative farming, 123, 133–35, 220

corruption, 164–65

Council on Economic Priorities, 158

"crowding out problem," 76–80

CSR (Corporate Social Responsibility): in apparel/footwear, 4, 147, 166; and commodity roundtables, 140–43, 211, 214; and fairwash, 4–5; at HP, 194–95; in supply chains, 10–12; voluntary, 41

cultural opportunity structures, 52, 56–57

DAP (Desarrollo Agrícola Paraguaya), 140–41

DEC (Digital Equipment Corporation), 184

deforestation: agriculture in, 103, 211; FSC certification in, 102–103; in global warming, 225; impact of labels on, 110; and palm oil plantations, 108–109; problem of, 85, 86–87; in Southeast Asia, 91, 103; tropical, 6–7, 85, 103, 105

Dell, 186, 191, 192

Democratic Republic of the Congo, 87, 99, 102, 189–90

Denmark, 40

developmental states, 186–87, 206, 208, 223

Dodd-Frank Wall Street Reform and Consumer Protection Act, 190

Dominican Republic, 152, 174–75, 221

Dow Agro-Sciences, 129

Eastern Europe, 51, 55, 152, 186. *See also* individual country names

eco-labels: availability of, 55; certification of, 20–21; for food, 115; growth of, 62; limits of, 76; markets for, 64–65; origins of, 109–10; and overconsumption, 73–74, 79–80; proliferation of, 2, 216; and self-interest, 31; on wood and paper, 87

economic opportunity structures, 52, 54–56, 57–58, 69–71, 210

education, 47, 82

egalitarianism, 62, 71, 76–77, 81, 82
EICC (Electronics Industry Citizenship Coalition), 7, 26, 181, 191–94, 195–96, 198–99, 216
El Salvador, 152, 154
electronics industry: activism against, 6–7; alternative production in, 193, 207–208, 219–20, 221; conflict minerals used in, 33, 189–90, 207, 214; defined, 241n2; environmental dangers of, 181, 188, 192; exploitation in, 179–80, 206; forced labor in, 189–90, 192, 195; key features of, 212–13; labor standards in, 181–82, 188–89, 191, 195; markets, 183–86, 193, 200–201, 207–208, 215; obsolescence of products in, 185, 202; production and consumption in, 33, 182–90, 218; reform of, 224; retailers in, 7, 200–201, 217; rules and unruliness in, 190–98, 215; supply chains in, 191–92, 218; waste from, 192; working hours in, 198–206, 214
energy efficient appliances, 62, 64
Enough Project, 189, 190
environmental activists and movements, 6–7, 53–54, 79, 90–91
Equal Exchange, 125–26
Ethical Consumer (UK), 9
ethical consumption, 2, 5, 31, 61, 66, 210
ethical fashion, 147, 176
ETI (Ethical Trading Initiative), 156–57, 158–59, 162–63, 165, 166, 168, 170
Europe: anti-sweatshop activism in, 147; apparel/footwear in, 148, 160–61; electronics in, 182–83; forest certification in, 93–94, 98–99; markets for food in, 145. See also individual country names
European consumers: and apparel, 148; boycotting by, 58; and certified forest products, 86, 96; and electronics, 182–83; fair trade market, 66; and food, 114–17; individual beliefs in behavior of, 44–47; organics consumption by, 63; social structures in behavior of, 47–51, 48
European Social Survey, 38–39, 228–29
European Union, 104, 111, 116
exclusivity, 50, 72–73, 81–82, 131, 135, 210

factors in conscientious consumption, 39–40
fair trade certification: in agri-food, 32, 113–14, 124–32, 133–34, 137–45, 211; in alternative production, 113–14, 220; in apparel, 175–76; competition in, 27, 127–28; consumption, 66; in cotton, 175; effectiveness of, 132–33; fairwash, 19; history in, 221; limits of, 30; mainstreaming of, 27, 43, 113–14, 127, 217; market for, 65–66, 132; movement and markets, 7–8, 40–44; spending on, 41; standardization of, 43; standards of, 2; as status symbol, 72–73; work in as political engagement, 80. See also coffee, fair trade–certified
Fair Trade USA, 127–28, 145, 175, 211, 217
Fair Wear Foundation (FWF), 8, 157, 168
Fairphone, 207–208, 220, 221
Fairtrade Foundation, 43, 65–66
Fairtrade International, 126–27, 128, 135
fairwash, 4–5, 18–21, 211
farms, 113, 122, 129, 131, 141. See also agriculture; smallholder farms/farmers
Fauna and Flora International, 129
field experiments, 67–69, 222
FLA (Fair Labor Association), 19, 156–61, 165, 168, 181–82, 199
Flextronics, 186
FLO (Fairtrade Labeling Organization), 125–27
flowers, Fairtrade, 72
food/food industry: in commodity roundtables, 32, 128–29; demand for, 115–17, 238n2; and forests, 109; guides to, 224; key features of, 212–13; local initiatives, 81; meaning of, 32, 72, 112–13; perishability of, 216, 218; politicized markets in, 6–7; production and consumption of, 62, 114–23; retailers in, 114–15, 117–21, 129. See also agri-food global value chains
footwear industry. See apparel and footwear industry
forced labor, 126, 155, 189–90, 192, 195
Foreign Trade Association, 160
forest certification: alternative production in, 219–20; and biodiversity, 85, 102, 109; and boycotting, 92; competition in, 93–94;

and consumers, 86–87; effects of, 99–100, 102–104, 111; implementing standards for, 98–104; in Indonesia, 104–109; ineffectiveness of, 211; management plans in, 99–100; markets for, 94–98, 103; percentage-based model of, 96–97; rise of, 32. *See also* FSC (Forest Stewardship Council)

forestry: community-based, 8, 220, 221; standards, 22, 98–104, 219; sustainable, 4, 29–30, 91–94, 98–104

forests, 88, 101, 109, 225. *See also* deforestation; wood and paper products

Foxconn, 179–80, 186, 188–89, 204

France, 40–41, 96

freedom of association, 100, 156, 159, 168–71, 210–11. *See also* labor unions

Friends of the Earth, 90, 92, 95

fruit crops, 120–21

FSC (Forest Stewardship Council): and buyer-driven markets, 219; certification standards by, 2, 20, 86, 92–93, 98–104, 217; community roundtable approach of, 128, 129; in community-based forestry, 220; competition with, 27, 216; as a constituency, 26; growth of, 109–10; history of, 32, 91–94; limits of rule making by, 30; market campaigns by, 14; market support for, 8, 94–98; "Principles and Criteria" by, 92, 98–99

Fundación Moises Bertoni, 141–42

furniture production and sales, 89, 217, 219

FWF. *See* Fair Wear Foundation (FWF)

Gabon, 87

Gap, 154–55, 167

gender, 50, 82, 151–52, 196–97, 210, 242n18

General Agreement on Tariffs and Trade, 153

geographic mobility, 151–53, 167, 178, 214–15, 240n4

Germany, 40–43, 41, 42, 96

global commodity chains. *See* global value chains

Global Exchange, 124

global value chains: activism affecting, 8–9; "buyer-driven," 10–11, 89, 149–50, 218–19; in electronics, 183–84, 186–87; lead firms

in, 24–25; local institutions in, 121–23, 215; in neoliberal globalization, 12–13; power of, 216–17. *See also* agri-food global value chains

global warming, 18, 85, 87, 225

Global Witness, 189

globalized localisms: in agri-food, 123–32; in apparel/footwear, 154–61; described, 27–28; in electronics, 190–94; in standards creation, 215; in wood and paper, 91–98

GMOs (Genetically Modified Organisms), 7, 24, 25, 131

Good Electronics network, 191

Goodguide.com, 8, 224

government institutions and policy: in agri-food, 121–22; in apparel/footwear, 151–52; case studies on, 223; in deforestation, 103; in electronics, 187, 206, 208; in global warming, 111, 225; in labeling, 236n13; in land-use policy, 224; in social change, 74; trust in, 45–46; in wood and paper products, 89–90, 96; on working hours, 205–206

green consumerism, 73–74, 79

Greenpeace, 14, 19, 95

greenwash, 4, 18–21, 87, 92, 131, 211

Groupo Lucci (Argentina), 129

GRSB (Global Roundtable for Sustainable Beef), 124

Grupo Andrew Maggi, 129

Guatemala, 117–18, 121, 152

Guthman, Julie, 50, 62, 72

health in organic choices, 47, 64

Home Depot, 6, 8, 90, 91, 94, 95, 106, 216

Honduras, 152, 153, 157

Hong Kong, 151, 152, 179, 191

HP (Hewlett Packard), 180, 183, 186, 191, 192, 194–98, 199–206

human rights activists and movements, 6–7, 53–54

Human Rights Watch, 14

IBM, 180, 183–84, 191, 192

ICT (Information and Consumer Technology), 180–81

ideology of conscientious consumerism, 3, 76–80, 81–82, 210, 224–25

IFC (International Finance Corporation), 140

IKEA, 89, 94–95, 103, 217, 218

illegal logging, 1, 4, 29, 90, 98–100, 102, 104–106, 111, 215

ILO (International Labor Organization), 13, 156, 159, 163, 177–78

income, 40, 47, 54–55, 70–71, 114–15, 122, 238n3

India, 89, 116, 153, 166–67

indigenous peoples, 22, 91, 93, 107, 110–11

individualization of responsibility, 13–14, 73

Indonesia, 1, 85, 87, 101–102, 104–109, 134–35, 152–53

industrial accidents, 146–47, 163–64, 178, 180

industrial context and structures, 23–25

industrial upgrading, 187

inequality: in apparel/footwear, 150–51; in consumerism, 81–82; economic, 130; income, 70–71, 114; in political engagement, 77; racial/ethnic, 49–50, 82; of small farmers, 136

INGOs (International Nongovernmental Organizations), 14–15. See also NGOs (Nongovernmental Organizations); names of individual organizations

innovation: case studies on, 223; in electronics, 180, 182, 183, 185, 186, 200, 207; in food, 115

Interfaith Center on Corporate Responsibility, 124, 191

internal compliance programs, 162, 177, 193

International Coffee Agreement, 37, 126

International Register of Certificated Auditors (IRCA), 193

International Sustainability and Carbon Certification System, 131–32

International Textile, Garment, and Leather Workers Federation, 158

"Internet of Things," 180

investors, 20, 122, 124, 143, 154–55, 191–92

ISEAL (International Social and Environmental Accreditation and Labeling) Alliance, 20

Japan, 121, 151

Kiss, Jemima: "The Real Price of an iPhone 5," 179, 206–207

Knights Apparel, 174–75

labor activists and movements, 6–7, 8, 53–54, 159, 179, 181. See also anti-sweatshop activism

labor law, 1, 172, 181, 199, 205–206

labor markets: in apparel/footwear, 172; discrimination in, 196–97, 242n18; in electronics, 33, 187, 203, 205–206, 208, 214; research on, 223

labor standards: in agriculture, 130; in apparel and footwear, 150, 177; case studies on, 223; in electronics, 181–82, 188–89, 191, 192, 195, 198; national regulation in, 122–23; willingness to pay for, 67–68

labor unions: activism supporting, 8; in agri-food global value chains, 122–23; in alternative production, 220; in anti-sweatshop rule-making, 155, 157; in the apparel industry, 154, 168–71, 176; in codes of conduct, 156, 163; factories run by, 220

land use rights and policy, 130–31, 135, 141, 144–45, 224

land values, 122, 140

Latin America, 117–18, 122, 127, 129, 134

lead firms, 24–25, 155–56, 159, 160, 165–67, 197–98, 218

LEED (Leadership in Energy and Environmental Design), 96

liberalization of markets, 122, 183. See also neoliberalism

lifestyle narratives in food markets, 115

local institutions, 121–23, 214, 215

localized globalisms: in agri-food, 135–43; in apparel/footwear, 168–72; described, 27–29; in the electronics industry, 198–206; political context in, 215; in wood and paper, 104–109

Locke, Richard, 150, 166–67, 188, 196–97

logging. See illegal logging; lumber industry

LOHAS ("Lifestyles of Health and Sustainability"), 16, 81–82, 115

Louis Dreyfus, 137
Lowes, 90, 94, 95
lumber industry, 89–90, 109, 219

mainstreaming: of alternative products, 8, 25; of fair trade certification, 27, 43, 113–14, 127, 217; of forest certification, 97, 101–102, 110; of stringent standards, 217–18
"Make IT Fair," 191
Malaysia, 85, 205, 206
management systems standards, 140–41, 171, 192–93, 195–96, 198
Mardi Gras: Made in China, 24
Marine Stewardship Council, 7, 14
markets: aggregationist approach to, 17; agri-food, 114–15, 123–24, 125, 132, 145; for certified products, 217; for electronics, 180, 183–86, 193, 200–201, 207–208, 215; moralization of, 13–14, 76; privilege in, 61–62; as regulators, 77; for standards, 15–16, 62–69; structures, 40–44, 54–56, 118, 144, 216; sustainable/fair niches in, 25; for "sweat-free" apparel, 60–61; for wood and paper, 65, 91, 94–98, 103, 110
Marks & Spencer, 24, 168
Mato Grosso Soybean Producers Association, 131–32
Mennonites in fair trade, 42
Mexico, 99, 117, 123, 152
Micheletti, Michele, 3, 16–17, 50, 59, 69–70
migrant labor: in agriculture, 71, 113, 129; in apparel and footwear, 156; in China, 168, 169, 170, 173; in electronics factories, 188–89, 202–205
milk, organic, 64
mobility of production. *See* geographic mobility
modularity in electronics, 184, 201–202
Monsanto, 120, 129, 131
Monterey Bay Aquarium, Seafood Watch guide, 9, 224
moralization of markets, 13–14
motivations of individuals, 44–47
Multi-Fiber Arrangement (MFA), 152–53
multinational corporations, 9–10, 11–12, 117–18

"Naming and Shaming," 154, 216–17
National Association of Grain Exporters, 131–32
National Consumers League, "White Label," 72–73
Nature Conservancy, 129
neoliberalism, 10, 12–14, 30, 41, 223
Nestlé, 11, 129
Netherlands, 40, 96
New York Times, 179–80, 181, 182, 191–92
Newsweek: Green Rankings, 194
NFD Agro, 140–41
NGOs (Nongovernmental Organizations): in agri-food, 123–24; in apparel/footwear, 155, 157, 169, 176–77; in commodity roundtables, 128, 129; on conflict minerals, 189–90; as constituencies, 26; and developmental states, 208; on electronics labor standards, 188, 190, 191–92, 198; in fair trade, 40–41; in forestry certification, 92, 99, 101–102; rules issued by, 10; in social change, 224–25
niche products, 25, 115, 138, 220
Nike: anti-sweatshop activism against, 154, 155; in brand auditing, 161–62; codes of conduct adopted by, 156, 163; media exposés of, 216; and standards, 160, 168; supply chain of, 10
NLC (National Labor Committee), 154
Nokia, 180, 183
North America. *See individual country names*

Office Depot, 90, 98
organic agriculture, 7–8, 63, 64, 133
organic food, 41, 47, 64, 74–75, 115, 236n6
overconsumption, 3, 18, 73–74, 79–80
overtime work, 149, 173, 189, 197–99, 204–205
Oxfam, 14, 40, 42–43, 124, 158

Pakistan, 153, 167
palm oil, 108–109, 124, 132, 134–35
paper products. *See* wood and paper products
Paraguay, 22, 112, 135–43
"Peace Corps–Paraguay mafia," 92
PEFC (Programme for the Endoresement of Forest Certification) System, 93–94, 216

personal beliefs, 44–47
personal efficacy, sense of in boycotting/buycotting, 46, 49
pesticides, 7, 64, 123–24, 126
philanthropic foundations, 95–96
Philippines, 152, 186–87, 203, 205–206
plywood, 67, 89–90
Poland, 55, 58, 99
political consumerism, 2, 5, 17, 44, 69–71. *See also* citizen-consumers
political context: affluence in, 53–54; in China, 172; in conscientious consumerism, 23; and consumer pressure, 216; domestic, 224; in fair trade sugar, 139–40; in Indonesia, 105–107; in labor rights, 167; in localized globalisms, 215; in Paraguay, 112
political efficacy, sense of, 45–46, 78, 210
political engagement, 46, 73–75, 77–79, 80, 210, 224–25
political opportunity structures, 52, 53–54
post-materialism, 44–45, 46, 52–53, 56–58, 58, 210
price of goods: in boycotting/buycotting, 47; in certified agriculture, 133; for certified products, 98; and concentrated retailing, 217; in food consumption, 114–15; in forest certification, 103; in illegally harvested wood, 90; importance of, 66–69; premium for certified products, 237n4; and "sweatfree" apparel, 60–61
private benefits for consumers, 66, 210
producer premiums for certified goods, 98, 103, 133
production standards. *See* standards for production
ProTerra Certification System, 131–32
PT Intracawood, 106–108
public relations campaigns, 19–20
pull-based ordering systems, 201–202, 203
"puzzle of rules," 29–30, 214, 215

racial inequality, 49–50, 82
Rainforest Action Network, 90–91, 92, 95
Rainforest Alliance, 105. *See also* SmartWood
R&D (Research and Development), 185, 187
recycled paper, market for, 65
Reebok, 169–79, 240n4

reflexive modernization, 49
regulation: in developing countries, 22–23; INGOs in, 14–15; of labels, 236n13; of labor in China, 198; voids in, 21–23
religion, 42, 43, 44, 124
resources, personal, 47–51
responsibility, 13–14. *See also* CSR (Corporate Social Responsibility)
"responsibilization" of consumers, 41
Responsible Agribusiness Institute, 131–32
retailers: of apparel/footwear, 148, 166, 178; in boycotting/buycotting, 55–56, 59; concentration, 182–83, 216–18; and fair trade, 41–44; global value chains in, 219; structure of, 55–56; top global, 118; voluntary rules adopted by, 7–8; of wood and paper, 89, 90, 92, 94–95, 117, 119
Rockefeller Brothers Fund, 95
RSPO (Roundtable on Sustainable Palm Oil), 7, 109, 113, 124, 128, 129–30, 134–35, 144
RTRS (Roundtable on Responsible Soy), 7, 113, 124, 128–32, 135, 140, 144–45, 239n20
rule making: in agri-food, 123–32; in apparel/footwear, 161–68, 176–77, 216; in electronics, 190–94; in the global economy, 29–30; global value chains in, 219
Russia, 1, 87, 99, 100–101, 104

SA8000, 158–59, 168, 170, 171–72
SAI (Social Accountability International), 7, 26, 156–57, 168, 170, 171–72. *See also* SA8000
Samsung, 183, 187
Scandinavia, 41, 51, 52
Schor, Juliet, 17, 77, 78–79
Scientific Certification Systems, 92
seafood, 7, 9, 224
Selfhelp: Crafts of the World, 42
SERRV International, 42
SFI (Sustainable Forestry Initiative), 19, 93. *See also* PEFC (Programme for the Endoresement of Forest Certification) System
shopping, 69, 209
Shopping Our Way to Safety (Szasz), 74–75
Singapore, 205
"slow goods" movement, 221

smallholder farms/farmers: in commodity roundtables, 129, 211, 214; and DAP, 141–42; fair trade-certified, 127, 211, 217; in food production, 114, 119, 121; globalization affecting, 113; in local political economies, 144; and palm oil plantations, 134–35; in Paraguay, 136, 141; and retail concentration, 217; and RTRS, 130, 135, 144–45; in the sugar industry, 137–40. *See also* agriculture; farms

smart phones, 33, 183

SmartWood, 20, 107. *See also* Rainforest Alliance

Social Accountability International, 158–59, 193

social class, 40, 48–49, 71–73, 122, 210

social context of consumption, 17, 39, 57, 59

"social desirability bias," 66

social engagement, 74–75

social justice, 61, 71, 115, 124

social labeling, 20–21, 31, 55, 62, 76, 115, 216

social movements, 6–9, 53–54, 111, 123–24, 145, 216–17

social responsibility, 140–43, 174–75. *See also* CSR (Corporate Social Responsibility)

social structures of consumption, 47–51, 53, 210

Soja Plus, 131–32

Solidaridad, 125, 129

Sony, 180

South Africa, 118, 123

South Korea, 121, 151, 186–87

Southeast Asia, 91, 103, 122, 161, 187, 202–204

Southern Cone Common Market (MERCOSUR), 137–38

Southern Europe, 51, 55

South-South trade networks, 116

soy, 112, 116–17, 120, 130–31, 132, 135–37, 140–43

Spain, 40

standards for production: activism improving, 7–8; alternative, 101–102, 113–14, 219–20; community roundtables in, 128; compliance certification, 20–21; in eco-labeling, 2; effectiveness of, 222–23; egalitarianism in, 81; for food, 124; for forest certification, 92–93; global or local, 27–29;

globalized localisms in, 215; implementation of, 4, 21–23, 98–104, 209; markets for, 15–16, 62–69; power of companies in, 147; "puzzle of rules" in, 29–30, 214, 215. *See also* voluntary standards

Staples, 90, 98

status-oriented consumption, 61, 71–73, 81

Stichting Onderzoek Multinationale Ondernemingen, 191

students, 77–78, 124, 154, 191

Students and Scholars Against Corporate Misbehavior, 191

subcontracting, 12, 25, 166–67, 218

subsidies, 41–42, 99, 103, 187

sugar, 137–40, 238n4, 239n23

supermarkets, 25, 43, 55, 117, 118–19, 120

supply chains: in agri-food, 143–44; in apparel/footwear, 149, 161, 175–76; codes of conduct in, 10–12, 155–56; in electronics, 180–81, 191, 194; structure of and activism, 24–25; in wood and paper, 104, 106. *See also* global value chains

surveys of consumers, 30–31, 38–39, 60, 66–67, 222

sustainability: in agri-food, 143–44; alternative production in, 219–21; assurances of, 110; claims of, 4–5; defining, 27; as fair/greenwash, 18–19; in logging, 1, 91; market fragility for, 63–64

sweatshops, 60–61, 148–51. *See also* antisweatshop activism

Sweden, 40, 58, 77–78, 96

Switzerland, 51, 52, 55, 58

Taiwan, 121, 151

Ten Thousand Villages, 42

Tesco, 117

Thailand, 122, 153, 181, 205

toy manufacturing, 161

trade policy, 152, 225

Traidcraft, 40, 43, 80

Transfair, 42, 124

transnational advocacy networks, 6, 14–15

transnational corporations. *See* multinational corporations

Triangle Shirtwaste Factory fire, 146, 154

trust, 45–47, 52–53, 56–57

Underwriters Laboratories, 9
Unilever, 128–29
UNITE (Union of Needletrades, Industrial, and Textile Employees), 154, 158
United Kingdom, 40–44, *41*, 86, 96, 173
United Nations, 13, 190
United States: agri-food in, 114, *116*, 117, 145; and apparel/footwear, 147, 148, 155, 160–61, 173–74; electronics in, 182–83; fair trade consumption in, 40–43, *41*; military and foreign policy in, 151–52, 154; wood and paper in, 86, 87, 88, 96, 104, 111
United Students Against Sweatshops, 154
unreflective consumerism, 18, 214, 215
unruliness, 29–30, 147, 164–68, 177, 215
US Green Building Council, 96

values, personal, 3, 57–58
vegetable crops, 120–21
Vietnam, 1, 165
violence in the forest products industry, 91
"volume credit" certification, 97
voluntary standards, 7–8, 9, 15–16, 147, 192–94, 214
"voting with your dollars," 45–46, 62, 69–71, 93
"voting with your fork," 145

wages: in apparel/footwear, 152–53, 158, 162; in codes of conduct, 155; in electronics, 188–89, 196, 197
Walmart, 10, 89, 117, 118, 154, 166–67, 217
Wang, 184

Whole Foods, 74, 115
Williams-Sonoma, 95
willingness to pay, 66–69, 96
Women Working Worldwide, 158
wood and paper products: boycotting of, 85–86, 105; certified, 7, 86, 211; globalized localisms in, 91–98; key features of, *212–13*; markets for recycled, 65, 91, 94–98, 103, 110; production and consumption of, 87–91; rules and unruliness in, 29, 91–98, 215, 216; standards for, 98–104; timber trading networks in, 218
Woodworkers Alliance for Rainforest Production, 92
workers' rights: in apparel and footwear, 20, 157, 161, 162–63, 167, 168–71; in codes of conduct, 161, 162–63; in electronics, 180–81, 191; in FSC certification, 100, 110–11
working conditions: in agri-food, 122; in apparel/footwear, 150–51, 159, 167–68, 172, 178; in codes of conduct, 155, 161; in electronics, 180, 181, 188, 195–96, 197, 207, 214; in forest certification, 99
working hours in electronics, 198–206, 214
World Bank, 99, 140
WRAP (Worldwide Responsible Accredited Production) Program, 157, 160
WRC (Worker Rights Consortium), 8, 157, 159, 168, 174
WTO (World Trade Organization), 13, 22, 225
WWF (prev. World Wildlife Fund/Worldwide Fund for Nature), 92, 95, 99, 128

TIM BARTLEY is Associate Professor of Sociology at Ohio State University.

SEBASTIAN KOOS is Assistant Professor of Corporate Social Responsibility, Department of Politics and Public Administration, University of Konstanz.

HIRAM SAMEL is Associate Professor of International Business at the Saïd Business School at the University of Oxford, where he is also a fellow in Management at Lady Margaret Hall.

GUSTAVO SETRINI is Assistant Professor of Food Studies at New York University.

NIK SUMMERS is a PhD candidate in Sociology at Indiana University–Bloomington.

www.ingramcontent.com/pod-product-compliance
Lightning Source LLC
Chambersburg PA
CBHW071733270326
41928CB00013B/2655